In memory of our fathers–
Edgar Seligman and Sidney Benjamin

ORDINARY FAMILIES, SPECIAL CHILDREN

ORDINARY FAMILIES, SPECIAL CHILDREN

A Systems Approach to Childhood Disability

Second Edition

MILTON SELIGMAN
ROSALYN BENJAMIN DARLING

THE GUILFORD PRESS
New York London

©1997 The Guilford Press
A Division of Guilford Publications, Inc.
72 Spring Street, New York, NY 10012
www.guilford.com

Printed in the United States of America

This book is printed on acid-free paper.

Last digit is print number: 9   8   7   6   5   4   3

Library of Congress Cataloging-in-Publication Data

Seligman, Milton. Ordinary families, special
   children: a systems approach to childhood disability
   / Milton Seligman, Rosalyn Benjamin Darling.
   —2nd ed.
      p.   cm.
   Includes bibliographical references and index.
   ISBN 1-57230-155-4 (hc.)   1-57230-466-9 (pbk.)
   1. Handicapped children—United States—Family
relationships.   2. Parents of Handicapped
children—United States.   3. Family social
work—United States.   I. Darling, Rosalyn
Benjamin.   II. Title.
   HV888.5.S45   1997
   362.4′043′083—dc20   96-38683

Preface

OUR PURPOSE in writing this second edition is the same as it was when *Ordinary Families, Special Children* was published in 1989. Now, as then, we examine the intertwined child, family, ecological, and sociocultural variables that contribute to the response of families to childhood disability. We attempt to shed light on those elements of family and community life that facilitate or detract from the family's ability to assume a satisfactory lifestyle. Another goal is to describe relevant intervention strategies and services for families when such help is being sought. A third goal is to update the research and to describe new programs and approaches that have emerged during the past several years.

In this edition of *Ordinary Families, Special Children*, we endeavor to include studies that have been published in recent years as well as older studies, clinical reports, and theoretical articles that contribute to our understanding of childhood disability and the family. The book also includes parent, sibling, and grandparent observations. In the professional literature in recent years we have witnessed an increased focus on family members who have heretofore been relegated to a peripheral role. There is updated information on these family members as the knowledge base about their concerns, aspirations, and contributions has grown.

There have been changes in counseling approaches to help families cope with childhood disability. Cognitive strategies, for example, have proven to be useful in helping families modify their thinking patterns and hence their coping abilities. Furthermore, there has been a burgeoning interest in group approaches in the area of family and disability. Groups for parents, and separate ones for fathers, siblings, and grandparents are now offered to help ease the family's adjustment.

Since the original edition was published, there have been new resources developed for families. One newer resource that is being used increasingly by families and professionals is the Internet. Through electronic mail, subscribers to various lists can now get both information and support regarding children's disabilities. In several chapters, we have included material from such lists to illustrate the family experience.

This new edition also reflects legal changes that have occurred since 1989. Laws in the fields of early intervention and maternal and child health are becoming increasingly family centered. In response to both legal mandates and evolving ideology, practitioners in the field of early intervention in particular have been developing more system-based methods for assisting families in identifying their resources and concerns. The last chapter in this edition reflects newer legal language as well as an updated presentation of methods for developing Individualized Family Service Plans.

This edition of *Ordinary Families, Special Children* reflects a shift in the language used to refer to persons with disabilities. Person-first language focuses on the personhood of one's being. Therefore, although this language is occasionally awkward, this book uses person-first language to acknowledge that one is a person first—a person who happens to have a disability.

We considered changing the title of this second edition to, simply, *Ordinary Families*. The phrase "special children" seemed offensive, at least to some families and professionals. Many adults with disabilities have taken offense at the "supercrip" image promoted in the media, which suggests that people who "overcome" their disabilities and achieve occupational or personal success are extraordinary in some way and should be placed on a pedestal. The preferred image in recent years has been one of ordinariness: people with disabilities are simply people who, like others in society, represent part of the normal range of human diversity (cf. Irving Kenneth Zola's book *Ordinary Lives*, among other published statements).

Similarly, many parents of children with disabilities have resented people who have said to them, "Oh, you have to be special people to have a child like that." Certainly, some parents have taken comfort in such explanations. A poem entitled "Heaven's Special Child" has been circulated among parents for a long time; it suggests that a family must be specially selected before being entrusted with the care of a child with a disability. Many parents who do not share the religious orientation of the poem have found it offensive.

Some have suggested that "special" is a euphemism for "disabled," or even, "inferior." Certainly, "special" education has had that connotation at times, and some in the field have advocated changing the name. In fact, as inclusive practices have become more accepted, the need for a substitute word has diminished. Why not simply call it "education"?

Because of our concern about the word special, we decided to do some informal research. We asked for opinions by posting our concern on a number of Internet lists that are used by both parents and professionals. We received over eighty responses! The results were mixed: some felt very strongly that the title should be changed, and others felt, just as strongly, that it should not. Because of the logistic and marketing difficulties involved in changing the title of a second edition (in fact, with a new title, the book would not technically be a second edition at all) and the mixed reaction we received, we decided to keep the original title. However, we would like to share a small sampling of the responses that appeared in our electronic mail boxes over a period of about a month in the Spring of 1996.

From an adult with a disability:

> When the word "special" is applied to children/people in that general, yet somehow specific, context, it does seem to me to imply a virtuous, or superior, quality dispensed to them . . . potentially it may increase the idea in people's minds that there is this super-human "aura" around children . . . an ethereal uncrossable gap between them and the rest of the human race . . .

From a parent of a child with a disability:

> We parents of children with disabilities get a lot of "you are so wonderful as parents taking care of Scott/Heather (you supply the name). I don't see how you do it all . . . working, doing all the stuff for your child, and keeping a home. I know I could never do it."

> "You must be special people to get a child like that. He is such an angel. He smiles all the time and is so happy." Well, few people ask for a child "like that." You just look at what has to be done and do it. If the other person had a child with a disability, he/she would do what has to be done. If people have these high expectations for me as a parent, then I have to make it look like everything is going wonderfully. I can't relax and tell a friend my feelings about my child because everything must come up sunny expectations. And that "little angel" probably has days that just drive you up the walls. Try a child taking black permanent marker and writing x's all over the walls, white velvet chairs, carpet, and photos . . . But I don't share these kinds of things with my friends who have typical kids. The image is important.

From a professional:

> What about a compromise—put the word "special" in quotations.

From a parent of a child with a disability:

> Don't know why, but the first thing that popped into my head was "Ordinary Families, Extraordinary Children." While "special" does

carry some unpleasant connotations for some of us, I think every parent of a disabled child would agree that their child(ren) is indeed "extraordinary."

From a parent of a child with a disability:

I think any parent of any child thinks their child is special. I don't find the connotation offensive or derogatory at all.

We really appreciate the feedback from so many people, both in the United States and elsewhere, and thank them for taking the time to write.

We want to acknowledge the voices of family members that helped to enrich the concepts we have tried to communicate in this book. We would also like to express our gratitude to Roberta Allen and Angie Shiring for their help in typing portions of the manuscript and to Denise Morrin for facilitating secretarial assistance and for helping out during moments of crisis. We want to acknowledge Keri Carnahan and Jim Yaworski who assisted in the clerical transition from a first edition that was not entirely computer based. Keri also provided additional assistance with the preparation of the reference list and other parts of the book. Finally, we want to thank Rebecca Strong for capably preparing the index. As always, our spouses, Karen and Jon, provided a supportive milieu.

MILTON SELIGMAN, *Pittsburgh, PA*
ROSALYN BENJAMIN DARLING, *Indiana, PA*

Contents

xi

∼

Introduction and Conceptual Framework: Social Systems and Family Systems

T<small>HE</small> <small>CONCEPT</small> of systems, long a focus of sociologists, has increasingly become a leading perspective in psychology and other "helping professions" such as nursing and social work. Particularly in the realm of understanding family relationships, the fields have come to share a "systems approach." In psychology, this approach has been marked primarily by the development of family systems theory and the social ecology model. In sociology, *all* theory relates to a model of interacting individuals and groups or "systems."

The following discussion will focus primarily on systems models in psychology and the helping professions and their relation to families of children with disabilities. At the end of the discussion, we will note the convergence between these models and some major currents of thought in sociology. The resulting synthesis will provide a broadly based conceptual framework for understanding and working with families of children with disabilities.

THE SYSTEMS PERSPECTIVE IN PSYCHOLOGY AND THE HELPING PROFESSIONS

It is only in recent years that conceptions of family functioning have been taken seriously by professionals who work with families containing a

1

member with a chronic disability. The major drawback of focusing on the person with a disability is that other affected family members are neglected. In some instances, a family member who is nondisabled may be coping poorly. The concentrated focus on the family member with a disability is also shortsighted in that it neglects the dynamic nature of family functioning. A problem experienced by one family member affects the entire system (and, in turn, affects the family member with a disability).

The reluctance in the past to embrace a broader, or ecological, perspective may have been partially a consequence of the psychoanalytic tradition, where the focus was on the individual and on intrapsychic rather than interpersonal processes. In addition, psychoanalytic theory generally focuses on the mother, with a particular focus on the mother–child relationship. Fathers were ignored purposely because of the assumption that they were less important than mothers in influencing the developing child (Parke, 1981). Extant theories reflected the traditional conception of the remote father. Furthermore, the mother was seen as the first and most important object of infant attachment and fathers played a supporting role for the mother (Bowlby, 1951). Another contributing factor may be that, with few exceptions (Minuchin, 1978), family theorists and family therapists have not studied or shown a particular interest in persons with chronic illness or disabilities within the context of the family. Others implicate professionals who narrowly define the unit of care as the ill or disabled individual (McDaniel, Hepworth, & Doherty, 1992). Whatever the reasons for this heretofore narrow perspective, there is presently considerable interest in integrating theories of family systems with the available information about persons with disabilities and their families (see, e.g., Elman, 1991; Ramsey, 1989; Rolland, 1993; Seligman, 1991b; A. P. Turnbull & Turnbull, 1990).

The purpose of the remainder of this section is briefly to trace the history of family-centered health care, and to provide a conceptual framework for understanding family functioning in general as well as family functioning when a child with a disability is present.

HISTORY OF FAMILY-CENTERED HEALTH CARE

Doherty (1985) provides a useful overview of early family intervention programs, beginning with the first organized effort to provide family-based care, the Peckham Experiment. Southeast London was the site for this project, which began in 1926 and was terminated in 1939. The Peckham Experiment consisted of an interdisciplinary team led by physicians whose unit of intervention was the family. The primary goal was to study and promote health by strengthening the family. The team engaged in social and recreational activities as well as physical evaluations. The Peckham Experiment ended with the beginning of World War II.

In the same year that the Peckham Experiment ended, the Cornell Project began in New York City. The project was a 2-year study of 15 families examining the relationship between health and family patterns and ways to treat families in interdisciplinary teams. Like the Peckham Experiment, World War II ended this project when the United States entered the war in 1941.

Motivated by the Peckham Experiment, the Montefiore Medical Group conducted a study and service project from 1950 to 1959. They studied 100 families and controls. The study families were seen by a team consisting of an internist, a pediatrician, a public health nurse, and a social worker. The Montefiore group focused on disease prevention by working with the family unit. Because of difficulties of team coordination and the reluctance of professionals to try out new roles, the project never fulfilled its potential.

None of these innovative multidisciplinary family intervention projects had an effect on health care services in North America during the first half of this century (Doherty, 1985). Post-World War II medicine continued to emphasize specialization and the biomedical aspects of patient care. The new specialty of family medicine, initiated in 1969, brought the idea of family-centered care nominally to the surface. But only in the 1980s has this discipline explored and utilized models for integrating families into patient care.

According to Doherty, nursing and social work evidenced a resurgence in family interventions during the 1980s. Historically, nursing has been sensitive to the patients' physical and social environment (M. A. Newman, 1983). In many health care settings nurses are the primary providers of health education to the family. The study of the family system is presently integrated into the nursing curriculum in many programs.

Social work was founded with a family emphasis but lost it during the discipline's middle years (Hartman & Laird, 1983). Social work in the 1920s was marked by an interest in mental hygiene and psychoanalysis. The emergence of family systems theory in the 1970s motivated social work to regain a family emphasis.

The Peckham Experiment, the Cornell Project, and the Montefiore Medical Group had a seemingly modest impact on family treatment as it presently exists. The conceptual and treatment bases of family interventions in health care did not begin to develop systematically until family systems theory and family therapy emerged in the 1950s, although H. B. Richardson's book, *Patients Have Families,* published in 1945, inspired a new subspecialty in medicine—family medicine (Doherty, 1985). The focus then, which has continued through the decades, has been the treatment of families experiencing psychosocial problems. In concert with the emerging research literature pointing to family factors in health and illness, family intervention has brought the issue of the family in health care to the forefront of interest in social work, psychology, psychiatry, and rehabilitation (Doherty, 1985).

Turk and Kerns (1985) claim that the large body of research on the impact of illness on the family and the role of the family in the maintenance of health and the response to illness has not been integrated into developing disciplines. Furthermore, this knowledge remains the domain of such areas as public health, psychosomatic medicine, and medical sociology while at the same time the conceptualizations of family theorists have received little attention in behavioral medicine and health psychology (Turk & Kerns, 1985). Turk and Kerns concur with Doherty (1985) to some degree that the family perspective is presently gaining more acceptance in applied fields. In fact, the present authors believe that family systems theory is making inroads in several fields, including psychology, special education, and early childhood intervention.

We believe that there is a significant increase in interest in the family and its impact on family members with chronic conditions. The particular focus of this book, and hence this chapter, is on families with a child or adolescent with a disability. To further understanding of these families, professionals need to be better informed about family dynamics and especially about the dynamics of families with a child who has a disability.

We noted above that there has been some effort to join concepts of family systems with knowledge about families affected by childhood disability. Contributors to the professional literature have made attempts to promote a better understanding of such important concepts as stress as it affects family functioning (Crnic, Friedrich, & Greenberg, 1983; Wikler, 1981) and the effects of social support and social networks on the family (Holroyd, 1974; Kazak & Marvin, 1984). These important issues will be addressed later in this chapter, building on the work of family systems theorists. But Ann Turnbull and her associates have developed a useful conceptual framework, marrying family systems constructs with information about families with children who have special needs. We now turn our attention to the work of Turnbull as well as other key contributors to the professional literature.

FAMILY SYSTEMS THEORY

Some years ago, Minuchin (1974), in a brief paragraph, captured the essence of the interactive nature of the family:

The individual influences his context and is influenced by it in constantly recurring sequences of interaction. The individual who lives within a family is a member of a social system to which he must adapt. His actions are governed by the characteristics of the system and these characteristics include the effects of his own past actions. The individual responds to stresses in other parts of the system to which he adapts; and he may contribute significantly to stressing other members of the system. The individual can be approached as a subsystem, or part of the system, but the whole must be taken into account. (p. 9)

The family, then, operates as an interactive unit and what affects one member affects all members. In contrast to earlier theories, a family systems approach distances itself from the view that linear relationships characterize family life and that the only important relationship is that between a mother and her child. Instead, families are viewed as interactive, interdependent, and reactive; that is, if something occurs to one member in the family, all members of the system are affected. As one family therapist observes, families can be likened to a baby's mobile that hangs over a crib (Elman, 1991). When one of the objects of the mobile is touched, all of the other objects are disturbed. General systems theory holds that each variable in any system interacts with the other variables so thoroughly that cause and effect cannot be separated. Writing about deafness in the family, Luterman (1984) writes, "This notion implies that when a deaf child is born into a family, to some extent, everybody is deaf" (p. 2). Von Bertalanffy (1968) observed that all living systems are composed of interdependent parts and that the interaction of these parts creates characteristics not contained in the separate entities. Others concur that the family is more than the sum of its parts (E. Carter & McGoldrick, 1980). Therefore, family life can best be understood by studying the relationship among its members. Few would argue against the idea that the family is the primary and the most powerful system to which a person ever belongs:

The physical, social, and emotional functioning of family members is profoundly interdependent, with changes in one part of the system reverberating in other parts of the system. In addition, family interactions and relationships tend to be highly reciprocal, patterned, and repetitive. (McGoldrick & Gerson, 1985, p. 5)

However, before one can grasp the dynamic nature of family functioning, it is imperative to have an understanding of the characteristics, both static and dynamic, that comprise most family units. We turn, then, to Turnbull and associates' conceptualization of the family (A. P. Turnbull, Summers, & Brotherson, 1986; A. P. Turnbull & Turnbull, 1990). These authors have made a noteworthy effort to apply family systems theory to the study of families with a child who has a disability.

Family Structure

Family structure speaks to the variety of membership characteristics that serve to make families unique. This "input" factor includes membership characteristics, cultural style, and ideological style.

MEMBERSHIP CHARACTERISTICS

Much of the literature on families with members who are disabled is based on the assumption of family homogeneity (A. P. Turnbull et al., 1986). Families, however, differ with regard to numerous membership characteristics: extended families with members who either reside in the household or are geographically apart; single-parent families; families with an unemployed "breadwinner," a member with a major psychological disorder such as substance abuse or mental illness, or a deceased family member whose influence continues to assert itself on the family ideology.

Although membership characteristics of families with members who have disabilities have been studied, little has been done to investigate the relationship of these attributes to either successful or unsuccessful family interaction. In regard to family membership, it is important to remember that membership characteristics change over time. For example, the exiting of a family member will precipitate different communication and relationship patterns, just as an addition to the family increases the membership, the communication patterns, and the dynamics.

CULTURAL STYLE

The family's cultural beliefs are possibly the most static component of the family and can play an important role in shaping its ideological style, interactional patterns, and functional priorities (A. P. Turnbull et al., 1986). Cultural style may be influenced by ethnic, racial, or religious factors or by socioeconomic status. In her review of the literature, Schorr-Ribera (1987) points out that culturally based beliefs affect the manner in which families adapt to a child with a disability, and these beliefs also can influence families' usage and level of trust of caregivers and caregiving institutions. Cultural factors as they affect families will be discussed in more detail in Chapter 7.

IDEOLOGICAL STYLE

Ideological style is based on a family's beliefs, values, and coping behaviors and is influenced also by cultural beliefs. Some Jewish families, for example, place a great deal of emphasis on intellectual achievement (McGoldrick, Pearce, & Giordano, 1982). Academic achievement may be sought by Jewish families, in part, to enable one to pursue professional opportunities designed to escape the repercussions of discrimination; therefore, college attendance is strongly urged. Some Italian families tend to emphasize family closeness and affection, thus college attendance may be viewed as a threat to family cohesiveness. Other beliefs and values may be handed down from generation to generation and influence how family members interact with one another and with other families and other systems (such as schools and governmental agencies). However, it is important to bear in mind that families from the same ethnic, religious, or cultural background can differ considerably.

The response of the family to a child with a disability is influenced by ideological style, but the reverse may also be true, namely, that such a child may influence a family's values. For example, when a child with a disability is born, a family not only responds to the event itself but must also ultimately confront its beliefs about people who have disabilities. Because chronic illness and disability do not discriminate on racial, cultural, or socioeconomic grounds, a child with a disability may be born to a family that is very dogmatic and prejudiced. In such an instance, the family must grapple with what the child's disability means to them psychologically and practically (Marshak & Seligman, 1993). In addition, family members must also examine their beliefs about persons with a minority group status, namely, persons with disabilities. The birth of a child with a disability thus results in a double shock to the family. In the wake of disability in the family, it is not unusual for persons who hold prejudicial attitudes toward "the handicapped" to emerge gradually as spokespersons and advocates for this same population. Darling (1991) refers to this pattern of advocacy as a "crusadership role."

As a family confronts a chronic disability, they must also cope with their beliefs about what and who can influence the course of events (Rolland, 1993). It is helpful to know if the family believes the control of the disability is in their hands, in the hands of others, or purely chance. Their views will influence their interpretation of events related to the disability, their help-seeking behavior, and their approach to caregiving. Rolland (1993) believes that professionals should assess the family's views about what caused a disability or illness and what might influence the outcome. Strongly held opinions that someone is to blame or feelings of shame and guilt may negatively influence the family's ability to come to grips with chronic illness or disability.

Ideological style influences the coping mechanisms of families. Coping behaviors can motivate the family to change the perceived meaning of the situation (A. P. Turnbull et al., 1993). An illustration of potentially dysfunctional coping strategy comes from a study that revealed that fathers of adolescents who were mentally retarded, compared to a matched control group of fathers with nondisabled adolescents, employed significantly more withdrawal and avoidance behaviors to cope with their anxiety (Houser, 1987).

According to McCubbin and Patterson (1981), coping styles can be classified into internal and external strategies: *Internal* strategies include passive appraisal (problems will resolve themselves over time) and reframing (making attitudinal adjustments to live with the situation constructively), whereas *external* strategies include social support (ability to use family and extrafamilial resources), spiritual support (use of spiritual interpretations, advice from clergymen), and formal support (use of community and professional resources). In a book on cognitive coping for families, A. P. Turnbull et al. (1993) describe a family member with a disability as a source of happiness, love, learning life's lessons, fulfillment, pride, and strength. The thrust in the aforementioned book is in response to the negative and pathological views of persons with disabilities that characterize some of the literature.

Family Interaction

It is important for professionals to realize that children with disabilities do not function in isolation. This reaffirms the notion that people live within a context—the family—and that, when something happens to one member of the family, everyone is affected.

To say that a family is a unit comprised of a certain number of individuals and that they function in a dynamic interrelationship is to provide only a partial picture of how a family operates. A. P. Turnbull et al. (1986) elaborate on the four components of the interactional system: subsystems, cohesion, adaptability, and communication.

SUBSYSTEMS

Within a family there are four subsystems:

1. Marital: Husband and wife
2. Parental: Parent and child
3. Sibling: Child and child
4. Extrafamilial: Interaction with extended family, friends, professionals, and so forth

The makeup of subsystems is affected by the structural characteristics of families (e.g., size of extrafamilial network, single mother or father, number of children) and by the current life-cycle stage.

Professionals need to be cautious when they intervene in a subsystem.

An intervention designed to strengthen the bond between a mother and her child, for example, can have implications for the mother's relationship with her husband and other children. Strategies need to be considered within the context of the other subsystems so that the resolution of one problem doesn't bring about the emergence of others. Perhaps such difficulties can be minimized by including (rather than excluding) family members and by communicating the purpose and expected outcome of a particular intervention.

COHESION AND ADAPTABILITY

The subsystems describe *who* in the family will interact, whereas cohesion and adaptability describe *how* family members interact.

Cohesion can best be characterized by alluding to the concepts of enmeshment and disengagement. Highly enmeshed families have weak boundaries between subsystems and can be characterized as overinvolved and overprotective (Minuchin, 1974). Such families have difficulty allowing for a sense of individuality. Overly protective families can have deleterious effects on children with disabilities. Such families experience considerable anxiety in "letting go" of their children and hence may keep them from participating in growth-promoting activities.

Conversely, disengaged families have rigid subsystem boundaries (Minuchin, 1974). Interactions in these families may be characterized by underinvolvement. Involvement creates anxiety, and disengaged families tend to avoid anxiety. Therefore a person with a disability may feel free to initiate independent activity but he or she rarely feels supported or loved.

Well-functioning families are characterized by a balance between enmeshment and disengagement. Boundaries between subsystems are clearly defined and family members feel both a close bonding and a sense of autonomy. Enmeshment and disengagement then represent the outer boundaries of a continuum and the approximate middle of the continuum is where one finds well-functioning families.

Adaptability refers to the family's ability to change in response to a stressful situation (Olson, Russell, & Sprenkle, 1980). Rigid families do not change in response to stress, and chaotic families are characterized by instability and inconsistent change. A rigid family would have difficulty adjusting to the demands of caring for a child with a significant impairment. The father's rigid "head of household" role, for example, would not allow him to help with domestic chores or to assist with the child ("woman's work"), thereby placing an inordinate burden on the mother. The mother, thus, must put all of her energies into caregiving responsibilities, leaving little time for the other children in the family or for interacting with other people. This family is in jeopardy of becoming isolated and dysfunctional.

Chaotic families have few rules to live by, and those that do exist are changed frequently. There is often no family leader, and there may be endless negotiations and frequent role changes (A. P. Turnbull & Turnbull, 1986). Chaotic families can move quickly from enmeshment to distance and hostility–disengagement. Families who interact in a functional way maintain a balance between emotional unity and autonomy, between reacting to change and a sense of stability, and between closed and random communication.

COMMUNICATION

From a family systems perspective, communication breakdowns reflect a problematic system rather than faulty people. Communication problems reside in the interactions between people, not within people (Turnbull & Turnbull, 1986). When working with families from a systems point of view, the emphasis is on changing patterns of interaction and not on changing individuals. There is an avoidance of placing blame on one family member or another and instead efforts are made to explore the factors that contribute to problematic communication patterns. Families sometimes believe that a particular family member is responsible for the problems they are experiencing, but they usually discover that difficulties often reside in faulty communication. Often, blaming a family member is less anxiety-provoking than examining dysfunctional communication patterns for which all family members bear a responsibility.

Family Functions

Family functions are products or outputs of family interaction (A. P. Turnbull et al., 1986). They reflect the *results* of interaction in terms of the ability to meet the needs of the family's members. To carry out functions successfully requires considerable interdependence between the family and its extrafamilial network. Also, families differ with regard to the priorities they attach to different functions, and they differ with regard to who will carry out certain functions.

The following reflect typical family functions (A. P. Turnbull & Turnbull, 1990):

1. Economic (e.g., generating income, paying bills, and banking)
2. Domestic/health care (e.g., transportation, purchasing and preparing food, medical visits)

3. Recreation (e.g., hobbies, recreation for the family and for the individual)
4. Socialization (e.g., developing social skills, interpersonal relationships)
5. Self-identity (e.g., recognizing strengths and weaknesses, sense of belonging)
6. Affection (e.g., intimacy, nurturing)
7. Educational/vocational (e.g., career choice, development of work ethic, homework)

In the family, a child with disabilities, especially a child who is severely impaired, can increase consumptive demands without proportionately increasing its productive capability (A. P. Turnbull et al., 1986). As a result, a child residing in the least restrictive environment (namely, the family) may have the unintended consequence of generating a restrictive environment for family members in carrying out their functions.

Furthermore, it is conceivable that a child with a disability can change the family's self-identity, reduce its earning capacity, constrict its recreational and social activities, and affect career decisions. One can see in fairly concrete terms how a child with a disability can affect the family by reflecting on the family functions noted above. This discussion also puts into perspective the notion that well-functioning families need to be flexible, open to change, and resilient (Singer & Powers, 1993).

The discussion thus far reflects on potential family problems. It is just as conceivable that children with disabilities can have a positive effect on family functions (Featherstone, 1980; Marshak & Seligman, 1993; A. P. Turnbull et al., 1993). For example, in one study Turnbull, Brotherson, and Summers (1985) report that families perceive a major positive contribution of a retarded member to be related to guidance, affection, and self-definition. In their study, parents and siblings described positive attitudinal and values changes that they attributed to the retarded family members. In H. R. Turnbull and Turnbull's (1985) book, *Parents Speak Out*, contributors identified numerous positive benefits that a child with a disability had on parental and sibling values. Jane Schulz (1993) quotes her daughter, Mary, as she writes about her own brother, Billy, who has Down syndrome:

> Bill has four beautiful, admirable qualities which often stir my intentions toward self-improvement. They are all aspects of character which I think are seldom found among us in the genuine way they are combined in Billy.
> The first is his truly generous spirit. He does Christmas the way it is meant to be done: He shops until he says, "My sister would love that" (and he's always right, because he pays close attention to those

he loves). The cost of the gift, whether a little or a lot, is immaterial, and Billy would truly rather give than receive—he always digs under the tree for the gifts he's giving to distribute first.

The second quality Billy has is a deep concern for the feelings of other people. He has a kind nature, and I cannot remember ever hearing a malicious word leave his mouth. When anyone in the family travels, Billy calls to be sure we arrived safely. And when someone has a problem, is ill, or has died, Billy's sincere sympathy is heartwarming.

Billy's natural, abiding faith in God and love of church is the third quality I admire in him. He always *wants* to go, as opposed to our feelings often that we'd rather do something else but *ought* to go to church.

And the last, most wonderful and enviable trait Billy reveals is a contentment with his home, his work, his family. He accepts his retardation not with resignation, but with aplomb. He has a routine at home that looks so peaceful to me, and he'll smile and say to me with a happy sigh, "I *like* my life." (p. 38)

In terms of family functions, some authors question the emphasis placed on the role of parents as teachers of their children (e.g., Seligman, 1979; A. P. Turnbull et al., 1986). It is important to remember that the educational function is only one of nine functions. Parents have many roles to play and many functions to perform, and one needs to be concerned about how the overemphasis of one role or function affects the others. Also, in asking parents to assume an educational function it is useful to inquire about the parents' wish to take on that role, whether they are comfortable with it or feel prepared to assume it. Parents are sometimes asked to do more at home with their child than the family system can tolerate. Too much stress may be placed on the family when professionals fail to coordinate the activities they ask the family to assume (Laborde & Seligman, 1991). With certain types of childhood impairments, a family may be given "homework" by the teacher, speech therapist, and physical therapist, among others. There needs to be some monitoring of the functions professionals ask a family to assume and a recognition that overburdening one aspect of family function can negatively impact the successful functioning of the other aspects.

Family Life Cycle

It is difficult to understand family behavior without an appreciation of the family life cycle. This developmental concept of family functioning is particularly important because it transects other family dynamics. As a family progresses over time, changes occur in its structure and function. These changes, in turn, affect the way the family interacts (B. Carter & McGoldrick, 1989).

The family life cycle is a series of developmental stages in which, during a particular stage, the family's lifestyle is relatively stable and each member is engaged in developmental tasks related to that period of life (Duvall, 1957). For example, a family with two late adolescent children is coping with the usual intensity and ambivalence of adolescent life in addition to the concerns that characterize adult (the parents') midlife. Change occurs for this family when one of the children leaves home, which affects the family structure (e.g., changing from four to three persons at home) and may affect other aspects of family life such as family interaction and communication.

One can hypothesize that certain family dynamics will change if the adolescent who left is a nondisabled sibling. The parents may, for example, become more focused on the child with a disability, restricting their own activity and blocking any moves their remaining child might make toward independence. Once the nondisabled sibling is gone, the burden of caretaking may become more intensified for the parents or, conversely, this change in family status may motivate grandparents to become more involved in the family. Furthermore, if the nondisabled child has played a major caregiving role in the family, he or she may experience guilt and loss in leaving. At any rate, this life-cycle change has the potential of setting in motion a series of family responses. For most families these changes result in some initial turmoil followed by achieving an equilibrium characteristic of that stage.

Theorists have identified from 6 to 24 developmental stages (B. Carter & McGoldrick, 1989). Olson and colleagues (1984) identified 7 stages, which are discussed here and include the following: couple, childbearing, school age, adolescence, "launching," postparental, and aging.

Each stage has its own developmental tasks; for example, parenting is important during the childrearing stage and nonexistent during the postparental stage. If launching fails to occur when it normally does (and it may not with children with severe disabilities), parents may need to extend their parenting beyond the usual period. The failure to launch can result in problems for family members if the parents resent remaining in a parental role and the youth with disabilities is unable to achieve independence. The nondisabled children may feel burdened by a family member's disability. They may have to assume caregiving roles for their brothers or sisters with disabilities. These children may feel that life is passing them by and that they are unable to achieve goals and dreams or perhaps even engage in fulfilling relationships.

Life cycle functions are highly age related; for example, physical care by parents is essential during infancy, and educational and vocational guidance are important when children are in high school and college.

Whereas bonding and attachment are vital in infancy, "letting go" is important when children reach late adolescence. Thus a key aspect of life-cycle stages is the change in function required of family members over time.

Developmental transitions (moving from one stage to another) can be a major source of stress and possibly even family dysfunction. According to a study by Olson et al. (1984), launching creates the greatest amount of family stress. But one should not assume that all families negotiate life-cycle changes and transitions successfully. We know that some families of children with disabilities may not be able to move beyond the parental stage. Likewise, poor African American families may experience numerous blocks to a fulfilling family life because "their life cycle constitutes a virtually endless series of crises and their adaptive capacities are often pushed beyond human limits" (Hines, 1989, p. 514). Hines goes on to say that

> members of multiproblem Black families are interdependent financially as well as emotionally. Survival as well as success for one person depends on others. Stress is persistently high and families are consistently experiencing demands for change and flexibility. When the impact of these external stressors is heightened by normal developmental stressors and the vertical stressors of unresolved family issues, the odds are great that developmental movement forward will be thwarted for both individual family members and the family unit as a whole. (p. 514)

A. P. Turnbull et al. (1986) related the developmental stages derived from systems theorists to the stress that families of children with disabilities experience. Below, for each stage identified by Olson et al. (1984), are listed some potential additional stress factors:

1. *Childbearing:* Getting an accurate diagnosis, making emotional adjustments, informing other family members.
2. *School age:* Clarifying personal views regarding mainstreaming versus segregated placements, dealing with reactions of child's peer group, arranging for child care and extracurricular activities.
3. *Adolescence:* Coping with the chronicity of the child's disability, dealing with issues of sexuality, coping with peer isolation and rejection, planning for the child's vocational future.
4. *Launching:* Adjusting to the family's continuing responsibility, deciding on appropriate residential placement, dealing with the lack of socialization opportunities.
5. *Postparental:* Reestablishing relationship with spouse (i.e., if child has been successfully launched), interacting with disabled member's residential service providers, planning for the future.

THE SOCIAL ECOLOGY MODEL

Early studies of childhood behavior were often conducted in laboratory settings where the many variables that effect human subjects could be controlled. However, there is some question as to whether relationships demonstrated under laboratory conditions hold true in the natural environment (Vasta, 1982). One of the leading critics of traditional laboratory research argues that "the emphasis on rigor has led to experiments that are elegantly designed but are often limited in scope. This limitation derives from the fact that many of these experiments involve situations that are unfamiliar, artificial, and short-lived, and that call for unusual behaviors that are difficult to generalize to other settings" (Bronfenbrenner, 1979, p. 18).

In the early studies of families with children who have disabilities, researchers have fallen prey to a somewhat similar problem by defining the unit of study or intervention in very specific terms. They did this by focusing exclusively on the child, neglecting the family as a legitimate unit of study. Later studies focused on the mother, with a particular emphasis on mother–child bonding. The consideration of the family as a dynamic, interdependent unit was a major step forward and yet there continued to be something missing in the conceptualization of the family. We know that young children with disabilities do not live in isolation. Likewise, the family lives in a broader context, namely, their immediate community and beyond. The formulation of the family within a social ecological framework has been discussed extensively by Bronfenbrenner (1979), and has more recently been discussed in relation to families of children with disabilities (Bubolz & Whiren, 1984; Hornby, 1994; Mitchell, 1983).

Similar to what occurs within the family, as delineated by the family systems model, the basic tenet of the ecological paradigm is that a change in any part of the ecological system affects subparts of the system, creating the need for system adaptation (equilibrium). The ecological environments for the family furnish the resources necessary for life—and make up the life support and social support systems.

Similar to boundary concerns in the family systems model, the ecological model is also concerned with the permeability of the family in interacting with environmental systems. An illustration of this concept is where a family with a child with a disability is or is not open to the supportive influences of other similarly situated families (e.g., support groups) or whether they are amenable to being assisted by social agencies or other sources of help.

There is a social ecology theory in which the family is viewed as a system nested within a number of other societal systems (Bronfenbrenner,

1979; Hornby, 1994; Mitchell, 1985). A key tenet of the social ecological point of view is that if one wishes to change behavior (perhaps, in this instance, the behavior of the family), one needs to change environments. The social ecological view further asserts that a child or family can be affected by events occurring in settings in which the person is not even present. An illustration of this phenomenon is where a young child can be affected by the conditions of parental employment. The parents' employment status can be the consequence of the health of the local economy. And the health of a local economy can in turn be affected by events occurring on a national (a severe economic downturn) or even international scale (a war). Thus, the behavior of a child or a family unit can be influenced by a variety of external and remote events. This view encourages a broad conceptualization of the forces that impinge on the family. Such a framework incorporates contributions to the literature that focus on the social policies that affect families of disabled children.

The subsystems of a social ecology model include the microsystem, mesosystem, exosystem, and macrosystem (Bronfenbrenner, 1979). Mitchell (1983) has applied Bronfenbrenner's concepts of a social ecology model to the study of families of children who have disabilities. A discussion of Mitchell's adaptation is presented below.

The *microsystem* constitutes the pattern of activities, roles, and interpersonal relations experienced by the family. In it one finds the following components: mother–father, mother–disabled child, mother–nondisabled child, father–disabled child, father–nondisabled child, disabled child–nondisabled child. This pattern of subsystems resembles the family systems theory already explored. Regarding the subsections of the microsystem, some of the potential problems of families with a child with a disability are mentioned below:

1. *Mother–father:* How well parents cope individually and as a couple before birth of a child with a disability; acceptance of child's disabilities.
2. *Mother–disabled child:* Mother's depression, guilt, and self-blame, how enmeshed or disengaged she may be with child.
3. *Mother–nondisabled child:* How much attention nondisabled children receive; using sibling in compensatory way, giving child excessive caretaking responsibility for disabled sibling.
4. *Father–disabled child:* Whether father withdraws or is psychologically and instrumentally present.
5. *Father–nondisabled child:* See #3 above.
6. *Disabled child–nondisabled child:* Feelings of guilt, shame, and fear of catching the disability or believing that one has caught it; disabled sibling enslaving nondisabled brother or sister; nondis-

abled sibling's feelings of ambivalence toward disabled brother or sister.

The microsystem (basically the family) functions in a *mesosystem* comprising a wide range of settings in which a family actively participates. The following comprise the mesosystem:

1. *Medical and health care workers:* How the child's diagnosis is handled; professionals' depth of knowledge and availability; attitudes of professionals toward families with children who have disabilities; professionals' skill in being honest with parents but also kind, humane, and helpful.
2. *Extended family:* Grandparents' degree of acceptance/rejection of grandchild with a disability; grandparents' and other extended family members' willingness to relieve parental stress by providing psychological and instrumental support.
3. *Friends/neighbors:* Community acceptance and support to help parents cope with their feelings of shame and embarrassment.
4. *Work/recreation associates:* Family members treated as normal and equal and not as an extension of child's disabilities.
5. *Early intervention programs:* There has been high praise for early intervention programs—more accessible in some communities than others.
6. *Other parents:* Social, psychological, and practical help is available from support groups for parents and siblings; can collectively affect social policy through collective action.
7. *Local community:* Availability and coordination of services—differ markedly in urban and rural communities and in poor versus affluent communities.

In the *exosystem,* there are settings in which the family is not actively involved, yet they can affect the family; for example:

1. *Mass media:* The mass media can affect attitudes about persons with disability—can portray them as poor souls, incapable, and undesirable, or as able, likable, and reliable.
2. *Healthcare:* Families of children with severe impairments in particular are dependent on health care systems.
3. *Social welfare:* For some families, financial and other governmental supports are essential for family well-being; Supplemental Security Income (SSI) disability payments also help maintain living standards for needy families.

4. *Education:* The existence of enabling education; sometimes adversarial relationship between parents and schools.

And, finally, there is the *macrosystem,* which reflects the values inherent in social institutions:

1. *Ethnic, cultural, religious, and socioeconomic:* Ethnic, cultural and religious values can affect how disability is viewed by family members and can play a role in how family chooses to interact with the service delivery system; socioeconomic status (SES) may determine or reflect a family's instrumental resources.
2. *Economic and political:* Health of the economy and the political atmosphere can have an important impact on programs for persons with disabilities and their families.

The core of an ecological orientation reflects a concern with the progressive accommodation between a growing organism and its immediate environment (the family) and the way this relationship is mediated by forces from more remote regions in the larger social and physical milieu (Bronfenbrenner, 1979). Thus, a major shift in a government's philosophy can, when the philosophy is translated into legislation, affect the availability of funds for social programs designed to help families. Similarly, and on a more local scale, an impasse between parents and the school over a child's proper educational placement affects not only the family, which feels frustrated, angry, and powerless, but also school personnel, who are distraught about the parents' resistance and defensiveness.

To understand families with children with disabilities, it simply is not sufficient to study only the child, the child and his or her mother, or the dynamics occurring within the family: It is becoming increasingly important to examine the family within the context of larger social, economic, and political realities.

In applying a social ecology model clinically, Hartman (1978) developed a diagrammatic assessment of family and community interactions. This graphic assessment tool is called an Eco-Map (see Figure 1.1). Hartman believed that a graphic representation of the family's reality would avoid simplistic, reductionistic cause-and-effect views of relationships: "Such linear views reflect the limitations of thought and language rather than the nature of the real world, where human events are the result of transactions among multiple variables" (p. 466).

The Eco-Map is a simple paper and pencil simulation that demonstrates the existence and flow of resources. According to Hartman, the Eco-Map "highlights the nature of the interfaces and [it] points to conflicts to be mediated, bridges to be built, and resources to be sought and

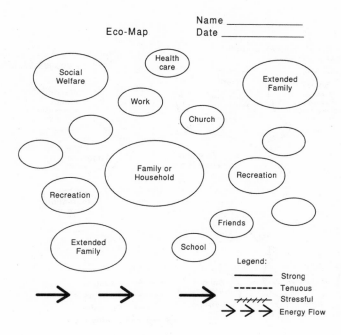

FIGURE 1.1. Hartman's Eco-Map. From Hartman (1978, p. 469). Copyright 1978 by Families International, Incorporated. Reprinted by permission.

mobilized" (p. 467). Figure 1.1 provides the basic schema of the Eco-Map and Figure 1.2 illustrates the case of "Jim," his family, and their present reality. Like a genogram, the Eco-Map can help the professional conceptualize a family's circumstances and consider appropriate intervention strategies. In clinical work, Hartman recommends that a copy of the Eco-Map be given to family members so that they can see themselves in relation to factors outside of the nuclear family. It can also be used in a pre–post fashion to determine the effectiveness of a particular family intervention.

RELATED CONCEPTS

There are a number of important aspects of family life that will be discussed in the following pages. These dimensions reflect aspects of life that can contribute to either family adaptation or family dysfunction. The following discussion will center on several key concepts that are often

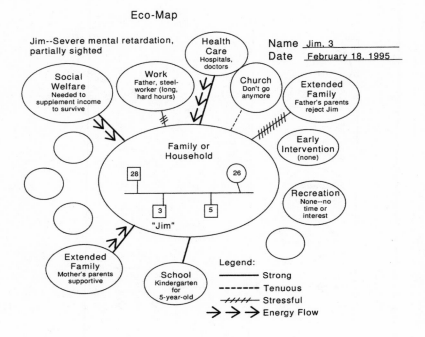

FIGURE 1.2. Eco-Map illustration of "Jim."

cited in the literature and relate directly to families of children with disabilities.

Stress

The concept of stress has already been broached. Stress has been mentioned in relation to life-cycle changes and is implicated also in events occurring within the family's social ecology. R. Hill (1949) developed a theoretical model of stress that is often cited in the family literature (McCubbin & Patterson, 1983; Wikler, 1981) and has been designated as the *ABCX* family crises model: *A* (the stressor event) interacting with *B* (the family's crisis-meeting resources) interacting with *C* (the definition the family makes of the event) produce *X* (the crisis).

The *A* factor (the stressor) is a life event or transition impacting on the family that can produce change in the family system. The family's boundaries, goals, patterns of interaction, roles, or values may be threatened by change caused by a stressor (McCubbin & Patterson, 1983). A stressor event, for example, may be the family's need to generate more income as a result of the economic burdens brought on by the realities of having a child with a disability. This "hardship" can place demands on the roles and functions of family members, alter their collective goals, and affect the family's interactions.

The *B* factor (family resources) has been described as the family's ability to prevent an event or change in the family from causing a crisis (McCubbin & Patterson, 1983). The *B* factor is the family's capacity to meet obstacles and shift its course of action. This factor relates directly to the notion that the family's flexibility and quality of relationship prior to the presence of the child with a disability may be an important predictor of its ability to adapt. Resources can also be acquired outside of the family by initiating contact with community services.

The *C* factor is the definition the family makes of the seriousness of the experienced stressor. The *C* factor reflects the family's values and their previous experience in dealing with change and meeting crises. This factor resembles a key component of Ellis's (1987) rational emotive therapy. He asserts that it is not the event itself that is disturbing to an individual but that the meaning attributed to the event constitutes the source of distorted thinking. Recent literature explores cognitive coping strategies that contribute to adaptive responses to family problems (Singer & Powers, 1993; A. P. Turnbull et al., 1993).

Taken together, the three factors all influence the family's ability to prevent the stressor event from creating a crisis (the *X* factor). A crisis reflects the family's inability to restore balance and stability. It is important to note that stress may never become a crisis if the family is able to use existing resources and defines the situation as a manageable event.

Family Adjustment and Adaptation

Along the same theme as the *ABCX* model, Patterson (1988) describes the Family Adjustment and Adaptation Response Model (FAAR). FAAR asserts that families attempt to maintain balanced functioning by using their *capacities* to meet their *demands*. A critical factor is the *meaning* (similar to the *C* factor above) the family gives both to a situation (demands) and to what they have for coping with the situation (capacities). A crisis happens when demands exceed existing capacities and an imbalance occurs. Balance can be restored by (1) acquiring new resources or learning new coping behaviors, (2) reducing the demands that confront the family, and/or (3) changing the way the situation is viewed.

In illustrating how symptoms or behavioral patterns serve as feedback mechanisms that become part of the pile-up of demands, Patterson (1988) describes the reciprocity between a diabetic child and his family:

> Hyperglycemia in a diabetic child may contribute to his or her emotional lability and thus to a greater incidence of conflict with siblings or parents. Conversely, parental conflict may contribute to internalized tension on the part of the diabetic child and a neuroendocrine response leading to hyperglycemia. (p. 79)

SOCIAL SUPPORT

Social support is often viewed as a mediating or buffering factor in meeting the demands of a stressful event (Cobb, 1976; Crnic, Greenberg, Ragozin, Robinson, & Basham, 1983). The presence of a child with a disability is considered a stressful event (Crnic, Greenberg, et al., 1983) and one that is chronic in nature (Olshansky, 1962). Social support is an external coping strategy that has been shown to reduce family stress (Beckman & Porkorni, 1988).

Researchers such as Crnic, Greenberg, et al. (1983) have examined social support in terms of three ecological levels: (1) intimate relationships (e.g., spousal), (2) friendships, and (3) neighborhood and community support. For example, in their study designed to assess the relationship of maternal stress and social support, these authors found that mothers with greater social support were more positive in their behavior and attitudes toward their infants. Intimate (spousal) support proved to have the most positive effects (Friedrich, 1979; Kazak & Marvin, 1984; A. P. Turnbull & Turnbull, 1990).

Kazak and Marvin (1984) and Kazak and Wilcox (1984) developed an innovative conceptualization of social support networks and applied this model to the study of families with children who are disabled. Kazak and Marvin (1984) elaborate on three components of social networks: network size, network density, and boundary density.

Network size is defined as the number of persons perceived as offering different types of support such as spiritual, medical, psychological, or instrumental support (Kazak & Marvin, 1984). These authors contend that, in general, the larger the social network, the greater the possibility of successful adaptation. Researchers determine network size by asking respondents for a list of names of supportive persons in categories (such as friends, family, professionals, etc.; Krahn, 1993).

Network density refers to the extent to which members of an individual's social network know each other, independent of the focal person. Density provides an indication of the interrelatedness of the social network. In their study of families of children with spina bifida, Kazak and Wilcox (1984) found that the social networks of families were fairly dense, suggesting that the people from whom help was sought knew and interacted with one another. When fewer friends are available to families, the role of formal helpers (e.g., community agencies) may be crucial.

The third characteristic of social networks is *boundary density*, which is a measure of that portion of the network membership that is shared by the individuals (e.g., parents) involved. That is, the boundary density is determined by the number of network members whom both parents knew and utilized. One method of determining boundary density is to ascertain to what extent spouses list the same network members. Kazak and Wilcox (1984) report that network overlap (high boundary density) tends to be associated with marital stability.

Two other characteristics of social networks are discussed by Kazak and Wilcox (1984) and Krahn (1993): network reciprocity and network dimensionality.

Network reciprocity is the degree to which affective and instrumental aid is both given and received, including the direction of flow in supportive exchanges (Krahn, 1993). Kazak and Wilcox (1984) provide an illustration of this concept: "Asking a friend to watch a child requiring specialized care may contribute to network drain and may not be matched by requests of a similar magnitude from the network" (p. 649).

Network dimensionality is the number of functions served by a relationship. Network members who are able to provide multiple types of help are viewed as being supportive and contributing to positive adaptation (Kazak & Wilcox, 1984).

Kazak and Wilcox assert that there are three areas of concern relevant to understanding the ecological context of families which relate directly to the notion of social networks. First, it is important to specify the precise nature of existing stresses and to integrate this knowledge into a family model. Implied here is that an examination of the social support network needs to be undertaken by professionals and factored into existing models of family functioning. Hartman's (1978) Eco-Map (see Figure 1.1) is a valuable tool for the practitioner to help achieve an understanding of the sources of support and stress contained in a family's environment. Second, although these families are sometimes characterized as socially isolated from their support networks, greater specification is needed in terms of the nature, extent, and consequences of this isolation. Third, the dissatisfaction families express regarding their relationships with professional personnel (Chapter 9), on whom they are often dependent, underscores the importance of examining more closely the availability of informal sources of support.

Childhood disability can have an isolating effect on families. "A diagnosis of mental retardation often seems to serve as a familial membrane that quarantines the family from mainstream society" (Marsh, 1993). Some of the reasons for this isolation are as follows: the emotional and physical exhaustion of families; the assumed stigma on the part of family members, social exclusion coming from a lack of acceptance and understanding, the support needs of extended family members, and the specialized needs of children with disabilities (Marsh, 1993; Parke, 1986). It is the availability of social support that helps to buffer some of the more arduous effects of childhood disability.

Both formal (e.g., social service agencies) and informal (e.g., family, friends) support can contribute to coping and adaptation. By the same token, certain supports can add stress to the family. Rejecting grandparents (informal) and cold, distant, noncommunicative professionals (formal) can burden the family with their lack of support and unsympathetic attitudes. Generally speaking, social support reduces the subjective distress of families; encourages positive personal, family, and child functioning (Dunst, Trivette, & Cross, 1986); and enables parents to maintain a sense of normalcy and coping effectiveness (Schilling, Gilchrist, & Schinke, 1984). Also, peer-led self-help groups are a powerful resource for family members (Seligman, 1993). These groups provide a forum for catharsis, education, mutual aid, and advocacy. More will be said about support groups in later chapters.

Developmental Transitions

The family life cycle was discussed earlier as a component of family systems theory. To briefly review, the family life cycle refers to seven life stages described by Olson et al. (1984) including couple, childbearing, school age, adolescence, launching, postparental, and aging. Because of the nature and severity of a child's disability and the family's response to it, families with children who have disabilities must concern themselves with a series of stages that, at least to some extent, are unique to them. For some families it is not possible to apply any type of developmental or stage theory model because of new major events that continue to occur throughout the child's lifetime. This may be true, for example, in a family with a hemophiliac child where periodic "bleeds" can cause considerable ongoing stress. Such events trigger a new cycle of upset, changing demands, and new adaptations.

Children with disabilities will be slower accomplishing certain life cycle or developmental milestones and some may never achieve them (Farber, 1975; Fewell, 1986). As the child approaches critical periods, parents may experience renewed anxiety or sadness. Fewell (1986) describes six periods that are particularly stressful to parents of children with disabilities:

ENCOUNTERING THE DISABILITY

The nature of a child's disability generally determines when the parents learn about it. Genetic disabilities, such as Down syndrome, are apparent soon after birth, therefore parents become aware of their child's condition early. Conditions such as deafness and language and learning disabilities may not be discovered until the child is older. Also, families may be confronted with disability caused by an accident or developing when their child is older. The confirmation of a serious and chronic problem often precipitates a crisis and affects the entire family. Immediate reactions may include shock, great disappointment, anxiety, and depression (Hornby, 1994). The loss experienced because of having a child who is different than expected may precipitate a mourning period much like the death of a family member (Marshak & Seligman, 1993). Contact with physicians and health care workers is particularly intense at this stage. It is also during this time of considerable stress that the family needs to inform other family members, friends, and work acquaintances of their situation. The awkwardness some family members feel can lead to isolation during a stressful period when social support is very helpful. A father who found out that his daughter had Down syndrome writes:

> I didn't want to see my friends. We became very isolated as a result of it. We drifted away from a lot of the friends we had—I found that I couldn't talk to friends. I couldn't face them—I think this is a little bit sad in the sense that I was very close to quite a few guys who had played soccer with me since I was very young—after Sally was born they just completely faded out of existence. (Hornby, 1994, p. 57)

Related to the initial encounter is the notion that a child's disability is an unanticipated event. Generally speaking, adults have expectations of proceeding through the normal life cycle events. Adults "internalize expectations of the consensually validated sequences of major life events— not only what these events should be but when they should occur" (Neugarten, 1976, p. 18). An unanticipated life event (birth of a child with a disability) is likely to be experienced as traumatic. Major stressors tend to be caused by "off time" events that fall outside of the family's expectations (Marsh, 1993).

EARLY CHILDHOOD

The early childhood years can be difficult ones for the family as they anxiously watch for their child to achieve certain developmental milestones. The chronicity of a child's disabilities and what it means to the family is a major part of the early childhood years. The nature and severity of the disability may play a key role in the family's perception and behavior (Fewell, 1991; Lyon & Lyon, 1991). In regard to a child's developmental delay, Fewell (1986) observes that

> The task of diapering a three-year-old is simply not as easy as it was when the child was one year old. The larger and heavier child requires more energy to lift and carry. The emotional burden is also great: parents anticipate the end of diapers and two o'clock bottles, and when these things don't end, it can shatter dreams and invite questions about the future. (pp. 16–17)

A parent's concern about the future is vividly portrayed by educator and parent Helen Featherstone (1980):

> I remember, during the early months of Jody's life, the anguish with which I contemplated the distant future. Jody cried constantly, not irritable, hungry cries, but heartrending shrieks of pain. Vain efforts to comfort him filled my nights and days. One evening when nothing seemed to help, I went outside, intending to escape his misery for a moment, hoping that without me he might finally fall asleep. Walking in summer darkness, I imagined myself at seventy, bent and wrinkled, hobbling up the stairs to minister to Jody, now over forty, but still crying and helpless. (p. 19)

Although early intervention programs are generally applauded, Fewell (1986) notes that a crisis may develop when a child enters an early intervention program, because of the following:

1. Families see older children with a similar condition and wonder whether their child will resemble them as he or she develops.
2. Families who share their experiences with other families realize that they may need to "fight" for the services their child needs, further draining the family's resources.
3. Families learn that they are often expected to be their child's primary caregivers and teachers.

In this latter regard, A. P. Turnbull and Turnbull (1990) quote a mother who says:

> I found the infant stimulation program to be very helpful in providing an opportunity to learn parenting skills. (Peter was our first child.) It also helped our morale in that it gave us specific things to teach Peter, and so we could see steady progress in his development. This created strong feelings of guilt in me because I felt that if I wasn't working with him at every opportunity, then I wasn't doing enough. If his progress was slow, I felt it was my fault. (p. 51)

During this phase, parents come into increasing contact with professionals, who may treat parents as patients who need treatment rather than as experts who are parents and caregivers (Alper, Schloss, & Schloss, 1994; Seligman & Seligman, 1980). Perhaps most discouraging at this stage is the realization of the chronic burden a child might be for parents and siblings as they view the future with some degree of uncertainty and anxiety. However, early intervention programs help to prepare the family for the marathon ahead.

SCHOOL ENTRY

Parents may experience another setback or period of adjustment when they realize that their child fails to fit into the mainstream of the traditional educational system. A child may require special education classes and a separate transportation system. Siblings may find this a particularly difficult period as more of their schoolmates learn that they have a disabled brother or sister. This stage can be characterized as the period when the family "goes public," as they venture beyond the boundaries of the family. And finally, parents, if they have not done so already, must adjust the educational and vocational goals they had envisioned for their child. However, parents should be reassured that as some doors may be closed to their children, others will open.

It is important to note that the difficulties parents experience depend on both the nature of the child's disability (e.g., there may be relatively few adjustments if the child is moderately physically disabled) and the preparedness of the school system to provide adequate educational and adjunct services for special needs children. Also, during this period, parents may debate the merits of a segregated versus an inclusive educational setting for their child.

ADOLESCENCE

Adolescence marks the period when children begin to separate from their parents. This period also reflects the time when adolescent children experience considerable change, turmoil, and ambivalence (Marshak, 1982). For families of children with disabilities, this stage can be a painful reminder of their offspring's failure to traverse this life-cycle stage successfully and their continuing dependence.

Peer acceptance or the lack of it may be particularly painful for the entire family during the adolescent years. Peer acceptance may determine the extent to which the child may feel rejected and isolated, which in turn may contribute to the stress parents and siblings experience.

> Adolescence is a particularly difficult phase of life for many with disabilities. The value placed on conformity during adolescence typically causes considerable distress because of the difference inherent in having a disability. Differentness becomes bad. An additional source of distress is the heightened importance placed on attracting a member of the opposite sex. Issues of independence and emancipation also become pronounced and a source of considerable turmoil. (Marshak & Seligman, 1993, p. 15)

BEGINNING ADULT LIFE

Public education offers both children and parents several benefits. It helps the child gain important educational and vocational skills and independence, and provides respite for the parents. But as a child's education draws to an end, parents must make some difficult choices. Because of limited vocational possibilities and inadequate community living arrangements, some families may be left with few choices. This is a stressful period in that the spectre of the child's future looms and can cause considerable concern and anxiety.

MAINTAINING ADULT LIFE

Where an adult with a disability will live and the level of care needed characterize the family's concerns at this stage. A major concern is the future care of their adult child as parents worry about the ensuing years when they may not be able to be active overseers or when they are deceased. One of the authors (M. S.) wrote about his fears regarding his young adult daughter when he is no longer alive:

> Tears come to my eyes when I think of Lori without her parents. She is so accustomed to having them [us] around. I try to suppress the apprehension that wells up in me when thoughts of Lori's future come to mind. But I can't deny the reality that anxieties about Lori's future are relentless. (Seligman, 1995, p. 182)

Mental health professionals are particularly important here to help families plan for their child's future in terms of vocational and leisure time activities, and in terms of living arrangements. Adult siblings as well as other extended family members may be useful resources and should be explored as potential helpers during this period. Although community support services are always needed, their availability and accessibility may be particularly acute here.

In a fitting conclusion to her discussion of the aforementioned stages, Fewell (1986) notes that when a family has a disabled child, all the actors in this support network must adapt to the extended needs of the disabled member. The adaptations family members make are often significant, and individual destinies may be determined by the experience. Family adaptations change as the child matures; the stress at various periods may affect family members differently, for much depends on the familial and environmental contributions to the dynamic interactions of adaptation at a given point in time. (p. 19)

Rolland's Model of Family Adjustment to Chronic Illness

Rolland's (1993) model of family adaptation to chronic illness relies on an understanding of a series of life-cycle and illness-related variables. According to Rolland, it is helpful for professionals to be knowledgeable about the characteristic and general patterns of an illness or disability over the life course of the condition. The following discussion will delineate illness characteristics as they intersect with aspects of the family life cycle.

An illness can have an acute or gradual *onset*. For acute onset problems (e.g., stroke, accident), families are forced to cope with the situation in a short period of time. Family members need to mobilize their resources quickly to cope with the situation, whereas a gradual onset illness may develop more slowly and require patience and a tolerance for ambiguity as symptoms are experienced. For gradual onset illness, the patient and the family may have to endure rounds of medical tests and examinations before a diagnosis is known.

The *course* of an illness is another disease variable that should be considered. For example, illnesses can be progressive, constant, or relaps-ing/episodic. In a constant-course illness, family members face a fairly stable and predictable situation, whereas in an episodic-course illness, family members may find it stressful to cope with the transitions between crisis and noncrisis and the uncertainty of when an episode will occur.

Two additional illness factors are *outcome* and *incapacitation*. In terms of outcome, a condition can be fatal (e.g., AIDS) or chronic and nonfatal (e.g., arthritis). The key difference between these outcomes is the degree to which family members anticipate loss (Rolland, 1993). In terms of incapacitation, an illness or disability can affect one's cognitive abilities (e.g., Alzheimer's disease), mobility (e.g., stroke, auto accident), or sensa-tion (e.g., blindness), or can create stigma (e.g., AIDS) or disfigurement (e.g., burns). The timing, extent, and type of incapacitation imply differ-ences in the degree of family stress (Rolland, 1993).

Illnesses also have *time phases*, such as crisis, chronic, and terminal. During periods of *crisis*, families are particularly vulnerable. Professionals have enormous influence over a family's sense of competence during this phase. Rolland (1993) views the initial meetings with professionals (diagnosis and advice) as a "framing event." He advises professionals to be very sensitive in their interactions with family members at this stage. For example, who is included during these early meetings can influence family communication patterns about the illness.

The *chronic* phase may be marked by constancy or by periods of episodic change or even death. The chronic phase challenges the family to maintain a semblance of a normal life while living with uncertainty. Chronic illnesses can strain family relations as expectations and personal life/career goals may need to be altered.

Families that adapt well to the *terminal* phase are those who are able to shift from trying to control the illness to "letting go" (Rolland, 1993). Being open to one's experience and dealing with the numerous practical tasks that need to be done characterize a family that is coping well.

A key component of Rolland's (1993) model of family adaptation to chronic illness is the concept of centripetal versus centrifugal family styles and phases in the family life cycle. These concepts describe typical and normative periods of family closeness (centripetal) and periods of family disengagement (centrifugal). Centripetal periods are characterized by an emphasis on internal family life. During centrifugal periods, the family accommodates the family members' interactions with the extrafamilial environment. Within the concept of the family life cycle, the family is seen at its centripetal best after the arrival of a newborn. A generally acknowledged centrifugal period is after the family's children are launched when both children and parents pursue interests outside of the nuclear family. Rolland (1993) discusses the implications of centripetal and centrifugal phases on family dynamics in the following passage:

> If a young adult becomes ill, he or she may need to return to his or her family of origin for disease-related caretaking. Each family member's outside-the-family autonomy and individuation are at risk. The young adult's initial life structure away from home is threatened either temporarily or permanently. Both parents may have to relinquish budding interests outside the family. Family dynamics, as well as disease severity, will influence whether the family's reversion to a centripetal life structure is a temporary detour within their general outward movement or a permanent, involutional shift. A fused or enmeshed family frequently faces the transition to a more autonomous period with trepidation. A chronic illness provides a sanctioned reason to return to the "safety" of the prior centripetal period. For some family members, the giving up of the building of a new life structure that is already in progress can be more devastating than when the family is still in a more centripetal period in which future plans may be at a more preliminary stage, less formulated, or less clearly decided

upon. An analogy would be the difference between a couple discovering that they do not have enough money to build a house versus being forced to abandon their building project with the foundation already completed. (p. 448)

In his writing, Rolland (1993) discusses other implications of disease onset, course, incapacitation, and so forth, as they interact with individual and family life-cycle phases. In the face of chronic disease, one needs to be mindful that the demands presented by an illness can seriously interfere with the personal life goals of family members. A balance, if possible, between meeting the requirements of the disease and achieving dreamed-of personal goals would be an optimal situation. To help achieve such a balance, Rolland (1993) suggests that

> it is vital to ask what life plans the family or individual members had to cancel, postpone, or alter as a result of the diagnosis. It is useful to know whose plans are most and least affected. By asking a family where and under what conditions they will resume plans put on hold or address future developmental tasks, a clinician can anticipate developmental crises related to "independence from" versus "subjugation to" the chronic illness. (p. 454)

THE SOCIOLOGICAL PERSPECTIVE

In some ways, sociological theory is similar to the perspectives just described. In other ways, it is very different. In this section, we will provide a brief overview of two major sociological approaches that will be applied in later chapters: structural–functionalism and symbolic interactionism. We will also suggest similarities and differences between these approaches and the systems perspectives described in previous sections. Finally, we will examine the differing foci of the psychological and sociological perspectives and suggest why both are valuable in understanding and working with families of children with disabilities.

Social Structure

The "structural–functional" school of thought in sociology has been most closely identified with the "systems" concept. This school traces its American roots primarily to Talcott Parsons and his colleagues at Harvard and to Robert K. Merton and his colleagues at Columbia during the 1950s and '60s. In the structural–functional perspective, society is regarded as a network of interconnected groups. The structure is held together by shared values that shape the roles the people play.

Each part of the system has a *function* that contributes toward the working of the whole. Functions may be *manifest*—generally acknowledged—or *latent*—not known or acknowledged. For example, the manifest function of a preschool program may be to provide an early educational experience for children; its latent function may be to provide a few hours of respite for parents.

In the structural–functional view, the actions of individuals are explained by their place in the social structure, and society has certain expectations about the behavior of people in different roles. Some of the determinants of these culturally based expectations include age, gender, ethnicity, and SES, among others. The values of the larger society, then, shape the ways in which parents relate to their children, husbands relate to their wives, and employers relate to their employees.

Much of the literature in the field of the sociology of the family looks very much like recent literature from the family systems perspective in psychology. Writings in both fields share a concern with family roles and functions, and with life-cycle stages and transitions between stages. The social ecology literature in psychology also resembles Parsonian systems theory in its concern with concepts like interdependence, equilibrium and disequilibrium, and the role of culture.

A structural–functional perspective is used later in this book in discussions of "opportunity structures" (Chapter 3) and professional and parent roles (Chapter 8).

Social Process

Another important current of thought in sociology has suggested that structural–functionalism does not adequately account for the dynamic nature of society. These theorists suggest that social change is the norm and that social interaction is a process in which "reality" is constantly being renegotiated. In this view, roles are not static sets of behaviors based on predefined values and expectations; rather, roles are continually being recreated by those who play them, based on situational contingencies. All "fathers" do not always act in exactly the same way, nor do all "mothers," "teachers," "doctors," or "patients," and the same father may act differently at different times or in different places.

The sociological perspective that has been most concerned with the determinants of these social processes is *symbolic interactionism*. This perspective is used, and will be elucidated further, in Chapters 2 and 3 to explain the "career" path followed by families from the prenatal period, through the birth of a child with a disability, through the preschool and school years, and into adolescence and adulthood. The symbolic interactionist perspective is used again in Chapter 8 to describe the process of interaction between families and professionals. The concept of stigma, used in several chapters, also has its roots in the symbolic interactionist literature.

Related Concepts

The concepts of stress and social support discussed earlier have received considerable attention in both the psychological and sociological literature. Sociological studies of disability, in particular, have typically regarded social support as a major mediating variable. These studies will be discussed in Chapters 2 and 3.

How the Perspectives Complement Each Other

Although sociologists and psychologists have developed similar perspectives in trying to understand families of children with disabilities, their focus in practice tends to be different. For psychological practitioners, the object of intervention is usually the "client" (in this case, the family). Intervention, in the form of counseling, therapy, or treatment, is intended to bring about changes in the family system or its individual members. For the applied sociologist, on the other hand, the object of intervention is often some aspect of the larger social structure. Sociologists generally focus on social change to create more opportunities for families.

Because of the difference in focus, *both* sociology *and* psychology (and other helping professions) are important in working with families. The helping professions (primarily psychology and social work) are important, because family members need to learn to use *existing resources* and to adjust to or *cope* with situations that may be unchangeable. For example, the family that devotes all its time to finding a "cure" for a child's Down syndrome may need assistance in redirecting its efforts.

On the other hand, in many situations, the family would be able to cope very well without assistance if enough supports or resources were available to them. The sociological perspective encourages the professional to assist families in *creating new resources* and expanding their "opportunity structures." For example, if no appropriate classroom for children with disabilities existed in a neighborhood school, the sociologically oriented practitioner might engage in advocacy for families by working with the school to develop the means to establish an appropriate classroom. Sometimes, situational factors are so overwhelming that intervention at the family level is not at all helpful. Extreme poverty resulting from larger societal conditions, for example, cannot be eliminated by family counseling; much broader social change is needed in such a case. At other times, needed social structures are in place yet the family continues to experience stress, marital disharmony, and major communication problems. Such feelings as guilt, shame, embarrassment, anxiety, and depression may be impossible to shake. In such instances, psychotherapy or family therapy may be indicated.

Some families need both counseling and advocacy; some families need neither. What the family "needs" is coming more and more to be defined by families themselves rather than by professionals. In the field of early intervention, for example, "family centered" is coming to mean "family driven." As one of the authors has described elsewhere (Darling & Darling, 1992), early intervention has shifted dramatically in recent years from a clinical, or professionally directed, field to one in which *parents* generally determine the desired outcomes of intervention for both the child and the family (see Chapter 10 for a further discussion of the process of outcome determination). Similarly, in the field of medical care for children with special health needs, recent legislation and policy have dictated a more family-directed approach (see Darling & Peter, 1994, for an in-depth discussion of models using this approach in medical education). Social work, education, and other fields have also been moving toward family-centered models (Adams & Nelson, 1995).

Both psychology and sociology, then, are today using a family-centered perspective in relation to families of children with disabilities. Both fields have also moved beyond a simple family-centered approach to a consideration of the larger social system within which families live. Professionals working with families need to be aware of the various levels on which intervention can occur. Those counseling families need to be sure that the problem is within the family itself, and not in the family's larger (and perhaps changeable) social situation. Conversely, professionals who focus on social change and advocacy need to have the skills to help families cope with limited opportunities. In either case, successful intervention requires an understanding of the systems perspective and an ability to provide broadly based interventions.

SUMMARY

This chapter has attempted to present several conceptual perspectives on families of children with disabilities. From the foregoing discussion, we have learned that families are remarkably complex and dynamic, as there are many factors that make up and impinge on family life. The family does not remain static but changes as new events occur. Also, families change as they progress through the life cycle. A contributor to family stress is disability/disease, which influences the life goals of family members. To be successful in interventions with families with children who have disabilities, professionals must be well grounded in the static and dynamic features of family life.

The approach to be taken in the following chapters, then, will be a systems approach. Derived from both the psychological and sociological literature, this approach views the child as part of a family system of interacting units and a social system of interacting families, individuals, and social institutions. Chapters 2 and 3 will employ a sociological perspective to look at how family reactions to the birth and rearing of a child with a disability are socially shaped. Using the principles of family systems theory, Chapters 4, 5, and 6 will explore the effects of childhood disability on various members of the family system and on the family as a whole. Chapter 7 will focus on counseling as a family-based intervention practice. In Chapters 8 and 9, we will return to the larger social systems perspective and look at interactions between families and others, both within and outside their social worlds. Finally, Chapter 10 will illustrate the application of a social systems perspective to assisting families in defining their resources, concerns, and priorities. By combining the systems literature from two fields, we hope to provide the reader with a broader and deeper understanding of families of children with special needs.

Becoming the Parent
of a Child with a Disability:
Reactions to First Information

THE FATHER of a child with a disability (Abraham, 1958) has written:

> No event in your entire babyhood could rival the despair of its first
> day. That, in itself, is consolation for parents who find out the worst
> right at the start. There is no lower depression than the day of being
> told. (p. 64)

Various writers have suggested that certain crisis periods are especially
traumatic for parents of children with disabilities (see, e.g., MacKeith,
1973; Chapter 1, this volume), including when parents first learn or
suspect that their child has a disability, school-entry age, time of leaving
school, and when parents become older. Of these, the crisis of first
information or suspicion of disability is probably the most difficult, and
families' needs for support are greatest at that time. In this chapter, we
present a sociological view of family reactions to the news of their child's
disability and suggest a model of family reactions during the infancy
period using an interactionist perspective.

Various psychological theories have attempted to explain family
reactions to the birth of a child with a disability (see Chapter 4). Perhaps
the most popular is "stage theory," (see Blacher, 1984a, for a review of

studies using this model), which suggests that parents progress through a series of "stages" in adapting to a child's diagnosis. Some writers have suggested that the sequence is variable, and others have argued that the model does not fit the adaptations of all parents. Stage theory is discussed further in Chapter 4.

Another popular strand in the literature concerns correlates of family adjustment. These studies suggest that certain kinds of families and/or certain kinds of children contribute to a family's ability to accept a child's disability. Some studies, for example, have suggested that a family's size, composition, SES, or ethnicity determines the reaction to the birth of a child with a disability; other studies have suggested a connection between the sex, age, birth-order position, or severity of a child's disability and family acceptance. Some of these studies are presented in Chapter 4.

Because of the great diversity among families, no single reaction or sequence of reactions can be found in all parents of children with disabilities. (The effects of subcultural diversity are explored further in Chapter 7.) In addition to predisposing characteristics that shape parental reactions, situational contingencies play an important role in parental response. These contingencies are discussed later in this chapter.

Symbolic interactionism, the theoretical perspective used here, is a sociological approach to social psychology that derives from the work of George Herbert Mead, Charles Horton Cooley, and others. This approach suggests that beliefs, values, and knowledge are socially determined through interaction and the ability of individuals to "take the role of the other," or understand the meanings attached to situations by other people. The symbolic interactionist view of human behavior focuses on social process rather than on static characteristics of individuals, such as gender, ethnicity, or personality type. When applied to families of children with disabilities, parental reactions would be interpreted within the context of the parents' interactional histories prior to their child's birth and their experiences afterward. Parents attach meanings to their experiences as a result of definitions they have encountered in their interactions with others.

Not all interactions are equally important. Among the most important are those with *significant others*, usually close family members and friends. When significant others define their situation positively, parents are likely to define it positively as well. The effects of interactions with significant others, along with the broader interactional context, will be explored later in this chapter as we trace the development of parental reactions from the prenatal through the postpartum periods.

THE PRENATAL PERIOD*

Prior Knowledge about Disability

Prior to their child's birth, most parents have had only limited experience with individuals with disabilities. In general, they have been exposed primarily to the stereotypes and stigmatizing attitudes toward disability that pervade our culture. S. A. Richardson (1970) and others have shown that almost all groups in the population have negative attitudes toward people with physical disabilities, and Gottlieb (1975) and others have shown that people with mental disabilities are also negatively labeled in our society.

During the prenatal period, then, most parents dread the possibility of giving birth to a child with a disability. As one mother of a child with Down syndrome said, "I remember thinking, before I got married, it would be the worst thing that could ever happen to me" (Darling, 1979, p. 124). Parents' concerns are sometimes even greater when they know of other families who have had children with disabilities:

> I've always been worried about having a child who was handicapped—one of our friends has a terribly retarded child, terribly retarded. We were concerned. We just wanted a healthy child. (Parent of a child without a disability, reported in Darling, 1979, p. 127)

In some cases, mothers claim to have had premonitions that something was wrong with their baby:

> I always said if it wasn't a girl, there was something wrong [this mother already had two boys without disabilities]. It just felt different from my other pregnancies, and my sister-in-law had just lost a baby at seven months.

> I felt very strongly that she was deformed. . . . She didn't kick as much as I thought she should.

> I thought something might be wrong because I was sick all the time and I wasn't sick at all during my first pregnancy. (Darling, 1979, pp. 125–126)

In these cases, concerns seem to be based on experience. These mothers' definitions of "what pregnancy should be like" did not fit their actual

---

*Some of the quotes from parents used in the following sections are taken from research conducted by one of the authors (R. B. D.) in the late 1970s. Although these quotes are over 18 years old, they could easily have come from parents of young children today; any "dated" material in the original source was not included here.

experience of pregnancy. Such parents are not typical, however, and most anticipate the birth of a healthy baby.

When parents express concerns about the health of their unborn child, these concerns are usually discounted by friends, relatives, and others. Even a mother who had four children with the same genetic disorder managed to rationalize her fears during each successive pregnancy with the help of physicians who assured her that her bad luck was not likely to recur. With regard to her third pregnancy, she said: "I was unrealistic. I said, 'He's going to be a Christmas baby. There won't be anything wrong with him' " (Darling, 1979, p. 143). In general, then, parents' fears about the health of their unborn baby are usually neutralized through interactions with others, and most approach the birth situation anticipating a healthy child.

Expectations that a baby will be "normal" are also promoted by prepared childbirth classes. Although these classes typically cover the possibility of unexpected events during labor and delivery, the end product of the birth process that is presented to prospective parents is generally a typical, healthy baby. The possibility of birth defects is usually not mentioned at all.

Most parents, then, are poorly prepared for the birth of a child with a disability. In some cases, parents are not even aware of the existence of their child's disability prior to the baby's birth. As one parent said, "I never heard of Down's. . . . Mental retardation wasn't something you talked about in the house. . . . There wasn't much exposure" (Darling, 1979, p. 124). Similarly the parent of a child with dwarfism recalled this initial reaction:

> I heard Dr. Z use the word "dwarf" outside the room when he was talking to the resident. When he came in, I said, "Dwarf? Are you saying my child's a dwarf?" What dwarf meant to me was a leprechaun. Whatever would that mean? Would you have to send them to a circus? (Ablon, 1982, p. 36)

In other cases, parents can recall having heard of a disability, but only in a limited, and typically negative, way: "I'd heard of it from a book. It was just a terrible picture on a certain page of an abnormal psych book that I can still sort of picture" (Darling, 1979, p. 25).

With the advent of modern technology, some childhood disabilities are being diagnosed prenatally. Through techniques such as amniocentesis, ultrasound, and maternal serum testing, parents are able to learn of problems prior to their child's birth. In cases of prenatal diagnosis, anticipatory grieving may be tempered by the hope that "maybe they made a mistake," and the baby will be all right after all. One mother, who was told after an ultrasound screening late in her pregnancy that her baby had hydrocephalus, said she was "shocked, sad, and depressed" after hearing the news but "hoped they were wrong" at the same time (Darling & Darling, 1982, p. 98). After she saw the baby's enlarged head in the delivery room, she no longer doubted the diagnosis.

Pregnancy as a Social Role: Expectations and Dreams

Attitudes toward pregnancy and birth vary among cultural and subcultural groups. Rosengren (1962) has shown, for example, that lower-class women are more likely than upper-class women to engage in "sick-role" behavior during pregnancy. The value placed on pregnancy is also likely to vary according to the value placed on children or large families in different groups. Within a context in which families are highly valued, as among some Italian Americans, for example, pregnancy is also likely to be highly valued, and the pregnant woman is likely to occupy an esteemed status. Within other cultural contexts, such as that segment of the urban American middle class in which one-child or two-child families are the norm, some pregnancies may be disvalued. Certainly, whether a pregnancy is planned or unplanned, whether the parents are married or not, and other circumstances surrounding the pregnancy and birth situations will shape parental reactions, regardless of whether or not the child is born with a disability.

LaRossa (1977) has argued that a couple's first pregnancy creates a crisis that is a potential strain on the marital relationship. Similarly, Doering, Entwisle, and Quinlan (1980) claim that a first pregnancy is a progressively developing crisis. The threat is generally not serious enough to destroy an otherwise strong marriage, but we should keep in mind that pregnancy and birth are stress-producing situations, even when a baby is perfectly healthy.

Expectant parents also typically fantasize about their unborn baby. They may imagine the baby's gender, appearance, personality, or other attributes:

> This is the dream child you have been waiting for since you yourself were a little girl playing with dolls. At long last, you will become the perfect mom . . . preparations begin . . . Lamaze classes, wallpaper, baby clothes, wooden cradle. . . . You fantasize about who this dream child will be. Tennis star, astronaut, literary genius. You read volumes of books on child care and parenting. . . . A colicky baby is your worst fear. (Spano, 1994, p. 29)

Interactions with friends and relatives help to shape parents' fantasies. Folk wisdom sometimes plays a role, interpreting the pregnant woman's shape or size or the baby's prenatal movements as indicative of the child's gender, size, or temperament.

Parents enter the birth situation, then, with a particular base of knowledge, attitudes, expectations, and hopes. They possess varying degrees of knowledge about disabilities; various attitudes toward people with disabilities and toward their own status as expectant parents; differing expectations about the birth situation, parenthood, and the attributes of their unborn child; as well as hopes and wishes relating to those attributes.

THE BIRTH SITUATION

A number of studies (see, e.g., Doering et al., 1980; Norr, Block, Charles, Meyering, & Meyers, 1977) have suggested that parents who have taken prepared childbirth classes are more likely to define the birth situation in a positive manner. More prepared parents, however, are also likely to be more aware of deviations from normal delivery room routine that may occur in the case of a baby with a problem.

Rothman (1978) has argued that, although prepared childbirth might seem more meaningful to the parents, it in fact places them in a situation as powerless as that of parents in the traditional, medically controlled birth situation. She suggests that hospital births are always medical events and the care of the mother and child are scheduled to fit institutional rhythms. Mothers' feelings of powerlessness are increased by admission procedures, such as stripping the woman of her clothing and jewelry, shaving the pubic area, and administering an enema. Danziger (1979) argues that medical control is also expressed through stimulation of labor and intervention in delivery. In the delivery room, then, even prepared parents may be intimidated by the professionally controlled setting. Feelings of powerlessness are likely to be magnified when a baby's problems are detected immediately after birth. As this mother's report shows, the parent has little control over events in the delivery room:

> When Billy was born I heard the nurse say, "Is it a boy or a girl?" and I knew right away something was wrong. . . . They wrapped him up so I could just see his head and they said, "We're going to bring him to the nursery now." I let him go because I knew something was wrong and I wanted him to be taken where he would get attention. (Darling, 1979, p. 132)

Typically, concerns about a baby are not revealed directly to parents in the delivery room. Rather parents become suspicious as a result of unintentional clues given by physicians and nurses:

> I remember very vividly. The doctor did not say anything at all when the baby was born. Then he said, "It's a boy," and the way he hesitated, I immediately said, "Is he all right?" And he said, "He has ten fingers and ten toes," so in the back of my mind I knew there was something wrong. (Darling, 1979, p. 129)

D'Arcy (1968) and Walker (1971) note clues, such as "the look on the nurse's face," consultations between nurses in hushed voices, and nurses who "looked at each other and pointed to something."

In rarer cases, the clues are not so subtle:

> When the baby was born, they said, "Oh my God, put her out." That's the first thing they said, "Oh my God, put her out" . . . and the next thing I remember was waking up in the recovery room. . . . I had my priest on my left hand and my pediatrician on my right hand . . . and they were trying to get me to sign a piece of paper. . . . I just couldn't believe that this was happening to me and I said to my priest, "Father, what's the matter?" and he said, "You have to sign this release. Your daughter is very sick," and I said to the pediatrician, "What's the matter with her?" and he said . . . she had something that was too much to talk about, that I shouldn't worry myself. . . . Nobody was telling me what this was. . . . I was very depressed. (Darling, 1979, p. 130)

Although more common in the past, such extreme examples of professionals withholding information from parents occur only rarely today.

Parental reactions in the immediate postpartum situation, then, may be characterized in many cases by the sociological concept of *anomie*, or normlessness. Because even prepared parents are unable to make sense of atypical events in the delivery room, the birth experience is stressful for almost all parents of children whose disabilities can be detected immediately by medical personnel. McHugh (1968) has shown that the components of anomie are *meaninglessness* and *powerlessness*, and both are commonly experienced by parents of newborns with disabilities.

As Chapter 8 shows, physicians have sometimes deliberately created meaninglessness and powerlessness in the belief that they were protecting parents, who were "not ready to hear the truth" so soon after birth. Yet, as Chapter 8 also reveals, studies show that most parents do want to know their child's diagnosis right from the beginning; uncertainty and suspicion may be more stressful than bad news. Although most physicians today do suggest a diagnosis before the baby leaves the hospital, occasionally the period of suspicion is protracted:

> He was born on Tuesday, and by Thursday, I was suspicious. Nurses would come in and ask to see pictures of my first child; then they would leave quickly. . . . The baby wasn't eating well, and once when a nurse came in after a feeding, I told her I was worried. She said, "It's all due

to his condition." I asked, "What condition?,," but she just walked out. . . . Then, the doctor asked me when I was going home. When I said "Tomorrow," he said "Good. That will give us more time to observe the baby." . . . The obstetricians kept asking me if I noticed any difference between Joey and my first baby . . . I asked to see the house pediatrician. . . . Then my husband arrived to take me home and he said to the doctor, "She doesn't know yet. I'll tell her later." [He had just been told himself.] (Darling, 1979, p. 129)

Again, such reactions by hospital staff were more common in the past than they are today.

Parents' immediate reactions to the birth of a child with a disability, then, may involve suspicions created by interactions with professionals. The birth situation generally occurs in medically controlled settings in our society, placing parents in a state of submission to professional authority. As a result, they are likely to feel powerless and to experience stress when events do not proceed according to their expectations. As the next section shows, anomie may be a continuing reaction even after a diagnosis has been established.

THE POSTPARTUM PERIOD

Early Reactions

As many studies have shown, parents' initial reaction to the news that their child has a disability is likely to be negative. Rejection of the baby during the early postpartum period is common, as these statements illustrate:

I was kind of turned off. I didn't want to go near her. It was like she had a disease or something, and I didn't want to catch it. I didn't want to touch her. (Mother of a child with Down syndrome)

I saw her for the first time when she was 10 days old. . . . She was much more deformed than I had been told. At the time I thought, "Oh my God, what have I done?" (Mother of a child with spina bifida) (Darling, 1979, pp. 135–136)

The fact that parents have chosen to deny life-saving treatment to such children in the well-publicized "Baby Doe" cases is not surprising. Attachment to the baby is probably lowest during the first few hours after birth. Parents are also very vulnerable during the immediate postpartum period and likely to be highly susceptible to suggestions by professionals that their children not be treated. Lorber (1971), a British physician who advocated "selective treatment" for children born with spina bifida, has in fact written that he preferred to present his case for nontreatment to parents immediately after birth, before bonding had occurred.

Theories of parent–child "bonding" have recently been questioned (see, e.g., Eyer, 1992). Parents do not automatically develop an attachment relationship with their babies. Even when a baby has no disability, "bonding" between parent and child is not always an immediate reaction. LeMasters (1957) found that most of the parents of typical infants in his study had little effective preparation for parental roles and had romanticized parenthood. Shereshefsky, Liebenberg, and Lockman (1973) quote a new mother:

> I don't think I was prepared at all because you read in books and you talk with people and you think that all of a sudden there is going to be this motherly surge of love, which is not true. . . . I had this colicky baby that spit up, and we had to stay home. It took me a long time. (p. 175)

Dyer (1963) has noted that 80% of the parents he studied "admitted that things were not as they expected them after the child was born" (p. 200).

With any baby, disabled or not, attachment grows out of the process of parent–child interaction. When babies respond to parental attempts to feed and cuddle them, parents feel rewarded. Attachment is further enhanced when babies begin smiling and making sounds in response to parental gestures. Infants with disabilities, however, may not be able to respond to their parents' efforts. Bailey and Wolery (1984), Blacher (1984c), Collins-Moore (1984), Robson and Moss (1970), Waechter (1977), and others have suggested that the following characteristics of some childhood disabilities may impede the formation of parent–child attachment:

- The child's appearance, especially facial disfigurement
- Negative response to being handled (stiffness, tenseness, limpness, lack of responsiveness)
- Unpleasant crying
- Atypical activity level—either lowered activity or hyperactivity
- High threshold for arousal
- No response to communication
- Delayed smiling
- Feeding difficulties
- Medical fragility
- Presence of medical equipment, such as feeding tubes or oxygen supplies.
- Life-threatening conditions

- Prolonged hospitalization and consequent separation
- Impaired ability to vocalize
- Inability to maintain eye contact
- Unpleasant behaviors, such as frequent seizures

Abnormal response patterns in infants may result in withdrawal by parents. As Stone and Chesney (1978) have written: "The failure of the handicapped infant to stimulate the mother leads to the failure of the mother to interact with the infant" (p. 11). Frodi (1981) has shown, further, that child abuse is disproportionately high in the instance of "premature, disabled, and otherwise deviant" infants.

The tremendous adaptive capacity of families is evidenced by the fact that, given all the obstacles to parent–child attachment present in the case of childhood disability, the vast majority of parents *do* form strong attachments to their infants with disabilities. In general, all but the children with the most severe disabilities are able to respond to their parents to some extent—by sound, gesture, or other indication of recognition. In addition, attachment is usually encouraged by supportive interactions with other people. For example, members of parent-to-parent groups in many communities visit parents of newborns with disabilities shortly after birth.

The mother of the infant with Down syndrome quoted earlier explained:

> I talked to a nurse and then I felt less resentment. I said I was afraid, and she helped me feed the baby. . . . Then my girlfriend came to see me. She had just lost her husband, and we sort of supported each other. . . . By the time she came home I loved her. When I held her the first time, I felt love and I worried if she'd live. (Darling, 1979, p. 136)

Similarly, the mother of the child with spina bifida reported:

> As time goes on, you fall in love. You think, "This kid's mine, and nobody's gonna take her away from me." I think by the time she was two weeks old I wasn't appalled by her anymore. (Darling, 1979, p. 136)

Waisbren (1980), Marsh (1993), and others have reported the important role of social support in promoting parents' positive feelings about their children. One father of a child with Down syndrome said that, at first, he and his wife had decided not to send birth announcements, but then "everybody was saying he was so lucky to have us as parents." The parents then printed announcements that looked like theater tickets for a hypothetical play entitled "A Very Special Person" (Darling, 1979, p. 136). Minde (reported in Collins-Moore, 1984) also found that parents in a support group interacted more with their infants than other parents.

Various situational contingencies may also affect attachment. As Waechter (1977) and other have noted, the timing of the baby's birth in relation to other family events is important. Another member of the family may be ill, the family may be experiencing financial difficulties, or the parents may be having marital problems. The amount of time and energy available to parents for the new baby will depend on these contingencies. Professionals need to be aware of the family's situation when they look at parenting practices and parent–child relationships so that expectations are not unrealistic.

The Case of Delayed Diagnosis

Not all disabilities are diagnosed in the immediate postpartum period. Some developmental disabilities, such as cerebral palsy or mental retardation, may not be readily apparent shortly after birth. Other disabilities occur as a result of accidents or illnesses later in infancy or childhood. In still other cases, professionals delay in communicating a known diagnosis to parents for a variety of reasons (these are discussed in greater detail in Chapter 8). In general, parents have said that they were better able to adjust when they were aware of their child's diagnosis from the beginning. The process of redefining as disabled a child once defined as "normal" appears to be a very difficult one for parents.

Most of the time, however, parents suspect that a problem exists before they receive a diagnosis, and diagnostic delay only protracts the period of suspicion and its attendant stress. The experience of one family is illustrative:

> The mother, who was a nurse and had an older child, felt from the time of birth that something was wrong with the baby. Her daughter would not nurse, her eyes were crossing, "and she always seemed to be looking at her right side." The mother asked her pediatrician about the baby's vision and hearing but was told that nothing was wrong. When the baby was three months old, she kept falling asleep, [and the mother suspected that a photographer who took her picture at that time knew something was wrong]. The mother again questioned her pediatrician and was told that nothing was wrong. At five months, the baby began to have seizure-like periods, and the mother became increasingly concerned. Both her husband and her pediatrician continued to deny the problem. Her husband said, "I thought she was a little paranoid about it. . . . When you're not home all day, you don't see the [baby's] lack of activity or anything like that." As a result, the mother tried harder to rationalize and began blaming herself, feeling

that perhaps she had been neglecting the baby in favor of her older child. Finally, when the baby was six months old, the mother "broke down and started crying" in the pediatrician's office. [The child was finally diagnosed as having mental retardation.] (Darling, 1983, p. 127)

In such cases parents tend to be relieved rather than shocked when they finally receive a diagnosis. This reaction is apparent in these families of children with mental retardation quoted by Dickman and Gordon (1985):

> When the doctor told us he couldn't believe how well we accepted the diagnosis. All I can say is that it was such a relief to have someone finally just come out and say what we had feared so long! We felt now that we could move ahead and do the best we could for Timmy.

> When James turned six months old, my husband and I decided to change pediatricians. The second doctor was an angel in disguise. She spotted the problem immediately. . . . The reason I called her an angel was that she finally put an end to the unknown. The not knowing exactly what was wrong was driving me crazy. (pp. 31–32)

Similarly, in a study of 131 families with children with mental retardation, Baxter (1986) found that most parents who experienced little or no worry after a diagnostic encounter had gradually become aware of their child's "differentness" or had sought a diagnosis to confirm their own suspicions.

Sometimes, a child's diagnosis is elusive, even when medical professionals are sharing all of their knowledge and suspicions with parents. Medical knowledge simply is not yet at the point where all childhood disabilities can be definitively labeled. In such cases, anomie-related stress may be protracted indefinitely. A parent writes about her need for a "label":

> Sometimes I wish my son had cerebral palsy or Down syndrome— something definite and preferably a little visible. . . . It is . . . the elusiveness of our son's problems that causes so much pain. So, as awful as it sounds, I have thought of what it might be like to have a child with a defined disability. (Gundry, 1989, pp. 22–24)

In cases of disability resulting from accidents or illnesses occurring later in infancy or childhood, parents typically react in ways similar to those of parents receiving diagnoses earlier in infancy. In some cases, the sense of loss may be even greater, because the child has already been defined as "normal." However, parents still experience feelings of meaninglessness and powerlessness until they completely understand the nature of their child's disability and have embarked on a course of treatment.

THE POSTDIAGNOSIS EXPERIENCE

Although a diagnosis may relieve the stress associated with meaningless-ness and the suspicion that something is wrong, parents generally continue to experience anomie to some extent until issues of prognosis have been resolved and until the child is enrolled in an intervention program.

The Need for Prognostic Information

A father who had been told that his son would be "a slow learner" expressed the following concerns:

> [I was most worried about] how he would develop. It was the uncertainty of not knowing whether he'd be able to go to school and get a job or whether he'd always be dependent upon us. It was just not knowing what was likely to happen and what the future held for him and for us. (Baxter, 1986, p. 85)

Similarly, a mother whose child had been diagnosed as having Down syndrome reported:

> The whole first year we didn't see anyone or go anywhere. I was worried what she would be like when she grew up. Would she be toilet trained? Would she walk or talk or do things like that? Who would take care of her if anything happened to us? . . . Our pediatrician kept putting us off, saying, "She's still too young." . . . I went down to the Visiting Nurse Association just to get some information, a pamphlet, anything, about [Down syndrome]. (Darling, 1979, p. 148)

Today, most families do not experience a protracted period of concern with prognosis because they are typically enrolled in early intervention programs that provide answers to their questions. However, when parents receive only a diagnostic label or limited information from professionals, they generally continue to wonder, and worry, about what their child will be like in the future. Most parents are especially concerned about whether the child will be able to walk and talk, go to school, and play typical adult occupational and marital roles. Baxter (1986) has noted that the basic underlying factor in all expressions of parental worry is uncertainty. Parents of children with disabilities experience an ongoing need for information about the meaning of their child's condition—a need that professionals must meet. The parents in Baxter's study indicated that the most important type of help they had received from professionals was *information,* and that this help was more important than sympathy and emotional support. Similarly, Gowen, Christy, and Sparling (1993), and

Darling and Baxter (1996) report that parents' greatest need, especially during the infancy, toddler, and preschool periods, is for information.

The Quest for Intervention for the Child

In addition to providing information, professionals (early interventionists; speech, physical, and occupational therapists; physicians and other medical professionals) are also able to provide therapeutic intervention that will minimize the effects of a child's disability. Once they learn that their child has a disability, virtually all parents are eager to begin a program of treatment. When they receive diagnostic information, parents are relieved of the stress of meaninglessness; until they begin to do something about their child's disability, however, they may continue to experience anomie in the form of powerlessness.

Some of the early literature in this field suggested that parents sought treatment because they unrealistically wanted their children to be cured. Numerous studies refer to parents' "shopping around" for a professional or a program that would make their child "normal." When parents are questioned about such "shopping" behavior, however, most do not report curing as their goal. Rather, like parents of children without disabilities in our society, they are simply trying to be "good" parents and do whatever they can to improve their children's quality of life. This mother's explanation of her motivation for seeking treatment is typical:

> Because nothing was happening, and I was just sitting there with this baby, we got involved with the patterning program. . . . We were never told he would be cured. They were the first people who reacted to Billy as a person or called him by name. Up to that time he had done nothing. My pediatrician said, "You're just looking for hopes." I said, "No, I'm just looking to *do* something for him. I'm sitting at home doing nothing." (Darling, 1979, p. 153)

Similarly, the mother of a child with mental retardation in an early intervention program directed by one of the authors (R. B. D.) said, after her baby had died, that she was grateful for the program. She felt no guilt at the baby's death because she had done everything she could for him while he was alive.

As early intervention programs have become more widespread and publicity about them has increased, parents' quests for services have become shorter. Yet most continue to search until they are satisfied with their children's medical care and have secured needed services, such as physical therapy or special stimulation programs. The extent of parents' quests for services will be based largely on the resources available to them.

Most families have financial and geographic limitations that prevent them from searching endlessly for the "best" program for their child. Competing needs, such as other children at home or ill parents, may also prevent parents from enrolling their child in a time-consuming program or one far from home.

Sometimes, parents are overwhelmed by *too much* information. When daily schedules involve many therapy sessions (sometimes at different locations), in addition to normal routines of work and household responsibilities, parents may again experience anomie in the form of powerlessness. As one mother explained, "Your mind leaps forwards, backwards and sideways trying to sort out the deluge of information—the doctors' reports, nurses' instructions, conflicting or ambiguous diagnoses, appointment, feeding and laundry schedules" (McAnaney, 1990, p. 21).

During the early months, then, parents are typically motivated by a strong need to reduce their anomie, their sense of meaninglessness and powerlessness. As one mother said, "We wanted to get *us* in control instead of everybody else" (Darling, 1979, p. 147). Professionals can be most helpful to parents at this time by providing as much information as possible about diagnosis, prognosis, and the availability of intervention programs and other resources in the community—in as humane a manner as possible.

The Need for Emotional Support

One mother said:

> I met other parents of the retarded after we moved here. I felt that made the biggest difference in my life. . . . Down there [where we lived before], with my husband working so much and no other families with retarded children, I felt that I was just singled out for something, that I was weird. I felt a lot of isolation and bitterness. (Darling, 1979, pp. 162–163)

Similarly, another parent wrote:

> My five-year-old son has Down syndrome. . . . Craig is a very hyper child. He goes in his room and dumps toys all over the floor and throws things everywhere. . . .
>
> My husband works all day and most evenings until 10 P.M., and I feel like I'm going crazy! . . . I must keep my eyes on him every minute, so I never get my work done. I can't even go to the bathroom by myself! . . .
>
> I feel like I'm the only one in the world going through this. No one understands. . . . ("Down Syndrome," 1991, pp. 12–13)

The importance of social support in alleviating stress in families of children with disabilities has been well documented (see, e.g., Dyson & Fewell, 1986; Trivette & Dunst, 1982). Trivette and Dunst (1982) have shown that parents' personal well-being, perceptions of child functioning, and family integration are positively influenced by a family's informal social support network. They conclude that

> the negative consequences often associated with the birth and rearing of a child with developmental problems can be lessened or even alleviated to the extent that the members of a family's informal support network are mobilized to strengthen personal and familial well-being and buffer negative effects.

In some cases the birth of a child with a disability creates a rift in a family's relationship with former friends and family members. In other cases, even though friends and family are supportive, parents still need the special kind of support offered by others with children like their own.

SUPPORT WITHIN THE FAMILY AND OTHER EXISTING NETWORKS

One of the most difficult tasks facing new parents of children with disabilities is telling other family members and friends about their child's problem for the first time. Many have said that they "just didn't want to explain." In some cases, parents are afraid of upsetting elderly relatives or family members who are expecting the birth of their own child.

Negative reactions from extended family members (see Chapter 6, which discusses grandparents) and friends range from denial of the child's problem to rejection of the child:

> [My in-laws] to this day will not accept her as retarded. They will not say the word. They don't like us to talk about retardation. . . . She's their only grandchild. My mother thought that if she prayed hard enough Susan would be O.K.

> People think that retardation is a contagious disease. . . . I don't understand how it threatens them . . . the fact that a van pulls up in our driveway, picks up our daughter, and takes her to a program.

> When she was little, people were afraid to say anything. They would ask how [her nondisabled brother] was doing, but just asking about Julie was like a personal question. (Darling, 1979, pp. 145, 159, 160)

On the other hand, many families report that friends and relatives have been very supportive and helpful:

I called my mother as soon as I knew, and she came over. She was very supportive.

My father said, "What's the difference? She's yours."

The thing that surprised me was that everyone accepted it right off. (Darling, 1979, p. 146)

Receiving the support of family members may be more important among rural and small-town families, where extended family members tend to live in close proximity and serve as significant others and resources for one another. Heller, Quesada, Harvey, and Wagner (1981) found, for example, that among families living in the Blue Ridge Mountains of Virginia, the identities of nuclear and extended families were fused. Kin were the major source of social support, and involvement with relatives was obligatory. Urban "middle-American" families, on the other hand, were more "primary-kin oriented," and the opinions of extended family members were not as important to them. The relative importance of the extended family in various subcultures is discussed further in Chapter 7.

SUPPORT GROUPS

Most parents are able to get the support they need from friends and family. However, when friends and family react negatively or are unavailable, parents must look elsewhere for support. Even when members of existing social networks try to be helpful, parents may still feel that they do not *really* understand the parents' situation. Meeting other parents of children with disabilities thus becomes very important to some parents after they learn about their child's disability.

Support groups composed of adults with disabilities and parents of children with disabilities serve a number of functions, including (1) alleviating loneliness and isolation, (2) providing information, (3) providing role models, and (4) providing a basis for comparison.

As a mother quoted earlier said, before she became involved in a support group, she felt as though she was "singled out for something." Another mother said, "I was in a once-a-week mothers' group, and it was very helpful. You find out you're not the only person with this problem" (Darling, 1979, p. 161). This function appears to be served equally well by groups of parents of children with similar disabilities and parents of children with diverse disabilities. The fact of having a child who is "different" provides a common bond among these families.

Support groups also serve as sources of practical information. As the parent of a child with dwarfism explained:

> The technical aspect is the easiest thing. The doctors can tell you all about that. What makes it so difficult is what you do everyday and how you raise the child. And no one can tell you that except right here at this meeting. (Ablon, 1982, p. 43)

Similarly, the mother of a child with cerebral palsy said, "Meeting other parents you get the practical hints—like how someone got their child to chew—that normal parents take for granted" (Darling, 1979, p. 163).

At meetings, too, parents have an opportunity to see others who are coping successfully with their situation. These others provide a model for them to emulate. Sometimes parents who have been too timid to change physicians or seek additional services for their child may have the courage to do so after hearing how other parents have successfully challenged the system. The positive effects of encountering successful models among adults with disabilities is apparent in this statement by a parent of a child with dwarfism:

> At first we could not bring ourselves to go [to the meeting]. Maybe we didn't want to see what she was going to look like. . . . We . . . did go to the next meeting. . . . That was the turning point, because at that meeting we began talking to a number of dwarfs. That's when we found out it was going to be O.K.: that dwarfs live like other people— they married, they drove cars, they took vacations, they held jobs—they could be like other people. (Ablon, 1982, p. 38)

On the other hand, some parents are reluctant to meet adults with disabilities while their own children are still very young.

Finally, when they meet other families, parents discover not only those who are coping successfully but also those whose children's problems are worse than theirs. Most develop a greater appreciation of their own situation as a result:

> You don't feel sorry for yourself when you see some children that are just vegetables.

> We went to a couples' group where we saw that other children were a lot worse than Peter.

> I was active in the parents' association at the beginning. I needed the help more then. . . . Some had much more severe children than I did. I felt lucky to have Elizabeth. . . . Now I don't feel so sorry for myself. (Darling, 1979, pp. 161–162)

These parents are typically surrounded by friends and relatives whose children do not have disabilities, who may achieve developmental milestones much more quickly than their own children. Many have difficulty

watching their children's slow progress in comparison with the accomplishments of their friends' and relatives' children. Comparisons with
other children with disabilities, on the other hand, may be much more
favorable. The support group thus becomes an important reference group
for these families.

Although professionals may not be able to serve as a reference group
for parents, they can play an important role by helping parents locate
existing support groups—or starting new groups where none exist. A
number of parents have reported difficulty in finding other parents like
themselves. These stories are illustrative:

> We were walking on the beach and we saw four little people. I decided
> I'd follow them. I had to talk to them. I followed them a long way then
> I went up to the woman and said, "Excuse me, but I think my son is a
> little person"— I don't know what word I used, maybe "dwarf"—"like
> you are. . . . " The woman told us about Little People of America
> [LPA]. I had read about LPA in Life magazine before, but I didn't know
> how to contact them. When we got back we wrote to B. and she had
> a mother call us in a few days. (Ablon, 1982, p. 37)

> A friend of mine called and said she thought she saw a girlfriend of
> ours that we had gone to school with in the doctor's office, and she
> said that her daughter said there was a little girl that looked like
> Michelle. I thought about it . . . I hadn't talked to this girl since we
> graduated from high school. I called her up and said, "You have a
> daughter, right? . . . I want to ask you a question. I don't want you to
> feel offended," I said, "If I'm wrong I'm sorry." I said, "[Doesn't] your
> daughter [have Down syndrome]?" She said, "Yes she [does]. How did
> you know?" . . . She was our first exposure to other retarded people.
> . . . She told us about . . . the Association for the Retarded. (Darling,
> 1979, p. 148)

Professionals who inform parents about the existence of support groups
early in a child's life can be very helpful in avoiding the need for
protracted and often stressful searches. When no support groups exist in
an area, the professional should consider starting one. A further discussion of the professional role in relation to parent support groups can be
found in Chapter 9.

"Parent-to-parent" groups have also been effective in meeting the
information and support needs of parents, and many such groups now
exist throughout the country (see the appendix of Darling & Baxter, 1996,
for a list of such groups by state). Thus, professional control of support
groups does not appear to be necessary. Professional control, at least in
the early stages of group development, may be more important in the
case of parents who are less well educated or feel powerless for other
reasons.

Professionals can also make parents aware of opportunities for "long-distance" support through electronic mail networks, the pen pals column in *Exceptional Parent* magazine, and national support groups and organizations of parents of children with rare disorders (see the appendix of Darling & Baxter, 1996, for a complete listing of such resources).

INTERACTIONS WITH STRANGERS

After they have told friends and family members about their child's disability, parents must face having to explain to strangers on the street, in restaurants, and in shopping malls. Most parents have said that taking their child out in public was very difficult for them in the beginning. These reports are illustrative:

> We took her to a store downtown, and she had a hat. . . . I wanted to make sure that hat would stay on so no one would see her ears. . . . We didn't want people to look at her. We didn't want to explain.

> I used to go to the laundromat . . . and so many people would say, "Your little girl is so good to sit there so quietly in the stroller." . . . I would just like, sit there, and my insides were like knots, and I would think, "Oh no, do I have to tell them about the cerebral palsy? Should I or shouldn't I? Should I just let it pass? . . . " All this is going through my mind. . . . I never told anybody. (Darling, 1979, pp. 155, 156)

Because children with disabilities sometimes look younger than their age, parents commonly avoid explanations by lying to strangers:

> He just looked like a little baby, even at two or three. People would ask how old he was—especially waitresses—and then they were embarrassed. So I started lying, and the waitresses would say, "Oh, he's so cute!"

> We bought a car last February. Joey was 15 or 16 months old, and the salesman asked, "Is the baby eight or nine months old?" I said, "Yes." [My daughter] said, "He's one." I said, "Sh." I've been a little too hesitant about telling people. (Darling, 1979, p. 157)

Some come to resent this situation:

> For five years I drew in my breath, narrowed my eyes, and proceeded to explain, in grim detail, Annie's premature birth, from weight and length right down to time spent on a ventilator. The EXPLANATION. Complete with the harrowing account I felt I was required to give to perfect strangers, as though this information was due them. And all

because of the simple question, "How old is she?" (Nelson, 1991, p. 23)

Eventually, most parents become more comfortable explaining to strangers about their children's disabilities. Professionals can help them develop explanations they can use in these situations; support groups can also be helpful in sharing explanations that other parents have used.

LEAVING INFANCY: MOVING TOWARD NORMALIZATION

Parent's reactions to the news that their child has a disability, then, will vary according to their interactions with other people—before, during, and after the time that the news is received. The meanings they attach to their child's disability will continue to change as their child grows and they encounter new interaction situations.

The ability of individuals to cope with any situation depends on how they define the situation. Definition of the situation is one of the most difficult tasks facing new parents because of the degree of meaninglessness and powerlessness usually present. Because the birth of a child with a disability is generally an unanticipated event, parents must rely on other people to establish meaning for them. Professionals play an important role by providing parents with diagnostic, prognostic, and treatment information.

By the end of the infancy period, most parents have resolved their anomie. They may still be angry or disappointed by their children's disabilities, but they are beginning to understand them. If their search for an intervention program for the child has been successful, they are also beginning to feel in control of their situation. At this point, the child's disability may decline in importance in their lives; the all-consuming need to make sense of an unexpected and painful event will eventually be replaced by the resumption of concerns with other family members, careers, and leisure activities.

The extent to which families will be able to return to a "normalized" lifestyle after the infancy period will vary according to the nature of a child's disability, available social supports, and other factors. These are discussed in the next chapter.

CHAPTER THREE

Childhood and Adolescence: Continuing Adaptation

Parenthood of a retarded person . . . is a kaleidoscope of feeling and experience.

It has its beauty, but it is always changing. It is irritation at ineffectual hands plucking endlessly at a knotted shoe-lace. . . .

It is guilt at the irritation. . . .

It is a surge of love for this person who needs your protection: and a surge of horror that he will always need it. . . .

It is a glowing admiration for his learning achievements, against such odds.

It is horror at the inexorable ticking of the developmental clock.

It is a prayer that he will painlessly cease to live.

It is the desperate rush to the doctor because he is looking ill. . . .

It is 365 days a year.

—MAX (1985, pp. 261, 262)

NORMALIZATION: GOAL OF THE CHILDHOOD YEARS

By the end of the infancy period, the resolution of anomie is complete for most families. As their children move through the preschool years, parents generally try to resume activities that were disrupted by their child's birth and the period of anomie that followed. The mother who has left a job may wish to return to work; the parents may resume social activities; the family may want to take a vacation or pursue other recreational activities. Parents are encouraged to maintain a "normal-appearing round of life" (Birenbaum, 1970, 1971) by other parents, friends, and professionals. Voysey (1975) argues that parents have a normality perspective because they are *expected* to be "normal" by other agents in society: parents' associations, magazine articles, clergy, and various helping professionals. These agents help parents rationalize their situation and teach them that they are *supposed* to be "coping splendidly" with their child's disability.

Voysey states that families develop an ideology of normalization, which contains the following elements: (1) acceptance of the inevitable ("It could happen to anyone."), (2) partial loss of the taken-for-granted ("taking it day to day"), (3) redefinition of good and evil ("There's always someone worse off."), (4) discovery of true values ("You appreciate your child's progress more when you don't just take it for granted."), (5) positive value of suffering ("It brings you closer together."), and (6) positive value of differentness ("It's for his own good.").

Although the components of normalization vary by social class and other subcultural factors, in general a normalized lifestyle for families with school-aged children in American society includes the following:

- Employment for either or both parents
- Appropriate educational placement for children
- Access to appropriate medical care
- Adequate housing
- Social relationships with family and friends
- Leisure time
- Freedom of movement in public places
- Sufficient financial resources to maintain their basic lifestyle

The presence of a child with a disability in the home can prevent a family from attaining any or all of these components.

The ability of families to achieve a normalized lifestyle will be determined by their opportunity structure, that is, their access to resources. Society provides a variety of resources, ranging from financial aid to respite care for children with disabilities. These resources are not equally distributed in the population, however, and for many families, life is a constant struggle. We suggest in this chapter that, regardless of the nature of a child's disability or of the personality or coping ability of the parents, the most important determinant of normalization for most families of children with disabilities is the availability of supportive resources in the community.

OBSTACLES TO NORMALIZATION

In a study of 330 parents of children with mental retardation, Suelzle and Keenan (1981) found that perceptions of unmet needs varied over the life cycle. Perceived needs for family support, respite care, and counseling services were higher among parents of preschoolers and young adults and lowest among parents of school-aged children. In a study of families of children with autism, DeMyer and Goldberg (1983) found that the need for respite remained relatively constant during childhood and adolescence. In general, practical problems seem to replace coping difficulties as parents' primary concern as their children get older. These include (Morney, reported in Mori, 1983) additional financial hardships, stigma, extraordinary demands on time, difficulties in such caregiver tasks as feeding, diminished time for sleeping, social isolation, less time for recreational pursuits, difficulties managing behavior, and difficulties performing routine household chores, among others. These and other problems, which serve as barriers to normalization, will be discussed in greater detail below.

Continuing Medical Needs

Children with disabilities generally require more specialized medical care and more frequent hospitalizations than others. In addition, these children may need medically related services, such as physical, occupational, and speech therapy. The availability of these services varies from one geographic location to another. Butler, Rosenbaum, and Palfrey (1987) have written that "where a child lives has become more than ever a predictor of the affordability and accessibility of care" (p. 163). They note a study showing that 12% of low-income children among the most severely disabled third of special-education students in Rochester, New York, did not have a regular physician and 7% did not have insurance coverage; in Charlotte, North Carolina, on the other hand, 34% of the same group had no regular physician and 32% had no insurance coverage. The study showed further that use of health care services was related to access: "Even for the most severely impaired group, the likelihood of seeing a physician was 3.5 times higher if the child had insurance coverage" (p. 163).

Obtaining insurance coverage for children with disabilities is often problematic. Some private insurance plans automatically exclude children with disabilities, and not all children are eligible for government-sponsored assistance, such as Medicaid. Some children "fall through the cracks," as illustrated by the following Internet communication (Internet, Children with Special Health Care Needs list, December 14, 1994):

> Linda and her husband have a four-year old daughter with Down
> syndrome. She has been denied medical insurance coverage under the
> family's group (employee funded) medical plan (because she has Down
> syndrome) and has also been denied coverage by New Jersey's AC-
> CESS plan (state funded high-risk pool) because she is her father's
> dependent and "should be" covered under his plan.

Even in areas where health care is readily available, parents may have
difficulty locating a physician who is interested in treating children with
disabilities. Pediatricians especially tend to prefer treating nondisabled
children with acute, curable diseases. As a result, parents of children with
disabilities may engage in lengthy searches before they find a physician
with whom they are satisfied. As one disgruntled father of a youngster
with a severe disability commented, "It's like when you take your dog to
the vet. . . . Not many doctors pick him up and try to communicate with
him as a child" (Darling, 1979, p. 151). For a discussion of other issues
relating to health care difficulties for children with disabilities, see Darling
and Peter (1994).

Eventually, most parents do obtain satisfactory health care for their
child. After their search is ended, parents may be reluctant to move to a
new location, where they would have to search once again. Opportunities
for career advancement may be limited as a result. Families' freedom of
movement may also be limited in other ways by their children's special
medical needs:

> There are things we'd like to do with [our two nondisabled children].
> We'd like to take some trips before [our daughter] goes to college. . . .
> But we can't do that now. . . . It's hard to travel with Billy now. . . .
> Because of his medical problems, I'm fearful to leave. I don't want to
> end up in a strange hospital somewhere. Everyone knows Billy at
> University Hospital now, and that's very relieving. (Darling, 1979, p.
> 182)

Special Educational Needs

The quest for medical services may become less of a priority as children
approach school age, but the search for appropriate educational programs often becomes more important at that time.

PRESCHOOL EDUCATION

For the child with a disability, formal education may begin shortly after
birth. With the proliferation of early intervention programs in recent years,
many children have begun receiving services soon after or even before,

they are diagnosed. These programs may be either home based or center based, although programs of both kinds typically involve parents as teachers for their own children. Some programs include specialists, such as physical or speech therapists, in addition to specially trained teachers.

In some cases, however, parents do not discover early intervention programs until well into their children's preschool years. As one mother said:

> [The doctor] said, "Just take him home and love him." . . . I wondered, Isn't there anything more? . . . When he was $2\frac{1}{2}$, I read in the newspaper about a preschool program for retarded children. (Darling & Darling, 1982, p. 133)

Although less commonly than in the past, parents may engage in extensive searches to find a preschool program that is appropriate for their child:

> We were in the_____Regional Center Area. They said when he was three years old, they would take him in a program. . . . There was a bus that would have taken him but it would have been two hours one way and three hours the other, because we were at the very end of the line. . . . That's when we decided, "If he's going to have school, we're going to have to move." . . .
>
> It was very difficult to get information. I called the state agencies, but they didn't give me anything. I finally had to go to every single town, every director of special ed, in the . . . area, and I visited just about every preschool they had. . . . Just about every one I went to, there were some little kids sitting nicely, learning about their colors and shapes and everything . . . and there was this one little kid crawling around in the corner playing with the wastebasket, . . . and I knew that was Brian. . . .
>
> If you live in_____and have a handicapped child, you move, because they don't have any programs. . . . I wasn't going to be the one that fought the system. . . .
>
> At_____Program, the profoundly retarded were being shown books. . . . They weren't just left in a corner. . . . We could have afforded to live elsewhere more easily, but we moved to_____, because that's where the_____program was. (Darling, 1979, pp. 174–175)

Today, Public Law 99-457 (discussed further in Chapter 10) and other funding sources have made preschool education more available, and physicians and other professionals are better informed about the existence of local programs. Some gaps in the quantity and quality of these programs remain, however. Generally, by the end of the preschool years, parents have found a satisfactory program for their children. However, concerns about the quality of available educational programs are likely to arise again when children reach kindergarten age. Parents of children without disabilities make take for granted the fact that the school system will provide an appropriate education for their children; parents of children with special needs who have similar assumptions often learn that local programs do not meet those needs.

THE SCHOOL YEARS

Prior to the passage in 1975 of Public Law 94-142, the Education of All Handicapped Children Act (later renamed the Individuals with Disabilities Education Act), guidelines for the education of children with disabilities were vague, and parents' rights were not clearly stated. Because of difficulties they had in obtaining an appropriate education for their children, many parents of teenage and adult children feel bitter and resentful toward the school system and, in some cases, even toward parents of younger children who have benefited from newer legislation and programs. The following stories, related by parents of adult children, illustrate some of the difficulties they have faced:

> In her old school, Karen had been in the same [trainable] class for three or four years. There were toys in the room. . . . The trainable teacher had been trying to teach Karen and a few others to read, but the special education director they had at the time said, "No, these children can't read." . . . A psychologist had once told us that Karen would be able to read some day, and she wanted to learn. We didn't think that Karen would get any more out of the trainable class. We begged them to test her. . . . We petitioned the Board. . . . A psychologist from the state said, "She's not ready." I felt like crying. . . . [A year later] we had her tested by a private psychologist. . . . He said that her speech needed improvement but that her vocabulary was almost normal rather than retarded. . . . He thought she should be in the educable class. . . . They finally moved her. (Mother of a child with Down syndrome, reported in Darling, 1979, p. 175)

> At Children's Hospital, Tony was in a class with active, bright kids. . . . He just sat in the corner and played in the sandbox. . . . Then he went to the School for the Blind, which is geared for the totally blind child. . . . They mostly concentrated on teaching Braille. Finally, Tony. . . . had to leave the school. They said [he was] retarded. . . . After Tony [was] labeled retarded by the School for the Blind, [he] started in the [city] Public School System, but they had no appropriate program either. . . . After three years we started fighting. . . . The Board of Education said, "We've got all kinds of retarded programs. We'll just put [him] in one of those." . . . I visited the programs, and there wasn't one child in a wheelchair. . . . I said, "How [is my child] going to get around? How [is he] going to go down these stairs? . . ." They kept saying "No" to us. . . .
> We were lucky at this time because [my husband had changed jobs and] was in the school system and knew a lot of people. And they were guiding us and telling us where to write, each step of the way. We went

right to the top. . . . A program was established within two weeks. (Mother of a child with multiple disabilities, reported in Darling, 1979, pp. 176–177)

Michael started first grade at the Oakmont School [a facility that served all children with disabilities within the region]. It was an old, noisy building . . . and it seemed that each year he did the same thing as the year before. . . . There was no separation by age. They just didn't know what to do with our kids. . . .

I talked to everyone, even [our state senator]. . . . He said, "You can't expect things to happen overnight." . . . After awhile . . . parents got together. We decided we wanted our kids in our own school district. . . .

Several parents got together and went to [our school district]. They were building a new elementary school. . . . I didn't know if mainstreaming would be better. I only knew it couldn't be worse. . . . They weren't going to put in an elevator. They wanted to build a tennis court instead. . . . They didn't want to provide transportation. . . . Then, we couldn't get him on and off the bus. . . . They supplied a helper. . . . You eventually get what you need . . . if you're very persistent, but they always leave you with the feeling that they are doing you a favor . . . to provide your son with an education. (Mother of a child with spina bifida, reported in Darling & Darling, 1982, pp. 137–138)

Special-education legislation of the 1970s, 1980s, and 1990s (Public Laws 94-142, 99-457, 102-119) has mandated that children with disabilities receive a free and appropriate public education in the "least restrictive environment." However, for a number of reasons, including ignorance, fear, and the limited resources of school districts, the promise of the legislation has not become a reality for many children. Because of poor knowledge about their legal rights, many parents have not challenged their children's educational placements. Public awareness has been growing, however, and more and more parents are questioning educators about their children's programs.

One study (Orenstein, 1979) of parents who did challenge the system found that many parents waited months before securing an evaluation. After evaluations were completed, parents were sometimes pressured into accepting inadequate educational plans by school personnel who used

tactics such as blaming the parents for their child's problems, claiming that the child had emotional problems . . . rather than learning problems, using excessive jargon, . . . and offering only minimal levels of special services until parents complain or threaten to use appeals processes.

Parents may challenge their children's educational plans for a variety of reasons. One common complaint involves placement in an inappropriate setting. Parents may wish to have their child placed in an inclusive setting rather than a special school or classroom; in other cases, they want more special programming for their children. The former case is illustrated by this experience, related by the mother of a child with spina bifida:

> When Ellen entered kindergarten, she was in a special needs class in the morning and mainstreamed in the afternoon. . . . [In the special needs class], she was with children whose needs were much more demanding than Ellen's. . . . Some were retarded. . . . At the end of the year we had a meeting. The first grade was on the second floor [Ellen was in a wheelchair]. . . . They said we should keep her in the special needs class. I was furious. . . . She had done so well in the mainstreaming class. . . . I wanted her in a regular first grade and I suggested moving the class downstairs. . . . They wanted Ellen in the special needs class because it was easier for them, not for any other reason. (Darling & Darling, 1982, p. 140)

Another common parental complaint involves the lack of coordination among the various educational settings through which children move during the school day. In the past, when children in special-education were completely segregated from children in regular instruction, coordination was not a problem. With the implementation of newer legislation, however, working relationships have had to be developed between special-education administrators, evaluators, and teachers on the one hand, and regular classroom teachers, principals, and guidance counselors, on the other. As Scanlon, Arick, and Phelps (1981) have shown, regular classroom teachers often do not attend conferences at which children's Individualized Education Plans are developed. Parents commonly complain that regular classroom teachers are not prepared for children with disabilities.

Another type of problem involves disagreements about the kinds of services schools are required to provide to children with disabilities. Parents may believe that related services, such as physical therapy, are needed in order for their children to receive an appropriate education; school systems may disagree. Some children require special health services in order to attend school. Children with spina bifida, for example, may require catheterization one or more times a day. In the past, parents had to come to the school to perform this simple procedure, often at great inconvenience. As a result of one family's persistence, however, the Supreme Court ruled several years ago that Clean Intermittent Catheterization is indeed a necessary related service that must be provided by the school district.

In some cases, families living in rural areas have had more difficulty than urban families in obtaining appropriate educational services for their children (Capper, 1990). Kelker, Garthwait, and Seligman's (1992) quote from a mother living in rural Montana is illustrative:

> We like this small community. Mark and I both grew up in this area and we want our children to experience the same close-knit, family-oriented upbringing that we enjoyed as children. However, with Jeff's special needs we are questioning more and more whether we are doing the right thing by staying here. (p. 14)

Some of the problems faced by rural school districts include difficulty in finding qualified staff, funding inadequacies, and transportation difficulties (Helge, 1984). As a result, rural families of children with disabilities often face special challenges.

Behavior Problems

Baxter (1986) found, in a study of families of children with retardation, that the major stressors associated with the care and management of the child were (1) behavior management problems and (2) the child's continued dependence. The first is discussed here and the second, in the next section.

Baxter found that although concern about the child's physical needs tended to decrease with the age of the child, worry about the child's behavior in public increased over time. Behavior management problems commonly occur in conjunction with such disabilities as mental retardation and autism. The following description of a child with both deafness and blindness illustrates some of the forms that these problems may take:

> When he gets off the bus Friday afternoon after a week at the residential school for the blind, he lies on the sidewalk kicking and screaming while his mother runs frantically to and from the house with various foods which might appease his anger. Over the weekend no one in the household is permitted to make program selections on the television because Johnny takes charge of the dial. Most of the night the family lies awake to the sound of ear-piercing screams, and the hours of quiet when they at last lapse into grateful sleep bring the morning rewards of ransacked kitchen shelves and mutilated books. (C. Klein, 1977, p. 310)

Such nonnormative, disruptive behavior may limit the family's opportunities for social participation. As one mother of a child with mental retardation and cerebral palsy explained:

> He's hard to take with us. I always have to get a babysitter or I'll stay home. . . . It's really like having a little baby, only he doesn't outgrow it. . . . And we don't as a rule have people over—because he doesn't go to sleep. (Darling, 1979, p. 171)

DeMyer and Goldberg (1983) have reported that the aspect of family life most affected by a child with autism is family recreation. Baxter (1986) has noted that parents are most willing to take such children to gatherings involving family and friends and least willing to take them to places involving other persons.

Baxter found that certain social situations produced considerable stress:

1. Formal social occasions where the child does not conform to norms
2. Other persons' homes where coping with the child's behavior is difficult
3. Public settings where behavior management is a problem
4. Restrictive settings that do not readily allow parents to withdraw from the situation
5. Social situations where the child engages in deviant forms of interaction with other people

Parents feel stress when their child's behavior calls attention to the family. Although most try to explain the child's disability to friends or strangers, some simply control their feelings and say nothing or move away from the distressing encounter. Birenbaum (1970) has shown that some parents may try to hide their children's behavior problems by cleaning the house before the guests arrive or controlling the home setting in other ways.

Although the extent of a child's behavior problems may be related to the nature of the child's disability, even families with children with severe disabilities may be able to achieve some degree of normalization if they have adequate social support. Bristol and Schopler (1984) have shown that family adaptation is more closely related to perceived adequacy of informal support than to the severity of the child's disability in the case of children with autism, and families without support may suffer considerable social isolation as a result of their children's behavior. As Bristol (1987) has shown, single parents may be especially vulnerable to such stress, although we should not assume that social support is lacking in all such cases. Baxter (1986) has shown, too, that small families tend to experience greater stress in care and management than larger families.

Continuing Dependence

As children without disabilities grow older, they become less dependent on their parents. By the end of the preschool years, they are able to feed and dress themselves and take care of their toileting needs. Later they become able to go about the neighborhood without supervision, and eventually they can stay home alone, without the need for babysitters. Demands on parents' time thus decrease. Disabilities may limit the ability of children to achieve such increasing independence, however. One study (Barnett, 1995) found, for example, that, in comparison with other parents, those who had children with Down syndrome spent more time on child care and less time in social activities. Mothers allocated less time to paid employment as well.

Even families with highly dependent children can achieve normalization if they have access to good support services such as low-cost, specially trained babysitters or respite care. A special camp in Arkansas, for example, cares for school-aged children with disabilities 48 weekends a year in order to provide relief for the families:

> Julie Mills, a severely mentally handicapped 10-year-old with a speech impairment, attends the camp.
>   "It allows us to be together the whole weekend, to go shopping at our will or just sit around and watch television," Julie's mother, Sherry Mills, said of time alone with her husband, Carl. "We become a little closer, get to know each other. It's almost like a date."
>   Susan and Mike Walker send their 7-year-old daughter Rachel to the camp so they can spend time with their 9-year-old daughter Dawn.
>   Rachel suffers from seizure disorders and mental and physical disabilities, Mrs. Walker said, and caring for her can deprive Dawn of attention. ("Camp Cares," 1986)

On the other hand, when such resources are not available, maintaining a normalized lifestyle can be difficult, as in the case of these parents of children with deafness and blindness:

> Several sets of parents have admitted they have never been on a vacation alone, and very few go out on the weekend because it is nearly impossible to locate a babysitter who will tackle this unusual charge for a reasonable fee. Respite care is a rare and dear luxury. With the deaf–blind youngster functioning as the focal point in these otherwise uneventful weekends, many parents become rivals in finding means to compensate for the child's lack of sensory input. (C. Klein, 1977, p. 311)

Financial Burden

Childhood disabilities have an economic impact on families in addition to their psychosocial costs. This impact includes both direct costs, such as expenses for child care, medical care, therapy, and special equipment, and indirect costs, such as lost work time, special residential needs, and interference with career advancement.

DIRECT COSTS

In a nationwide survey of 1,709 families with children with physical disabilities, Harbaugh (1984) found that the largest single out-of-pocket expense was for babysitting. This finding is not surprising, considering the continued dependence of children with disabilities discussed in the last section. Yet because of the costs involved, some parents of children with disabilities may actually use babysitters less than parents of children without disabilities, even though their needs are greater.

Harbaugh reports that, after babysitting, physical and occupational therapy costs were the greatest out-of-pocket expense of the families in his study. These and other medically related services are not always covered by health insurance, and Harbaugh found that the average monthly cost to families for these services (in 1984) was $162—a significant portion of the family budget for many.

Physician visits and hospitalizations are also expensive for these families, especially when they are not covered by private health insurance or public medical assistance. In one study (Butler et al., 1987), only 22% of privately insured children with disabilities had all their visits to physicians paid by their insurance plans. Another study (Select Committee on Children, Youth, and Families, reported in Morris, 1987) estimated that 10.3% of children with disabilities and 19.5% of disabled children in poverty have no health insurance. In addition, 40% of all children with disabilities below the federal poverty level are not covered by Medicaid (this figure may be even higher if Congress passes new legislation they are considering at the time of this writing). A survey by the National Center for Health Statistics (NCHS; reported in "NCHS Studies," 1992) indicated that low income and Hispanic chronically ill children with special needs were less likely to have insurance coverage than other children. Butler and colleagues (1987) also note that continuity of insurance coverage is a problem for both publically and privately insured families. For privately insured families, job changes may mean discontinuity in coverage. The U.S. Congress's Select Committee on Children, Youth and Families (reported in Morris, 1987) found that the annual expenses for hospital and physician services for a child with a disabling chronic condition range from $870 to $10,229, depending on the condition's severity. In contrast, the cost of these services for a nondisabled child averages about $270 a year. (For a further discussion of hospital costs, see Darling, 1987.)

Medical equipment and supplies are also very expensive. The cost of a standard child-sized wheelchair, for example, is currently approximately $900. Children with severe physical disabilities may also need special equipment for feeding, toileting, and other activities of daily living. Computerized equipment, which can greatly improve quality of life, is even more expensive. A computerized system that can synthesize speech, for example, currently costs between $4,000 and $5,000. Most health insurance plans do not yet cover such items.

Many insurance plans have limits as to the dollar amounts they will cover. Health maintenance organizations (HMOs) often have similar limits. As one grandmother related,

> My 7-year-old granddaughter's HMO limits the amount of PT [physical therapy] she can get (she was born with spina bifida). . . . My daughter has been "banking" her PT as she is going to need surgery for scoliosis and will need a great deal of PT then . . . we find the HMO most restrictive. For instance, they have a $5,000 cap on wheelchairs. She's still using the first chair she received through a different coverage but has had to have new seating on it through her new HMO so is already into her $5,000 max by about $3,000. Consequently when she gets her next chair, within a year or two, she is [going to exceed the cap]. (Internet, Children with Special Health Care Needs List, November 22, 1994)

Although medically related costs will vary by the disability, two studies found total expenses of this nature to be over $100,000 to raise a child to age 18. In a study of families of children with spina bifida, the total cost of medical care and equipment from birth to age 18 was $108,000 to $192,000 in 1982 dollars (Lipscomb, Kolimaga, Sperduto, Minnich, & Fontenot, 1983). Similarly, a study of families of children with cerebral palsy (Morris, 1987) found an average cost of $126,631 for disability-related expenses over the same time period.

OTHER DIRECT COSTS

A child's disability may also require housing or vehicle modifications, such as ramps, lifts, or widened doorways to accommodate a wheelchair. C. Klein (1977) notes, too, items such as locks for cabinets and bars for windows in the case of children who are deaf–blind. Additional items are noted by the father of four teenagers with a cerebral palsy-like syndrome:

> Our kids have a phone. It's essential. Other kids can go out and play. We can't afford it but we have it. . . . We also can't afford the swimming pool, but water's the best therapy. . . . Where else can they go and swim almost every day in the summer? The city don't have it, so I have it. (Darling, 1979, p. 180)

INDIRECT COSTS

Other, hidden costs may also be associated with childhood disability. Because these children require access to services and greater commitments of their parents' time than other children, the family's overall economic situation may be adversely affected.

As a mother quoted earlier in the chapter noted, her family moved to a more expensive community than they could afford because a good preschool program was located there. Similarly, another parent has written:

> We were forced to leave the Aurora . . . Public School District for the express purpose of obtaining an appropriate public school education for our son. . . .
> The private sector is willing to educate these children—at huge expense. As one professional said to me: "Our attitude even here is, we'll take your house and your second car. Your husband has to get a second job; then we'll help you with your child." Thus, we left Aurora . . . knowing that we would eventually lose our home if we didn't. ("Reader's Forum," 1985, p. 7)

Some parents may reject opportunities for career advancement because services for their children may not be as good in a new location. The amount of parents' time required by a child's special needs may also interfere with career advancement or a parent's having a job at all. Lipscomb and colleagues (1983) found that the average weekly work reduction among parents of children with spina bifida was 5 hours for fathers and 14 hours for mothers. In 1982 dollars, the resulting average annual income loss for these families ranged from $8,000 to $ 17,000. Morris (1987) notes the cases of a mother who forfeited an annual salary of $30,000 to transport her child to speech and physical therapy and a parent who quit work and stayed home for 15 years to care for her disabled child.

One father has written:

> I think there is a common perception amongst the public that the costs of raising a child with a disability are only in the costs incurred for medical care, etc. This is hardly true.
> We know exactly what the loss to society, and our family was, in dollar terms: $5.2 million. (Our daughter is a quad.) We know because a certified economist carefully considered all factors involved in the loss as part of legal proceedings. . . .
> In terms of the things we definitely notice every day, however: my spouse had to drop to half-time. . . . Because she had to drop to half-time, and because there is a bias against half-time people, and because our frantic schedule means we don't have time for commuting so we need to work close to home, she earns significantly less than half

of what she could full-time. Originally, we had both planned on working full-time after the kids were 10 or so, to provide for the kids' college, get ready for retirement, and do some things we had wanted to do while we were still young enough to have the physical vigor to do them.

I have not advanced as far in my work as I had expected to, before the birth of our daughter. I believe my salary is significantly lower than it would be otherwise, because my first priority is care provision and advocacy, not what I do at work. Many of the people I work with know and respect that, however the bottom-line is that you get paid for what you do at work, not for what you do at home. (Internet, Children with Special Health Care Needs List, March 15, 1995)

Although estimates of the total cost of rearing a child with a disability vary according to the method used, one recent estimate of both direct and indirect costs per child ranged from $294,000 for spina bifida to $503,000 (in 1992 dollars) for cerebral palsy (Waitzman, Romano, Scheffler, & Harris, 1995).

Continuing Needs for Support

Needs for social support may be ongoing among families whose opportunities for inclusion in "normal" society remain limited. Such families may be geographically or linguistically isolated or may have children whose disabilities are rare or pose unusual difficulties in obtaining needed services. These electronic mail requests (all from the Children with Special Health Care Needs List) are illustrative:

One of my son's therapists called me yesterday and asked me if I had any ideas about finding some support for one of her families. . . . The family would love to find someone to talk to but have been unable to find any other people locally. . . . Speaking from experience (my son has an even rarer syndrome . . .) it makes *so* much difference in your coping abilities when you have someone to talk to who has *been* there. (January 26, 1995)

One of my son's therapists . . . asked me to put in another request about this, because they are having trouble finding someone to interact with a family of a . . . child. The major problem in this instance is that the family speaks almost no English at all—they are Hispanic. There is another child in this area with the same syndrome, but they don't speak Spanish. (April 27, 1995)

Thanks to all who sent me private e-mails about my [children's disabilities]. It really made me feel less alone, and I got some useful resources to look into (it is hard to find out about resources when you don't live in a big city). (November 10, 1994)

Stigma and Its Consequences

As noted in Chapter 7, individuals with disabilities in our society are likely to encounter stigma in their interactions with others. Goffman (1963) has shown, further, that parents and others who associate with people with disabilities are likely to bear a "courtesy stigma" of their own. As children get older, their disabilities generally become more visible and, thus, more stigmatizing.

Baxter (1986) found that the attribute most likely to attract attention to a child with a disability was speech, not appearance or behavior. Parental stress was also related to the quality of their child's speech. In order to prevent stigma-producing encounters, then, families may have to structure their lives to avoid social situations that would require their children to speak or perform roles that would otherwise call attention to their disabilities. Such children, then, may not be taken to see Santa Claus at Christmastime or to visit casual acquaintances. Parents' lifestyles may be limited as a result.

Physical Barriers

A final obstacle to normalization involves physical barriers in the environment. Individuals with disabilities and their families may be prevented from full social participation by stairs, narrow doorways, and hilly terrain. Our society is structured, both socially and physically, to meet the needs of people without disabilities. Although accessibility has been increasing in recent years, families of children with disabilities are still limited in their housing choices, vacation destinations, and general freedom of movement.

In a small number of families, normalization is delayed when family members themselves do not agree about their needs and their child's needs. For example, parents may disagree about the appropriate school placement for a child. In such cases, professional counseling may be required to resolve the difference. This option is discussed in Chapter 9. In general, though, socially imposed obstacles are the major deterrents to normalization for most families.

CATALYSTS TO NORMALIZATION

The strength of families is demonstrated by the fact that, given the many obstacles that exist, most are still able to achieve a nearly normal lifestyle: normalization is, in fact, the most common mode of adaptation in our society. Achievement of a normalized lifestyle may be related less to the degree of a child's disability or parents' coping abilities than to the *opportunity structure* within which the family resides.

Opportunity Structures

All families do not have equal access to opportunities for normalization. These opportunities include the following:

- Access to satisfactory medical care and medically related services
- Availability of an appropriate educational program
- Supportive relatives and friends
- Access to respite care and day care, if needed
- Adequacy of financial resources
- Presence of accepting neighbors
- Quantity and quality of household help
- Access to behavior management programs, if needed
- Availability of appropriate recreational programs
- Access to special equipment, if needed
- Presence of friends and social opportunities for the child
- Adequacy of available transportation

Families' opportunity structures can be changed. Such changes may occur when a family moves to a new neighborhood or encounters a helpful professional. Opportunity structures are also changed by new laws and court decisions and through parental activism and disability rights movements. Professionals can play an important role in working with families to change their access to existing opportunities and to help them create opportunities where none exist.

Changes in Support Networks

As we noted in the last chapter, parents commonly become immersed in support groups consisting of others like themselves when their children are young and newly diagnosed. Continued immersion in such homogeneous groups can eventually become an obstacle to normalization, or integration in "normal" society, however. As a result, parents often decrease their involvement in segregated support networks as their children get older. As one mother explained:

> We went to the Association pretty regularly for two years. But after awhile we felt that they did not have that much to offer . . . as far as

help to us. . . . We just got too busy to go to the meetings. Karen didn't
have a lot of problems. (Darling, 1979, pp. 161–162)

Parents may also decrease their involvement with other families of
children with disabilities by encouraging their children's friendships
with children without disabilities in the neighborhood or at school. As
one mother of a child with spina bifida explained, her daughter has
some friends at "myelo" clinic but she does not see them elsewhere.
"They live too far away," and the mother will not go out of her way
because she wants her daughter to be "as normal as possible" (Darling,
1979, p. 193).

Although parents may choose to become integrated into "normal"
society, their success will depend on their opportunity structures—"normal"
society must accept them. A summary description of the family of
the child with spina bifida described above illustrates such a successful
adaptation:

> The mother reported that relatives thought the baby was "fantastic"
> and were very supportive during the first few months. Elizabeth
> attended a nursery school with children without disabilities and was
> then in an inclusive public school classroom. She has always been well
> accepted by the other children. Grandparents and other family mem-
> bers live nearby and continue to be highly supportive. They babysit so
> that the parents can take short vacations alone. The parents have
> decreased their involvement in a parents' association and, at the time
> they were interviewed, were preoccupied with the "normal" concerns
> of running a business, wanting to buy a house, and preparing for a
> new baby. (Based on Darling, 1979, pp. 191–193)

Placement Out of the Home: A Form of Normalization

In writing about families of children with severe mental retardation,
Farber (1975) describes a "principle of minimal adaptation." He argues
that families disrupt their patterns of living as little as possible to adjust
to a problem situation and that parents who have difficulty living with a
child with severe retardation move through a progression of minimal
adaptations:

1. *Labeling phase:* The bases for existing role arrangements are
   removed.
2. *Normalization phase:* This is based on the pretense of maintaining
   normal roles (most families remain in this phase and do not
   proceed further).
3. *Mobilization phase:* Normality claims become difficult to maintain.

4. *Revisionist phase:* This involves isolation from community involvements and role renegotiation.
5. *Polarization phase:* Parents attempt to locate the source of their difficulty within the family.
6. *Elimination phase:* Normality is maintained by excluding the offending person.

Farber notes that parent-oriented families are more likely than child-oriented families to reach the elimination phase, as are families that were coping poorly prior to the birth of the child. Movement through phases is also influenced by social and cultural expectations, not only by internal family dynamics.

Movement from one phase to another may occur more frequently at turning points in family life. If a mother becomes chronically ill, for example, she may not be able to continue caring for a child with a disability. Similarly, if a family's support network changes (as, e.g., in the case of the death of a grandparent who had helped with child care), the parents will be more likely to move toward the elimination phase, opting for an alternative, such as institutionalization of the child.

Changes in the child can also lead to placement out of the home. As nonambulatory children grow and become heavier, caring for them at home becomes more difficult. Some children with severe retardation also become more difficult to handle as they grow and become more mobile. In some cases, parents may come to believe that a child's special needs can be better met in a residential treatment facility than at home. Meyers and colleagues (reported in Blacher, 1984a) have noted that the proportion of children with severe and profound mental retardation residing in their natural homes drops sharply at school age.

Seltzer and Krauss (1984) note four characteristics associated with residential placement:

1. Child characteristics (level of retardation, behavior problems, age, degree of care needed)
2. Family characteristics (SES, race, marital satisfaction)
3. Informal supports (friends and family)
4. Formal supports (social and psychological services, respite care, skills training)

MacKeith (1973) suggests three principles that can be presented to families to help them make decisions about residential placement:

1. In our culture, most people live with their families and do better if they do so.

2. People go away from home if thereby they are able to get treatment and education that are better—and sufficiently better to outweigh the disadvantages of being away from home.
3. People go away from home if other people in the family are suffering from their continued presence.

Questions about residential placement are more likely to arise at turning points in the lives of children and their parents—at school-entry age, at the time of leaving school, and when parents become older and unable to care for their child at home.

Residential placement enables some families to achieve normalization when alternatives are not available or acceptable. Through some means, then—social support, access to resources, or removal of the child from the home—most families are able to have a normalized lifestyle. *Normalization is the most common mode of adaptation among families with children with disabilities during the childhood years.* In the next section we look at other adaptations and present a typology of family adaptations based on a model of differential opportunity structures.

TYPOLOGY OF ADAPTATIONS

The Crusadership Mode

Although normalization is the most common parental adaptation through most of the childhood years, for some parents normalized routines remain elusive. In particular, parents whose children have unusual disabilities, continuing medical problems, or unresolved behavior problems may have difficulty finding the social supports necessary for normalization. Some of these families adopt a *crusadership* mode of adjustment in an attempt to bring about social change.

Unlike parents who have achieved normalization, these parents may become *more* involved in disability associations and segregated support groups as their children get older. In a study of families of children with birth defects, C. I. Goodman (1980) found that parents who acknowledged serious problems in their lives and the lives of their children were more likely to be involved in parent groups. Parents' associations tend to draw their active membership from parents of younger children (who have not yet achieved normalization) and a smaller number of parents of older children with unresolved problems. When normalization cannot be attained, associations and the activities they provide may fill important needs. As the father of four teenagers with disabilities said: "The [Association] is our kids' only social life. . . . I'm on the Board and I'm referee of the soccer team" (Darling, 1979, p. 162). Such parents sometimes come to play leadership roles in state and national disability groups.

The goal of crusadership is normalization, and families who adopt this mode strive to achieve that goal in a variety of ways. Some become involved in campaigns to increase public awareness of their child's disability. Others testify before congressional committees in an attempt to promote legislation favorable to people with disabilities. Still others wage legal battles or challenge the school system to establish new programs. Crusaders, then, are advocates who try to change the opportunity structure for their own and other people's children. (For a further discussion of crusadership and parent activism, see Darling, 1988.) Some eventually achieve normalization and withdraw from involvement in advocacy groups and roles; a few, however, may continue to advocate on behalf of others in an altruistic mode.

Altruism

Because the ultimate goal of most parents is normalization, altruism is not common. As noted above, parents generally decrease their involvement in organizations and activities that emphasize their stigmatized status in society as their children get older. The departure of families who have achieved normalization from these organizations is unfortunate for the parents of younger children in need of successful role models. Not all such families abandon organizational activity, however.

A few families who have achieved normalization remain active in segregated groups for the sake of others, and individuals from such families are often found in leadership roles in national disability associations. Their motivations vary. Some are truly caring, humanistic people; some have a strong sense of justice; some are applying the principles of their religion; and others simply enjoy the social aspects of participation or the prestige resulting from their leadership roles. Altruists, then, are those who *choose*, for whatever reason, to associate with people with disabilities and their families even though they have access to opportunities for integration into "normal" society. Perhaps families adopting this mode of adaptation will increase in coming years as the disability rights movement becomes more and more successful in removing some of the stigma associated with disability in our society.

Resignation

At the opposite pole from the altruists are the families who, despite their inability to achieve normalization, never become involved in crusadership activity at all. In her study of parent groups, C. I. Goodman (1980) found that many parents did not participate as a result of lack of knowledge. Such parents are doubly isolated: They are stigmatized by "normal" society, and yet they never become integrated into alternative support groups. Some may become fatalistic, whereas others may have mental health problems resulting from stress.

Parents who become resigned to their problematic existence may lack access to supportive resources for a number of reasons. Some may live in isolated rural areas where no parent groups exist. Others may not be able to search for support because of poor health, lack of transportation, or family problems apart from the child with a disability. In the lower socioeconomic classes, especially, the burdens of daily life—of simple survival—may take precedence over concerns relating to a child's disability. Families who are isolated from the mainstream of society, because they do not speak English or because the parents themselves have disabilities, may not have access to the lay or professional referral networks that provide information on available resources. Crusadership and altruism are luxuries that presuppose some free time and the absence of competing demands on that time, often making those modes of adaptation most appropriate for middle- and upper-class families.

A Model of Modes of Adaptation

By the time their children have entered adolescence, then, most parents have adopted a characteristic mode or style of adaptation to their children's disabilities. These modes are shown in Table 3.1. The reader should keep in mind that these modes are ideal types that are only approximated by real families. Some families move back and forth between modes as their needs and opportunities change. Ideal types help

TABLE 3.1. Modes of Adaptation among Parents of Children with Disabilities

Mode of adaptation	Type of integration[a]	
	"Normal" society	Alternative subculture (disability as a "career")
Altruism	+	+
Normalization	+	−
Crusadership	−	+
Resignation	−	−

[a]+, integration achieved; −, integration withdrawn or not achieved.

us to understand family lifestyles, but they should not be used to stereo-type families or to predict their responses in any given situation.

All parents, then, have differential levels of access to two opportunity structures: (1) "normal," or mainstream, society and (2) the smaller disability subculture, consisting of parent support groups, advocacy or-ganizations, special-needs media, and state and national associations. In general, parents who have equal access to both structures will choose a normalization mode rather than the segregated mode of altruism. Par-ents who do not have equal access to both structures will choose crusad-ership if their access to normalized structures is severely restricted and resignation if their access to the disability subculture is restricted as well.

These modes of adaptation, first proposed by one of the authors over 15 years ago (Darling, 1979), are similar to those described by Radley and Green (1987) in the case of adjustment to chronic illness. Normali-zation is paralleled by their "active-denial" mode, which is characterized by fighting the illness and by retaining social activities and minimizing symptoms. Altruism is paralleled by "secondary gain," wherein the illness becomes the context for the pursuit of other rewarding activities. Crusad-ership is similar to "accommodation," which is characterized by changes in lifestyle ("illness as an occupation"). Finally resignation mirrors the "resignation" mode, in which the loss of social activity is accompanied by a sense of being overwhelmed by the illness and subject to its vicissitudes. Radley and Green suggest that these modes reflect a psychological process of self-acceptance. In the case of parents of children with disabili-ties, access to social resources may be a more important determinant of mode of adaptation than parents' levels of "acceptance."

More research is needed to increase our understanding of how parents become integrated into different opportunity structures. The social processes involved may not be significantly different from those found in studies of social movements or social networks in general. Kazak and Wilcox (1984) found that networks of families of children with disabilities tended to be more dense than those of comparison families, suggesting that various members of these families' support networks knew each other. A more "dense" or closely knit network may serve to isolate families from contacts with resources outside of the network. Kazak (1987) suggests that a greater understanding of social networks would be helpful to professionals interacting with these families.

As children with disabilities approach adolescence, the adjustment strategies adopted by their families during the childhood years may become problematic. When children leave school, parents are faced with planning for the future and confronting questions about whether their children will be able to play adult roles. These concerns are discussed in the next section.

APPROACHING ADULTHOOD: A THREAT TO NORMALIZATION

Adolescence is a stressful time for most families, whether their children have disabilities or not. Blumberg, Lewis, and Susman (1984) identify a number of tasks that adolescents must accomplish: (1) establish identity, (2) achieve independence, (3) adjust to sexual maturation, (4) prepare for the future, (5) develop mature relationships with peers, and (6) develop a positive self-image and body image. In addition, Brotherson, Backus, Summers, and Turnbull (1986) note some tasks that are unique to families with young adults with developmental disabilities:

- Adjusting to the adult implications of disability
- Deciding on an appropriate residence
- Initiating vocational involvement
- Dealing with special issues of sexuality
- Recognizing the need for continuing family responsibility
- Dealing with the continued financial implications of dependency
- Dealing with a lack of socialization opportunities for people with disabilities outside of the family
- Planning for guardianship

Continuing Dependence

The hardest part is at night, when he's lying there peacefully and you're thinking the 100,000 thoughts of what could have been and all the reasons why this happened. You think that from day one, and I think you ask that all your life. And it goes on 24 hours. It does not end. (A 72-year-old mother of a 49-year-old son with mental retardation; Krauss & Seltzer, 1993)

In the typical family, the "launching" stage, when children leave home creates stresses that have been called the "empty-nest syndrome." As the child becomes an adult, all of the parental energies that have been bound up for so long in childrearing are no longer needed for that purpose. Many parents, and especially those who have not developed occupational or other interests outside the home, experience some anomie during this period in their lives. On the other hand, A. W. Clemens and Axelson (1985) have noted that in families of children *without disabilities,* the continued presence of adult children in the home can be stressful because it violates social expectations—parents expect the empty-nest syndrome to be only a temporary crisis in their lives. Parents of children with disabilities may find themselves in a similar situation as their children approach adulthood. The empty-nest syndrome is an experience they would welcome. As one father said:

> We'll never reach the stage that other people reach when their children leave home, and that's depressing. . . . I wonder what will happen to Brian when he no longer looks like a child. (Darling, 1979, p. 184)

The reader should be cautioned, however, that, as A. P. Turnbull and Turnbull (in press) and others have suggested, expectations about independence are culturally determined and not all families react negatively to an adult child's continuing dependence.

Although some children with disabilities who do not have intellectual limitations, *do* achieve independence during later adolescence and adulthood, many are not able to do so. Those with mental retardation or physical problems that prevent the mastery of self-help skills will continue to be dependent on others to some extent for the rest of their lives.

Most parents of children with disabilities begin to have concerns about the future from the day they suspect that something is wrong with the child. Some have suggested that these concerns occur more commonly among fathers than mothers during the early years (see, e.g., D. J. Meyer, 1995). During the infancy and childhood periods, however, parents develop rationalizations that enable them to see the future in positive terms or they push it out of their minds. Until their children reach middle adolescence, most parents of children with disabilities seem to adopt an ideology of "living one day at a time." This ideology is expressed by the mother of a 9-year-old with spina bifida:

> In high school, Ellen's going to be excluded. I always picture Ellen as being left out. So far, it hasn't happened, but as kids get older, being alike is so much more important. She'll probably have trouble in school—and what happens when she gets out of school? I don't like to think about it. We just take each year as it comes. (Darling & Darling, 1982, p. 155)

As a child moves through adolescence and approaches adulthood, parents are forced to begin thinking more seriously about the future. Some parents who had hoped that their child would someday be independent may reassess their situation at this time and come to realize that independence is an unrealistic goal. The parents of a 15-year-old expressed these concerns:

> We've been a little down . . . in the past year. . . . He's getting to be an adult. . . . He's never going to make it on his own. . . . The present is fine. We can manage it. . . . Our basic concern is the future. . . . We are getting older. We need babysitters constantly. . . . It's a continuation

of care. . . . Joe really can't be left alone. . . . What if something
happens to us? That's our basic fear. (Darling & Darling, 1982, p. 156)

Some families envision economic and lifestyle consequences as a result
of their child's continuing dependence:

> When our daughter is through the school system, it's highly likely my
> spouse will have to stop working altogether, and I may try to go to a
> 32-hour week, due to the wretched support for adults with severe
> disabilities in this state. We might consider moving to another state at
> that point. Among older people we know with severely handicapped
> children, except those who are wealthy, the norm seems to be to care
> for the child at home as long as possible—often well into the 70s or
> even 80s. (Father of a child with quadriplegia) (Internet, Children with
> Special Health Care Needs List, March 15, 1995)

Parents such as these typically embark on a search for solutions that
is similar in some ways to the searches undertaken by younger parents
whose children have just been diagnosed. They search for such things as
appropriate living and employment arrangements; financial and legal
advice; and social, recreational, and, when deemed appropriate, sexual
opportunities for their children. Suelzle and Keenan (1981) found that
perceptions of unmet service needs were more widespread among parents of young adults than among parents at any other time in the life
cycle. As noted earlier, they found that needs for family support and
services such as counseling and respite care exhibited a U-shaped function: They were high among parents of preschoolers and young adults
and lower among parents of school-aged children. As adulthood approaches, then, the normalization adaptation, so common among families during the childhood years, is likely to be threatened by a new
awareness of unmet needs.

Exploring Alternatives for the Future

LIVING ARRANGEMENTS

Although they have physical disabilities, many adults without significant
intellectual limitations are able to live independently with supports such
as personal assistants or modified housing, equipment, or vehicles. These
individuals need to be included in planning for their own futures, and
some may become involved, like their parents, in crusadership to make
normalized ways of life more accessible to them.

For the adult who cannot achieve true independence, a number of
alternatives may be available, depending on where they live and their

financial resources. At one extreme is institutionalization; at the other are various forms of community-living arrangements. Although residential alternatives have continued to grow during the last two decades, studies indicate that most adults with major disabilities still reside in relatively large settings (Krauss & Giele, 1987). Waiting lists for group homes and other smaller, community-based programs and for personal assistant services are often long. In more rural areas, such facilities may not even exist at all. Parents have also expressed concerns about the high rate of personnel turnover in some group homes and the qualifications of staff there (Darling & Darling, 1982).

In cases such as the one noted above, parents decide to keep their adult children with them for as long as they live; some expect siblings to accept this responsibility; and others rely on various members of the extended family. Most parents realize that none of these arrangements is necessarily permanent, yet many delay in exploring residential alterna-tives, continuing the wait-and-see ideology so common among parents of younger children. Many of these parents are ambivalent—knowing that eventually their child will have to enter another living situation but also dreading that time. These remarks by the parents of an adolescent with moderate mental retardation are illustrative:

> He's never going to be self-sufficient, which means as long as we are alive, he'll be with us. I'll never permit institutionalization. Perhaps eventually he'll be in a group home situation . . . maybe an adult day program. . . . His brother and sister are being trained to want to take care of him. I don't want them to have him live with them but I want them to keep close ties. . . . We haven't really explored things for the future. . . . We live for today. (Darling & Darling, 1982, p. 158)

EMPLOYMENT OPPORTUNITIES

Normalization for adults in most segments of society includes inde-pendent employment. Yet individuals with disabilities may be limited, either by their disabilities or by employer attitudes, in their quest for jobs. Parents' concerns about their children's ability to achieve independence generally include the world of work, as evidenced in these comments by the mother of a young adult with spina bifida:

> Right now we're not sure what he'll be able to do and what's available for him to do. . . . I've thought for years, "What will Paul do?" His father and I won't always be around to take care of him. Paul's got to have a reason to get up in the morning. . . .
>   Eighteen seemed like a long time away when he was four years old. . . . Now he doesn't have any inkling as to the value of a dollar. . . . I'm concerned about what he will do. . . . Sometimes, I get so angry

at Paul. . . . He's waiting for me to come up with an answer. (Darling & Darling, 1982, p. 162)

In some cases, parents must readjust their goals for their children in accordance with their children's disabilities. The mother of a child with Down syndrome said:

> There was a Down's woman who was a dishwasher at work. My first reaction was, "My daughter will not wash dishes for somebody else." Later, I thought, "Well, maybe she'd like washing dishes." I just want her to do whatever she wants to do. (Darling, 1979, p. 184)

Other parents may become involved in efforts to enforce the implementation of the Americans with Disabilities Act (ADA) in order to increase their children's opportunities for employment.

Some individuals with disabilities may not be able to achieve competitive employment at all but may be able to work in sheltered or supported employment situations. Still others may not be capable of any kind of work. Being able to work for a living is a basic expectation deeply rooted in the American way of life. The capitalist ethic suggests that those who do not work are in some way morally inferior to those who are employed. Consequently, the realization that a child might not ever be able to do any productive work is a difficult one for some parents.

SOCIAL OPPORTUNITIES

Parents' concerns about social acceptance for their children include a variety of interactional areas: friendship, dating, marriage, recreational opportunities, and opportunities for sexual activity. Getting information may be difficult. As one mother said:

> I made a feeble attempt to discuss Bruce's sexual development with the pediatrician, but he seemed more embarrassed than I and suggested that I not borrow trouble. . . . Few medical and other professional people seemed interested in the impact which sexuality has on the entire family of a retarded person. (J. Y. Meyer, 1978, p. 108)

Questions of normalization arise when adolescents with disabilities attempt to establish relationships with their nondisabled peers:

> Like most teenagers, I became very self-conscious about my appearance and physical state. In childhood, my family and others had accepted my physical limitations with little or nothing said; in my teens, these same limitations started cutting me off from the world. I think

the first boy–girl parties that my age group started having were probably the beginning of the social and emotional difficulties that have been greater than my physical ones. (Kiser, 1974, p. 54)

My cousin and Judy's steady egged me to ask her for a date. I told them I didn't think it was right for me to ask a nonhandicapped girl to go on a date because I was in a wheelchair. (Chinn, 1976, p. 75)

Such experiences may be slowly changing as society works to include children with disabilities in "normal" social opportunities from earlier ages.

Adolescents' attempts to achieve normalization have included rejection of the "disabled" peer group:

When I graduated from special school, I said, "Thank God, no more handicapped people." And I slipped into college. The first year I didn't have any friends. My parents said, "Why don't you invite the old high school friends?" I said, "No, I'm not going to be associated with handicapped people anymore. I'm finished with that." (S. A. Richardson, 1972, p. 530)

In other cases, the peer group of others with disabilities has become the locus of the adolescent's social life:

His best friend has spina bifida too. He lives [nearby], and they talk all the time. He doesn't really have any other friends that he sees. . . . He goes to a spina bifida meeting once a month at City Children's Hospital. . . . He has a girlfriend in the spina bifida group. They write and talk on the phone between meetings. (Darling & Darling, 1982, p. 166)

More recently, some parents of young adults who were in inclusive settings in school have attempted to create opportunities for social inclusion for their children after they have finished school. Ann Turnbull, for example, has spoken at conferences about her family's attempts to create an inclusive peer group for her adult son. Others have tried to combine living arrangements with opportunities for social inclusion by finding roommates without disabilities for their adult children with developmental disabilities.

LEGAL/FINANCIAL NEEDS

When parents realize that their children with disabilities may outlive them, they usually become concerned about providing for their children's future legal and financial security. Finding an estate-planning specialist who can help them plan for the future is not always easy.

Beyer (1986) notes that if parents leave their assets directly to their child, the child may not be eligible for government benefits, such as SSI or Medicaid. He recommends instead that parents establish a trust for the child, naming a sibling or other person as the trustee. In all cases, parents should seek out a good lawyer, preferably one experienced in planning in situations of disability.

An alternative to family or public guardianship of the individual with a disability is corporate guardianship (Appolloni, 1987). These programs have been developing in various areas throughout the United States and have a number of advantages, including standards relating to quality of life and the possibility of a lifetime commitment.

FAMILY CAREERS IN PROCESS:
AN OVERVIEW OF EMERGENT PATTERNS

Several consistent patterns or styles of adaptation emerge from a review of the lifestyles over time, or *careers,* of many families of children with disabilities. This usage of the term "career" derives from the sociological literature and does not refer to an occupational sequence. The major determinant of the career path that any given family will follow is the social opportunity structure. When supportive resources and services are available to parents, they are most likely to choose a lifestyle based on normalization. When the opportunity structure is limited, on the other hand, they may engage in various forms of seekership (discussed below) or crusadership in an attempt to achieve normalization. The modes of adaptation that families adopt commonly change in a patterned sequence over the course of a child's life cycle. These career changes are shown in Figure 3.1.

Immediately after a diagnosis has been issued, parents are generally in a state of anomie; that is, they experience both meaninglessness and powerlessness in relation to their situation. Anomie is also felt by parents who suspect that something is wrong with their child and whose suspi-

Time in child's life cycle	Postpartum	Infancy	Childhood	Adolescence	Adulthood
Mode of parental action	Anomie →	Seekership →	→ Normalization → Altruism → Crusadership → Resignation	→ Seekership →	→ Normalization → Altruism → Crusadership → Resignation

FIGURE 3.1. Career paths of parents of disabled children.

cions are not confirmed by a physician or other professional. Most parents experience meaninglessness because they have little knowledge about disabilities in general or their child's disability in particular.

Parents feel powerlessness even after they have satisfied their need for meaning. Once they have obtained a diagnosis, most parents ask, "What can I do about it?" Most parents have a strong need to do all that they can to help their children. However, most parents of infants with disabilities have little knowledge of intervention programs or educational or supportive services. All too often the professionals who issue the diagnoses are themselves unaware of available programs.

Human beings constantly strive to make sense of their experiences. When events seem random and we feel out of control, most of us try to rationalize our experiences and reestablish order in our lives. Consequently, when parents feel anomie, they are likely to engage in behaviors that will restore their sense of meaning and purpose. During their children's infancy, then, most of these parents become engaged in a process of *seekership*—they read books, they consult experts, they write letters, and they make telephone calls—in an attempt to find answers to their questions and alleviate the anomie that they feel.

Most parents find the answers they are seeking. As a result, most parental quests end in *normalization*. By the time their children have reached school age, most parents have obtained an accurate diagnosis, found an acceptable pediatrician, and enrolled their child in an appropriate educational program. Many parents have also found support through talking to other parents of children with similar disabilities. Most parents, then, are able to achieve a nearly normal style of life during the childhood years.

Although the majority of parents choose normalization when it is available to them, a few remain active in parent groups or other advocacy organizations in an attempt to help other people achieve normalization. Such parents forgo the comforts of a normalized routine and adopt an *altruistic* mode of adaptation.

Because of a limited opportunity structure, some families are unable to achieve normalization. Sometimes their children have more severe or unusual disabilities or they live far away from treatment facilities. When parents do not have access to good medical care, appropriate educational programs, or other services, they may adopt a mode of prolonged seekership, or *crusadership*, and attempt to change the opportunity structure. These parents may join national organizations, go to court to demand that their children's needs be met, or use other means to create necessary services.

Finally, some parents who do not have access to services for their children may also not have access to the means for bringing about change.

These parents who are doubly isolated adopt a mode of *resignation*. They struggle alone with difficulties created by the child with a disability and often with other problems as well. Resignation is probably a more common outcome among the poor than among parents in the higher social classes.

When the child with a disability reaches adolescence, normalization is likely to be threatened. During the childhood years, most parents adopt an ideology of "living one day at a time." Once a child approaches adulthood, however, problems raised by the child's continuing dependence must be faced. Regardless of the adaptation they adopted during the childhood years, then, all parents must eventually make decisions about their child's future. At this time, seekership commonly resumes, as parents search for living arrangements, employment opportunities, or other services that their children will need when they are no longer willing or able to care for them.

Finally, for some parents, the normalization equilibrium will be reestablished after they have located a satisfactory residential setting for their child. Other parents may choose to continue in an altruistic mode and remain active in organizations for people with disabilities even after they have found a place for their own child. Finally, some parents may not be able to locate a satisfactory setting at all and may keep their adult child with them while they adopt a crusadership or resignation mode.

Ideally *all* families should achieve normalization. Social change in the form of more and better services for people with disabilities could bring normalization to the crusaders and to those who are resigned to their fate. Altruism would, consequently, be eliminated as well for lack of need. Professionals should explore ways to help families expand their opportunity structures, with the goal of making normalization available to all who seek it.

⌘

Effects on the Family
as a System

ALTHOUGH RESEARCH continues, given our present state of knowledge it may be misleading to draw firm conclusions about the problems and stresses experienced by families of children with disabilities. It is also difficult to ascertain whether these families are better or worse off than comparable families where no special needs child or adolescent resides. The research in this area is beset by many methodological problems (Crnic, Friedrich, et al., 1983; Berger & Foster, 1986), which has resulted in mixed and contradictory results. Nevertheless, the "sense" one gets from some contributors to the professional literature is that the trauma and unrelenting stress of coping with a youngster who is disabled can be difficult at best if not immobilizing. This view is reflected in such commentary as the following:

> Some parents overprotect and do not stimulate the child to use the abilities he has. Others are so depressed that they cannot do much for the child. In still others, the sadness is interwoven with a kind of impotent rage toward the world. Many parents are angry at the retarded child, though they try to cover this up, hating to admit feelings of anger toward a helpless child. Most try to do their best in spite of their personal sense of loss and sadness, but some become cool and distant and withdraw from the retardate the sustained warmth and stimulation that he requires even more than other children. Some parents try to quash their own sadness and embark on brisk programs, pushing the children relentlessly toward speech training, toilet training, nursery school, exercises, and a host of other "stimulating" activities. If they push too hard, they overwhelm a

vulnerable child and tend to make him withdraw even further. (Bernstein, 1978, pp. 58–59)

N. Hobbs, Perrin, and Ireys (1986) write:

> Families with a chronically ill child confront challenges and bear burdens unknown to other families. The shock of the initial diagnosis and the urgent and compelling need for knowledge; the exhausting nature of constant care unpredictably punctuated by crises; the many and persistent financial concerns; the continued witnessing of a child's pain; tensions with one's spouse that can be aggravated by the fatiguing chronicity of care; the worries about the well-being of other children; and the multitude of questions involving the fair distribution within the family of time, money, and concern—these are challenges that parents of chronically ill children must face. (p. 80)

After their comprehensive literature review, Crnic, Friedrich, et al. (1983) conclude that even though there are inconsistent and contradictory findings, in general, the available literature suggests that families of children who are mentally retarded are at risk for numerous difficulties in comparison to families with nonretarded children. Patterson (1991) seems to agree when she notes that numerous studies report negative sequelae of disability on family members. She cites studies reporting that parents of children with disabilities have more health and psychological problems and experience a diminished sense of mastery. Furthermore, mothers seem to be vulnerable when they absorb family stress and protect the rest of the family from it. And although divorce rates are comparable to those of other families, there tends to be more reported marital distress among families of children with disabilities (Patterson, 1991).

Some of what is presently known about families is derived from empirical data but much of it is anecdotal. Family members, often writing in the most poignant terms, describe their experiences of parenting a child with a disability (see the magazine *The Exceptional Parent*; H. R. Turnbull & Turnbull's book *Parents Speak Out* [1985]; Helen Featherstone's *A Difference in the Family* [1980]; D. J. Meyer's *Uncommon Fathers* [1995]; and Moorman's *My Sister's Keeper* [1992], among others). No one would challenge these personal accounts in terms of their veracity, rich insights, and poignancy, yet from a research perspective one needs to question how representative these views are of the broader population of families with children who have disabilities. Furthermore, most accounts from family members are written by highly educated and articulate persons.

Much of the research has been from the mother's perspective and it is not unusual for mothers to be asked about the adjustment of other family members (Hornby, 1994). A mother's view of another family member's functioning has value, but this type of information should not take the place of nor should it be interpreted as necessarily accurate information about other family members.

Much of the early research was conducted on families of children who are mentally retarded and especially with children who are severely mentally retarded (Farber, 1959, 1960b; Ross, 1964). This left a major gap in our understanding of families of children with other disabilities. Although there continues to be a disproportionate number of studies published about families of children with mental retardation, the situation is changing as publications in other areas are being reported with greater frequency—hearing impaired (Israelite, 1985; Sloman, Springer, & Vachon, 1993), epilepsy (Lechtenberg, 1984), chronic illness (Rolland, 1994; Travis, 1976; Turk & Kerns, 1985), spina bifida (Fagan & Schor, 1993; Tew, Lawrence, Payne, & Rawnsley, 1977), autism (Harris, 1994; Schopler & Mesibov, 1984), hemophilia (Varekamp et al., 1990), and mental illness (MacGregor, 1994). These developments are important yet their segregated nature imply that families with children with different disabilities are more dissimilar than alike. We examine this assumption more closely later in this chapter.

The point to be made here is that separate lines of inquiry are developing and that these imply that some disabling conditions exert a greater stressful influence on the family then others. The truth probably is that we know little about the differential impact of children and youth with dissimilar conditions but the research, with its segregated literature, may contribute to misleading conclusions. We have also not sufficiently explored the effects of mild–moderate versus severe disability on the family, although a few authors have made attempts to examine this area (Fewell, 1991; Lyon & Lyon, 1991). This topic will also be explored in this chapter.

As noted above, mothers' experiences have been explored with far greater frequency than those of other family members (Foster & Berger, 1985) and many of the studies cited in this chapter used mothers as subjects. That is beginning to change also, as more attention is being paid to siblings (Grossman, 1972; Seligman, 1991; Stoneman & Berman, 1993; Wasserman, 1983), fathers (Lamb & Meyer, 1991) and even grandparents and other extended family members (Seligman, 1991a, 1991b; Sonnek, 1986).

Our understanding of families of children with disabilities has changed from a singular focus on the mother to one which explores family dynamics and now even broader ecological factors (see Chapter 1). This expansion in perspective makes it imperative that we study the multitude of influences on families and not resort to linear and simplistic explanations of family functioning. For example, the research on social support networks and their buffering effect on family stress is but one example of the promising lines of research to be explored (Kazak & Marvin, 1984; Krahn, 1993; Kazak & Wilcox, 1984).

In addition to the factors already enumerated, the changing nature of the family has made it even more difficult to study the effects of childhood disability on the family. Another area that needs more research attention is the examination of family adaptation over time (longitudinal studies). The implementation of innovative research models also needs to be considered more seriously. For example, Goode (1984), in examining in depth the public presentation of a family with a deaf–blind child, utilized a naturalistic/observational research design to study this phenomenon. There are only a handful of studies that have used an observational model. And finally, research on families from other cultures and different ethnic groups is in short supply (Harry, 1992a; Mary, 1990).

Against this backdrop, then, which suggests that research on families of children with disabilities is riddled with problems and raises more questions than answers, we shall attempt to examine the factors that have been reported to affect family adjustment.

STAGES OF MOURNING

Chapter 2 discusses in depth the effects of first knowledge of disability on the family. However, this section will briefly review the stages parents are thought to experience after learning of their child's disability. This chapter will also explore a few additional concepts related to early knowledge to augment the discussion in Chapter 2.

Stage theory, as it has been applied to parents of children with disabilities, has been subject to some controversy (Blacher, 1984b; Mary, 1990; Olshansky, 1962; Searle, 1978). For example, stages are conceptually confused by some, in that what one researcher calls "denial," another may call "guilt." Another problem is that most of the studies have been done with white, middle to upper-class subjects. An exception to this is Mary (1990), who found in her small-scale study that only 25% of the African American mothers of children with disabilities felt that they had experienced a progression of emotions (stages) over time, compared to 68% for whites and 75% for the Hispanic mothers. Mothers who had had some education and experience in utilizing human services seemed better at articulating a stage theory model—or perhaps in reflecting a stage theory model that had been proposed to them. The stages noted below have been used in reference to families of children with disabilities in response to the observation that the birth of a infant with disabilities is often experienced by the parents as the death of the expected normal, healthy child (Solnit & Stark, 1961).

Duncan (1977) adapted Kübler-Ross's (1969) stages, which characterize reactions to impending death. The stages must be viewed flexibly due to the complexity of families and the unpredictable impact an event may have. Knowledge of these stages can help professionals understand family response to a crisis so that their behavior is understood in context and not regarded as inappropriate, chaotic, or pathological. Also, being aware of these stages enables the professional to intervene in a timely and appropriate fashion.

Kübler-Ross's (1969) stages are as follows:

1. Denial
2. Bargaining
3. Anger
4. Depression
5. Acceptance

Shock and *denial* are a parent's initial response. Denial appears to operate on an unconscious level to ward off excessive anxiety. Denial serves a useful, buffering purpose early on but can cause difficulties if it persists. If, over time and in the face of clear evidence, parents continue to deny the existence of their child's disability, one needs to be cautious that children are not pushed beyond their capabilities; parents do not fail to enroll their child in early intervention programs; and parents do not make endless and pointless visits to professionals to get an acceptable diagnosis.

During this stage, parents report feeling confusion, numbness, disorganization, and helplessness. Some parents are unable to hear much of what they are told when the child is diagnosed:

> One mother told me that when the pediatrician told her that her 18-month old son had cerebral palsy, she "burst into tears" and didn't hear anything else. Another mother recalled how she had listened very calmly as the neurologist explained the extent of the brain damage her 14-year old daughter had sustained as the result of a car accident. Then she got in her car and began to drive home, but after a few hundred yards, as she was crossing a bridge, she felt sick and her legs felt like they'd turned to jelly, so she got out of the car and leaned over the side of the bridge to get some air. (Hornby, 1994, p. 16)

It is important for professionals to realize that, after they have communicated a diagnosis, parents may not be in an emotional state that allows them to hear the details of the disability. Explanations about etiology, course, and prognosis may fall on deaf ears. Professionals need to deliver the diagnosis (honestly and with compassion) and respond to any questions the parents may have. The questions parents ask at this juncture probably reflect the answers they are prepared to hear. Most importantly, the professional involved during this initial diagnosis stage (usually a physician) should consider scheduling another meeting where he or she can review the details of the disability and respond to any questions the parents may have. For a further discussion of communication in diagnosis, see Darling (1994) and S. D. Klein (1994).

The *bargaining* phase is characterized by a type of magical or fantasy thinking. The underlying theme is that, if the parent works extra hard, the child will improve. A child's improved condition is compensation for hard work, being useful to others, or by contributing to a worthy cause. During bargaining, one may see parents join local groups in activities that benefit a particular cause. Another manifestation of the bargaining phase is that parents may turn to religion or look for a miracle.

As parents realize that their child will not improve significantly, *anger* develops. There may be anger at God ("Why me?") or at oneself or one's spouse for having produced the child or for not helping. Anger is frequently projected onto professionals for not healing the child (doctors) or for not helping their child make significant learning gains (teachers). Anger can also come from angry feelings due to an unsympathetic community, insensitive professionals, inadequate services, fatigue due to long hospital stays, and the like. Excessive guilt can sometimes turn anger inward, so that a parent blames her- or himself for the disability. Anger turned inward often results in depression. It is essential that professionals allow or even encourage parents to express their normal and understandable anger. This means that professionals need to be comfortable with anger, which is not easy for those who have learned from their families of origin that anger is a negative emotion. Perhaps most important is the notion that, by not expressing deeply held emotions, family members can become more and more isolated from each other, and feelings of depression may deepen.

Expressing anger is often cathartic and cleansing and can reduce anxious feelings, but when parents realize that their anger doesn't change their child's condition and when they accept the chronic nature of the disability and its implications for the family, a sense of *depression* sets in. For many parents depression is temporary or episodic, although Olshansky (1962) speaks about the "chronic sorrow" parents experience. Depression may coincide with a particular stage of the family life cycle. Developmental transitions imply change and invite comparisons with other children and families. These periods are time bound and the seriousness of one's depression depends on how the family interprets an event and on their coping abilities. Also, it is very important to be able to distinguish between clinical depression and milder and normal forms of dysphoria.

Hornby (1994) asserts that for some, *detachment* follows anger when parents report feeling empty and nothing seems to matter. Life has lost its meaning. This reaction is thought to indicate that the parent is reluctantly beginning to accept the realty of the disability. This then is a turning point in the adaptation process.

Acceptance is achieved when parents demonstrate some of the following characteristics:

1. They are able to discuss their child's shortcomings with relative ease.
2. They evidence a balance between encouraging independence and showing love.
3. They are able to collaborate with professionals to make realistic short-and long-term plans.
4. They pursue personal interests unrelated to their child.
5. They can discipline appropriately without undue guilt.
6. They can abandon overprotective or unduly harsh behavioral patterns toward their child.

In applying these stages, one needs to be mindful that families are not homogeneous and that these stages may not be a good fit for some families. For some, these stages are cyclical and recur as new developmental milestones are achieved, or when a crisis occurs (e.g., a child's condition worsens). Other factors that affect the manifestation of these stages include whether they are determined in part by one's culture, whether all family members experience the same stage at the same time, how long a particular stage lasts, and what accounts for differences in duration. According to Hornby (1994), "Some parents appear to work the process in a few days, whereas others seem to take years to reach a reasonable level of adaptation. Just as for any major loss it is considered that most people will take around two years to come to terms with the disability. However, some parents seem to take longer and a few possibly never fully adjust to the situation" (p. 20).

The literature on this topic is fairly extensive and reflects an interest in the initial and continuing experiences of parents (Blacher, 1984b). In addition to the precautions noted above, another difficulty has been with the measurement and validation of these stages.

Some authorities have indicated that, when families experience stages of adaptation at all, they may complete the entire process within a short period of time (Darling, 1979; Hornby, 1994; Kennedy, 1970). On the other hand, Olshansky (1962) suggests that chronic sorrow is a *normal* reaction to parenting a child with a disability and it is a more meaningful concept than the overly simplistic notion of acceptance/rejection. In this view, a parent who continues to experience sadness about a child's disability can still be a competent and caring parent. Too often, professionals have been quick to label parents as unaccepting or poorly adjusted when they are, in fact, reacting normally to their continuing burden.

A final variation of adjustment to disability suggests that, while one reaction may be the most dominant one, certain amounts of the other reactions will also be present (Hornby, 1994). For example, when parents' predominant emotion is one of anger, they may also be experiencing some denial and sadness at the same time.

CHRONIC BURDEN OF CARE

A major distinguishing feature of families with a child who has disabilities from families that are confronting other crises is that of the chronicity of care such families anticipate. As noted in Chapter 3, for some families the care is 24 hours a day, 7 days a week, for many years. The stresses can be relentless and drain the family physically and psychologically. Add to this the financial worries that may exist, and the family has the potential of being at risk. The degree to which the family is in trouble may depend on how it conceptualizes or reframes its life circumstance, how supportive family members are of each other, and how much social support is available outside of the family.

For some families, the burden of care is not only chronic; it can be experienced as a dark cloud that engulfs the family now and for years to come. Family members may see little relief when they look to their future. Instead of independence, growth, self-fulfillment, and differentiation, a family may see only despair, dependence, and social isolation. Family members who are distressed and depressed may need family counseling (Elman, 1991). "The mental health needs of exceptional parents may be cumulative. That is, living with a handicapped child over many years can take its toll psychologically, physically and financially" (Seligman & Meyerson, 1982, p. 108).

In facing the future, family members must decide how they plan to negotiate their special life circumstance. As we noted in Chapter 1, flexibility, adaptability, and open communication between family members are important to successful family living. Family members may need to assume roles that were not anticipated. For example, siblings may need to help with caretaking more than they otherwise would, and fathers may need to assist instrumentally more often and also be psychologically supportive of the mother. Mothers, so that they do not become en-meshed, have to learn to facilitate, without undue guilt, as much growth and independence as their child is capable of achieving. All in all, over the family's life span, members need to adapt, negotiate, and communi-cate. This is sound advice for all families but it has special relevance to families where there is a chronic stressor.

In addition to seeking help within the family, the family system needs to be permeable enough to allow for outside help, such as respite care, when such help is needed and is available. For example, Wikler (1981) reports that respite care leads to a decrease in negative maternal attitudes toward the child and increased positive family interaction. Others rein-force the importance of respite care services and advocate a spectrum of types of respite care to meet different family needs (Upshur, 1991). Receptiveness to outside intervention and help is important in enabling the family to cope with a chronic and potentially stressful situation. And it is within this context that professional psychologists, counselors, social workers, nurses, and physicians need to help families adapt to their situation. They may also have to help families *create* such resources where they do not exist (Darling & Baxter, 1996; Darling & Darling, 1982; Laborde & Seligman, 1991).

STIGMA

Mark Twain once wrote that "there is something that he [man] loves more than he loves peace—the approval of his neighbors and the public. And perhaps there is something which he dreads more than he dreads pain—the disapproval of his neighbors and the public" (Clemens, 1963, p. 344).

In American society today, persons who are physically and mentally disabled are often judged on the same basis as nondisabled persons, resulting in a degradation or *stigmatization* of persons with disabilities. To the extent that individuals deviate from the societal norm of physical and mental perfection, they are likely to be shunned, ridiculed, avoided, ostracized, and discriminated against. To illustrate, the following letters to Ann Landers were written in response to one of her columns:

> Dear Ann: Usually you're right, but you were wrong to get huffy with "Chicago Reader." . . . The sight of a women with food running down her chin would make me throw up. I believe my rights should be respected as much as the rights of the person in the wheelchair—maybe even more so, because I am normal and she is not.

> Dear Ann: In my opinion, restaurants should have a special seating section for handicapped people, partially hidden by palms or other

greenery so they are not seen by other guests. (Ann Landers, October 1986)

The conditions of stigmatization vary for different disabilities. Goffman (1963) suggests that some disabilities are "discredited" whereas others are "discreditable." A "discreditable" condition is one that is not readily apparent to a lay person. A child with a disfigurement hidden by clothing or a disease such as cystic fibrosis might be able to "pass" as normal in many situations and thus avoid stigma. On the other hand, a child with a more visible disability such as Down syndrome or spina bifida would be "discredited" immediately, although the degree of discreditation may vary for different conditions.

Individuals with discreditable disabilities and their families will sometimes engage in what Goffman calls "impression management" to appear normal. Voysey (1972) mentions the mother of an autistic child who was able to conceal the severity of her child's condition from even the closest family members by cleaning him and the house before visits. Parents may dress a child in contemporary clothes that reflect the mores of the day, or they may groom her in a modern hair style. These are efforts to offset any noticeable characteristics of the disability. Of course, some parents dress and groom their children well because this is how their other children are clothed and groomed and not because they are particularly concerned about the opinion of others.

In the case of "discredited" conditions, which are immediately obvious to strangers, the problems of "impression management" are different. "Passing" as "normal" is not possible in these cases. Davis (1961) has suggested that when those with visible disabilities come into contact with people who are not disabled, a kind of mutual pretense takes place: Both the stigmatized and the nondisabled person act as though the disability did not exist. Davis calls this mode of interaction *fictional acceptance* because the nondisabled person does not *really* accept the person with a disability as a moral equal.

In these studies, interaction between the stigmatized and nonstigmatized person never moves beyond a superficial level. People may be hesitant to become close to the family of a stigmatized person because they, in turn, might be stigmatized. Goffman (1963) suggests that close associates of stigmatized persons come to bear a "courtesy stigma" and may suffer similar reactions of avoidance, rejection, or ridicule. For this reason, stigmatized individuals and their families may choose their friends from among what Goffman (1963) calls "their own"—others who already share a similar stigma.

The notion of social stigma does not apply exclusively to persons with disabilities but also to minority group members. Although persons with disabilities share certain commonalities with members of other minority groups, important differences exist (Wright, 1983). For example, persons with a disability differ from other minority groups in that their disability is not likely to be shared by other family members or perhaps even by others in the immediate environment. In contrast, members of minority groups are often surrounded by other persons with whom they share common attributes, such as skin color.

Nevertheless, the experience of difference felt by children with disabilities is also, by association, felt by other members in the family, namely the parents, siblings, and grandparents. In a social or interactional context, these families feel devalued, which can result in a sense of shame and stigma. One reaction to this is to distance oneself from the family member who is disabled, whereas another might be to seal the family from interactions with others—a "gather the wagons" mentality.

Studies have rather consistently shown that persons with disabilities are viewed negatively by the general public (Marshak & Seligman, 1993; Resnick, 1984). Research has also demonstrated that certain disabling conditions are more acceptable than others and, furthermore, that professionals hold attitudes that are negative (Darling, 1979; Resnick, 1984). Indeed, Resnick (1984), based on his literature review, reports on the negative attitudes held by teachers, counselors, social workers, and physicians. A prodigious researcher in the area of attitudes toward persons with disabilities states that "professionals, like most people, prefer working with the 'beautiful people'—those who are most like themselves intellectually and socially" (Siller, 1984, p. 195). Furthermore, the generally held negative attitudes toward persons with disabilities are reinforced by training in medical schools and other professional training programs, which may account, in part, for the negative attitudes professionals hold (Darling, 1983).

Thus, the predominant social attitude toward those who are different has been one of stigma, and stigmatized persons are regarded as morally inferior to those who are "normal" (Goffman, 1963). As J. Newman (1983) has pointed out, "In early societies, illness and disability were seen as the work of evil demons and supernatural forces—disease and disability [were seen] as the scourge of God, as punishment for sin" (p. 9). In today's society, stigma may be decreasing somewhat as a result of greater public awareness and acceptance of disability. In fact, chronic illness or disability has personally touched many families.

Gliedman and Roth (1980) believe that the destiny of children with disabilities is to suffer from a greater likelihood of unemployment, underemployment, and lower wages than able-bodied peers. They may also be the victims of limited upward mobility, poverty, marital separation and divorce, frequent hospitalizations, low educational attainment, and social isolation. These outcomes, Gliedman and Roth contend, are not due to one's limitations alone, but more importantly, are a consequence of individual and societal response to disability. Through social activism and major legislation, the dire consequences noted by these authors may be less applicable in the mid-1990s than they were in the early 1980s.

Families must develop competence in managing uncomfortable social situations (Marshak & Seligman, 1993; Wikler, 1981). Wikler notes that family members may "face hostile stares, judgmental comments, murmurs of pity, and intrusive requests for personal information whenever they accompany their child to the grocery store, on the bus, or to the park." (p. 282) She notes further that families with a child with mental retardation are subject to an increase in the number of stressful encounters as the discrepancy between the child's size and mental functioning increases.

It is probably true that the rather positive portrayals of persons with disabilities in films and television have positively affected attitudes. Nevertheless, our present state of knowledge regarding public and professional sentiment about these persons informs us that attitudes continue to be negative. Thus, for some families, stigmatizing attitudes and social ostracism may be added to the other burdens families must bear.

One study found that adolescents who suffered from cystic fibrosis had major difficulties with their self image compared to similarly aged victims of asthma or cancer (Offer, Ostrov, & Howard, 1984). Cystic fibrosis is a lethal genetic disease in which chronic respiratory and digestive problems delay growth and sexual development, resulting in a noticeable difference in physical appearance. In speculating on their findings, Offer et al. (1984) remark "that in illnesses in which the social stigma is easily noticed by others (i.e., cystic fibrosis), the self-image system is impaired. The greater the stigma, one might assume, the greater the impairment" (p. 72). In her review of the research on families of adolescent victims of cystic fibrosis, McCracken (1984) reported that families often experience poor communication; a general lack of time and energy for personal, marital, and family activities; marital discord; depression; and repressed hostility. Thus, the child's difficulties due to the characteristics of the disease and the associated social stigma affect the entire family.

Such sobering information about attitudes toward persons with disabilities must be factored into our conception of the family with a child who has a disability. At a minimum, we as professionals must carefully examine our own attitudes toward disability and toward families with special-needs children lest these attitudes interfere with our performance in subtle ways. Personal examination of our own attitudes is important and an appropriate arena for beginning to explore these would be in professional training programs.

MARITAL ADJUSTMENT, DIVORCE, AND SINGLE PARENTHOOD

Divorce adds to the stress of illness and many persons with disabilities live in households with only one parent (N. Hobbs et al., 1986). There is a growing population of single parents (including never married parents) in society in general, and single parents of children with disabilities would appear to experience greater stresses in their family system than parents in two-parent families (Simpson, 1990; Vadasy, 1986). Yet most of the assumptions about single parenthood and childhood disability are intuitive; empirical data are scarce.

One study reported that single mothers of children with disabilities felt that there were too many time demands, which hindered their personal growth (Holroyd, 1974). These mothers also felt that they had many problems, that the family was not well integrated, and that they had significant financial problems. Another study found that single mothers reported more stress than control mothers (Beckman, 1983), and another one reported that mothers rated that their greatest need was for respite care, then financial assistance, and, thirdly, personal and social support (Wikler, 1981). Wikler also found that these mothers were less likely to be employed, were more likely to be on welfare, and felt that they would not remarry. Indeed, a number of authors claim that divorce and single parenthood lead to financial, psychological, and instrumental problems. However, one needs to bear in mind that divorce does not have the same impact on all family members, and that the effects of divorce may depend on when in the family life cycle it occurs and the degree of dysfunction in the family before marital breakup (J. B. Schulz, 1987; Simpson, 1990).

One outcome of divorce exists in families in which one or both parents in the original family remarry (Visher & Visher, 1988). Blended families may be faced with an array of family variations and emotional situations (A. P. Turnbull & Turnbull, 1990). New rules and roles may need to be adopted, loyalty issues to the biological and nonbiological parents need to be negotiated, new lines of authority need to be established, financial responsibilities may need to be reconsidered, and the like. When a child with a disability resides in a blended family, other issues, such as caretaking and primary responsibility for the child, among other issues, need to be negotiated.

In two-parent families, the role functions assumed by family members are shared, thereby decreasing the burden on any one family member. Perhaps the most support a single parent can expect from family is from his or her own parents. Generally speaking, problems for single parents of children with disabilities include economic, physical, and emotional needs. Researchers, practicing professionals, and those responsible for social policy should seriously address the needs of this under-served population (Vadasy, 1986).

The information regarding marital problems and divorce in families of children with disabilities is sparse and contradictory (Crnic, Friedrich, et al. 1983; Patterson, 1991). Gabel, McDowell, and Cerreto (1983) report that the onset of marital difficulties is one of the more frequently reported adjustment problems. Their research review shows that marital problems included more frequent conflict, feelings of marital dissatisfaction, sexual difficulties, temporary separations, and divorce. Farber (1959) found marital conflict to be common, especially in families containing a retarded boy aged 9 or above. Conversely, some families of children with disabilities report no more frequent problems than comparison families (Bernard, 1974; Dorner, 1975; Martin, 1975; Patterson, 1991; Weisbren, 1980), and some marriages have been reported to improve after the diagnosis of a child's disability (Schwab, 1989). In regard to the latter point, Marsh (1993) observes that "there is increasing recognition among professionals that catastrophic events are inherently challenges that can serve as catalysts for the emergence of regenerated and enriched lives. Although a diagnosis of mental retardation may involve the disintegration of existing modes of functioning, it also provides opportunities for personal and familial reintegration" (p. 89).

Although the data regarding marital satisfaction and divorce in families of children with disabilities are contradictory, we do know that some marriages are under stress but remain intact, others simply fail, while still others survive and are even enhanced. Our task should probably be to understand why some families disintegrate while others thrive. Some believe that future investigations should help differentiate the child and family characteristics and other ecological factors that distinguish families that cope well from those that do not (Crnic, Friedrich, et al., 1983). In a study involving 479 families, Boyce, Behl, Mortensen, and Akers (1991) found the following:

- The child's functioning level was not a predictor of parent-related stress but it was related to the level of stress experienced by the child (functioning level was defined by the child's ability to take care of him- or herself, relate to others, communicate with others, and perform motor and cognitive functions).
- Having a son with disabilities was more related to parent stress than having a daughter with disabilities.
- Parents of children with disabilities experienced increased levels of stress compared to parents of children without disabilities.
- Increased age of the mother was related to less stress.

- The number of children with disabilities in the family was related to increased stress.

Zucman (1982) speculates, for example, that in attending to the needs of an infant or child with disabilities, the mother unwittingly moves away from her husband. Feeling abandoned, a husband may turn to others for solace or at least distance himself from the family as a means of self-protection (Houser & Seligman, 1991). An often-reported sibling response to a parent's excessive attention to a brother or sister with a disability is to feel angry and resentful; perhaps the same general dynamic operates with spouses.

A family's focus on the child with a disability as a source of family problems may in fact be a "red herring" that leads the parents away from more fundamental issues about their relationship (S. L. Harris, 1983). Harris makes the cogent point that professionals need to discriminate between family problems related to childhood disability from those that would have arisen under any circumstances. Problematic marital relationships can be made considerably worse by the birth of a child with a disability. Schipper (1959) found that in those families who had serious personal and/or financial problems *prior* to the birth of their child with Down syndrome, the child sometimes became "the straw that broke the camel's back." It is probably a myth that such a child or any child for that matter can bring a troubled marriage together.

After a thorough review of the literature on families of children with severe disabilities, Lyon and Lyon (1991) concluded that these families must contend with a number of stressors but in general the research reveals mixed conclusions regarding the impact a child has on the family. These authors, as well as other contributors to the literature, have noted the major methodological problems inherent in much of the research and conclude that, in the absence of clear evidence that these families are coping badly, professionals should focus on such practical matters as concrete information, respite services, financial help, and other supportive services to help with logistical problems. "Rather than to continue to view these families as functioning pathologically we might better and more productively focus upon those practical matters that are of great concern to the families themselves" (Lyon & Lyon, 1991, p. 254).

From the above overview, what then can we conclude about marital harmony/dysfunction among families of children with disabilities? One conclusion may be that marital dysfunction might have occurred even without the presence of disability. Another is that in some families a child with disabilities may aggravate latent problems. Another conclusion is that many families can cope successfully with the help of family and community supports. And, finally, marital discord may result in divorce and single parenthood, areas that deserve much more attention than they have thus far received.

FAMILIES WITH CHILDREN WITH DIFFERENT HANDICAPS

Although research on families with children with differing disabling conditions is increasing, the available research is too contradictory to draw any definitive conclusions. Recently, there have been investigations conducted on children with a variety of disabilities in the same study to explore factors across disabling conditions that may influence parental stress and coping. Furthermore, there are studies that use terms such as "developmentally delayed," "developmentally disabled," or simply "disabled children" where the exact disability is unknown. Nevertheless, even though there are some studies reporting on families of children with more than one disability and others that employ ambiguous terminology, most studies explore parental response to a child with a specific disability. Therefore, based on the characteristics of a child's condition one may speculate on the effects that certain child attributes have on the family.

The unpredictability of the behavior of autistic children and the social–interpersonal ramifications experienced by families cause considerable stress (Bristol, 1984; S. Harris, 1994; Schopler & Mesibov, 1984). Even as we learn more about the biological bases of certain conditions, parents of autistic and schizophrenic children are still often considered responsible for their child's illness and thereby suffer the social stigma that accompanies this disorder. Schizophrenia was thought to have been the consequence of family interaction; this theory was based on a flawed belief and not on scientific evidence (Dawes, 1994). For families with autistic children, the following constitute high-risk factors: ambiguity of diagnosis, severity and duration of the illness, and lack of congruity with community norms (Bristol, 1984). Cantwell and Baker (1984) cite research that indicates that families are affected by the multiple failures of their autistic children, mothers appear the most severely affected, spousal affectional bonds tend to be weakened, siblings are affected, and family difficulties do not diminish as the child grows older.

One study showed that 27% (or 13 out of 47 subjects) of parents of head trauma victims had a diagnosable psychiatric disturbance, which became manifest after the offspring's accident (Tartar, 1987). The disturbance was primarily associated with high levels of anxiety and depression. Notably, it was the behavioral and not the physical aspect of the offspring's disability that was most closely associated with parental disturbance.

The unpredictability of seizures of children with epilepsy may result in a constant vigilance for seizure activity for family members (Lechtenberg, 1984). Public attitudes toward persons with epilepsy resemble those toward persons with mental illness, thereby creating a major stressor for the family. Families with a child with hemophilia need to be constantly vigilant about their child's bleeding episodes, and families with children with heart disease need to be cautious about bringing home infections (Travis, 1976). All of the above characteristics of the child's disability may cause stress in the family and may precipitate a major family crisis when there are other existing family problems. As Tartar (1987) points out, the contribution of the parents' characteristics, together with the demand characteristics of the child's disability, "underscores again the complex dynamic and reciprocal relationship between parent and offspring with the characteristics of one affecting the reactions of the other" (p. 83).

As with most disabling conditions, the effects of a deaf child on the family are mixed (Luterman, 1984). However, hearing-impaired children are often also impaired in their communication which can be a source of considerable frustration for family members (Sloman et al., 1993). Levine (1960) reports that children who are deaf are often socially less mature than their hearing peers, and they are more than twice as likely to have emotional problems. Also, hearing-impaired youngsters are often educated in segregated environments that, on the positive side, enable them to develop communication skills, develop personally, and acquire academic knowledge. However, being apart from the mainstream can also serve to isolate these children from the larger, nondeaf community and remove them from establishing stronger ties with family members, although this view is not necessarily shared by members of the deaf community.

Fewell (1991) reports that the *degree* of visual loss in blind children has important implications for the child and the family's reaction to the child. Just as children with low vision try to "pass" as normally sighted, parents too are caught in the dilemma of not wanting to identify their children's differences. Although children who are blind may struggle with their mobility, and there is some evidence of delayed and aberrant social behavior, the fact that a blind child can think, communicate, and carry on with the chores of daily living makes blindness less devastating to the blind child and the family than other disabilities (Fewell, 1991).

For children with physical disabilities, it is their mobility that is most affected, which, in turn, may affect their ability to perform self-care functions. Physical impairments can take a variety of forms such as a loss of limbs or a paralysis due to accident or disease. The nature, characteristics, and severity of the physical impairment may determine the type of adjustment the child and the family must make (Marshak & Seligman, 1993). For example, a child with quadriplegia holds numerous implications for how family members choose to assist with frequent caretaking duties. A child with muscular dystrophy, a degenerative disease, creates a need for the child and family to adjust to an increasing level of dependency as the disease progresses. Numerous other physical disorders, many that are rare and leave the family with few others to identify with, may cause problems for the family.

A relatively new medical procedure has been reported that allows children and adolescents who have end-stage renal disease to perform dialysis at home (LePontois, Moel, & Cohn, 1987). Four or five exchanges are required daily for these children, yet home treatment permits them to reduce hospital visitations and to be ambulatory, active, and more in touch with family and peers. Although the dialysis procedure shifts somewhat in responsibility from the parents to the patient during adolescence, the family experiences "burnout" from years of home care, and they may lose hope in the possibility of a satisfying future for themselves. Conflicting messages from professionals, such as the caution that needs to be exercised in maintaining sterile techniques to prevent serious illness combined with the message that the family should not become anxious and should allow separation and individuation to occur, can result in feelings of hopelessness, helplessness, and depression in family members.

Mullins (1979) reports that the physical needs of children with cancer affect the entire family. "The medications, hospitalizations, repeated transportation for treatment, and extended care at home will be a drain on family finances and physical resources" (p. 266). If the cancer is terminal, the family needs to prepare for the child's imminent death. This can be a crisis of major proportions and requires considerable family adjustment before and after the child's death occurs.

Cystic fibrosis, one of the most common chronic diseases of childhood, requires the family to comply with a prescribed home regimen. This disease results in pulmonary dysfunction and also involves the pancreatic and gastrointestinal systems and presents serious challenges for the coping skills and adjustment of the family as a whole (Brinthaupt, 1991). The home care of the child is difficult and chronic, and failure to carry out treatment can contribute to the progression of the disease and eventual death (Dushenko, 1981). In regard to compliance with home treatment for children with cystic fibrosis, Patterson (1985) reports that age is a factor in that children are more reluctant to adhere to prescriptions as they grow older. Also, the family's commitment to home treatment may wane in the face of the reality that their child is moving into the terminal stages of the disease. Communication in these families often declines in a situation that is difficult and requires the continued expression of hope and mutual support (Patterson, 1985). McCracken (1984) reports that families with children with cystic fibrosis have multiple problems and Offer et al. (1984) argue that an adolescent's problems are exacerbated by short stature and appearance of lower maturational level. Social stigma, as noted earlier, adds to the stress of the disability.

It is impossible to conclude with any certainty how the particular type of a child's disability will affect the family. Factors other than severity of disability may play an important role in determining family adaptation (Crnic, Friedrich, et al., 1983). We know from Rolland's (1993) model (Chapter 1, this volume) that onset, course, and prognosis, as well as other illness/disability-related variables, may influence family response. Researchers report that the quantity and quality of community resources and family support have an impact on the family's ability to cope with childhood disability (Darling, 1991; Korn, Chess, & Fernandez, 1978; Wortis & Margolies, 1955). More recently, researchers have sought to determine more specifically how and which aspects of social support are most helpful to families (Kazak & Marvin, 1984; Kazak & Wilcox, 1984; Krahn, 1993).

According to one researcher, mothers of children with disabilities experienced significantly more stress if their offspring had a greater number of or unusual caregiving demands, were less socially responsive, had more difficult temperaments, and displayed more repetitive behavioral patterns (Beckman, 1983). Beckman's research is important in that it represents a departure from other studies by examining specific child characteristics rather than medical labels, although within any one disability category we would find a wide range of behaviors and other child attributes. Beckman's results support those of Tartar (1987), who found that it was the behavioral, not the physical, aspects of a child's disability that were most distressing.

In a study of 111 parents of children who had hemophilia, researchers found that the burden caused by their child's illness was rather small (Varekamp et al., 1990). In fact, 45% of the parents reported that their marriage had improved, in contrast with 4% who felt that the marriage had gotten worse. With hemophilia, bleedings are mostly unexpected and require immediate attention. The risk of bleeding places the parents in an internal struggle between wanting to protect the child and also wanting to avoid limiting the child at play or hindering the child's personality development. Yet the stress of coping with a child's bleeds seems to be less problematic to parents than dealing with children who isolate themselves, do not communicate, have outbursts, and experience behavior problems (S. Harris, 1994). Blacher and Bromley (1990) agree that child characteristics that may influence parental stress include the severity of mental retardation and the degree of maladaptive behavior.

In the face of inconclusive research data, we feel that it is incumbent upon us to educate professionals regarding the numerous variables that may affect family adjustment and to persuade them to keep these variables in mind when evaluating a family's level of functioning. However, as further research avenues are explored, it seems to us that Beckman's (1983) observations deserve attention. The effects that specific attributes of children (or the demand characteristics of the disability) may have on the family is a more productive line of inquiry than to lump all children with a particular label into one diagnostic category and assume that they are all alike. However, it appears from the review thus far that the caregiving demands and the aberrant behavior of the child lead to more stress than any other aspects of the disability. Finally, Patterson (1991) asks the cogent question of why some families cope poorly while others actually become stronger in the face of childhood disability. Patterson responds to her own question by noting that "it is the nature of high stress, particularly chronic stress, to exaggerate the direction a family was going—pushing them to extremes of their preexisting style of functioning" (p. 133).

THE SEVERITY OF DISABILITY

Perhaps a more productive avenue for research than type of disability is the impact the severity of disability has on family functioning. Severity has implications for caregivers in terms of dependency, increased attention for the child with a disability (perhaps at the expense of other family members), frequent contact with medical personnel and other service providers, the prospect of lifelong care, and, in some cases, coping with difficult behavior.

The placement of children with mild, moderate, and severe disabilities into categories is somewhat arbitrary. Diagnostic ambiguity is particularly evident between the mild and moderate categories. However, Fewell (1991) briefly differentiates these categories:

1. *Mild:* Includes children whose disabilities require special services but who have substantial areas of normal functioning.
2. *Moderate:* Includes children who are markedly deficient in at least one area while functioning normally in others.
3. *Severe:* Includes children with disabilities that pervade most, if not all, areas of functioning.

According to Fewell (1991), children in the less severe categories are more difficult to assess educationally and in terms of emotional adjustment, and thus treatment alternatives are less obvious. Furthermore, the ambiguity of the diagnosis may cause families to go to many sources in search of a favorable diagnosis ("shopping"), thus delaying initiation of a treatment plan and thrusting the family into a state of stress. The more "normal" a child appears the more likely that parents may be "stuck" in the denial stage and engage in more "shopping" (Hornby, 1994; Seligman, 1979). Parents who deny their child's disability seem to experience more tension with professionals (especially school personnel). For children with mild to moderate disabilities, treatment may need to be modified as the child develops and other problems appear, decrease, or increase. Moderate disabilities may become worse over time or improve.

Children who are mildly or moderately disabled (especially those who fall into the "mild" category) are often considered "marginal" in that they do not clearly fit into either the disabled or the "normal" category (Marshak & Seligman, 1993). A person who is "marginal" can claim partial membership in two worlds but is not completely acceptable to either (Stonequist, 1937). Based on a review of several studies, Fewell (1991) argues that people who are intermediately disabled will have more adjustment problems than individuals with more severe disabilities. Marginality implies ambiguity not only in terms of diagnosis but also in terms of the parents' concerns about the future, social acceptance, and level of functioning. But it seems that social adjustment may have the most severe impact on the child and family. In this regard, Watson and Midlarsky (1979) speculate that a mother's overprotective behavior toward her child with mental retardation is not caused by guilt; it is the consequence of her perception that "normal" individuals have negative attitudes toward people who are retarded. Fewell (1991) makes the cogent point that the family's difficulty with the social destiny of their stigmatized child is inevitable and normal, and is not a sign of pathological functioning.

A child with a less severe disability creates stress for the family due to the "uncertainty of not knowing in a given situation whether the child will be accepted or rejected" (Fewell & Gelb, 1983, p. 178). Certainly, in school situations and in one's immediate community, concerns about acceptance and belonging are paramount, especially during adolescence. A child who is not disabled but who has a physical disfigurement, say, cleft palate or facial scars, certainly will face ridicule and experience shame from peer reactions. On the other hand, children who have invisible conditions (epilepsy, autism, diabetes) have consistently been found to have more emotional problems than those with disabilities with more visible limitations or deformities (Blum, 1992). The concealment of a minor or invisible impairment can create considerable stress for some youth in their interactions with others (Marshak & Seligman, 1993). It is not unusual for a person with a mild disability to define him- or herself entirely by the disability. It's almost as if a deformed limb implies that one is a defective person.

As suggested earlier, a family who has a child who is devalued due to a disability also may experience a sense of stigma and lower status:

> The effect of the moderate disability on functioning is, according to
> our definition, limited. The moderately handicapped are not of them-
> selves socially deviant. They are penalized, however, by virtue of the
> "handicapped" label. They are identified with the severely handi-
> capped, although they could as easily be identified with the nondis-
> abled. Their social isolation is no less palpable for being undeserved,
> and it strongly affects their parents. (Fewell & Gelb, 1983, p. 179)

A study of mothers of thalidomide-deformed babies found that social
factors were a major concern in the parents' reactions (Roskies, 1972)
and, as time went on, the importance of social factors for the mothers
increased.

The concept of "spread" has relevance to children with milder
disabilities and, by association, their families. Dembo, Leviton, and
Wright (1956) introduced the term *spread,* which refers to the power of
single characteristics to evoke broader inferences about a person. If a
person has an undesirable characteristic and is viewed as less adequate
only in that regard, the judgment would be a realistic one. But the realistic
appraisal of others is more the exception than the rule. For example,
physique (being obese or fit and trim) evokes a wide variety of impressions
and feelings about people. Specific characteristics may be inferred from
physique (an obese person may have physical restrictions), but also the
person *as a whole* is sometimes evaluated (for example, the obese person
is also viewed as depressed, socially isolated, low in self-esteem, and
lacking in sexual relationships). Global devaluations are problems of some
magnitude, in that persons with atypical characteristics are considered to
be less worthy, less valuable, and less desirable (Marshak & Seligman,
1993).

Early research indicated that the characteristics, traits, and behaviors
of persons with a disabilities are inferred beyond the disability (Musseen
& Barker; Ray, both cited in Wright, 1983). Because of spread, the degree
of disability is often perceived as more severe than it actually is. An
illustration of spread is when a sighted person speaks unusually loudly to
a person who is blind, as if blindness implies a hearing impairment as
well.

The phenomenon of spread is implicated in the way parents of
children with disabilities are sometimes viewed. As noted earlier, Goffman (1963) calls this phenomena "courtesy stigma." As a consequence of
disability in the family, some parents are as subject to spread as are their
sons and daughters who are disabled. Parents of these children may be
viewed as deeply troubled and burdened—or as extraordinarily brave and
courageous. The numerous factors that contribute to family adjustment,
as well as the complex nature of their interactions, are typically disre-
garded. By association, then, certain characteristics may be attributed to

family members of children who have mild disabilities. The all-too-ready judgment, on the basis of disability in the family, that a person's life is a tragedy from which there is no reprieve may be a fairly common perception.

In their contribution on parenting children with moderate disabilities, Fewell and Gelb (1983) discuss family adjustment to children who have vision and hearing problems, physical impairments, and learning disabilities. They conclude their review of these conditions by stating that "In most cases, the presence of a child with a moderate impairment creates the following concerns: the dilemma of being educated with the nondisabled or the handicapped; the stress of heavy involvement in physiotherapy; the stress of acknowledging the existence of the handicap or simply covering it up" (p. 192).

Lyon and Lyon (1991) report that children with severe disabilities constitute an extremely low incidence population and are really a heterogeneous population with different characteristics, needs, and abilities. Although children with severe disabilities are heterogeneous, there are a number of problems and difficulties that characterize them and their families' responses to them.

Intellectual deficits are one characteristic of this population. These children may be substantially delayed cognitively and may not even acquire the most rudimentary conceptual abilities. In addition, they may remain extremely limited in the acquisition and use of language.

Another problem common among children with severe disabilities is the presence of physical disabilities. Chief among these is cerebral palsy, which, along with other physical impairments, can affect basic movements such as walking, using one's hands, speaking, and eating. The presence of major physical disabilities is exceedingly restrictive to the impaired child and places a great burden on the family.

A third characteristic is sensory impairment. Many have various degrees of visual and/or auditory deficits. It is not uncommon for children with sensory impairments also to have varying degrees of retardation and physical disabilities as well.

A major consequence of severe impairment is that these children also manifest great difficulty in developing appropriate social skills. Social skill deficits may be associated with mental retardation or childhood autism. These children characteristically demonstrate bizarre behavior through unintelligible or repetitive speech, self-stimulation, and even self-destructive behavior. These behaviors are difficult to treat and often necessitate extensive effort and commitment for the family to remedy or even tolerate (Harris, 1994; Lyon & Lyon, 1991). We already know from the research of Beckman (1983) and Tartar (1987) that a child's behavior can be a major stressor in the family.

It would seem from this review of children with severe disabilities that the consequences for the family would be insurmountable. For some families this may be so, but the evidence regarding negative impact is unclear. Much of the fault for this equivocation lies in the fact that research in this area is not abundant (although the research has increased somewhat since the first edition of this book in 1989) and that which has been reported is poor from an empirical point of view (Hauenstein, 1990). Nevertheless, the literature does provide some preliminary evidence as to how children with severe disabilities affect the family.

Several researchers conclude that children with severe disabilities have a negative effect on siblings. For example, older sisters were reported to have a higher incidence of psychiatric disturbance (Gath, 1974), while some siblings may experience a variety of negative emotional reactions such as fear, death wishes, and anxiety (Grossman, 1972). One consistent finding has been that older female siblings may experience difficulty due to excessive caretaking (Lyon & Lyon, 1991; Moorman, 1994). On the other hand, other investigators found no evidence of negative impact on siblings (Caldwell & Guze, 1960; Kibert, 1986). (A more detailed discussion of siblings appears in Chapter 5.)

In terms of the family, Farber's (1959, 1960b) pioneering studies showed that overall integration of families who kept their children with severe retardation at home was affected negatively. Another study found that families of children with severe disabilities evidenced more negative emotions (Gath, 1974), while other researchers have reported role tension, increased divisiveness within the family, negative emotionality, and increased financial burden, as well as restrictions in family activities, more physical health problems, and more marital distress (Caldwell & Guze, 1960; Dunlap & Hollinsworth, 1977; Farber, 1960b; Hormuth, 1953; Patterson, 1991). In a study designed to compare families of children with severe mental retardation, educable mental retardation, and trainable mental retardation, Blacher, Nihira, and Meyers (1987) found that parents of children with severe retardation reported the greatest amount of negative impact on family adjustment. Family adjustment was defined as the "extent to which the retarded child affects the atmosphere in the home, relationships among family members, agreement as to discipline of the child" (p. 315). The excessive caretaking responsibilities of family members of children with severe retardation apparently influenced family adjustment. However, on the measures of marital adjustment ("extent to which the retarded child has influenced the parents' marriage" [p. 315]), no differences were found between the three groups. Blacher and colleagues' results reinforce those found by others who explain that the demanding care of a child with severe disabilities was more likely to disrupt family routines and social lives than contribute to significant marital problems. A further finding was that there were no differences among the three groups on the coping scores, reflecting an equal ability to deal with day-to-day events. A number of professionals argue that the negative effects have been over-stated and the positive effects have been ignored (Jacobson & Humphrey, 1979; Lyon & Lyon, 1991; Schwab, 1989).

Lyon and Lyon (1991) note that problems frequently reported by families of children with severe disabilities include financial difficulties and the burden on the practical day-to-day operations and logistics of the family. They concur with others that these families have been patholo-gized too often in the past and that, with adequate services (and these families need many), families with youth who have severe disabilities do manage to cope. When families experience severe stress, they argue, it is usually due to the failure of the service delivery system and not necessarily a consequence of the child's disability. Indeed, of the many services needed by families with a child who has severe impairments perhaps one of the most critical and, in some communities, least available is respite care (Lyon & Preis, 1983; Upshur, 1983).

In contrast to the aforementioned authors, Blacher (1984b) con-cludes from her comprehensive literature review that "[t]he impact of a severely impaired child on the family appears to be profound, pervasive, and persistent. It is reasonable to assume that parents feel the effects of such a child throughout infancy, early childhood, during the school years, and beyond into adult life" (p. 41). And Crnic, Friedrich, et al. (1983) comment that the "research in this area suggests that parents of retarded children are at the least a group at high risk for emotional and personality difficulties" (p. 128).

Although Blacher (1984b) and Crnic, Friedrich, et al. (1983) tend to view the effect of a child with severe disabilities more negatively than others do they note that extrafamilial and intrafamilial support buffer the hardships. The availability and quality of social support is generally viewed as a critical factor in a family's ability to cope—a fact that should be noted by those in a position to affect public policy.

It seems that a characteristic that differentiates families with children with severe impairments from those with children with more moderate disabilities is the burdensome, unrelenting chronicity of care. The burden of multiple needs can also place stress on the family system. For families with children with mild or moderate disabilities, the "marginality" of the child and the impact this has on social acceptance constitutes a major obstacle. The evidence to date supports the conclusion that marital harmony is comparable across levels of severity. And, finally, the caregiv-ing demands together with the aberrant behavior of the child cause stress in the family no matter how mild or severe the disability is.

In the end, perhaps, as one considers whether it is best to posit type of disability or severity of disability as more debilitating to the family, the most useful construct may come from R. Hill's (1949) model of stress. Recall from Chapter 1 that a key to a family's experience of stress is the C factor, which refers to how the family interprets a particular event. This is similar to Ellis's (1962) conception of neurotic behavior in individuals, which holds that the event itself does not determine one's response but that the meaning attributed to the event determines how one will respond. These views of human behavior would suggest that a key intervention with distressed families would be to help them to reorganize their thinking, which in turn would affect their outlook and thus their behavior. There have been several recent publications that reflect a cognitive approach to help families cope (Singer & Powers, 1993; A. P. Turnbull et al., 1993). Perhaps a combination of constructive thinking about their situation and adequate family and community support would constitute a meaningful strategy for professionals to consider in helping families. However, due to mounting tensions in the family and relentless burdens, some families may need extensive psychotherapeutic help as well (Marsh, 1993).

One conclusion from this review is that it is too simplistic to base one's evaluation of family functioning on whether a child has a particular type of disability or whether the disability is moderate or severe. Phenomenological thinkers have argued that the most meaningful reality is that which the person, or in this case, the family, perceives. It is only by "walking in the shoes" of another that we can truly understand another's reality.

OTHER FACTORS THAT AFFECT THE FAMILY

Stress, its causes and consequences, has probably been studied more than any other construct with regard to families of children with disabilities (Beckman, 1983; Friedrich, 1979; Friedrich & Friedrich, 1981; Houser, 1987; Patterson, 1991; Wikler, 1981). Stress can manifest itself in a number of ways:

> When people are under severe stress it tends to first affect any areas of physical or psychological weakness which a person has. For example, the first sign that I get that stress is getting the better of me is when I begin to experience a mild form of the stammer which I had as a child. With other people the signs of too much stress may be problems with their stomach or difficulty in sleeping at night. Some people experience unusual and sometimes frightening physical symptoms such as numbness in a limb or a sensation that one has suddenly become heavier and fatter. (Hornby, 1994, p. 182)

One author has identified 11 characteristics that differentiate major from normal stressors (Figley, 1983):

1. Little or no time to prepare
2. Slight previous experience
3. Few sources of guidance
4. Experienced by few others
5. Interminable time in crisis
6. Lack of control and sense of helplessness
7. A sense of loss
8. Disruption and distraction
9. High dangerousness
10. High emotional impact
11. Presence of medical problems

Marsh (1992) believes that, based on Figley's criteria, a diagnosis of mental retardation is potentially a catastrophic stressor for family members because it is usually an unanticipated event, there is little time to prepare, and there has been little or no previous experience. Moreover, there are few sources of guidance, limited understanding by those who are not family members, the disability generally lasts for a lifetime, there is a strong sense of helplessness, and medical problems may exist. Over time, however, family members do not continue to experience the disability as a catastrophic event as the family adapts, although some families adapt and cope better than others.

For some, the research indicates that stress is a major factor in the lives of family members in that the presence of a disability in the family causes great stress. Other studies report the reverse to be true. Houser (1987), for example, reported that fathers of adolescent children with mental retardation were no more stressed than a control group of fathers of adolescents without retardation. This positive outcome conflicts with other studies on fathers (Andrew, 1968; Cummings, 1976; Holt, 1958b). Dyson and Fewell (1986) found that parents of young children with severe disabilities were significantly more stressed than a control group. Beckman (1983) reported that single mothers reported more stress than mothers in two-parent homes but found also that two child characteristics, age and sex, were not related to the amount of stress experienced by mothers, a finding that contradicts that of other studies (Bristol, 1984; Farber, 1959). These studies once again reflect the mixed and contradictory results found in the literature.

In understanding stress in context, it is important to acknowledge that stress is a common human condition and is caused by both familial and extrafamilial factors. Furthermore, based on the available evidence we cannot say that these families experience more or less stress than the general population, although certain factors (e.g., lack of support, child characteristics) do seem to contribute to chronic stress for family members. However, it is misleading to assume, even in studies that demonstrate stress in families of children with disabilities, that stress is necessarily dysfunctional. Low levels of stress over relatively short periods of time may be perfectly adaptive. High levels of stress over long periods of time, however, are another matter:

> Considerable evidence suggests that high stress levels, if chronically sustained, may contribute significantly to a lowering of one's energy levels, ineffective cognitive processes, performance failures, ruptures in interpersonal relationships, flattened affect, a weakened immune system, and degenerative diseases of various kinds (Matheny, Aycock, Pugh, Curlette, & Cannella, 1986, p. 500)

Perhaps the research question that needs to be asked is whether stress levels of family members are high or low and whether they are sustained over long periods of time, rather than simply assessing whether stress exists or not. Clearly, the exploration of this phenomenon has captured the interest of researchers but different questions regarding stress and families need to be formulated before meaningful conclusions can be reached.

The interest in stress research has sparked a corresponding interest in coping behaviors (Folkman, Lazarus, Dunkel-Schelter, DeLongis, & Gruen, 1986; Houser & Seligman, 1991; A. P. Turnbull et al., 1993). Coping, which can take several forms, has social support as a major component. Indeed, social support, both within and outside of the family, is generally viewed as buffering the effects of stress. In assessing families, then, a useful approach would be to evaluate the demand characteristics of the child's disability, determine the coping resources within the family, and ascertain the social supports available to help reduce negative effects. In this regard, Matheny et al. (1986) provide an in-depth discussion of coping resources (e.g., social support, beliefs/values, and self-esteem) and coping behaviors (e.g., assertive responses, tension reduction strategies, and cognitive restructuring).

Zucman (1982) believes that professionals should be concerned about families that are socially isolated. She asserts that social isolation has a tendency to increase as the child grows older but feels that a major contributor is the "insufficient help received from the social and professional environment" (p. 29). Linked to the family's withdrawal is the denial of the child's disability and concomitant unrealistic view of the child's future. Presumably, when families defend against the reality of their child's disability, they remove themselves from needed services and withdraw from relationships with other families. Their withdrawal would indicate, however, that there is some unconscious recognition of the child's problems. Whatever the cause, a family's withdrawal from social interaction is a serious concern.

Although the evidence is inconclusive, there is some indication that children with physical disabilities are at risk for abuse or neglect (Morgan, 1987; White, Benedict, Wulff, & Kelley, 1987). One problem with the research in this area is the failure to determine more precisely whether child or family characteristics—or perhaps a combination of the two—are linked to abuse and neglect. The most consistently reported demographic factor associated with reported child abuse or neglect is low SES (White et al., 1987). However, child abuse among high-SES families tends to be underreported. Stress is a consequence of poor economic conditions, too much change too quickly, poor general coping, inadequate parenting skills, and social isolation. A major child characteristic in child abuse is low birth weight or prematurity. Premature infants are ill more often, cry more, and are more irritable; they may thus overwhelm their parents (Morgan, 1987). It is also important to keep in mind that some infants and children become disabled after an abusive attack. This brief review of issues pertaining to child neglect and abuse again reinforces the notion that family dysfunction can have its roots in a number of child or parent factors.

Although some of the literature in this field has stressed the negative impact of childhood disability on the family, other studies have noted benefits created by the presence of such a child in the home (Singer & Powers, 1993; A. P. Turnbull et al., 1993). Some of the positive aspects include (1) increased family cohesion, (2) increased "involvement" and (3) personal growth (Darling, 1986). The literature on the negative impact of children with disabilities must be balanced by a greater recognition of family strengths. More research is needed on the positive effects that arise from childhood disability. We are pleased to report that since the publication of the first edition of *Ordinary Families, Special Children* in 1989, we have detected a move in the direction of discerning family resilience, strengths, and coping abilities.

CHAPTER   FIVE

Effects on Siblings

In the late 1960s, in a sermon on equality, William
Sloane Coffin said, "Am I my brother's keeper? No, I
am my brother's brother." His concept was one that I
instinctively understood and long for: A relationship of
mutuality, based on respect, that neither diminished
nor augmented either participant.

—MOORMAN (1994, p. 47)

Since PUBLICATION of the first edition of *Ordinary Families, Special
Children* there has been considerable attention paid to sibling issues in
the professional literature when one of them is disabled and the other
one is nondisabled. Siblings who share in the anticipation and excitement
of a new child in the family also share in the grief and pain that
accompanies the birth of an infant with a disability. There is now a
considerable literature on family adaptation, which has primarily focused
on the parents, with a particular emphasis on mothers. Research and
comment on siblings, however, suggest that, while many cope well, others
may be "at risk" psychologically (Deluca & Solerno, 1984; Lobato, 1990;
Moorman, 1994; Powell & Gallagher, 1993; Seligman, 1991b; Stoneman
& Berman, 1993; Trevino, 1979).

The study of the effects of a brother or sister with a disability on
nondisabled siblings has emerged as a significant area of research and
concern. In the first edition, we wrote that "We need considerably more
research before we fully understand disabled and nondisabled brothers
and sisters, their respective roles in the family, and the reciprocal effects

118

they have on each other" (p. 111). It now appears that some reasonable speculations can be made about sibling relationships based on a reasonable body of research, commentary, and "the voices" of siblings.

The following section, then, is an examination of the factors that appear to influence sibling relationships. The first part of this chapter will review sibling relationships in general. We then go on to discuss the sibling relationship when one sibling has a disability.

THE SIBLING BOND

Sibling relationships are usually the longest and most enduring of family relationships. The permanency of this relationship makes it possible for two individuals to exert considerable influence over each other through longitudinal interactions. As Powell and Gallagher (1993) note, "Siblings provide a continuing relationship from which there is no annulment" (p. 14).

Like any intense, long-term relationship, sibling relationships are cyclical. Bank and Kahn (1982) observe that siblings follow a life cycle of their own. They provide a constant source of companionship for one another during the early childhood years. During the school-aged years, it is common for siblings to extend themselves to others outside of the immediate family as they exercise the social skills they have developed together. During adolescence, siblings manifest ambivalence about their mutual relationship yet they still rely on each other as confidants and advisors. In adulthood, siblings may interact less often due to marriage and/or geographical distance. Even so, during this period siblings may provide long distance support and encouragement as they embrace the vicissitudes of adult life. In addition, as aunts and uncles they provide unique support networks for each other's children. And finally, in old age when children move on to increased independence and spouses pass away, siblings continue to provide a social network for each other (S. Harris, 1994). It is not unusual in this stage for sibling relationships to become reestablished or to intensify once again in a manner similar to the first stages of their lives together.

The many changes in contemporary family life add to the importance of studying sibling relationships. Bank and Kahn (1982) suggest that the following realities of family life may result in increased sibling contact and emotional interdependence:

1. Because fewer children are born, family size is decreasing. Also, children tend to be closer in age, resulting in more intense contact between siblings.

2. Siblings provide a source of support to each other over the life span.
3. Siblings may rely on each other more because of frequent moves by the family and the resulting difficulty in developing friends.
4. Siblings are confronted with family disintegration and new configurations as divorce and remarriage rates remain high. Such changes in family structure surely affect sibling relationships, although the nature of these changes is not well known.
5. Parental stress affects the availability of parents to their children. Such periods of parental emotional absence influence sibling relationships.

Children are growing up in a mobile and complex world where opportunities for contact, constancy, and permanency have decreased. "Children are biologically propelled by these biological needs . . . to turn for satisfaction to any accessible person. In a worried, mobile, small-family, high-stress, fast-paced, parent-absent America, that person can be a brother or a sister" (Bank & Kahn, 1982, p. 15).

In the past we have not sufficiently acknowledged the intense, long-term, and complex nature of sibling relationships. Now that we have begun to focus on this subsystem of the family, we are beginning to comprehend the immense value in understanding sibling relationships and in fostering their positive growth (Kahn & Lewis, 1988). It may well be that in families where a child with a disability resides we need to be particularly sensitive to the siblings' experience. In this regard, Marsh (1993) observes that siblings share with their parents the loss that accompanies the birth of a child with a disability. In some ways, however, they are less vulnerable than their parents, who will likely assume financial and caregiving responsibilities. In other ways, they are more vulnerable due to their age because it carries with it a special susceptibility to the stress and disruption that often accompany the experience of other family members. Although many siblings are unaffected by or even benefit from this experience, other siblings simply do not fare well. However, linear cause and effect explanations of the impact siblings have on each other are misleading. Instead we agree with Stoneman and Berman (1993) when they observe that

> the sibling relationship is directly affected by specific characteristics of the individual siblings, by characteristics of the family in which the children live, and by the childrearing strategies used by the children's parents or primary caregiver. The child rearing strategies used by parents, in turn, are influenced by several factors, including characteristics of the parents and the emotional climate of the family and of the individual siblings. (p. 4)

In the following pages we will examine the sibling relationship from both a research and a personal perspective. Our plan is to explore the various factors mentioned in the literature that have a bearing on sibling response to a brother or sister with a disability.

THE NEED FOR INFORMATION

Due to the parents' reluctance to communicate, siblings may have a limited understanding of their brother's or sister's condition. In her review of studies on siblings, Wasserman (1983) noted that there is a startling lack of information about the disability, its manifestations, and its consequences. Limited or poor information confuses siblings in regard to several factors:

1. Feeling responsible for a particular condition
2. Whether the condition is transmittable
3. If and how one should communicate to family and friends about the disability
4. What implications the child with a disability has for the siblings' future
5. How one should respond to discomforting feelings such as anger, hurt, and guilt
6. How to relate effectively to one's brother or sister and to others in one's environment

In their book, *Living with a Brother or Sister with Special Needs: A Book for Sibs,* D. Meyer, Vadasy, and Fewell (1985) have published a sensitive and down-to-earth contribution that addresses the many feelings and questions siblings have about their special circumstances. Such areas as the following are addressed in their book: typical sibling concerns regarding the future, services for children and their families, and a discussion of feelings that siblings often experience. In addition, the authors provide short, readable, and accurate explanations of the etiology, manifestations, and prognosis of a number of disabling conditions.

Parents may be neither able nor willing to share information with their nondisabled children. A colleague of the authors' had been told as a youngster that her sister suffered from asthma. Her sister had cerebral palsy. Asthma was a more acceptable condition than cerebral palsy in a family where social appearances were paramount. When parents are unable to inform their children about another child's disability, siblings may seek information on their own. Sometimes they search for information without knowing that they are doing so:

In addition to taking two elective classes in special education, I volunteered to work as a tutor and aide. I worked with slower kids in teaching them to read and began to see learning problems at all levels. I volunteered at the child development center and saw small children who were "developmentally delayed" and learning to crawl. I also went to a local chapter of retarded citizens to stuff envelopes and stood on city street corners collecting money. I see now that these must have been early attempts to collect more information about Mary Louise's condition, information that I never got from my parents. (Hazi, 1992, p. 12)

In regard to the provision of information, Murphy, Paeschel, Duffy, and Brady (1976) observed in their discussion groups with siblings of children with Down syndrome that the type of information requested appears to be related to age. From ages 6 to 9, children asked questions about motor development and speech, discussed what their brothers and sisters could and could not do, and were interested in the medical and biological information presented to them. Concerns about the future became evident among the 10- to 12-year-old children, while the older adolescents showed concern about their own chances of bearing a child with a disability. A child's cognitive abilities may place limits on understanding, especially for very young children.

Siblings have sought to be more open about their circumstances, their feelings, and their need to be better informed. They have found that they are not alone and indeed have discovered that disability in the family—and the family's reaction to it—is shared by others. Along with discovering that others share this life situation, siblings are speaking out so that parents and professionals will understand their special challenge. And finally, siblings—aided by such resources as the Sibling Information Network[*] and the magazine *The Exceptional Parent* —are encouraging a wider dissemination of basic information about disabling conditions and their emotional impact so that siblings, parents, and professionals are better informed. It is only with accurate and fairly complete knowledge that professionals can move toward stated treatment goals. And armed with this knowledge siblings will be in a better position to perceive their situation unambiguously and with less fear. Service providers need to understand that children will respond with less anxiety when they are

---

[*]Sibling Information Network, CUAP, 991 Main Street, East Hartford, CT 06108. The Network publishes a newsletter that, in addition to providing information, allows siblings to share their feelings and experiences regarding their life with a brother or sister who is disabled. Similarly, the Committee of the National Alliance for the Mentally Ill publishes a newsletter, *The Sibling Bond.* This newsletter reviews relevant publications, provides information, and publishes sibling essays. Their address: National Sibling Network, 5112 15th Avenue, South Minneapolis, MN 55417.

presented with accurate information in a compassionate and understanding manner.

The chore of informing a nondisabled child about her brother's or sister's disability often falls to the parents. However, parents are not always well informed. "My parents never talked to me about Sally's illness. They couldn't have explained it to me even if they'd wanted to, for no one adequately explained it to them" (Moorman, 1994, p. 42).

According to Powell and Gallagher (1993), siblings need a way to get information at various stages of their lives. They need a system that is responsive to their personal questions instead of to generic, predetermined questions. Their information system has to be a longitudinal one—one that reflects their changing needs. For example, children at age 7 may request some basic information; children usually ask their parents for answers to important questions. In contrast, a 47-year-old sibling may seek answers to questions about lifelong care and estate planning.

CAREGIVING

Another important issue is the responsibility children often bear for their sibling with a disability. Excessive caregiving can result in anger, resentment, guilt, and, quite possibly, subsequent psychological problems, especially if it is combined with limited parental attention. A friend of the author's (M. S.), in her late 60s, mentioned that she still harbors angry and resentful feelings about her youth due to the attention her diabetic sister received from her parents. The friend expressed surprise that her feelings felt very distant in time yet continue to evoke strong negative reaction.

A child with a disability absorbs a great deal of time, energy, and emotional resources. Before they are ready, children may be pressed into parental roles they are ill prepared to assume. As Myers (1978) notes, such youngsters may move too rapidly through the developmental stages so necessary for normal growth.

> From the time Roger began going to physicians and consultants, it seemed to me that I carried a five-hundred-pound lead weight around in the front of my brain. Never out of my mind was the idea that my brother was retarded, needed special attention, needed special care, and that I had to provide some of it.
>
> My role in those days was someone who was always around to help care for Roger. That was my mother's phrase. My father called me his "good right arm." Roger himself called me "Dad" before he corrected himself and called me "Bobby."
>
> I never felt I dressed like a kid, never felt comfortable with the clothes I wore, never felt I knew how to act as a boy or a teenager. I was a little man. (p. 36)

The tremendous burden visited upon children as they assume responsibility of a sibling with a disability is vividly expressed by Hayden (1974):

> The responsibility I felt for Mindy was tremendous. One year, when my "babysitting" duties involved periodic checking on my sister, Mindy wandered away between checks. After a thorough but fruitless search of the neighborhood, my mother hysterically told me that if anything happened to Mindy, I would be to blame. I felt terrified and guilty. I was seven. (p. 27)

Kirkman's (1985) study of adult siblings showed that resentment and anger regarding caregiving is not unidirectional. In her Australian study, she found that a few of her 151 sibling subjects reacted negatively to their parents because of *parents'* failure to provide adequate attention to the brother or sister who was disabled. One sibling said, "I feel angered at both my parents for lack of understanding and effort to truly help him. They have neglected their responsibility to their son and have lost my respect in this regard" (p. 3).

Unlike Kirkman's study, much of the literature focuses on the responsibilities some children assume in a family as a result of having a brother or sister with a disability. There is relatively little information on adult siblings and their experience of burden, guilt, and fear. Although some adult siblings live lives relatively free from excessive anxiety and fear, others do not:

> Whenever I tentatively imagined her [mother's] death, and myself returning to Virginia to take over Sally's care, I instantly thought of suicide. I was convinced I would have to give up my life; I just wasn't sure which way I would do it. (Moorman, 1994, p. 44)

> We all have to worry. Who else is going to be there? I will have to worry and it will be my responsibility; I think about it all the time. I think about the person I am going to marry: When I meet someone, they are not going to just marry me, but they are going to have to love my brother and know he is going to be around all my life. (Fish, 1993)

It can be a challenge for adults who have a child with a disability to accept their circumstances when they compare their lot to other adults who do not share this experience. Some children find their life with a sibling who has a disability even less comprehensible when they compare their family circumstances to others with nondisabled children:

> The whole situation is profoundly unfair. It is unfair that the family must live with schizophrenia, autism, blindness, or retardation while others do not. It is unfair that some children must function as adjunct

parents even before they go to school, while others successfully avoid
responsibilities of all sorts well into their second decade. The brothers
and sisters of the handicapped child learn to cope with this unfairness,
and with their own response to it, the sorrow and the anger. (Featherstone, 1980, p. 162)

Parental injunctions regarding the care of a child/adult with a
disability can haunt siblings well into their adult life:

My hope is that I will have future choices and that I can see some
shore. What is on the shore? A group home placement may come up
within the distant future. Foster care may exist. I may be able to take
on an advocacy role in my community, fighting for my sister's rights
and my own. As a single, unmarried, professional woman, I will be
able to hire someone to permanently live with us. This last option is
my father's preferred future vision. Mine is the first, but his unshakable
"When I die . . . " message and fear controls my sister's future and my
own. (Hazi, 1992, p. 21)

Siblings may experience "survivors' guilt" due to their healthy lives
which sharply contrasts with those of ill or disabled children (Bank &
Kahn, 1982). As noted by D. J. Meyer and Vadasy (1994), a sister's secret
prayer might be something like the following: "Dear God, why did this
have to happen to Colleen? She's so little and so sweet and now she's in
the hospital with all these tubes coming out of her. She has all these
seizures and seems in such pain. She doesn't deserve this. Why couldn't
it happen to me?" (pp. 14–15). Siblings may experience considerable guilt
over the advantages they have and the only recourse to expiate such guilt
lies in taking care of the ill sibling. The danger is when the well sibling
remains "in the service" of a brother or sister through much of life
because of guilt and forced obligation.

Family size seems to be related to the extent to which a sibling
experiences caregiving responsibility. This clinical observation is borne
out by Grossman's (1972) research, namely, that the college students she
interviewed from two-child families found life with a sibling who is
retarded as more stressful than did those with a number of other, normal
siblings. It could be that in larger families where more children are
available to help there is more shared responsibility and less pressure on
each sibling to excel in compensation for a brother's or sister's disability.

Research also reveals that the gender of nondisabled brothers and
sisters plays a significant part in caregiving. Female siblings are more
subject to caregiving behavior than males and may thus be more prone
to psychological maladjustment. However, this early observation of the
relationship of gender and maladjustment has been questioned by recent
information that males sometimes fare more poorly than females and that

sibling age, age spacing, and gender may interact in complex ways (Simeonsson & Bailey, 1986). Nevertheless, when it comes to caregiving, females probably do assume these roles more frequently than males, but perhaps this does not necessarily lead to maladjustment.

Indeed, McHale and Gamble (1987) speculate that problems should not be attributable to caregiving per se; rather, how children with disabilities behave when they are being cared for by their siblings may create tensions. Therefore, these authors would discourage a realignment of family roles and responsibilities and instead teach children behavior management skills. McHale and Gamble also report from their research that children were more depressed, anxious, and had lower self-esteem when they were dissatisfied about how their parents treated them relative to the other children in the family. These findings held for siblings of both disabled and nondisabled brothers and sisters. Parental "fairness" is an important concern for siblings in general (D. J. Meyer & Vadasy, 1994).

Stoneman and Berman (1993) report on a series of studies they and their colleagues conducted. They found that older siblings experienced an increase in conflict between them when they had greater child care demands. This finding applied only to child care responsibilities and not to household chores. Also, contrary to the expectation that younger siblings in caregiving roles will experience "role tension" characterized by anxiety and conflict (Farber, 1960a), younger nondisabled siblings who assumed more caregiving roles had less conflicted relations than did siblings with fewer responsibilities (Stoneman, Brody, Davis, Crapps, & Malone, 1991). Generally speaking, these researchers concede that nondisabled siblings have more caregiving duties than other children who do not have a brother or sister with a disability, but that engaging in these activities does not uniformly result in negative outcomes.

Grossman (1972) found that SES may be related to the amount of responsibility nondisabled siblings might assume for a brother or sister. The more financially able a family, the better prepared they are to secure necessary help from sources outside the family.[*] Families that are less secure financially must rely on resources within the family. Financial problems produce additional stress and can detract from general stability when excessive and unreasonable demands are placed on family members. In families worried and stressed primarily because of limited financial resources, a child with a disability may even be blamed as the source of the financial woes. In such instances, service providers must be alert to the potential for abuse of the child with a disability.

---

[*]It is worth noting here that, due to family values, there may be considerable resistance to securing outside help, irrespective of the family's financial situation. Some families believe that the cornerstone of their survival lies within the family, not outside of it.

The burdening of siblings with the care of chronically physically ill children seems to be common (Travis, 1976). Travis reports that siblings who have been excessively burdened may leave home during their adolescence. She observes that signs of mounting resentment among siblings can be seen in hasty or unkind physical care. Relatedly, Stoneman and Berman (1993) observe that they are surprised "by the force with which some children with disabilities attack their siblings, sometimes causing physical harm even when under the direct supervision of an adult" (p. 16). In an informal study by Holt (1958a), nondisabled children were reported to have suffered repeatedly from unexpected physical attacks by their siblings. Some chronically ill children enslave their physically normal siblings—"Hand me this, pick up that." Children with chronic illnesses have been observed to be verbally abusive toward their nondisabled siblings, presumably because of envy and confusion. However, in close-knit families, the care of a child with a disability is viewed as a shared responsibility.

During adolescence, the willingness of siblings to accept care from and give care to each other can become a source of conflict (Rolland, 1994). Caregiving and -receiving during this sensitive developmental stage, when becoming more independent from the family is an essential task, can result in increased anger and resentment. Heightened concern about one's appearance and public image can increase fears for nondisabled children and embarrassment and humiliation for the child with a disability as they interact in giving and receiving roles. Instead of increasing the caregiving of their nondisabled child because they increasingly trust their judgment, parents should realize the special vulnerabilities of adolescence. A case in point is provided by the following observations by Moorman (1994), as she reflects on her adolescent years with her mentally ill sister, Sally:

> I saw her as a disturbance, an embarrassment. She seemed to speak in non sequiturs that caused conversations to jerk to an abrupt stop. She was overweight and ungainly. She had no friends. I was entering adolescence, and I wanted friends—neat friends. I was afraid that Sally's strangeness would get in the way of my social life. For me, Sally was a liability and I all but stopped speaking to her. If I could behave as if she were invisible, she might disappear.
>
> As a teenager, I earnestly pursued the fantasy that I was an only child. Denying Sally's very existence enabled me to concentrate on trying to make my own life seem as normal as possible, but it eventually took a toll. I couldn't bear to be alone, and I was often unable to concentrate. In my early teens, I began to have trouble studying, and, by the time I reached high school, I could barely keep up with my classes. I was often deeply depressed. (p. 42)

Responsibility for the physical well-being of a chronically ill child can be taken to great lengths. In instances where the sick child must be guarded from infection—say, in chronic heart disease—Travis (1976) reports that mothers warn their healthy children to avoid crowds for fear of bringing home infections. Such responsibility for the welfare of one's ill brother or sister places an inordinate burden on children, with possible implications for their subsequent adjustment. Siblings in a family with hemophilia, for example, may bear an enormous amount of responsibility in helping the family prevent their brother's or sister's "bleeds."

Siblings may be burdened by excessively high parental aspirations to compensate for parental disappointments and frustrations. The responsibility for high achievement may fall on the shoulders of nondisabled siblings, some of whom may intellectually or psychologically not be able to attain in a manner compatible with parental expectations. One study showed that pressure to achieve was especially in evidence when the child with a disability was a son (Grossman, 1972), while another one indicated that older, only daughters are prone to dual stresses (Cleveland & Miller, 1977). These daughters experienced pressure to compensate for the parents' unfulfilled hopes while also assuming parent-surrogate responsibilities. Interestingly, Coleman (1990) found that siblings of children with developmental disabilities scored higher in the need for achievement than siblings of children with only physical disabilities and than those of children with no disabilities.

Michaelis (1980) observes that a child's schooling may fall to nondisabled siblings:

> Although using the services of the siblings to help implement the education programs for the handicapped child may at first seem like an obvious solution, it may be the beginning of more problems for the school, the family, the siblings, and even the handicapped child. It is important that siblings are not expected to be their "brother's keeper" to the extent that their own social and academic learning is hampered by the responsibility. (p. 102)

All parents reflect on the future of their children—their education, marriage, career. Parents of children with disabilities worry even more about the future as they fret about many of the same issues parents of nondisabled children do; in addition, they are concerned about such issues as the extent to which their child will be able to achieve independence, how they will be able to care for their offspring with a disability in their later years, and who will care for the child once one or both parents are deceased.

In instances where a sibling needs lifelong care or supervision, nondisabled brothers and sisters understandably look anxiously to the future. They wonder whether the responsibility their parents at present assume will later fall to them. They wonder whether they can cope with the decisions that need to be made in future years, in addition to worrying about whether they can physically or psychologically manage to care for their brother or sister. As noted earlier by Fish (1993), another related concern is the worry siblings may have about whether one's future or present spouse will accept or be able to cope with a brother or sister who has a disability.

As noted earlier, some nondisabled siblings may resent the caregiving roles they play in the family, especially, when in addition to providing care, there is a significant imbalance in the amount of parental attention received. Parental inattention to one child coupled with excessive concern over another one may shield some parents from the problems their nondisabled child may be experiencing:

> She missed the signs of depression in me, her well and happy, outgoing and successful child, because I never revealed my suicidal thoughts and always appeared to have a new and plausible plan for my future. To the day she died, Mother was proud—no, thrilled—to introduce me as her daughter, as if to say, "See? I wasn't so bad, after all." She depended on me to clear her name, to show the world she was capable of being the mother of a healthy child. She didn't see that I was not so healthy inside—I was happy enough for her. "Peggy could always take care of herself," Mother liked to say, "I never had to worry about her." (Moorman, 1994, p. 43)

Sibling responsibility for a brother or sister who is disabled should thus be a major concern for the professional. Exploring the extent to which a sibling feels or expects to assume responsibility for a disabled family member is very important. How a sibling envisions the way one will manage life's future demands depends in part on whether there are vestiges of resentment and anger toward the parents and from earlier interactions. Professionals ought to help siblings consider how much responsibility should be assumed if there are other able family members. For some a central issue will be whether one can, without guilt, abandon the powerful burden of responsibility their parents may have placed upon them out of their own anxieties about the future care of their child.

IDENTITY CONCERNS

In the wake of a disability, young children may be concerned about "catching" the disability. Featherstone (1980) notes that anxiety about this is exacerbated when siblings learn that the disability was caused by a disease like rubella or meningitis. In a videotape where parents talked about the effects cancer has on the family, one of the concerns voiced was that well children feared that they too would be stricken with the disease (Western Psychiatric Institute and Clinic, 1980). According to Rolland (1994), "A sibling's illness shatters children's myths that serious health problems and death happen when a person is old; they lose a sense of immunity. Siblings often develop fears or phobias that even the smallest symptoms may be serious" (p. 220).

The fear of taking ill with cancer runs high among siblings (Sourkes, 1987). Children need reassurance that there is little likelihood of getting the same disease and they need to be told that the illness is not contagious. Siblings are encouraged to pursue their own activities and relationships, which can help counteract the overidentification that occurs in sibling relationships.

Young nondisabled siblings may have anxieties that they will become blind or deaf in the future (Marion, 1981). As noted above, siblings may believe that if a disability can happen to a brother or sister, then it can happen to them. Children have been known to develop somatic complaints in their attempts to gain attention from their parents (Luterman, 1979; Marion, 1981; Rolland, 1994; Sourkes, 1987). In siblings of hearing-impaired children, it is not uncommon for them to develop a pseudosensory deficit as an attention-getting behavior (Luterman, 1979). Furthermore, siblings of children with epilepsy have an inordinate fear that they will develop the disorder—a fear disproportionate to the possibility that they will indeed acquire epilepsy or a seizure disorder (Lechtenberg, 1984). Reflecting anxieties about getting ill or becoming disabled, siblings can complain of sleep and appetite problems, headaches, and stomach pains (Rolland, 1994). Somatic complaints can also serve another function in the family system:

> In some families somatic symptoms may become a dysfunctional way of expressing a need for attention. A well sibling may feel that physical complaints are the only valid form of currency that can compete with a chronic disorder . . . Often a sibling . . . will protect parents by hiding his or her feelings or distracting them by acting out. Healthy children sometimes feel excluded from the family and different because they do not have physical symptoms. In response, they develop somatic complaints as a way to get attention. Frequently, this is not a conscious process, and may be resistant to change. (Rolland, 1994, pp. 220–221)

As a consequence of a strong identification, the nondisabled child may feel overly responsible to the sibling with a disability in order to justify psychologically the fact that he or she is not the afflicted one (Michaelis, 1980). Moreover, siblings have been known to feel responsible for the disability, particularly when a newborn is deeply resented and the child has fleeting thoughts about a brother's or sister's demise. The notion of overidentifying with a brother or sister who has a disability may be attributable in part to age, age spacing, and gender similarities between disabled and nondisabled siblings (Breslau, 1982; Breslau, Weitzman, & Messenger, 1981; Lobato, 1990).

The development of an identity for a nondisabled child separate from that of his or her sibling is of considerable importance:

> The issue of being similar to or different from the retarded sibling permeated many of the meetings and seemed to be a source of enormous concern for all of the group members. In fact the experience with this group suggests that the main task of siblings of defective children is to avoid identifying with them. (Grossman, 1972, p. 34)

Siblings who are poorly informed about the nature and consequences of their brothers' or sisters' disability may be confused regarding their own identity (Wasserman, 1983). If adolescents are ill informed of the nature of the disability, identity issues are sure to arise because this period of development is marked by considerable struggle over self-worth and self-identity. In her sibling support groups, Feigon (1981) consistently observed a strong identification with the sibling who was disabled that resulted in feelings that one is or will be disabled. Others speculate that relatively undifferentiated siblings may share symptoms with their brother or sister who is disabled, whereas siblings who have successfully separated tend to act more independently (Bank & Kahn, 1982). Furthermore, it is not unusual for a child to reflect a picture of a brother or sister that coincides with that of one's parents:

> My seven-year old mind figured that they were going to find out what was wrong with him, give him some medicine, and cure him, just as they did for me when I was sick. I fantasized that one day he would walk out of the elevator talking normally. In many ways, this is the picture my parents saw, and I was only reflecting their attitude. (Siegel & Silverstein, 1994, p. 7)

The type of disablement of chronically ill children may bear a relationship to the identity problems of siblings. Tew and Lawrence (1975) concluded from their study that siblings of children who were mildly disabled were most disturbed, followed by siblings of children who were severely and moderately disabled. It may be that identity confusion and one's ability to differentiate oneself from a brother or sister is a consequence of the perceived similarity of the other. In other words, the less disabled the sibling, the more likely issues of identity may surface. Others, however, point out that the research consistently supports the position that there is no simple linear relationship between severity and sibling adjustment (Kirkman, 1985; Lobato, 1983). The same conclusion holds when one considers the type of impairment (Lobato, 1983). For siblings of seriously emotionally disturbed children, Bank and Kahn (1982) comment:

> Every well sibling that we have interviewed has, at one time or another, feared the possibility of becoming like a seriously disturbed brother or sister. Some siblings do not dwell on this fear, while others allow themselves to be haunted and dominated by the possibility that they could wind up in serious trouble or in a mental hospital. (p. 253)

This observation is illustrated in the following quote:

> In college, I had consulted a school psychologist occasionally, but vigilantly guarded my deepest fears. I know now that I was terrified of becoming mentally ill myself and had been most of my life. I was afraid that if I sought help in a serious way, I would be "like Sally." It wasn't until I was in my thirties that I began therapy in earnest, perhaps because, by then, some small part of me felt confident that I would get better, not worse. (Moorman, 1994, p. 43)

Siblings may become confused regarding their role in the family (Powell & Gallagher, 1993). One source of confusion pertains to their dual role as sibling and as surrogate parent. As noted previously, caregiving responsibility may promote a child's self-perception as a parent surrogate when he or she is, in reality, a sibling.

With young children particularly, professionals should help parents understand the concerns of nondisabled siblings. As noted earlier, parents may be unaware of the needs of their nondisabled children. In this regard, one study found that parents thought their nondisabled children were coping considerably better than the children themselves thought they were (Wallinga, Paquio, & Skeen, 1987). The parents' participation in the study enabled them to realize for the first time how much they had neglected their healthy children.

Professionals can help siblings express their identity concerns and their worries about contamination. Support groups of similarly aged youngsters are a useful adjunct to individual counseling (D. J. Meyer & Vadasy, 1994; Seligman, 1993). Siblings may feel different or odd about their experiences and feelings but are comforted in a group context with others who share their experience.

The value of a support group for siblings is reflected in the following observations from Moorman (1994):

> Some years later, I found the Sibling and Adult Children's Network, a branch of AMI [Alliance for the Mentally Ill]. There, everyone talked

about what I had assumed were my own particular problems: dread of taking over, fear of having deeply troubled children, fear of relationships with lovers who might not understand or sympathize, inability to develop our own lives because we were expecting to have to drop them at a moment's notice to intervene in a crisis. When I aired my "secrets," which were commonplace in this group, I felt for the first time that I was with people who knew exactly what I was talking about. There was immense comfort in simply being in the room with my peers. (p. 44)

CAREERS

Basic life goals of nondisabled siblings may be affected when a child with a disability is present in the family. A child's career decision may be shaped by having interacted with and cared for a less able brother or sister. Nondisabled children are cognizant of others' reactions to their brother or sister, adding to their sensitivity to social relations. The continuous act of caring for a brother or sister with a disability, especially in a loving, attentive family, may become internalized to the extent that it influences career decisions in the direction of the helping professions (D. J. Meyer & Vadasy, 1994).

> I have found my upbringing to have been very positive, in spite of the emotional hardship that [my sister's] cystic fibrosis placed on the family. At the age of nine I perceived myself as being a vitally important participating member of the family. My parents encouraged me to assist in the care of my newborn sister and I learned to crush pills and mix them in applesauce, do postural drainage, and clean and fill the mist tent. Through this experience self-esteem was enhanced, responsibility was learned, and maturity was developed. Although I occasionally feel that I grew up too fast, for the most part the experience gave me a personal insight and compassion that I carry with me in my practice as a pediatric specialist. (Thibodeau, 1988, p. 22)

As Farber (1959) and Cleveland and Miller (1977) found in their studies, nondisabled siblings internalized helping norms and turned their career endeavors toward the improvement of mankind or at least toward life goals that require dedication and sacrifice. The following comments by a sister of a sibling with multiple disabilities reflects the thinking behind the decision to prepare for a service career:

> Having Robin as a member of our family caused me to undergo a great deal of introspection which led me to insights into certain aspects of my character that needed to be changed. My contact with him, coupled with some sound advice from my parents, also unquestionably influenced my decision to pursue a career in special education. I had originally intended to enter the field of chemistry, and indeed I

completed a bachelor's degree in that area. However, something about my choice bothered me. I enjoyed the lab work and the excitement of scientific discovery, but something was missing. It wasn't until my father, during the course of one of our "What are you going to do with your life?" discussions, pinpointed the problem when he quoted the following statement made by the philosopher Kierkegaard: "The door to happiness opens outward." What this meant to me was that one could find true happiness through serving others. The choice of a career then became obvious to me. What better way was there to serve others than to enter the field of special education where I could help people like my brother lead more fulfilling lives? (Helsel, 1978, p. 112)

Although Illes (1979) did not specifically investigate career objectives of siblings of cancer victims, she did report that her subjects exhibited compassion, tolerance, and empathy—characteristics valued in the helping professions. Indeed, Skrtic, Summers, Brotherson, and Turnbull (1984) speculate that a sibling's identification with a brother or sister who has a disability and a desire to understand his or her problems provides the impetus to choose a career in education or in the human services. In a recent study, however, Konstam et al. (1993) found that in a group of college-aged children, those with brothers or sisters with disabilities were not more likely to consider a human service career than a group of young adults who did not have a sibling with a disability.

Without adequate research data, the theoretical leap between the development of compassion, tolerance, and empathy and the selection of a particular career goal may be too great. In fact, siblings who have developed such attitudes and who believe they have already made a significant contribution to a difficult life circumstance may seek out fulfillment in fields outside of the helping professions.

In a videotape[*] of a group of siblings expressing their personal views of life with a brother or sister who has a disability, a sister of a brother with autism spoke about her wish to pursue a career unrelated to the helping professions. She felt she had contributed considerably to the welfare and development of her brother and now felt that she wanted something "for herself" in a profession that was not oriented toward the human services. Moreover, Israelite (1985), in a small-scale study of siblings of children with hearing impairments found that subjects indicated their desire to pursue careers that were unrelated to the human service professions. In his family of 10 siblings including a brother with autism, Laureys (1984) reports that he has one brother who is an art therapist, a sister in special education, a brother in a woodworking

---

[*]*The Other Children: Brothers and Sisters of the Developmentally Disabled.* Available from Siblings for Significant Change, 105 East 22nd Street, New York, NY 10010.

business, a sister who is a graphic artist, a brother studying business, a sister studying language and drama, another sister in journalism and literature, an undeclared high school star wrestler, and he himself is a lobbyist in government.

There is, thus, insufficient data for firm conclusions about the relationship between having a brother or sister with a disability and choosing a particular career path. There is only enough information for some armchair speculation about the impact of a child with a disability on a sibling's career choice.

ANGER AND GUILT

Anger is an emotion common to human beings. Some handle the expression of anger better than others, while some deny that they experience anger at all. Under certain circumstances, siblings of children with disabilities may experience anger more often and perhaps more intensely than siblings of nondisabled brothers or sisters. Whether siblings harbor or openly express their feelings of anger and resentment depends on a number of factors:

1. The extent to which a child assumes a major caretaking role in the family
2. The extent to which a child with a disability takes advantage of (manipulates) a nondisabled brother or sister
3. The extent to which the child with a disability may restrict a brother's or sister's social life or is considered a source of embarrassment
4. The extent to which a child with a disability requires excessive time and attention from the parents and takes time away from the other children
5. The extent to which the family's financial resources are drained by the child's needs
6. The number and gender of children in the family
7. The overall accommodation parents have made to their special circumstances

As reflected in the following observation by Featherstone (1980), anger may arise in relation to numerous factors:

Children feel angry at parents, at the disabled child, at the wider world, at God or fate, perhaps at all four. Some blame their mother and father for the disability itself (just as they blame them for any new baby). A

handicap creates unusual needs; many children envy their brother or
sister this special attention. And older children may rage secretly about
the sometimes colossal sums of money spent on diagnosis and therapy—resources that might otherwise finance family comforts and college tuition. (p. 143)

Reactions from acquaintances or strangers to a child with a disability
may lead to open expressions of hostility, as illustrated in the following
comments from a college student:

> I heard some guy talking in the back about Mark and how stupid he
> was, and you could make him do anything and he is so gullible, and
> all this kind of stuff. I walked back to the kid and slugged him in the
> face. . . . I always felt that I had to protect him from someone, from
> teasing, from fights, and any other kids trying to put things over on
> kids who are at a disadvantage to them. If you love somebody you
> cannot help but get emotionally involved in that. (S. D. Klein, 1972,
> pp. 12–13)

Siblings may be placed in a difficult bind. Parental demands that a
child should care for and protect the sibling with a disability clash with
those of the child's playmates, who encourage shunning. The nondisabled
child's ambivalent feelings (anger, guilt, love, protectiveness) toward his
or her sibling and resentment toward the parents for demanding that one
love and take care of the sibling with a disability result in a tension-filled
situation.

> Wherever I went, Mindy went too. . . . I was often excluded from
> neighborhood games because of my sidekick. And then there was the
> unwritten family rule that I must leave with Mindy whenever my
> playmates made fun of her. They often did mock her, of course, and
> we would leave—except for one time, which to this day gives my
> conscience no rest, when I joined in. I lost many playmates by having
> to side with Mindy. I felt neglected by my family and shunned by my
> peers. I was a very lonely little girl. (Hayden, 1974, p. 27)

Writing about his sister Stacey, Silverman (in Siegel & Silverman,
1994) notes below how Stacey's complaints about their brother Marc, who
had autism, were dismissed by their burdened parents. This increased her
sense of guilt and undermined her self-esteem:

> My brother's worsening behavior coincided with Stacey's adolescence,
> and our parents had very little reserve left over to deal with her
> "emotional turmoil." Her complaints about his walking around in his
> underwear, his going to the bathroom with the door open, or his
> tearing up her clothes were deemed selfish. If she didn't "understand"
> she was immature and ungrateful for being normal. She was expected

to adapt to his behavior accordingly, something that required a maturity beyond her years. She was to be a "little adult," denied the carefree days of childhood and adolescence. . . . If you grow up with your needs and concerns trivialized by others, you begin to trivialize them yourself, automatically. It's a pattern that will follow you to adulthood. (pp. 13–14)

Feeling ignored and unappreciated for one's achievements leaves lifelong scars on nondisabled children. Hayden (1974) continues:

Mindy's achievements always met with animated enthusiasm from our parents. In contrast it seemed, mother and daddy's response to my accomplishments was on the pat-on-the-back level. I was expected to perform well in every circumstance. I wanted my parents to be enthusiastic about my accomplishments, too. I didn't want to have to beg for praise. I didn't want to be taken for granted. I wanted to be noticed. (p. 27)

Angry feelings surface when siblings perceive that their mother must carry the burden of care for a child without their father's help. Work, business meetings, or committee and community involvement can keep fathers from contributing. In such instances, it is useful for professionals to distinguish between fathers who are legitimately occupied from those who are "too busy" because they wish to deny or avoid their anxiety-provoking family situation. Nondisabled siblings probably sense their father's motivations, which adds to their anger toward him (see Chapter 6 for more on fathers). It is important to determine the reason for the parents' absence or lack of involvement. It may be the parents' inability to cope with their child's disability, a reflection of marital problems, or family dynamics where one parent is the caregiver and excludes the other one from the parent–child dyad.

There are many reasons for nondisabled siblings to experience anger—and the guilt that often follows in anger's wake. Even so, there seems to be a deficiency in the area of helping siblings understand, tolerate, or accept and express the anger they so often feel. Professionals need to help siblings understand the source of their anger and to understand the universality of angry feelings. For siblings of emotionally disturbed children, Bank and Kahn (1982) note that

aggressiveness is one natural way through which siblings communicate. But when one sibling is defective, or is seen as defective and needs special treatment by parents, the well child must learn to inhibit, to refrain from aggressive taunts and actions. To establish himself as "well," he must give up and suppress these vital angry parts of himself, or submerge or hide them, lest he further injure his vulnerable sibling. Further, the well sibling learns not to rock the parents' boat, not to roil already troubled waters. Inhibition of anger also means that other forms of spontaneity—such as kidding, humor, and "messing around"— get squelched. The relationship between disturbed and rigidly avoidant siblings is serious and drab and lacks playfulness. (pp. 259–260)

Guilty feelings that one may have caused the disability and that one should be punished for it can lead to withdrawal, depression, suicidal thoughts, self-destructive and aggressive behavior, and declining school performance (Rolland, 1994). These feelings can be unwittingly reinforced by parents if a child is not allowed to express guilty feelings. Parents may suppress their child's feelings by reassuring him or her too quickly. Parents sometimes believe that in talking about an illness/disability their child will be upset, when in fact the child is already worried, anxious, and guilty and needs to express these emotions. By not allowing their children to reveal their feelings, parents may be actually protecting themselves from their own guilty thoughts.

Professionals should help parents facilitate the expression of anger and guilt by their nondisabled children and they should be sensitive to parents who discourage the open expression of feelings. It is also important to take note when parents are made anxious by their child's feelings and to communicate this observation to the parents sensitively. Again, sibling support groups are an excellent resource for coping with emotions like guilt and anger. A group of peers that share a particular life circumstance has powerful healing powers. However, the first line of action should take place within the family.

COMMUNICATION AND ISOLATION

Featherstone (1980) observes that the presence of a child with a disability in the family inhibits communication. She believes that the lack of communication within a family over a child's disabling condition contributes to the loneliness normal siblings experience. Siblings may sense that certain topics are taboo and that "ugly" feelings are to remain hidden; they are thereby forced into a peculiar kind of loneliness—a sense of detachment from those to whom one typically feels closest. Family secrets or implicit rules forbidding the discussion of a problem force normal siblings constantly to pretend that circumstances are other than they seem (Trevino, 1979). For some parents, discussing their child's disability with their nondisabled son or daughter is as threatening as a discussion of sex.

The child with a disability is a total family concern and siblings need to be involved in the total family communication process. Often decisions that bear on the disability are made without prior discussion with or explanation to siblings who may be affected by them. We, therefore, encourage open communication within the family to help reduce unpleasant side effects.

Some parents "teach" their children that aggression toward a sibling who is disabled is bad, disloyal, and rebellious. As a result, angry feelings are kept hidden or discharged in the parents' absence:

> Rather than invigorating the relationship with the give-and-take of insults and punches, easily dished out and quickly forgotten, the well sibling must be wary of hostile impulses toward a sick brother or sister, or risk being charged with kicking the crippled or hurting the handicapped. The well sibling, being presumed to have many riches and advantages, is expected to show restraint, charity, kindness, and loyalty. Being a true-blue Boy Scout is, of course, impossible; and well siblings may vent their dammed-up anger in sneaky and violent ways. (Bank & Kahn, 1982, pp. 260–261)

Powell and Gallagher (1993) concur that communicating to children about their brother's or sister's disability is difficult, yet not impossible. They offer the following communication guidelines to help the parent–child relationship:

1. Display active (not passive) listening.
2. Take the time.
3. Secure needed knowledge.
4. Be sincere and honest.
5. Respond in a comprehensive fashion.
6. Adopt an open attitude.
7. Provide balanced information.
8. Be aware of nonverbal communication.
9. Follow up earlier communication.

Communicating the nature of a disability to a child is difficult yet essential. Children sense underlying feelings regardless of the actual words used; therefore, open and honest communication is important within the family. Pearlman and Scott (1981) believe that what is communicated to children should be based on a child's age and what he or she is able to comprehend and assimilate. They believe that parents should be aware of certain key words in their communication to children. For example, the words "better" and "worse" invite comparisons, whereas "different" and "cannot" convey that limitations are not due to anything anyone did or did not do. Finally, these authors urge parents to begin a dialogue with their children as soon as possible. Children sometimes keep their worries and problems to themselves, which makes it difficult for parents or others to know about their private concerns (McHale & Gamble, 1987). Parents can, however, sometimes detect when a child is distressed by noting behavior changes such as an increase in belligerence, sleep disturbances, and school problems.

In regard to schoolwork, Michaelis (1980) notes that nondisabled siblings may resent that the brother or sister is "playing" when they themselves must work so hard. Explaining the educational methods used with the child and the skills that are being taught will help make it possible for the sibling to be supportive rather than critical and resentful. Also, young siblings may not understand that their brother or sister has certain cognitive limitations and as a result spends less time studying and in other learning activities.

Peer reactions may further isolate siblings from their social group. Children who feel rejected by their peers and are largely ignored by their parents are youngsters at risk. Add the caregiving responsibility siblings may assume, and the creation of emotional problems may be set in motion. And finally, Featherstone (1980) comments on the frustration and isolation siblings feel when they are unable to communicate with their brother or sister:

> The difficulty of "knowing" an autistic or profoundly retarded child, or the child with a severe communication disorder, can frustrate siblings as much as parents. They yearn for a relationship of equals, for someone with whom they can play and tell secrets, someone who shares their child-view of an adult world. Even when the normal siblings perform some of these functions, they sometimes imagine the special relationship they might have with this brother if he were more accessible. The able-bodied member of a two-child family may feel very much alone. (p. 159)

FOR BETTER OR WORSE

Trevino (1979) is unequivocal in her view that nondisabled siblings are children at risk. She believes that the research suggests several factors that contribute to emotional disturbance, such as the number of children in the family, sibling age and gender, parental reaction to the child with a disability, and the like. Other potential contributing factors have already been mentioned in this chapter. These and other variables have also been noted in several reviews of the literature (e.g., Boyce & Barnett, 1991; Lobato, 1990; Marsh, 1993; Powell & Gallagher, 1993; Stoneman & Berman, 1993).

Various researchers and clinicians view the potential for psychological harm differently. Poznanski (1969), Trevino (1979), and San

Martino and Newman (1974) are pessimistic about the impact a child with a disability has on sibling adjustment. Poznanski reports that psychiatrists treat more siblings than children with disabilities themselves. Trevino believes that children without disabilities who have a combination of certain characteristics and circumstances are, indeed, children at risk who require psychological intervention. For San Martino and Newman, guilt provides the foundation for subsequent difficulties siblings are likely to experience. From their interview of 239 families, Breslau et al. (1981) found conflicting results regarding sibling adjustment. As noted earlier, siblings who are ill informed about the nature of their brother's or sister's condition seem to be at risk for experiencing somatic complaints and excessive guilt and anger (Rolland, 1994).

Featherstone (1980), from personal experience and in recounting the experiences of others, and Grossman (1972) and Kibert (1986), from their research on brothers and sisters in college, take a more cautious view of the effects on nondisabled children. They believe that a child with a disability in the family may have differential outcomes: little impact, negative impact, or positive outcome on subsequent adjustment and coping. Farber's (1959, 1960a) research tends to support the same conclusion, which is further reinforced by S. D. Klein (1972) and M. Schreiber and Feeley (1965). Grakliker, Fishler, and Koch (1962) did not find any adverse effects reported by the siblings interviewed in their study nor did McHale, Sloan, and Simeonsson (1986) in their study of siblings of brothers and sisters with autism and mental retardation. This study is particularly noteworthy because it had 90 carefully selected subjects and included a matched control group. Although statistical differences between groups were not significant, children with brothers or sisters with a disability had more variable experiences, with some children reporting very positive and some describing very negative relationships with their brothers or sisters. McHale and colleagues note that children who reported difficult relationships worried about their brother's or sister's future (perhaps sensing some implication for themselves), perceived parental favoritism toward the child with a disability and experienced rejecting feelings toward their brother or sister. The children with a better outlook viewed their parents and peers as reacting positively to their brother or sister and they had a better understanding of the disability.

In another well-conducted study, siblings of children with a chronic illness were reported to be as well adjusted as control subjects (Tritt & Esses, 1988). However, the siblings of the ill children were perceived by their parents as having more behavioral problems, such as withdrawal and shyness. In another study using a matched control group, it was found that siblings of children with disabilities displayed the same level of self-concept, behavior problems, and social competence as the nondisabled control group children (Dyson, 1989). However, there were some differences between the study groups: siblings of children with disabilities were less active in extracurricular activities; brothers between the ages of 7 and 11 showed fewer fantasizing, deviant, and isolated behaviors; and for the age range of 12 to 15, brothers were less aggressive and hyperactive and tended to have fewer behavior problems than children of brothers or sisters who were nondisabled. Further, type of disability was associated with adjustment in that siblings of brothers or sisters with mental disabilities showed better behavioral adjustment, a higher self-concept, and more social competence than siblings of children with physical or sensory disabilities or siblings of children with milder disabling conditions. Also, the older the child with a disability, the more behavior problems of the sibling, and the larger the age gap, the better the sibling's adjustment. In addition, the larger the family and the higher the mother's education, the more social competence a sibling showed. Of particular interest in this study was the finding of variability in adjustment in both groups of children, suggesting that there are individual differences in adjustment among children whether they reside with a brother or sister who has a disability or not. And finally, the less depressed and emotionally troubled the mother, the better off are the children (Siegel & Silverstein, 1994).

Bank and Kahn (1982) observe that adjustment can be affected by the age and developmental stage of the nondisabled sibling. Furthermore, the chronicity of the condition determines whether the sibling must cope with a time-limited or more chronic situation, and the rate of onset, especially with a sibling with mental illness, can be the source of confusion. The stigmatizing aspects of a child's condition should also be considered. In a public situation, a well-behaved youngster with Down syndrome will be less noticed than a drooling, bent figure in a wheelchair.

From an empirical point of view, the question of whether siblings are not affected, are helped, or are harmed by the presence of a brother or sister with a disability remains open to speculation. Available data have not yet determined the prevalence of emotional problems among siblings residing with a disabled brother or sister compared with that in families where there is no disability. The factors that interact and subsequently lead to adjustment or psychological difficulties are many and combine in complex ways.

Although some contributors to the professional literature are uncompromisingly pessimistic about the effects of a child with a disability on family members, others are remarkably optimistic, especially parents and siblings who have written about their experiences. In reviewing much of the research and commentary about siblings one may be left with the impression that largely negative effects are to be expected. This is simply not true.

For examples, Illes (1979) reported that siblings of children with cancer were compassionate, tolerant, empathic to parents, and appreciative of their own health. Such positive sentiments underscore both the capacity of children to function under stress and the important contributions they make to their families. Glendinning's (1983) British study, in which she interviewed in depth 17 parents (mostly mothers) of children with severe disabilities revealed that siblings were seen to face life optimistically. Drotar argues that a child's chronic disability brings family members together (quoted in Wallinga et al., 1987). A common adversity tends to mobilize positive efforts on behalf of their child, which actually benefit the family. Furthermore, Simeonsson and Bailey (1986) note that siblings who have been actively involved in the management of their disabled family member tend to be well adjusted. It is difficult to integrate this observation with the studies that caution against excessive caregiving. It is possible that shared family caregiving and responsibility along with attention to and the expression of affection to *all* children in the family promotes a healthy, caring environment.

In their research Grossman (1972) and Kibert (1986) report that a number of college students who reported on their relationship with their brother or sister with mental retardation appeared to have benefited from growing up with their disabled siblings: "The ones who benefitted appeared to us to be more tolerant, more compassionate, more knowing about prejudice" (Grossman, p. 84). In support of Grossman's findings, Miller (1974) found a number of nondisabled siblings who had experienced involvement in the growth and development of a retarded sibling and exhibited a sense of pride that they had been a part of it. Diane, a nondisabled sibling, said the following in her interview with S. D. Klein (1972): "I always felt there was something very different about our family. Of course, you know, Cathy being that difference. Because of her difference there was a degree of specialness or closeness about us that, I do not know, it was sort of a bond that made us all very, very close. We all pitched in and helped each other out." (p. 25)

Another sister, this one of a boy with mental retardation, cerebral palsy, and epilepsy, has put her retrospective thought as follows:

I do not mean to imply that life with Robin has been all goodness and light. I have seen the strain that the responsibility of his constant care has placed upon my parents. I worry about the increasing frequency of his seizures and about what would happen to him should my parents become unable to care for him. Robin, himself, like all brothers I suppose, can be truly aggravating. It makes me angry to see him try to weasel his way out of doing things that I know he is capable of doing. Just the other day, I was scolding him for not clearing his place at the table. I guess my sisterly bossing was too much for him. He pointed at

me and angrily made the sign for handcuffs—his way of indicating that
I should be put in jail.

All in all, I feel that Robin has brought much good into the lives
of my family. He has taught us a great deal about acceptance, patience,
individual worth, but most of all about love. (Helsel, 1978, p. 112–113)

And after a lengthy discussion of brothers or sisters of youngsters
with disabilities and their adaptation to this special circumstance, Featherstone (1980) remarks:

> I have focused, up until now, on the difficulties that the able-bodied
> child faces. These problems are real enough, and assume major
> importance in the lives of some children. Nonetheless, the sheer length
> of my discussion creates a misleading gloomy impression. It may
> suggest that for the brothers and sisters of the disabled the develop-
> mental path is strewn with frightful hazards, that all but the most
> skillful parents can expect to see their "normal" children bruised
> irreparably by the experience of family living. The truth is quite
> otherwise. (p. 163)

And from her comprehensive review of the sibling literature, Lobato
(1990) concludes:

> Too many parents of young children, it may seem as though the child's
> illness or disability will do nothing but harm to the other children.
> However, this is actually quite far from the truth. As young siblings
> mature, evidence is clear that they usually do not have more problems
> than other children. In fact, many siblings show areas of great social
> and psychological strength. Their relationships with and behavior
> toward one another also tend to be more nurturing and positive than
> between many other sibling pairs. (p. 60)

From this review of the literature, one realizes that our knowledge
of sibling adjustment is further along than it was at the time of the first
publication of *Ordinary Families, Special Children,* yet it still leaves some
questions unanswered. However, we are not without some guidance for
professionals who should heed the admonition that sibling adjustment is
dependent on numerous intertwined variables and that simple answers
may be misleading. The impact of a child with a disability may be "for
better or for worse" and may depend on various mediating variables. We
feel even more supported in this conclusion now then we did in 1989.

Effects on Fathers
and Grandparents

IN STUDYING the family and disability, the focus of attention is often on the person with a disability. A present-day case in point is in the area of geriatrics where victims of Alzheimer's disease are the central focus. While research continues on those afflicted with this disease, there is a growing body of literature on family members who care for and must cope with Alzheimer's patients. Similarly, parents of children with disabilities, who fall on the other end of the lifespan spectrum from the ill elderly and their family caregivers, have been studied with increased frequency since the late 1950s. The fact that a child with a disability resides within a reactive system, affects it, and in turn is affected by it is increasingly acknowledged by researchers and practicing professionals in the field.

In the area of childhood disability and the family's response to it, mothers have been the most studied family member. This is probably due, in part, to their greater accessibility, but it also and perhaps more importantly reflects the fact that mothers give birth and are considered natural caregivers and nurturers. Also, in the past, most mothers stayed at home to raise the children while fathers worked outside the home. Within the context of a family systems perspective, which stresses that all family members are affected by a crisis, fathers, siblings and grandparents are now being considered important influences who are, in turn, influenced by childhood disability. This chapter, then, will examine the least studied family members, fathers and grandparents.

FATHERS

One author observes that fathering is the "single most creative, complicated, fulfilling, frustrating, engrossing, enriching, depleting endeavor of a man's life" (Pruett, 1987, p. 282).

Lamb and Meyer (1991) note that only after the publication of a 1964 study on infant attachment and a later paper reconceptualizing the "maternal deprivation" literature did there emerge a realization that in emphasizing mothers, researchers had lost sight of the broader context in which children are raised. Prior to that, the role of the father in child development and family functioning had been undervalued. The diminution of interest in the father's influence can be attributed, in part, to Freud's (1936) theories which promoted the mother as the primary influence in the development of children. Bowlby (1951) reinforced this belief by suggesting that the father's role in child development was secondary to that of the mother. Thus, until the 1970s, the mother's role in the family overshadowed that of the father.

Traditionally, men assumed an instrumental role while women were socialized into an expressive one. The instrumental role is task oriented and involves problem solving, independence, rational thought, and an unemotional stance (Darling & Baxter, 1996; Parsons, 1951). On the other hand, the expressive role involves attention to feelings, emotional needs, dependency, and cooperation. In regard to gender roles, families of lower SES have been reported to be more traditional whereas higher SES families have been reported to be moving toward less gender differentiation (Scanzoni, 1975). Some recent studies (see, e.g., Gerson, 1993) have suggested, however, that as many differences exist within social classes as between them. There have been some reported differences in roles by race and ethnicity as well (Darling & Baxter, 1996).

The last decade has witnessed a marked reversal in this trend. This evolution is illustrated in the widely read child care books written by Benjamin Spock (Hornby, 1988). In the 1946 edition, Spock stressed the support that fathers should provide mothers. In the 1957 edition, he suggested that fathers become involved in child care, though as secondary to mothers. In his 1985 book (Spock & Rothenberg), he suggested that the father's responsibility in child development should be equal to the mother's. Further evidence for the elevation of the importance of fathers has been the escalation of publications on fathers in the last several years (Darling & Baxter, 1996; Hornby, 1988; Houser & Seligman, 1991; May, 1991; D. J. Meyer, 1995).

The escalation of interest in fathers has come about for several reasons (Hornby, 1988; Pruett, 1987). Accompanying the increase in the number of mothers who work has come a corresponding focus on alternative caregivers for children, and a likely resource for alternative care would-be fathers. The shortening of the work week for some has meant that fathers are able to have more time to spend with their families. Furthermore, changes in child custody laws have led to an increase in the number of single-parent fathers who have joint custody. Traditional sex roles are more relaxed so that the identification of women with mother-hood and caretaking, and men with breadwinning is becoming less rigid. Also, the adoption of family systems models has meant that all members of the family are considered to be important contributors. And finally, as the following section illustrates,the dearth of information on fathers and fathering has encouraged researchers to investigate this family role from a number of perspectives.

The Father's Role

In the past, children were viewed as malleable organisms waiting to be shaped by outside socialization processes. A more contemporary view suggests that each child has individual characteristics that not only affect the way the child is influenced by external forces but that also cause the child to shape the socializers themselves (Lamb, 1983). Therefore, socialization is viewed as a bidirectional process with influences flowing in two directions.

According to reviews by Lamb (1983); D. J. Meyer, Vadasy, Fewell, and Schell (1985); and Lamb and Meyer (1991), nurturing emotions are not unique to mothers; fathers also seem to know instinctively how to interact with their infants and how to care for them. Furthermore, fathers are interested in their infants and want to be actively involved with them. In fact, during infancy the father's sensitivity to his infant's distress is just as acute as the mother's.

Other studies reviewed by these researchers reveal some differences between mothers' and fathers' behaviors with their infants that begin to emerge shortly after birth. Mothers tend to engage more in caretaking while fathers tend to play more with their infants. Fathers are more vigorous with their infants and they are more likely to pick up and toss their infants and generally be rougher than mothers, who are more likely to play such games as peek-a-boo or hide-and-seek. However, fathers, like mothers, adapt their play to their child's developmental level, suggesting that both fathers and mothers are equally sensitive to their child's developmental changes. These general observations would suggest that fathers are competent nurturers and caretakers.

Fathers and the Child with a Disability

There are only a modest number of studies of fathers whose children have disabilities (Marsh, 1993). Because of this, only the most limited conclusions can be made. In addition, the studies are compromised in a variety of ways (Lamb & Meyer, 1991). First, there are few observational studies of fathers whose children have disabilities. Findings are frequently based on maternal reports of paternal reactions. Second, many studies are methodologically flawed and often researchers provide few details concerning the procedures used and the range of disabilities represented. Third, studies have focused on the fathers' reaction to the diagnosis and on initial adaptation rather than on the impact on fathers of adolescent or adult children. Finally, there is a disproportionate interest in fathers with children with mental retardation to the exclusion of children with other developmental disabilities.

Change causes stress and the birth of *any* child is stress inducing for the parents. The birth of a child means that both parents must readjust their marital roles in order to assume new responsibilities. Feelings of elation and joy may give way to fatigue and doubt as the parents worry about their competence as parents, and they may experience ambivalence over their loss of freedom. Therefore, there are "normal" stresses preceding, during, and after the birth period. Add to this upheaval the birth of a child with a disability, and a full-blown crisis may be set in motion.

Lamb and Meyer (1991) note that fathers and mothers initially respond differently to the news that they have produced a child with a disability. Fathers tend to respond less emotionally and focus on possible long-term concerns whereas mothers respond more emotionally and are concerned about their ability to cope with the burdens of child care. In other words, fathers tend to perceive the diagnosis of the disability as an instrumental crisis whereas mothers see it as an expressive crisis. However, even though fathers may be more instrumental and mothers more expressive, some fathers are concerned about the day-to-day demands of the disability and some mothers worry about the costs of raising a child with a disability.

Generally speaking, fathers are more concerned than mothers about the adoption of socially acceptable behavior by their children—especially their sons—and they are more anxious about the social status and occupational success of their offspring. As a result, fathers are more concerned about the long-term outcomes of their children with disabilities than mothers are and they are probably more affected by the visibility of the disability (Lamb & Meyer, 1991; Tallman, 1965).

Because of the high expectations fathers have of their sons, they may be especially disappointed when they have a boy with a disability (Farber,

1959; Grossman, 1972). The behavioral consequences of this disappointment are manifested in extremes of intense involvement with and total
withdrawal from their sons, whereas fathers seem to have limited, routine
involvement with their daughters who are disabled (Chigier, 1972; Grossman, 1972; Tallman, 1965). A more recent study, however, does not
support the contention that fathers are more distressed by a boy with a
disability than a girl, suggesting that more research is needed in this area
(Hornby, 1995a, 1995b; Houser & Seligman, 1991).

In a frequently cited study, Cummings (1976) found that fathers of
children with mental retardation were more depressed and experienced
lower self-esteem and confidence in their roles as fathers than fathers of
nondisabled children. They also reported less enjoyment of their children
than the fathers of the control group. However, a more recent study
showed that fathers reported fewer symptoms of distress, higher self-esteem, and more internal locus of control than mothers (Goldberg, Marcovitch, MacGregor, & Lojkasek, 1986). The results of this study run
counter to those of Cummings and suggest that fathers may adjust more
favorably now than in the past. This may be due to more enlightened
attitudes and to the availability of greater support systems and programs
for fathers (D. J. Meyer et al., 1985). On the other hand, as the researchers
speculate, their findings might support the idea that men tend to deny
and suppress uncomfortable emotions (Goldberg et al., 1986). In a recent
study, Hornby (1995a, 1995b) found that fathers' adaptation to their
children with disabilities was related to certain personality characteristics,
for example, neuroticism. That is, the more neurotic (as measured by
Hornsby using the Eysenck Personality Inventory on 87 fathers) the less
adaptive they were to their family situation and the less satisfied they were
with their marriages. One explanation for these results is that fathers may
have been "neurotic" before the child's birth. Another is that the child's
disability may have triggered latent neurotic tendencies.

Fathers' reactions to their children with special needs may have
implications for the response of other family members. For example,
Peck and Stephens (1960) found a high relationship between the degree
of paternal acceptance toward the child and the amount of acceptance
and rejection generally observed in the home. This suggests that the
father's reaction might set the tone for the entire family. Lamb (1983)
speculates that this may reflect the fact that fathers obtain less satisfaction from children with disabilities than from nondisabled children.
Furthermore, it supports the notion that the fathers' involvement is
discretionary, that is, that fathers can increase or decrease their involvement whereas mothers are expected to show the same commitment to
all children. Not only is the development of the child with a disability
likely to be affected when fathers choose to withdraw, but the entire

family suffers. Indeed, Houser and Seligman (1991) found that the fathers who experienced higher levels of stress tended to cope by employing an escape-avoidance strategy.

Family systems theory would suggest that as the father pulls away, other family members will be affected and will respond in reaction to the father's behavior. As the father withdraws, the burden of care, for example, falls to other family members, particularly the mother. When this happens, feelings of anger and resentment will fester as tension in the family increases. The father's distancing behavior as family members struggle with the added pressures of coping with a child with a disability will set into motion a negative and dysfunctional dynamic. When their involvement decreases, fathers force mothers to cope alone with the emotionally and physically demanding tasks of attending to the child's needs. Fathers may thus bear a greater responsibility for allowing a child's special needs to have adverse effects on the marriage. If fathers reacted by becoming more involved, their own satisfaction and the integration of the family might both increase (Lamb & Meyer, 1991).

The father's emotional difficulties may be masked by his need to be stoic and in control of his emotions (D. J. Meyer et al., 1985). Some men may find it difficult to express sadness or grief because to express these feelings is often considered a sign of weakness. When the infant's mother is experiencing shock or depression, the father may suppress his own feelings because they are not manly and/or because he wishes to support his wife by being "strong." Some fathers suppress their emotions because it is not manly to express them, while other fathers may react stoically to the mothers' expressiveness at the time of diagnosis in an attempt to achieve some type of balanced presentation.

> My recollection of the early days is more selective than that of Lori's mother. I am not blessed with a particularly acute memory for detail. I'm better at forests than trees. Furthermore, I suspect that denial has helped me cover up painful emotions during the early years. The way I see it, Lori's mother was better at being "in touch" with her emotions, which may have motivated me to take a more stoic stance. This dynamic reminds me of the underfunctioning/overfunctioning that occurs in marriages. The more mom frets about a child's development, the more dad assumes a cool, "we can handle it" approach. The more dad becomes anxious about being on time for appointments, the more mom acts casually and unconcerned about this social transgression. It's predictable, when dad is overly anxious about something, mom will adopt a calmer attitude, perhaps in the interest of balance or to help lessen anxiety between parents. (Seligman, 1995)

A father's stoic behavior can be viewed by professionals as a more manageable reaction. The male physicians quoted below seem to feel more comfortable communicating distressing information to fathers than to mothers:

> Usually I prefer to tell the father. The mother is in an emotional state after having just given birth.
> If I had a choice, I'd probably prefer talking with the father first and let him help me make the decision about talking to the mother.
> I call the father and ask him what he wants me to do. I wait until I can reach the father before I talk to the mother.
> I try to talk to the obstetrician to find out if it's the mother's first baby or if she's anxious or apprehensive. . . . I always tell the father right away. (Darling, 1979, p. 206)

In terms of research, Hornby (1995a, 1995b) believes that many of the assertions about fathers require considerably more study than what is presently available. In his British study, Hornby evaluated adaptation, marital functioning, social support, stress, and personality of 87 fathers of children with Down syndrome. The mean age of the fathers was 41 years (range = 27–62 years); 64% of the children were boys, with a mean age of 9.2 years and a mean IQ of 40 (range = 7–63). The results from Hornby's research showed the following:

1. Fathers adapted equally well to their sons and daughters.
2. Fathers' adaptation was not related to the severity of their child's disability.
3. The stress experienced by fathers was not related to the ages of their children.
4. Fathers' adaptation was not related to the level of social support they received but to their satisfaction with the support.
5. Fathers' adaptation was significantly related to their levels of neuroticism.
6. The stress experienced by fathers was inversely related to the educational level and perceived financial adequacy but not to their social class.
7. The majority of fathers did not experience depression or major personality problems.
8. Fathers did not experience higher levels of marital distress nor were they more prone to divorce than the national average.

In his conclusion, Hornby (1995a) writes:

> Clearly these findings regarding fathers of children with Down syndrome provide quite a different view of the effects on fathers of children of disabilities than has appeared in the literature. Therefore, it is possible that the assertions about these fathers, on which there

was a consensus in previous reviews of the literature, provide a mostly erroneous view of their experiences. (p. 252)

In another study, Hornby (1995b) examined fathers' views about the effects of children with Down syndrome on themselves and their families. Taped interviews were obtained from 90 fathers (presumably the same ones as in his previous study) of children aged 7 to 14 years. A qualitative analysis of the data revealed the following:

1. The most frequent comment (46%) was about the cheerful personality of their child. The fathers' positive sentiments about their Down syndrome child may bear a relationship to their positive responses to raising a child with a disability in Hornby's first study. Fathers of children with other disabilities may have similar or markedly different reactions.
2. Forty-two percent of fathers mentioned the initial trauma they experienced following the diagnosis.
3. Forty-three percent of fathers complained about the restrictions imposed on the family by the disability.
4. Thirty percent commented that the child had minimal effects on family life.
5. Thirty-six percent of fathers expressed concern about providing for their child after school age or when the fathers become older, ill, or dead.

Although there were some concerns about family restrictions and what the future may hold, Hornby's (1995a, 1995b) research supports the contention that the fathers in his studies adjusted quite well to their Down syndrome child.

In his discussion groups, Smith (1981) found that the fathers distrusted male displays of emotion and that they learned as children that "men" are always in control of their emotions and that "big boys" don't cry. Smith believes that these masculine behaviors place considerable stress on fathers and make it harder for them to express and be attuned to their own feelings.

> For the men in the fathers' discussion groups, these facets of the stereotypic masculine role were quite restrictive and presented obstacles to the men's coming to terms with their children's handicaps and with their own feelings as parents of exceptional children. In particular, these men displayed stereotypical instrumental traits such as a reluctance to show one's emotions, a need for independence and self-reliance, and a need to "fix" problematic situations. (Smith, 1981, p. 12)

Smith points out that as fathers of children with disabilities these men experienced a variety of intense emotions, which they could not easily express or confront. For example, many felt anger at physicians who initially informed them of their child's disability, believing that these doctors were unnecessarily abrupt and unsympathetic. Furthermore, the fathers found themselves dependent on the expertise of professionals. This dependence was difficult for fathers because it made them feel less in control and less competent as parents. Males grow up to be "fixers" who actively confront problems. Passivity in the face of a crisis is threatening to men who have learned that they must be "strong," not show weakness (mainly by suppressing emotions), and be able to resolve difficult situations competently. Perhaps the most poignant frustration is that fathers simply cannot "fix" their child's disability, and, despite their anguish about this situation, they may not be able to express how they feel.

In a recent overview of a major conference on psychotherapy research, it was reported that the suppression of emotions contributes to a heightened intrusion of disturbing thoughts: "Keeping thoughts secret creates a suppression cycle: The thought immediately comes to mind, the person tries to suppress it again and the cycle continues. Wegner hypothesizes that disclosing suppressed thoughts may stop this cycle and prevent intrusive thoughts" (Azar, 1994, p. 25). Furthermore, suppressed emotions may have medical as well as psychological implications. Headaches, back pain, and a more vulnerable immune system have been linked to suppressed emotions. For most of the fathers, their involvement in the discussion groups led by Smith (1981) represented the first time they had acknowledged to anyone, including their spouses and even themselves, that they had such strong feelings resulting from the birth of their child. Smith believes that support/discussion groups for fathers are an important emotional resource that will benefit fathers and indirectly will have a positive effect on the entire family. Indeed, as D. J. Meyer and colleagues (1985) emphasize, the support that the father can provide to his wife and other family members is another reason it is important that fathers learn to cope with their child's disability.

Josh Greenfeld (1978) describes the powerful and contradictory feelings he experiences as he reflects on life with his son Noah, who has autism:

> I thought continually that soon I will have to kill Noah. The monster that has long been lurking in him increasingly shows its face. And just as the day may come when I can no longer bear to take care of him, I could not bear to see him mistreated—or maltreated—in a state hospital like Camarillo or Letchworth Village.
> He will become a hopeless grotesque with less than endearing manners. He keeps putting his fingers to his lips and then spit-touching

the nearest object or person. He pinches, he scratches, he pulls hair. This morning he suddenly pulled Foumi's [Greenfeld's wife] hair after she had chastised him for his finger-spitting. I heard her crying and rushed to free her from his grasp.

Killing him would be a kindness. His brain has stopped working; he has not been functioning anyway. I dread it but I see myself killing my son not as a myth but as a fact. My dreams now are dreams of prison. Isolation. A winding down of my life in solitude. It seems absurd, I know. But could I ever bear to see Noah suffer, killed softly and cruelly, day after day? No.

There is a man from Santa Barbara who killed his brain-damaged son a few years ago. He put a gun to the boy's head and squeezed the trigger, then called the police. He's in prison now. But he'll get out eventually. (pp. 282–283)

Noah is quick to scream, to clutch, to demand, to be unreasonable. He is a tyranny I will never learn to live with. He is an obsession I will never learn to live without. (pp. 94–95)

In terms of paternal vulnerability in the face of childhood disability, Marsh (1993) writes:

Their inability to serve as protectors undermines their self-esteem; their suppression of affect may prevent them from resolving their emotional burden; and their involvement increases their caregiving burden. In addition, the metamorphosis of male roles in recent years has undoubtedly added to the confusion that fathers experience when they are confronted with the disability of a child. (p. 155)

We know, then, that some fathers of children with disabilities may reject their child and withdraw; they may experience a lower sense of competence and self-esteem; and they may experience considerable frustration as they confront the masculine injunctions they have learned to exercise in the face of powerful emotions. The issues then become, how might a father learn to be more accepting of his child and how can he come to terms with emotions that are not easily expressed? Furthermore, how can intervention efforts be directed toward fathers more systematically than they have up until now? Certainly the discussion group model proposed by Smith (1981) seems to be one type of intervention that can help ameliorate some of the problems noted above. Another promising venture is the workshop format that has been developed at the University of Washington.

Starting in 1978, fathers of young children with disabilities in Seattle, Washington, were exposed to a group format that provided information and social support (Vadasy, Fewell, Greenberg, Desmond, & Meyer, 1986). The basic structure was that fathers met twice monthly for 2 hours. They

brought their child with them to sessions organized by two male facilita-
tors, one a professional and one a father of a child with a disability. The
meetings included activities in which fathers and children participated
together, such as songs, dances, and games. Time was set aside for fathers
to meet without their children so that they could discuss their concerns.
Guests were invited to speak on a topic selected by the fathers at some
of the meetings. Mothers were often invited to attend the presentations,
and special family meetings were scheduled at holidays and occasionally
at other times. This format allowed fathers to acquire information,
experience social support from other fathers, discuss feelings and practical concerns, and develop strong attachments to their child.

The fathers' workshop manual, developed by the investigators at
the University of Washington, describes in detail how to initiate a
fathers' group, select leaders, and plan for the various components of
the meetings (D. J. Meyer et al., 1985). Since 1980, participating families
have been the subjects of research on the program's impact on parents'
stress levels and coping abilities. One study reported showed that both
fathers and mothers who had been participating in the program had
lower stress and depression levels and higher satisfaction levels regarding their social supports than parents newly entering the program
(Vadasy, Fewell, Meyer, & Greenberg, 1985). In a later evaluation of 45
sets of parents, it was found that both mothers and fathers reported
significantly decreased depression (Vadasy, Fewell, Greenberg, et al.,
1986). Fathers reported a decrease in stress and grief but an increase
in pessimism about the future.

The fathers' information needs decreased over time and mothers
reported increased satisfaction with social supports, increased family
cohesion, and decreased stress and rigidity in family control over time
(Vadasy, Fewell, Greenberg, et al., 1986). The outcomes for the study were
very positive and support the value of fathers' groups. The unanticipated
finding regarding the fathers' increased pessimism, according to the
investigators, may be due to the fathers' acceptance of the child's limitations. It may also reflect the fact that knowledge is a double-edged sword.

Lamb and Meyer (1991) urge organizations serving children with
disabilities not to neglect the fathers' involvement in the family and in
programs promoted by agencies. Fathers have a need for information
about their children's disability, information about programs and services, and treatment that is equal to that of mothers (Darling & Baxter,
1996). Professionals need to make opportunities for paternal involvement
by scheduling meetings convenient for both parents, sending home
informative materials and newsletters addressed to both parents, and
actively soliciting fathers' opinions about their child, their concerns, and
their perceptions of the services provided.

Although it is important to urge fathers to become involved, it is equally important to be cognizant of cultural factors in developing programs with fathers in mind (see Chapter 7). For example, family privacy is a primary value in some cultures May (1991). Thus, a discussion group format is poorly suited for fathers who may be better served through natural systems of support (e.g., extended family, the church) or by reading material such as newsletters and the like.

In summary, as a result of some modest research efforts, we know that some fathers experience adverse reactions to the birth of a child with a disability. Fathers who are coping poorly themselves tend to find it difficult to be supportive of their spouses. When fathers experience stress and withdraw from their families, other family members (especially the mother) must take up the slack, resulting in family tensions. Furthermore, there is some evidence that fathers may cope better with a daughter than a son. A promising resource for fathers seems to be a support group format that can help fathers form more positive attachments to their young children with special needs, gain information, and discuss their common problems in a supportive context. Generally speaking, though, fathers appear to adapt to their children rather well. It seems that a majority of fathers have little trouble assimilating a child with a disability into their life, while others have learned great lessons and have grown from the experience. However, a minority struggle considerably with this occurrence. Even though most fathers cope admirably, their life experience is, in a variety of ways, dissimilar from fathers of children who are nondisabled. All of these reactions to childhood disability are reflected in the essays of fathers in D. J. Meyer's (1995) book, *Uncommon Fathers: Reflections on Raising a Child with a Disability*. However, much more research is needed on fathers to better understand their responses and coping behaviors to childhood disability.

GRANDPARENTS

A systemic view has to appreciate the complexity of intergenerational relationships affecting contemporary family life. Yet much of the literature on families has focused on the nuclear family, with little mention of grandparents. To conceptualize the family apart from its ancestral past is to ignore an integral aspect of the family's present life. Some argue that the influences from previous generations are of considerable importance for understanding the nuclear family's dynamics (Bowen, 1978). Others note that the grandparent–grandchild relationship has the potential for affecting the development of children in a way that is different from other relationships (Baranowski, 1982).

Traditional views of the role of the grandparent as the domineering, controlling family matriarch or patriarch have given way to a more positive view. Grandparents now view their roles as being less associated with power and more related to warmth, indulgence, and pleasure without responsibility Wilcoxon (1987). Contemporary roles, then, seem to be multidimensional and supportive. Kornhaber and Woodward (in Wilcoxon, 1987) identified the following grandparent roles:

1. Historian: A link with the cultural and familial past
2. Role model: An example of older adulthood
3. Mentor: A wise adult experienced in life transitions
4. Wizard: A master of storytelling to foster imagination and creativity
5. Nurturer/great parent: An ultimate support person for family crises and transitions

Furthermore, positive relationships between generations can add to a family's well-being:

> One of the most effective automatic mechanisms for reducing the overall level of anxiety in a family is a relatively "open" relationship system in the extended family. . . . Any successful effort that goes toward improving the frequency and quality of emotional contact with the extended family will predictably improve the family's level of adjustment and reduce symptoms in the nuclear family. (Bowen, 1978, pp. 537–538)

Becoming a grandparent confers a special status on a person. Grandparents witness the emergence of a new generation and this allows them the satisfaction of seeing their grandchild take on new and fulfilling roles—a source of considerable pride. In some ways, grandchildren provide a new "lease on life" for grandparents. The wish to survive is expressed concretely by the birth of a grandchild. As Gabel and Kotsch (1981) note:

> The sense of surviving through the grandchild may help soothe the increasing infirmities of advancing age and the approaching reality of death. Grandchildren also offer renewal, because grandparents can relive the joys of their own early parenthood as they watch their children in this early phase of life. Furthermore, playing with and occasionally caring for young grandchildren supplies grandparents with a revived feeling of importance and purpose in life. To the delight of many grandparents, this new lease on life is purchased at a relatively low cost. They can often enjoy their grandchildren without the burdens of the ongoing caretaking responsibilities and the stress of parenthood. (pp. 30–31)

People are becoming grandparents earlier in their lives and will continue in this role for longer periods than in previous generations (D. J. Meyer & Vadasy, 1986). The grandparent role can be assumed when one is in the 40s or 50s, younger than grandparents in the past. Seventy percent of persons over age 65 have grandchildren and more than a third are great-grandparents (Streib & Beck, 1981). Also, increased life expectancy means that some people will assume grandparent roles for almost half their lives. In terms of the diversity of grandparenthood according to age, some become grandparents at age 40, others at 50, and still others at age 80 (Pinson-Millburn, Fabian, Schlossberg, & Pyle, 1996).

Approximately three-fourths of the elderly live within 30 minutes of at least one child, making regular contact between nuclear and extended family a reality (Stehower, 1968). Almost half of U.S. grandparents see a grandchild every day (L. Harris & Associates, 1975). And state laws protecting grandparents' rights to continue their relationships with their grandchildren (after divorce) demonstrate how seriously grandparents regard their roles and how important this relationship is to them.

In recent years, grandparents have in some cases become the primary caretakers for their grandchildren. This new responsibility has resulted primarily from an increase in single parenthood. Often, a grandparent cares for a child while the parent works or goes to school. Grandparents also become caregivers when their grandchildren's parents are addicted to drugs, have children out of wedlock at very young ages, are guilty of child abuse or neglect, divorce, become unemployed, or die (Davis, 1995; Downey, 1995; Woodworth, 1994). Some of these grandparents who inherit a grandchild become "parents" of "healthy" children, whereas others assume parenting roles of children who have chronic health problems or who are disabled.

In summary, then, we know that there will be more persons becoming grandparents as this century comes to a close. Earlier views that grandparents are interested in control and tend to meddle in their children's lives have been replaced by the perception of grandparents as supporters and helpers to their adult children and nurturers to their grandchildren. Furthermore, and perhaps most important, grandparents are affected by what happens in the nuclear family and, in turn, they affect those family members.

Considering these various roles and meanings of grandparenthood, how might a grandparent be expected to react when confronted with a disabled grandchild? What meanings do they attach to this experience? How do grandparents cope with the grandchild? With their adult child? With their son- or daughter-in-law?

Grandparents and Childhood Disability

As one grandmother put it:

> There is a very special magic between grandparents and grandchil-
> dren. There is a joy, a delight, an unencumbered relationship. The
> responsibility of parenthood is over. Grandparents have an opportu-
> nity to sample the mysteries and watch with awe the unfolding of a
> new personality. This new unique human being is a stranger, but is
> hauntingly familiar. He is the link between our past and the future.
> But what happens when this link, this delight, this claim to immortality
> is born less than perfect? What is the relationship then between
> grandparent and grandchild? (McPhee, 1982, p. 13)

The remainder of this chapter will attempt to address the questions
posed by McPhee. Indeed, when a child with special needs is born,
grandparents, just like the parents, must face the disappointment of a
"less-than-perfect" baby and ponder the relationship between this child
and themselves. They must also reflect on their relationship with their
own children and how they will interact with this newly constituted family
of which they are a part.

A major concern of the parents is "How will our parents (or in-laws)
accept our baby?" Writing about her experience with her mother-in-law,
Pieper (1976) chronicles their reactions to each other after the birth of
her son. Pieper's mother-in-law was reluctant to visit her in the hospital
and later accused Pieper of burdening her son (Pieper's husband) for life.
Attempting to cope with such an assault, Pieper chose to try to understand
the special mother–son relationship rather than, in her own pain, strike
out at her mother-in-law:

> She is my husband's mother! Just as I could gaze on that son of
> mine—looking for all the world like a plucked chicken, even to the black
> sutures near his butt—and feel a fierce protectiveness, so she could feel
> nothing less for the son she had loved for so much longer. . . . I was
> supposed to present their son with a fine, healthy, and above all
> "normal" child. . . . Instead, I had given birth to a "defective baby." In
> so doing I had threatened her son's well-being—or her image of it. I
> had threatened his financial future, his emotional make-up, his posi-
> tion in the community and his independence. Her harsh words to me
> in the hospital were a way of expressing the same protectiveness toward
> her son that I was now feeling toward mine. (Pieper, 1976, p. 7)

A relationship that floundered had, with the insight and wisdom of
the mother, been restored. Pieper understood a mother's protective
feelings toward her son. She further understood that her mother-in-law
grew up when deviancy was tolerated even less than it is today. In

addition, the notion of the "bad seed" may have played a role, in that at some level the mother-in-law may have felt that *she* had passed on the defective gene, resulting in childhood disability. This can be threatening and anxiety provoking to a relative. As expressed by McPhee (1982), "That diagnosis set both sides of the family busy rattling skeletons trying to prove that each was pure and not responsible for the present suffering" (p. 14). Just like the parents, grandparents can harbor guilt feelings that last for a lifetime:

> My mother called to see how things went. I told her what they [the doctors] said, and she told me it was crazy, they were crazy, and she would never accept it. She hung up on me. She wouldn't talk to me. It took my mother years, and she has finally accepted it. I found out later my mother always blamed herself. My mother only recently told me that she feels that God punished her because she was always a very proud, vain person. Because she was that way, God was teaching her a lesson and bringing her down a notch. She still feels that guilt. I was totally stunned. I never knew she carried that all those years. (in Marsh, 1993, p. 173)

Generally speaking, an event that usually reassures grandparents—that the future will be carried on by a grandchild—instead introduces uncertainty about what the future holds for the family. The birth of a grandchild with a disability evokes certain emotions (D. J. Meyer & Vadasy, 1986). Grandparents experience a dual hurt, not only for the grandchild, but also for their child, whom they may see as burdened for life (Marsh, 1993). The grandparents' wish for their adult children's happiness is shattered as they see their offspring preparing to cope with a family crisis that won't go away and cannot be easily remedied.

Perhaps to avoid the pain of reality, grandparents may deny a grandchild's problem ("There's nothing wrong with her"), trivialize it ("She will grow out of it"), or have fantasies of unrealistic cures (D. J. Meyer & Vadasy, 1986). Grandparents who deny the existence of a child's special needs and those who reject the child can prove difficult burdens to the parents who are attempting to cope with the crisis. The parents must attend to their own pain while at the same time they are compelled to cope with their own parents' or their in-laws' reactions. Generally speaking, strong negative reactions from extended family members can lead to triangulation and cut-off between and within generations (Walsh, 1989). Grandparents siding with one or the other parent can lead to triangles that harm family functioning.

Although we know little about how grandparents react to the birth of a grandchild with a disability, it is likely that they experience a mourning period following the loss of the idealized grandchild that they had expected (Marsh, 1993). Just as the parents experience the "death" of the expected normal, healthy child, so too may the grandparents feel a great loss and mourn for the death of what they had wished for. They may go through similar stages as the parents: denial, grief, anger, detachment, and eventually acceptance. Reporting on the reactions of grandparents who attended the grandparent workshops at the University of Washington, Vadasy, Fewell, and Meyer (1986) report that their initial reactions were most often sadness (67%), shock (38%), and anger (33%). Although 43% reported that they continued to feel sad long after they first learned of their grandchild's disability, 57% eventually expressed acceptance.

Grandparents may be mourning at the same time the parents are grieving. In the crisis-laden initial period of discovery, both parents and grandparents may be experiencing great loss and grief; they may, therefore, be unable to be supportive of one other. Grandparents may be in a state of "diminished capacity" for providing help to their child's parents (Gabel & Kotsch, 1981). At this early stage of confronting childhood disability, professionals should remain alert to the varied experiences of family members, while helping them understand one another's pain and need to grieve.

Grandparents may experience negative emotion when a child with a disability enters the family. A pattern commonly emerges in which a paternal grandmother expresses her resentment toward her daughter-in-law, as noted in the relationship described above by Pieper. The hurling back and forth of accusations between family members heightens the sense of crisis. The mother may already feel guilty about the birth but she is made to feel even more burdened when she is accused by an in-law of destroying her husband's life. At a time when the mother needs support, she is instead confronted with hostility. The husband, in turn, is placed in a difficult position, feeling that he needs to be supportive of both his mother and his wife, while coping with his own pain, which is often unexpressed. Furthermore, children may view the mounting tensions between their parents and their grandparents with considerable apprehension. Partly as a consequence of grandparent reactions, the nondisabled children may be confused about how they should respond to the new and less-than-perfect addition to the family. In short, hostility between the parents and the extended family may, if not resolved, become a major source of continuing intergenerational conflict.

As noted above, perhaps the intergenerational family interaction that is discussed most in the literature is that between the mother and the child's paternal grandmother (Farber & Ryckman, 1965; Holt, 1958a; Kahana & Kahana, 1970). As in Pieper's (1976) situation, paternal grandmothers have been known to blame the mother for the child's disability.

Furthermore, Weisbren (1980) found that the father's relationship with his parents was more important than all other support sources. Weisbren also reported that fathers who perceived their parents as highly supportive engaged in more activities with their child, felt more positive about their child, and were better able or more willing to plan for the future than fathers who had unsupportive parents. She further found that mothers who perceive their in-laws as supportive also feel more positive about their child. This research suggests that grandparents may have much more influence on how parents respond to their child with a disability than originally believed.

Although resentment, guilt, and anger can be destructive, such feelings must be viewed in context. Negative emotions should probably be expected and accepted, especially early on. To discourage family members from expressing their pain through anger is to encourage its expression in subtle ways; thus, major underlying issues that are never directly confronted may affect the lives of family members in more camouflaged ways. At any rate, just as professionals must understand and be accepting of the parents' anger so too must they accept similar feelings from grandparents. One grandmother comments:

> Anger and hostility can be destructive forces to live with. Will anger and hostility be all this child will ever mean to me? I wondered. I suffered for him—for what he might have been, should have been. I resented what his birth had done to my lovely daughter.
>
> I cried a lot and prayed a lot and yelled at God a lot. Then, I said, "So be it. You're sorry for yourself, but look at that child. Just look at him. Not what he might have been, but what he is. Grow up, lady." (McPhee, 1982, p. 14)

Although grandparents typically enjoyed their own parenting years, they may have looked forward to the time when the parent role would cease. The birth of a child with a disability can suddenly thrust grandparents back in time, causing them to resume a role they thought had been fulfilled:

> When my own kids were little the chaos just all seemed to go with the territory—spilled milk, scattered cereal, orange peels behind the couch, lost socks, wall-to-wall toys. I cleaned it up a dozen times a day without a second thought. Now, just bending over sometimes sparks that second thought! We don't have the peace and quiet we sometimes think we'd like to have. Sometimes I find myself thinking, "I served my time at this! What am I doing here?" (Click, 1986, p. 3)

One grandparent who was thrust into a parent role due to the parents' drug addiction remarked, "I feel I've been cheated. I'm not ready for the rocking chair, but if I want to go out with friends, I can't. I feel like something has been stolen from me" (Minkler & Roe, 1993, p. 60).

We have suggested thus far that grandparents, by their reactions and lack of support, can be a source of considerable consternation to the nuclear family coping with childhood disability. The sense of threat and vulnerability, the loss they experience, the ambiguity the situation holds for them, their denial and lack of acceptance can indeed be burdensome for the family. In this regard, Hornby and Ashworth (1994) report that, in their small-scale study (n = 25 parents), they found that the perceived level of support from grandparents was low. A quarter of the grandparents were considered to have added to the parents' burdens and almost a third of the parents expressed a wish for more support from grandparents. However, perhaps for most families with a child who has special needs who have living extended family, the situation may be a more positive. Indeed, as Vadasy and Fewell (1986) report, mothers of deaf–blind children ranked their own parents high on their list of supports.

Grandparent contributions to the nuclear family can be many and varied. Some professionals conceive of grandparents as valuable resources to their grandchildren and the family (Vadasy, Fewell, Meyer, & Greenberg, 1985). Due to their experience, grandparents have much to offer in advising about child care, providing access to community resources, and in sharing coping strategies that helped them in the past. They also may have more time available so they can assist with shopping, errands, and child care; and any type of respite from the daily chores of caring for the child is welcome. Respite services are not available in some communities, making this a most valuable contribution. Furthermore, because of their community contacts, grandparents may be able to provide the family with access to services within the community. Through the grandparents' church group, for example, the family might gain access to child care, special equipment, and other types of support. And finally, as noted above, as a consequence of divorce, substance abuse, and violence, some grandparents serve as parents to children with disabilities (Simpson, 1996).

Perhaps the most important type of help from the extended family is emotional support. The support of grandparents during the initial diagnostic and "first knowledge" phase and throughout the child's development adds immeasurably to the parents' ability to cope, and it provides excellent role models for siblings as well:

> You think that after you've raised your children you can stop being a parent and become a person again. And then your adult child experiences tragedy or loss, and your heart aches with the knowledge of your own impotence and how you yearn to go back to the days when a bandaid and a kiss could fix anything. Who are we to try to advise our children? How can we see beyond the moment, how can we diminish

their pain or give them faith in the future? Mostly all we can do is wait, offer them our patience and our constancy, and try to keep our own hope alive. (Click, 1986, p. 3)

From the very beginning, there was no question that she was accepted, just like any other child born in our family. I remember how the whole family rallied. They said that she would be fine, and it meant a lot to us to have that family support. They sent us cards and flowers and gifts and did all the things you do when a baby is born. And I think that was so important, because, after all, she was a baby first, and then a baby who had problems. (in Vadasy, Fewell, & Meyer, 1986, p. 39)

Grandparents can thus be a source of emotional support and instrumental assistance; but as noted above, they can also add to the family's burden when they are not accepting of their grandchild and fail to be supportive. The question, then, is, how can professionals help those grandparents who wish to be involved and useful, as well as those who are struggling with their feelings and, as a result, find it difficult to come to terms with the family crisis? The grandparents' sense of threat or burden exacerbates the stress of parents. Several models and programs have been offered to help grandparents gain essential information and come to terms with their reactions.

Support Groups

George (1988) believes that grandparents can enhance the coping abilities of the entire family. She advocates a support group model whereby grandparents of grandchildren with disabilities exchange information and feelings with other grandparents who are confronting a similar crisis. In such groups, grandparents benefit through mutual support and increased knowledge about children with disability. They become better able to provide support to the parents, thereby alleviating stress. Moreover, the child benefits greatly from the increased acceptance by his or her grandparents.

A pilot support group for relatives of children with disability was formed at the University of Tennessee Child Development Center (George, 1988). The objectives of the group included the following:

- To provide education and opportunities for solving problems with regard to developmentally delayed children
- To provide a supportive atmosphere where feelings could be clarified and ventilated
- To aid and strengthen the family in coping with the birth of a child with a disability

- To promote networking and interfamily links with others in similar situations

The group sessions were held for an hour per week for approximately 8 weeks. Initially, relatives discussed their feelings in intellectual and superficial ways and tended to maintain a distance from other group members. At this early stage, members relied on leaders, other group members, or experts (guest speakers) for information. These initial informational sessions helped relatives to obtain updated information as well as to correct stereotypical attitudes.

During the second stage of the group process, grandparents discussed their adult children's reactions at the time of diagnosis. During the third stage, relatives began to express their own feelings of shock, anger, and sadness. The group climate became more intimate as members shared their personal reactions and sorrow. During this phase, participants also discussed possible resolutions to problems.

The final phase was characterized by ambivalent feelings as both members and leaders struggled with the impending termination of the group. The leaders noted attachment and bonding among members and encouraged members to maintain contacts outside the group.

Workshops

D. J. Meyer and Vadasy (1986) developed a workshop model for grandparents at the University of Washington in Seattle. Similar to George (1988), they reasoned that grandparents can create additional burdens for the family if they lack adequate information about childhood disability or have unrealistic expectations of their grandchild's potential. Moreover, accurate information can contribute to the grandparents' acceptance and support. It was also believed that grandparents needed a forum where they could receive emotional support.

These objectives led to the two major components of the workshop: grandparent roundtable and provision of information. Guest speakers were invited to present information, and the roundtable provided an outlet for grandparents to express their opinions and feelings. The following topics were typically discussed: family stress as a result of the child's diagnosis, difficulties of a single grandmother raising a child with a disability, frustration of a grandparent who could not help her daughter because of geographical distance, sharing the joy and closeness that a child with special needs can bring to a family, and so forth. After about an hour of roundtable discussion, a guest speaker generally presented information on a preselected topic. Cofacilitators, a professional and a grandparent, generally conducted the workshops.

Research indicates that grandparents want to be better informed about available therapies for their grandchild, want to know more about the child's disability, and want to have some idea of the child's potential (Vadasy, Fewell, & Meyer, 1986). Grandparents also wonder whether they are doing the right things for the grandchild and express anxiety about the future. Based on these concerns, a workshop or support group model effectively helps grandparents and their adult children cope with the crisis of childhood disability.

Extended Family Programs

The family-involvement program at the Atlanta Speech School includes a morning workshop for grandparents of infants and preschoolers with hearing disabilities who are enrolled in the school (Rhoades, 1975). Tours of the facility are conducted and presentations on the anatomy of hearing, hearing tests, the causes of hearing impairment, and so forth are presented. Another program designed to meet the needs of extended family members is the Family, Infant, and Toddler Project at Vanderbilt University (Gabel & Kotsch, 1981). At bimonthly meetings, grandparents and other family members obtain information on therapies and educational programs. A portion of each meeting is open for questions.

Other localities have expanded their programs for children with special needs to include nuclear- and extended family members (Sonnek, 1986). Thus there appears to be a slowly growing responsiveness to the needs of grandparents. However, research on the outcomes of such programs is needed.

Grandparents are important resources and their involvement benefits them as well as the nuclear family. We agree with Sonnek (1986), who says that grandparents have been an unrecognized and underutilized resource. Professionals should make every effort to look to the extended family as a resource and consider their potential contributions to the family.

$\sim$

Cultural Reactions to Childhood Disability and Subcultural Variation

T HE BIRTH of a child with a disability has different meanings in various societies throughout the world. Even within a single complex society, this event can have a variety of meanings that are shaped by subcultural values and beliefs. In this chapter, we briefly review some of the cross-cultural diversity in reactions to childhood disability and look more closely at the variety of meanings that are attached to disability in American society.

Understanding cultural diversity is important in a systems perspective. A family's definition of its situation and of the roles that various family members should play will vary considerably depending on the family's background. Although individual differences certainly exist, cultural values and meanings shape reactions to children with disabilities. Professionals need to know as much as possible about the potential differences they might encounter in the families with whom they interact.

CROSS-CULTURAL DIVERSITY

Values attached to disability have varied both geographically and historically. In ancient Sparta, malformed babies were thrown over a precipice; yet in some societies people with disabilities are believed to have supernatural powers and are held in high esteem. Safilios-Rothschild (1970) suggests that prejudice toward people with disabilities varies by (1) level of development and rate of unemployment; (2) beliefs about the role of government in alleviating social problems; (3) beliefs about individual "responsibility" (sin) for disability; (4) cultural values attached to different physical conditions; (5) disability-connected factors, including visibility, contagiousness, part of the body affected, physical versus mental nature of the disability, and severity of functional impairment; (6) effectiveness of public-relations efforts; and (7) importance of activities that carry a high risk of disability—for example, war. Chesler (1965) suggests that the higher the stage of a society's industrialization and socioeconomic development, the greater the tendency to value high intelligence and achievement. Some of the most highly industrialized societies generally have little tolerance for deviance from behavioral norms.

A sampling of variant reactions to disability in different cultures throughout the world illustrates the role of cultural values in shaping attitudes. Obesity in women is greatly admired in most African tribes yet stigmatized in the American middle class (Chesler, 1965). Among Middle Eastern Muslims, the term *saint* is applied to people with mental retardation, and they are given benevolent and protective treatment (Edgerton, 1970).

> Among the Wogeo, a New Guinea tribe, children with obvious deformities are buried alive at birth, but children crippled in later life are looked after with loving care. . . . Among the Palaung, an Eastern clan, "it is lucky to have extra fingers or toes, and extremely lucky to be born with a hare-lip." (Wright, 1983)

DeCaro, Dowaliby, and Maruggi (1983) found no difference between English and Italian samples in career expectations for children with deafness.

Dybwad (1970) has argued that level of technological development is insufficient to explain varying values toward mental retardation. He notes that infanticide of children with retardation exists in both primitive and industrialized societies, as does a belief in the divinity of people with retardation. Positive attitudes toward retardation can be found both in the primitive Truk Islands and in modern Denmark. He quotes an Indonesian report that could as easily have been written about a Western country: "the trainable child presents its problem. The child is mostly hidden. The parents are twisted by the conflict of guilt and shame" (p. 563).

Groce (1987) has suggested that disability issues in developing countries are different from those in the Western world. She writes:

> High tech, hospital-based, rehabilitative approaches to care, urban-based educational facilities, and even support groups, do little to reach the majority of the Developing World's disabled people, the vast majority of whom are poor and an estimated 80% of whom live in rural areas. (p. 2)

Many of the disabilities found in these areas are preventable, and those that are not worsen because of lack of early intervention and rehabilitative services. The difficulties faced by families as a result of a lack of resources, which have been noted throughout this book, are likely to be grossly magnified in the developing world.

HISTORICAL CONTEXT

J. Newman (1991) has suggested that attitudes and social policies with respect to persons with disabilities have resulted from historical processes. He argues that these processes have been guided by philosophies of utilitarianism, humanitarianism, and human rights. These philosophies have been a part of Western culture since primitive times and continue to shape attitudes and policy today.

Lazerson (1975) writes that the 19th century saw a shift in American society from home care of the child with a disability to institutionalization. He attributes this shift to the fears early and mid-19th-century Americans had about social disorder. The creation of institutions paralleled the influx of large numbers of immigrants into the United States. As families became more transient, institutions outside of the family began to assume certain welfare functions. Concurrently, any deviance from social norms, including disability, came to be defined as a social problem, not merely a family problem.

A common justification for residential care suggested that institutional services were better that those available in the community. A 1914 study (reported in Sollenberger, 1974) illustrates this thinking:

> We have no hesitancy in advocating the creation of a state hospital for crippled children in every state of the union. In no other way can the multitudes of crippled children outside of the large cities be reached.
>
> That the family home is the best place for well children is now generally recognized. But crippled children are conceded to be a special class, requiring in many cases surgical operations and in many cases very close physical supervision for months, often years. . . . Some surgeons insist that parents cannot be trusted to adjust a child's brace or even to bring him to the dispensary at the time ordered by the doctor. (pp. 8, 22)

Lazerson attributes the shift away from institutions that has taken place in the 20th century to the special education movement, which places the responsibility for educating children with disabilities onto community schools. In addition, inhumane conditions were found to exist in some large institutions. The success of some early efforts to provide family-based services to children led to the creation of more such programs. The success of community-based early intervention programs, in particular, began to be reported widely in the literature in the 1960s, resulting in the large-scale growth of these programs throughout the country. The availability of community resources, coupled with the spread of the ideology of normalization, has once again made the family the locus of care for children with disabilities in America today.

MODERN AMERICAN SOCIETY

As noted in earlier chapters, the most pervasive attitude toward disability in modern American society is stigma. As Goffman (1963) and others have written, individuals with disabilities have commonly been discredited and relegated to a morally inferior status in American society. Stereotypes are also prevalent. Gottlieb (1975) has noted, for example, that most people think of persons with mental retardation as organically different, "Mongoloid"-looking, and physically disabled or mentally ill. Safilios-Rothschild (1970) suggests that people with disabilities are a minority group in American society and share the following characteristics with other minority groups:

1. They are relegated to a separate place in society (encouraged to interact with their "own kind").
2. They are considered by the majority to be inferior.
3. Their segregation is rationalized as being "better for them."
4. They are evaluated on the basis of their categorical membership rather than their individual characteristics.

English (1971) reports the existence of such negative attitudes toward people with physical disabilities in over half of the able-bodied population, although, as the rest of this chapter will show, variations exist according to such subcultural factors as age, gender, and SES. Variations also exist according to the nature of the disability, with those with mental disabilities tending to be more stigmatized than those with physical disabilities.

Although stigma continues to shape much of the interaction between people with and without disabilities in American society, attitudes may be slowly changing. The disability-rights movement has had an impact in reducing some stereotypical thinking, and legislation such as the Individuals with Disabilities Education Act and the Americans with Disabilities Act has placed individuals with disabilities in the societal mainstream. In the remainder of this chapter, we look at variations in attitude toward childhood disability that exist within this larger, still negative, but evolving framework of society as a whole.

As we have just indicated, attitudes toward children with disabilities vary considerably from one culture to another. In a pluralistic society, various groups within a culture may also hold divergent views of these children. Although sharing some of the aspects of the culture of the larger society, these subcultures also have their own beliefs, values, attitudes and norms, which are learned through interaction among their members. Until fairly recently, most of the literature on families of children with disabilities ignored subcultural variation. Theories of stages of parental adaptation, for example, seem to imply that all parents pass through similar stages regardless of SES, race, or ethnicity. In the following pages, we examine the idea that families' views are in fact shaped by the segment of society within which they live.

Societies are stratified along a number of different dimensions, which are not mutually exclusive. Probably the most important dimension is SES, or social class. Although SES has a number of components, the most important are occupation, education, and income. Socioeconomic levels have been grouped in various ways, but a five-class system has been commonly used (see, e.g., Hollingshead & Redlich, 1958). Social classes are not separate subcultures in the same way as some racial and ethnic groups. Socioeconomic diversity is more a matter of differential access to opportunity than of different beliefs and values; this fact will be discussed further in the section on social class. In addition to socioeconomic stratification, subcultural groups also form along racial and ethnic lines. Religious and regional variation also exist. Members of these groups are more likely to interact with others like themselves than with members of other groups. Attitudes and behavior are thus shaped by the subculture.

THE BASIS FOR SUBCULTURAL VARIABILITY

Some subcultural differences appear to be innate. Freedman (1981) notes that even as young infants Caucasian and Chinese babies respond differently to stimuli. Differences have also been found between Navajo and Caucasian newborns. Mother–child interaction also varies among these groups, with Caucasian mothers vocalizing more to their infants than the others. Although parent vocalizations are certainly culturally conditioned, they may also be increased or inhibited through interaction with a naturally active or quiet baby.

An infant with a disability who was less responsive than most might thus be less alarming to an Asian or Native American mother whose experience had been with relatively quiet infants. Conversely, a disability resulting in an increased irritability or activity level might be more difficult for such a mother.

Responses to illness and disability are also subculturally patterned through experience and learning. Kleinman, Eisenberg, and Good (1978) and others have noted the difference between illness and disease. Disease is a physiological condition, whereas illness refers to the patient's perceptions of disease. Illness is a product of social learning, which determines meanings, expectations, values, treatment-seeking behavior, experience of symptoms, and other characteristics that we associate with disease.

As we have said, disability, like illness, is viewed in many different ways by different cultures throughout the world. Subcultural learning can be equally powerful in shaping views toward disability within a society. S. A. Richardson, Goodman, Hastorf, and Dornbusch (1961, 1963), for example, found that in American society, children learn at an early age to devalue disability and show the same preferential pattern for various types of disabilities as adults. However, an Italian subgroup ranked facial disfigurement less negatively than the general sample, and a Jewish subgroup ranked both facial disfigurement and obesity less negatively than the general sample.

Chigier and Chigier (1968) replicated the S. A. Richardson et al. study in Israel and found that SES was a significant factor in determining attitudes. Children of low SES tended to rank cosmetic disability less negatively than physical disability, and children of high SES ranked physical disability less negatively then cosmetic disability. The authors suggest that physical prowess is generally highly valued in lower-class communities and that middle-class children are more likely to be socialized to value appearance. Middle-class children probably also learn to value education and mental ability more highly than physical skill.

Another Israeli study (Shurka & Florian, 1983) looked at parental perceptions of their children with disabilities. The authors note that earlier studies had shown that Israeli families of Oriental origin had significantly more negative attitudes toward family members with disabilities than those of European origin. In this study, Arab parents perceived their young adult children with disabilities as needing more help, and Jewish parents perceived their children as more independent and capable of work. This finding is attributed to differences between the Arab and Jewish family systems. The Arab system is described as encouraging dependence on the parents and the extended family.

In American culture, too, subcultural socialization shapes family reactions to disability. Marion (1980) has noted that minority group parents are often not nearly as overwhelmed by the birth of a child with a disability as are parents in the cultural mainstream. Feelings of protection and acceptance of the child may be more common in these groups than the shock, disbelief, guilt, and depression that have been attributed to mainstream parents by many writers.

FAMILY DIVERSITY

What is a family? Certainly, the middle-class ideal—the nuclear family, consisting of a married couple and their unmarried children—is not universal in society today. Vincent and Salisbury (1988) have written, "Combining the incidence of divorce, widowhood, and single parenthood, 67% of the children born in America today will be raised by a single parent for part of their lives" (p. 49). They also note that perhaps 75% of all children under the age of 6 receive day care while their parents work. Thus, some traditional models of service provision to families may no longer be applicable.

Although diversity is not new, families today are more diverse than at any time in history. This diversity can be attributed to both cultural and structural factors (Zinn & Eitzen, 1993). Cultural factors have become more important as the United States has become more demographically diverse. Structural conditions have recently been rooted in economic changes that have had a major impact on the labor market.

In 1980, fewer than one in five Americans was a member of a racial or ethnic minority. In 1990, the ratio had changed to one in four, and demographic projections suggest that by 2030, the ratio will be one in three. As we will show later in the chapter, different racial and ethnic groups have different values, norms, and beliefs regarding children and disabilities.

Structural factors affecting families today result largely from a decrease in high-paying blue collar jobs during the past 20 years. Consequently, more married women with children are in the labor force, and mother-only households have become more common as a result of the postponement of marriage and increase in lifetime levels of divorce.

As Copeland and White (reported in Hanson & Lynch, 1992) have suggested, households today include single-parent, step- and blended, adoptive, foster, grandparent, and same-sex-partner families, along with married couples. These are all variants on the nuclear family. In addition, in some ethnic groups, the nuclear family was never the norm. Rather, households typically included various extended family members, or even "fictive kin" not related by blood or marriage to the nuclear family. In some American communities today, parents and children still live in close proximity to grandparents, aunts, uncles, and cousins. In others, homelessness and isolation from relatives are common.

Family diversity also encompasses wide variations in parent characteristics. Although many parents today postpone having children until they are in their 30s or 40s, teen pregnancy is also common. Often, grandparents are involved in the care of their teenage children's children. Parents also have varying educational levels. In some communities, few have finished high school; in others, most have graduated from college or have advanced degrees. Some parents have mental retardation or physical disabilities. Different family structures are also sometimes found in urban and rural areas. Professionals who work with families need to take this diversity into account.

THE INFLUENCE OF SOCIAL CLASS

Social class is not so much a matter of cultural diversity as of structural constraints. People do not become poor in the same way that they become African American or Latino American. Rather, class differences can be attributed to the differential allocation of opportunities in society. Given a choice, most people would want to be rich. However, economic changes resulting in a decreased need for semiskilled labor, and low wages for unskilled jobs have led, during the past decades, to an increase in young families living in poverty. Poverty severely limits the lifestyle choices available to families, and most of the attitudes and behaviors attributed to lower-class families in the literature are best explained by limited opportunities rather than differences in basic values.

Attitudes toward Disability

Families with children with disabilities come from all social classes. Professionals, on the other hand, are more likely to come from middle- and upper-class backgrounds. As a result, professionals and the families they serve may have highly divergent views of disability and its treatment. Perhaps the greatest conflict in this area has occurred in the field of mental retardation, especially in the mild ranges of retardation. Although parents and professionals from middle- and upper-class backgrounds may regard mild mental retardation as a devastating condition, lower-class parents may not even define it as a disability.

In a study of institutionalized children with retardation, Mercer (1965) found that the children who were discharged generally came from low-status families. High-status families were more likely to concur with official definitions of mental retardation and the need for institutionalization. The low-status families, who were not as achievement oriented, were able to envision their children playing normal adult roles. Downey

(1963) found, similarly, that more educated families tended to show less interest in their institutionalized children, because the children were unable to conform to the family's career expectations.

Lower-class families may have higher tolerance for deviance in general than middle-class families. Guttmacher and Elinson (1971) found, for example, that upper-class respondents were more likely than lower-class respondents to define a series of deviant behaviors as illness. Middle- and upper-class families tend to share the professional's perspective of mental illness, whereas the lower classes may see such behaviors as normal variants. Children with disabilities that result in nonnormative behaviors may be less accepted in middle- and upper-class families as a result.

As Hess (1970), Kohn (1969), and others have noted, middle-class parents expect independent behavior and achievement from their children. They have higher educational and occupational aspirations for their children and higher expectations that those aspirations will be attained. Socially appropriate behavior is also likely to be viewed by these parents as necessary for achievement. Holt (1958a) has written about families with children with retardation:

> The families that managed best were not those in the upper classes. These parents were ambitious for their children and never overcame their frustration and disappointment. The ideal parents were those who . . . did not have great ambitions. . . . They looked upon the child as a gift for which to be thankful whatever his condition. (p. 753)

This class-based pattern does not seem to occur as clearly in the case of physical disability. Dow (1966) found no correlation between social class and parental acceptance of their children with disabilities and notes that parents of all classes tend to have optimistic attitudes. These favorable attitudes are maintained by depreciating the importance of physique.

Intervention Issues

In working with families of different social classes, professionals should be aware of differences in lifestyle or in parent–child interaction that may affect acceptance of professional recommendations or reactions to the professional. Professionals working in home-based programs that use parents as teachers need to be especially aware of the varying teaching strategies employed by parents of different social-class backgrounds. Laosa (1978) found, for example, that in a group of Chicano families, mothers with more formal education tended to use inquiry and praise in teaching their children and mothers with less education were more likely to use modeling as a teaching strategy. Another study of mothers of low-SES preschoolers with mild retardation (Wilton & Barbour, 1978) found that they showed less encouragement of their children's activities than comparison mothers. Attempting to get such parents to use more "middle-class" techniques could result in lack of compliance with a treatment program.

Lower-class parents are also likely to have less time and money to spend on their children's disabilities than their middle-class counterparts. Resources such as transportation, employment opportunities, adequate or appropriate housing, and access to good medical care are limited in the lower classes. When the necessities of life are scarce, a child's disability may not be a family's number-one priority. The disability may be only one of the many problems faced by the family. Professionals who judge such families by middle-class standards are often unwittingly creating a situation of noncompliance by their unrealistic expectations.

Dunst, Trivette, and Cross (1988) found that low-SES families of children with disabilities had less family support and more physical, emotional, and financial problems than a higher-SES group. Without a strong support network to share the burden, such families are likely to experience considerable stress in managing their children's disabilities, regardless of their level of acceptance. Colón (1980) has suggested that the multiproblem, poor family has a truncated life cycle, with a greater loss of family members and greater shortening of life stages than the middle-class family and that the mother is commonly the organizing force in family life. The support offered by the professional can be important to such families.

At one time, researchers believed that a "culture of poverty" existed (see, e.g., O. Lewis, 1959). Since then, studies have generally indicated that poor people share most of the values of the larger society. However, the conditions imposed by a chronic shortage of cash affect lifestyles and can restructure the priorities of a group. "Getting ahead" is not a major concern when survival is uppermost in people's minds.

ETHNIC VARIATION

An ethnic group has been defined as "those who conceive of themselves as alike by virtue of their common ancestry, real or fictitious, and who are so regarded by others" (Shibutani & Kwan, reported in McGoldrick, 1982, p. 3). Ethnic identification may be based on race, culture, or national origin. Census data from 1989 indicated that the population of the United States was composed of ethnic groups in the following proportions (Harry, 1992a):

Group	Percentage of population
African American	12.0
Hispanic (of any race)	8.3
Asian, Pacific	2.8
Native American	0.7
White	84.1

These data indicate a decrease in the white population in proportion to the other groups, compared with data from the last census. Chan (1990) notes that shortly after the year 2000, one-third of the projected U.S. population will consist of people of color, and the white population of the state of California will be in the minority. Among the whites are people with various ethnic identifications, including Irish, Italian, Jewish, and German. Some members of ethnic groups may identify very strongly with the group, whereas others may think of themselves more as Americans than as ethnics. Because attitudes toward disability and toward children in general vary by ethnicity, professionals should be aware of the ethnic identification of the families they serve.

The following discussion is not intended to be an exhaustive or definitive review of the literature on various ethnic groups, but rather, to suggest the kinds of ethnic differences that may be relevant to professionals working with families of children with disabilities. A more detailed review of this kind can be found in an excellent book, *Developing Cross-Cultural Competence* (Lynch & Hanson, 1992).

African American Subculture

Much of the literature on African American families in America has focused on social class rather than ethnicity. Consequently, many of the patterns that have been uncovered have been socioeconomic. Tolson and Wilson (1990) have shown that African American families are not homogeneous and that considerable diversity exists among two- and three-generational families of varying socioeconomic levels. Although these families are disproportionately represented in the lower classes, an African American subculture does appear to exist apart from SES and can be found in African American middle-class families as well as in the lower classes. We need to be careful to distinguish these ethnic patterns from characteristics associated with poverty.

Because so many African American families are poor, the incidence of poverty-based disability resulting from poor nutrition and poor prenatal care is disproportionately high in these families. Edelman (1985) has noted that almost one in two African American children is poor compared to a poverty rate for American children in general of one in five. Infant mortality and low birth weight, a leading cause of childhood disability, are twice as high for African Americans as whites. In addition, three out of five African American children under the age of 3 live in single-parent households. Jones and Wilderson (1976) have noted that African American children are seven times as likely as white children to be placed in special educable mentally retarded (EMR) classes in school, a consequence of labeling, racism, and SES. Moore (1981) notes that African American children constitute 45% of EMR enrollment nationally. Poverty also contributes to stress, and Korn et al. (1978) found, in one sample of children with physical disabilities, that African American families were more vulnerable to stress than whites.

Studies of poor African American families indicate that teenage pregnancies are common and women tend to start families at early ages (Franklin & Boyd-Franklin, 1985; D. A. Schulz, 1969). These young mothers are probably poorly prepared to care for a child with a disability. However, as Dodson (1981); Franklin and Boyd-Franklin (1985); Harrison, Serafica, and McAdoo (1984); and others have suggested, childrearing in African American families has historically been a communal process, with a high level of involvement by the extended family. Mutual-help patterns are usually strong. Staples (1976) suggests that the "attenuated extended family," consisting of a single adult and her children as well as additional relatives in the home, is a common family form. This family is likely to be surrounded by a large kin network, including fictive kin as well as blood relations. A system of informal adoption also exists (Hines & Boyd-Franklin, 1982).

As Jackson (1981) has noted, in poor, urban African American families the mother is usually the person responsible for providing care for a family member with a disability. The female role in general in such families is associated with respectability, dependability, family, and home. The oldest female sibling is also typically recruited to help care for younger children (D. A. Schulz, 1969).

Foley (1975) has made a number of recommendations for therapists working with disadvantaged African American families. He suggests first that the therapist needs to win the family's confidence by bringing about some immediate success, such as helping the family receive SSI payments, better housing, or a clinic appointment. The therapist also needs to be aware of communication styles, including a high percentage of incomplete messages, speaking in generalities rather than specifics, or relying on nonverbal messages rather than verbal ones. Foley also notes that these families tend to label behavior in negative ways and that the therapist must help them relabel family members so that they may interact with those members more constructively. Pinderhughes (1982) has also cautioned the therapist about not compounding the powerlessness of such families. These recommendations apply to professionals other than therapists as well.

A number of studies have looked at African American families of all socioeconomic levels and backgrounds, not merely the urban poor. Billingsley (1968) has shown that such a perspective reveals that not all African American families are disorganized and headed by females. In another study, Heiss (1981) found that no major difference exists between African American and white women on attitudes toward marriage and family. Similarly, Scanzoni (1985) found that SES is a more important determinant than race in shaping parental values. African American parents were found to have the same values as whites of the same social class. Thus an African American middle-class family might be just as devastated as a similar white family by the birth of a child with mental retardation, for example.

However, some characteristics seem to emerge as distinctive of an African American subculture regardless of social class. Boykin (1983) has argued that African Americans have a distinctive culture marked by spirituality, harmony, movement, verve, affect, communalism, expressive individualism, orality, and a social time perspective. The importance of the extended family and the church as social supports have also been reported at all socioeconomic levels.

The support of significant others has been shown to be extremely important for families with children with disabilities. Manns (1981) has noted that African Americans of all social levels have more significant others than whites. They tend to have large, extensive kin networks, which support overall survival and coping efforts. When asked to name a significant other, African Americans are more likely to name a relative. Sudarkasa (1981) suggests that the roots of the African American family system lie in the African principle of consanguinity, which emphasizes the extended family over the conjugal relationship.

In naming significant others who are not relatives, half of the respondents in Manns's (1981) study mentioned an African American minister. Other studies (Franklin & Boyd-Franklin, 1985; Hines & Boyd-Franklin, 1982) have also mentioned the importance of religion in African American family life at all social levels. Hines and Boyd-Franklin (1982) have written:

> In the Baptist church, a Black family finds a complete support system including the minister, deacons, deaconesses, and other church members. Numerous activities . . . provide a social life for the entire family, which extends far beyond the Sunday services and provides a network of people who are available to the family in times of trouble or loss. (p. 96)

The willingness of the religious community to provide emotional support and help in caring for a child with a disability can greatly ease the burden on a family.

The roles of African American parents and children have also been studied at various socioeconomic levels. D. F. Hobbs and Wimbish (1977) found that adjustment to parenthood is more difficult for African Americans than for white couples. The most typical marital role pattern in the African American family appears to be egalitarian (Hines & Boyd-Franklin, 1982; Staples, 1976). McAdoo (1981) has argued, however, that African American fathers tend to be more authoritarian than white fathers, particularly with respect to their daughters. Bartz and Levine (1978) and Durrett (reported in Williams & Williams, 1979) also found that these parents are authoritative with their children. Studies (Bartz & Levine, 1978; Young, 1970) also suggest that African American parents encourage earlier independence training in their children than other parents. African American parents who expect accelerated development and early assumption of responsibility by their children may be disappointed by a child with a disability whose development is considerably slower than the norm.

In one report on African American families (University of Pittsburgh Office of Child Development, 1991) Sharon Nelson-LeGall suggests differences in African American and white communication patterns. She notes that, compared to whites, African Americans may use more hand and body gestures, avoid eye contact, and wait short times before speaking, resulting in overlapping speech patterns. These differences, if misunderstood, could lead to difficulties in family–professional communication.

Finally, some studies have looked at African American "folk culture." Folk beliefs of African Americans and other ethnic groups are dying in urban American society. However, the professional may still encounter individuals who subscribe to such traditional beliefs and practices. Jackson (1981) has noted that some lower-class African Americans of rural origin still believe in root medicine and root doctors. Spector (1979) also notes the belief in some African American communities that certain individuals have healing powers. The use of alternative healers could create conflict with standard medical treatment of children with disabilities. Another folk belief cited by Spector is the notion that eating clay or starch protects a pregnant woman and her child. Such a belief could give rise to feelings of guilt in a mother who gave birth to a child with a disability after failing to take this precaution.

Latino Subculture

Latino Americans constitute the second-largest ethnic minority in the United States. Although the Census Bureau uses the term "Hispanic," many members of this population group prefer the term "Latino." Harry (1992a) suggests that, although intragroup diversity exists, Latino Americans share a common language (Spanish) and worldview based on Catholic ideology, familism, and values of personalism, respect, and status. She suggests, further, that a strong sense of family pride sometimes makes acceptance of a severe disability difficult in these groups. Mild disability, on the other hand, may not be recognized by the family. One study (Mary, 1990) found that, in comparison with African American and white mothers, Hispanic mothers were more resigned and less angry about having a child with mental retardation. Although similarities exist among various groups of Latino origin, Mexicans, Puerto Ricans, and other Latino Americans have separate identities and subcultures. In this section, we consider the disability-related aspects of the Mexican American (Chicano) and Puerto Rican subcultures, which are common among large population segments in some regions of the United States.

MEXICAN AMERICANS

Mexican Americans tend to be geographically concentrated, with 85% living in five southwestern states (Alvirez & Bean, 1976). Wendeborn (1982) has written of this population:

> Unlike the European immigrants to America who were cut off from their prior homelands by the vast Atlantic Ocean, the Hispanic patient of Mexican heritage still has access to Mexico. Many still have immediate families and other relatives in Mexico. This proximity to Mexico lends itself to retention of the Mexican culture—thus the Hispanic of Mexican heritage is in many ways a bicultural person. (p. 6)

As in the case of African American families, a significant proportion of Mexican Americans live in poverty. As a result, they are prone to a certain amount of labeling by professionals. According to Jones and Wilderson (1976), Mexican American children are 10 times as likely as Anglo children to be placed in EMR classes. Such placements are attributable in part to assessment techniques that discriminate against non-English-speaking children and those whose culture differs from that of the majority. The poor Mexican American family may also lack access to treatment facilities and consistent care for a child with a disability. Guerra (1980) notes that "the case of the chronically ill or handicapped child, who often is seen in many different facilities and receives support from many programs and agencies, represents a very serious deficit in the system" (p. 21). He also points to the difficult transition from the "space age" technology of a neonatal intensive care unit to the "two-room *casa*" in the *barrio*, or neighborhood, as a situation marked by inadequate outreach to the culturally different family.

In addition to high levels of poverty, Mexican culture is also marked by language and lifestyle differences from the mainstream. As a result, Mexican American parents may find interactions with professionals difficult and may be uncomfortable in institutional settings. Stein (1983) reports that Hispanic parents do not participate as actively in the development of their children's Individual Education Plans as do Anglo parents or parents in general. Both schools and medical settings tend to be intimidating to these parents. Azziz (1981) notes that, to Hispanics, hospitals are places where the sick go to die. Hospital visiting rules, which exclude some family members, are also foreign to them. In addition, the Spanish-speaking patient may have difficulty distinguishing among various hospital personnel and may pay more attention to a technician who speaks Spanish than to a physician who speaks only English. Romaine (1982) notes, too, that time has a different meaning in Mexican culture, and Mexican Americans may not keep appointments, creating scheduling problems for professionals. Quesada (1976) notes, further, that Mexican Americans are attuned to short-range therapy, from which they expect immediate results. Consequently, they may not comply with long-term treatment programs. Quesada also mentions the concept of *dignidad,* a kind of reticence, which may result in a paternalistic dependence that is misunderstood by professionals. Differences in acculturation are related to SES, and middle-class Mexican Americans are more likely to speak English and have familiarity with the mainstream culture.

The traditional Mexican family has been characterized as marked by values of familism, male dominance, subordination of young to old, and person orientation rather than goal orientation (Alvirez & Bean, 1976). Guinn (reported in Williams & Williams, 1979) notes a number of additional differences between Mexican American and Anglo values: Mexicans stress being, and Anglos stress doing; Anglos value material well-being more than Mexicans; Mexicans have a present-time orientation, and Anglos have a future orientation; Anglos value individual action, and Mexicans value group cooperation; Mexicans are fatalistic, whereas Anglos value mastery of the universe. All these values may cause Mexican American parents to be more accepting of a child's disability than Anglo parents.

The importance of the extended family in Mexican culture has been noted by many writers. Heller (reported in Williams & Williams, 1979) states that the web of kinship ties imposes obligations of mutual aid, respect, and affection. Falicov (1982) notes that the family protects the individual and that the extended family members may perform many parental functions. Cousins may be as close as siblings. In addition, *compadres,* or godparents, play an important role. Lieberman (1990) also mentions the *madrina,* who is selected by the parents to share responsibility for the child. In a study of the extended family as an emotional support system, Keefe, Padilla, and Carlos (1979) found that Mexican Americans consistently relied on relatives more than friends, regardless of geographical proximity. Children are more likely to have close relationships with siblings and cousins than with extrafamilial peers. Both Falicov and Karrer (1980), and Keefe and colleagues (1979) note that Mexican women have a strong tendency to confide in female relatives. The young Mexican mother is likely to rely on her mother for advice and support. The support network provided by the family can be very helpful to parents of children with disabilities.

The proximity of the extended family can also create problems for parents, however. Falicov and Karrer (1980) explain, for example, that the presence of the extended family puts pressure on members to compare themselves with their relatives. The mother of a child with a disability who is surrounded by sisters, sisters-in-law, and cousins whose children do not have disabilities may be upset by the constant reminder of her child's "differentness." Keefe and colleagues (1979) also note that their Mexican American respondents sometimes resented their relatives' intrusion into their personal affairs. Friends who react negatively to a child with a disability can be avoided by parents; avoidance of close family is more difficult.

Mexican American attitudes toward childrearing also sometimes differ from those of the cultural mainstream. Falicov (1982) and Falicov and Karrer (1980) note a relaxed attitude toward the achievement of developmental milestones and self-reliance, along with a basic acceptance of the child's individuality. Such an attitude would certainly be favorable for a child whose development proceeded much more slowly than the norm or who was not able to achieve independence from the family. Other childrearing values stress the goal of socializing children to be respectful and well mannered (Castaneda, 1976; Williams & Williams, 1979). Traditionally, children are also socialized to play gender-specific roles: Girls are trained for the home, and boys are taught to be strong and to dominate the family. A child with a disability that affected behavior could have difficulty fulfilling parental expectations for politeness and respectful conduct. Parents could also be disappointed by a male child whose disability prevented him from playing his traditionally defined role.

Like other ethnic groups, Mexican Americans, depending on their degree of identification with the traditional culture, have folk beliefs about the nature of disease and disability. Spector (1979) notes, for example, that Chicanos may regard illness as a punishment for wrongdoing. Such beliefs could result in guilt, and, in fact, Wendeborn (1982) has noted the presence of guilt feelings in Mexican parents of children with mental retardation and cerebral palsy.

A social worker in a birth defects evaluation center serving a large number of Mexican American families describes several illustrative cases (H. Montalvo, personal communication, 1982):

Case 1: A young native Mexican couple presented to our Birth Defects
Evaluation Center with their 1-month-old baby girl. She had the typical
clinical picture of Apert syndrome and the diagnosis was confirmed
during the initial clinic visit. Unknown to the clinic staff was the belief
that this condition was blamed on a lunar eclipse that had occurred
sometime during the pregnancy. . . . Guilt, either implied or direct, is
assumed by the mother because it is her obligation to screen herself,
and the fetus, by properly warding off the "harmful" rays of the eclipse.
Most women normally wear one or several keys on their abdomen during
this period. If this is not addressed, and in a manner so as not to impose
one's value on a particular couple, it can prolong the deep sense of guilt
of both father and mother. Especially the mother, who must then also
accept her assumed oversight by caring for the defective member.

Case 2: A young couple, legal residents of the United States, arrived at
our clinic with their 4-year-old son. He was diagnosed as having classical
Schwartz–Jampel (Pinto–DeSouza) syndrome. This very intelligent couple followed our counseling session well and understood the autosomal
recessive transmission and the subsequent one-in-four risk of recurrence
for each pregnancy. However, it was not until the mother was alone with
the social worker that she intimated she had a severe *susto* (fright) during
her pregnancy. She noted that her husband, an activist in their native
Mexico, had been jailed over several days with no word available on his
release. Mrs. G. was concerned and afraid for her husband's well-being
and she felt this fright and anxiety may have infiltrated the fetus and
caused a gene mutation. Interestingly then, an articulate woman who
capably followed our concise and detailed session on autosomal recessive
transmission nevertheless felt a *susto* could also contribute to such a birth
defect.

J. M. Schreiber and Homiak (1981) also note the belief that children are
susceptible to *susto,* even *in utero,* and Prattes (1973) also mentions the
use of a metal key around the abdomen to prevent cleft palate caused by
a lunar eclipse.

A number of folk beliefs concern illness in children. One folk belief
in the Mexican American community is *mal ojo,* or evil eye. As Prattes
(1973) explains, "the belief is that if a person, especially a woman,
admires someone else's child and looks at him without touching him,
the child may fall ill of the evil eye" (pp. 131–132). Another common
belief is that *caída de mollera* (sunken fontanel) is caused by a fall or the
abrupt removal of the nipple from an infant's mouth (Chesney,
Thompson, Guevara, Vela, & Schottstaedt, 1980; Martinez & Martin,
1966; Rubel, 1960).

A less common belief among Mexican Americans suggests that

hydrocephalus is caused by a precious rock inside a child's head (Prattes, 1973). Because the rock is believed to be valuable, parents may refuse to give permission for an autopsy if the child dies. They believe that physicians will sell the rock.

Another preventative measure common in this group is the use of mittens on a baby's hands in order to avoid cutting the child's fingernails (Prattes, 1973). Cutting the nails is believed to lead to blindness or nearsightedness (C. Hill, 1982; Prattes, 1973), and the mittens prevent the baby from scratching his or her face.

Those who believe in folk medicine may employ the services of a *curandero* (folk healer) in addition to, or instead of, those of a health care professional. The *curandero/curandera* derives his or her ability to cure from the supernatural (Spector, 1979). Because these healers maintain a close, warm, personalized relationship with the family, they may be preferred over the impersonal medical professional who works in a clinic or hospital setting. Keefe and colleagues (1979) found, however, that among urban Mexican Americans in one sample, the use of the *curandero* as a means of emotional support was negligible.

Physicians, however, may be even less likely than folk healers to become significant others for parents. J. M. Schreiber and Homiak (1981) note that any diagnosis or treatment is likely to be evaluated and accepted or rejected by the patient's family and that Mexican women usually prefer to go home and discuss any proposed treatment with their entire family. When the professional recommendations are not highly valued, the family may seek other consultations. Wendeborn (1982) notes that Hispanic families of children with cerebral palsy have difficulty accepting the fact that the condition cannot be healed completely and may consult with numerous practitioners at considerable expense before accepting the approach of any professional or facility.

Although many Mexican American families may behave in the ways suggested above when they have children with disabilities, many others exhibit attitudes and behavior that do not differ significantly from those of Anglo or other non-Mexican families. One study of poor Mexican mothers (Shapiro & Tittle, 1986) found, for example, that, like their Anglo counterparts, their subjects experienced difficulties in the areas of social support, child adjustment, perceived stress, and family functioning as a result of their children's disabilities.

PUERTO RICANS

Perhaps even more than other ethnic groups, the Puerto Rican community relies very heavily on the family as a source of strength and support. García-Preto (1982) has written:

> In times of stress Puerto Ricans turn to their families for help. Their cultural expectation is that when a family member is experiencing a crisis or has a problem, others in the family are obligated to help, especially those who are in stable positions. Because Puerto Ricans rely on the family and their extended network of personal relationships, they will make use of social services only as a last resort. (p. 164)

The structure of the Puerto Rican family also differs from the nuclear family model of the larger society. The basic family unit is commonly extended among Puerto Ricans and may consist of *compadres* (godparents) and *hijos de crianza* (children of upbringing) in addition to blood relatives (Mizio, 1974).

Although the extended family is the primary source of help and social support, members of the Puerto Rican community may also approach friends, neighbors, or a neighborhood spiritualist. Secondarily, they may approach professionals whom they know well. Ghali (1977) suggests that Puerto Ricans will not confide in anyone until *confianza*, or a familial-type of trusting relationship, is established. Professionals working with such families must, therefore, work toward establishing a personal bond with them.

Another frequently noted aspect of the Puerto Rican subculture is fatalism (see, e.g., Fitzpatrick, 1976; García-Preto, 1982; Ghali, 1977). Submissiveness and acceptance of fate are encouraged, in contrast with the American values of achievement and aggressiveness. As in the Mexican American subculture, such fatalism may help parents cope with a child's disabilities.

Harwood (1981) has also noted a stricter gender-based division of labor among traditionally oriented Puerto Ricans than among other groups. Woman are expected to care for children at home, and men are expected to demonstrate *machismo*. A woman who must work outside the home may thus experience some conflict as a result. These patterns are reminiscent of those found in other Latino groups. In many ways Puerto Ricans are similar to other Latino Americans, yet in other ways their subculture is unique. The professional who works with these families must be careful, therefore, when generalizing from one group to another.

Harry (1992c) has noted that the low-income Puerto Rican families in her study did not accept professional definitions of their children's disabilities because of different meanings they attached to terms like handicapped or retarded. One parent said, "They say the word 'handicap' means a lot of things. . . . But for us, Puerto Ricans, we still understand this word as 'crazy'" (p. 31). Similar reactions have also been noted among parents in other groups.

Asian American Subculture

Just as one should not necessarily generalize from one Latino group to another, one must be careful in assuming that all Asian subcultures are alike. However, similarities do exist. In this section, we look at two important Asian American groups: Japanese and Chinese.

Like other ethnic groups, Asian Americans value the family very highly. Any problems are likely to be solved within the family. Family problems are regarded as private, and bringing them to the attention of outsiders is considered shameful (Shon & Ja, 1982). Professionals might have a difficult time attempting to counsel such families. On the other hand, reticence in revealing coping difficulties does not necessarily mean that a family will not accept more "technical" medical or therapeutic services. For example, a Vietnamese family in the early intervention program directed by one of us (R. B. D.) was very receptive to physical therapy and other services offered to their daughter, who has cerebral palsy.

Harry (1992a) has written that the essence of Eastern cultures is collectivism and harmony, and that modesty is important. She notes that major disabilities are traditionally interpreted in one of four ways: (1) as retribution for sins of the parents or ancestors, (2) as possession by evil spirits, (3) as resulting from the mother's behavior during pregnancy, or (4) as an imbalance in physiological function. Such disorders are therefore seen as bringing shame to the family and may be met with fatalism or folk healing. She notes, too, that Asian parents are protective of young children and may be reluctant to seek help for them.

In the Japanese family, the *ie*, or household unit, is the most important frame of reference (Kitano & Kikumura, 1976). Although the family is residentially nuclear, close ties to relatives are maintained. Children are expected to be respectful and considerate toward their parents and to have a high degree of self-control. Obligation to the family is also important (Harrison et al., 1984).

Kitano and Kikumura (1976) note that the Japanese are taught to defer to those of higher status, and open confrontation is avoided. As a result, members of this group are unlikely to challenge the professional, even when they do not agree with a recommended course of treatment. Shon and Ja (1982) note, too, that communication tends to be indirect.

Among Chinese Americans as well, the family—not the individual—is the major unit of society. Huang (1976) notes that Chinese children usually grow up in the midst of adults and are not left with babysitters. Lee (1982) writes that the mother–son relationship is particularly close in this group, even after a son marries. The oldest son usually has more responsibilities than other children in the family.

Like the Japanese, Chinese parents may not show their feelings for fear of "losing face," making interaction with a counselor difficult. Other group values, however, may encourage acceptance of a child with a disability. For example, the Chinese tend to be fatalistic and to believe in collective responsibility among kin (Gould-Martin & Ngin, 1981; Lee, 1982). Although the past is more valued than the future, Chinese parents do have high educational aspirations for their children (Harrison et al., 1984; Huang, 1976). Acceptance of a child with retardation could be problematic within such a value orientation, and Yee (1988) has, in fact, noted that denial of a child's disability is common in Asian families. Family counseling, rather than individual counseling, may be especially appropriate for those Asian American families who have a need and desire for counseling.

Professionals working with Chinese families should also note that they may not adopt the "ideology of normalization" common among Western families of children with disabilities (Anderton, Elfert, & Lai, 1989). In the area of education, Chan (reported in Harry & Kalyanpur, 1994) suggests that the mandate that parents participate in their child's educational planning may be "both alien and threatening" to those with a traditional Asian background. As in the case of other ethnic groups, however, considerable intragroup variability is likely to be present among Asian American families, especially those with long exposure to mainstream American culture.

Native American Subculture

Because of much intertribal variation, Native Americans cannot be regarded as constituting a single subculture. In some ways, however, various tribes seem to be more like one another than like the cultural mainstream. Attneave (1982) and others have noted, for example, that the Native American tends to be stoic and to accept fate. Attneave (1982), Harrison and colleagues (1984), Pepper (1976), and Price (1976), among others, have listed the following differences in values between Native Americans and the American middle class:

Native American	*American middle class*
Cooperation	Competition
Harmony with nature	Control over nature
Adult centered	Child-centered
Present time orientation	Future time orientation
Expression through action	Verbal expression
Short childhood	Extended childhood
Education for knowledge	Education for grades

Because these families are more accepting of fate and less achievement oriented than others in society, they are likely to have less difficulty coping with a child with a disability. Attneave (1982) has written, "Since children are considered precious and are accepted for themselves, a handicapped child is usually given all the support needed to reach his or her own level of fulfillment" (p. 81). Locust (1988) has noted that among the Hopi some of the gods in fact have disabilities and that the Native American belief system stresses the strengths of individuals rather than their disabilities. Harry (1992a) has observed that most Native American languages do not have words for disability.

In addition, these families are likely to have help and support in rearing a child with a disability. Traditionally among Native Americans, the extended family shares in childrearing duties. Williams and Williams (1979) have also noted that Native American children tend to be loved by everyone in the family. Anderson (1988) has suggested that grandparents may be even more important than parents in childrearing among Native Americans.

Joe and Malach (1992) note that developmental milestones are perceived differently by some Native Americans. They cite the example of a family that did not know when their child sat or walked but knew exactly when the child first laughed. The day a child laughs or is named is regarded as a major milestone.

Professionals involved with these families should be aware of a tendency toward reticence. Interactions may be marked by long silences and little self-disclosure (Attneave, 1982). In addition, some Native American families still make use of traditional healers, such as medicine men and shamans. The professional who desires to win the trust of these families should not belittle the efforts of folk healers. Spector (1979) has also noted that Native Americans may be offended by direct questions or note taking by professionals.

Native Americans, like other ethnic groups, may hold folk beliefs about various childhood disabilities. Kunitz and Levy (1981) have written that, among the Navajo, a child's illness is believed to be caused by a taboo broken by the mother during pregnancy. Seizures are called "moth sickness," which is believed to result from a broken incest taboo.

Varying beliefs about cause can result in positive or negative labeling of disability. Seizures, for example, result in stigma among the Navajo. As Kunitz and Levy (1981) note, some congenital malformations, such as cleft palate, are negatively labeled by the Navajo, and others like extra fingers or toes or hip displacement, are not labeled at all. In fact, these deformities may be regarded as normal variants, and parents may not comply with professionally recommended treatments. More serious physical disabilities, blindness, and deafness may be ignored by the Navajo because of the economic burden of long-term treatment.

Other Ethnic Subcultures

African Americans, Latino Americans, Asian Americans, and Native Americans are all generally regarded as minority groups in American society. Harry (1992a) has noted that, in general, (lower-class) minority parents are likely to exhibit a pattern of "passivity" in relation to their children's special education programs. Similarly, Sontag and Schacht (1994) found that minority (Latino and Native American) parents reported less participation than European American parents in their children's early intervention programs. The special education system and other mainstream systems are typically not structured to recognize the strengths of families whose behavior differs from normative expectations.

Although ethnic variation is also present among the white majority, value differences from the cultural mainstream may not be as pronounced—especially among the third, fourth, and fifth generations. Some ethnic differences in reaction to disability have been noted by various writers, and these are mentioned here briefly.

ITALIAN AMERICANS

In a classic study, Zborowski (1952) found that Italian Americans react to pain in an emotional and exaggerated way. Although the tendency to stereotype should be avoided, Italian culture can generally be characterized as valuing emotional expression more than some other American subcultures. Consequently, the reaction of Italian American parents to the diagnosis of a child's disability may be a strong one.

In describing Italian culture, virtually all writers refer to the central place of the family. Although family ties are strong in many ethnic groups, they are especially strong among Italians. Femminella and Quadagno (1976) have noted that such ties continue to be important even among third-generation Italian Americans. Rotunno and McGoldrick (1982) have written, "For Italians, the family has been the thread that has provided not only continuity in all situations, but also the training to cope with a difficult world" (p. 340). Italian parents of children with disabilities are thus likely to have a strong family support system. In addition, as Rotunno and McGoldrick (1982) have noted, "Italians have learned to utilize environmental support effectively and to extract whatever good is possible from a seemingly hopeless situation" (p. 360).

In addition to being supportive, the Italian family is often large and generally includes godparents as well as true relatives. The identity of the individual is based on the family rather than on education or achievement (Rotunno & McGoldrick, 1982). Such an environment is likely to encourage acceptance of a child whose disability prevents personal success.

Among the folk beliefs held by Italians are superstitions attributing congenital abnormalities to unsatisfied desires for food during pregnancy. Another belief suggests that if a pregnant woman bends or turns her body in certain ways, abnormal fetal development may result (Ragucci, 1981). A third- or fourth-generation Italian American mother may not accept these beliefs; however, she may have difficulty coping with a grandmother or other relative who does accept them.

Because the family is the primary source of support, Italian Americans do not make much use of professional support services. Rotunno and McGoldrick (1982) suggest that Italians do not trust professionals. Ragucci (1981) notes that professionals who are *simpatico* (warm, congenial) may be trusted, but that those who are *superbo* (arrogant, unapproachable) are likely to be avoided by members of this group.

JEWISH AMERICANS

In the study mentioned in the previous section, Zborowski (1952) also found Jewish patients to react to pain in an exaggerated and emotional way. Like Italians, Jews are generally noted for being highly verbal and emotional in response to both adverse and joyous occasions. Verbal expressiveness is one of four values of Eastern European Jewish families noted by Herz and Rosen (1982). The other values are centrality of the family, suffering as a shared value, and intellectual achievement and financial success. Generosity is also highly valued.

In contrast with the Italian family, which encourages dependence in children, the Jewish family encourages children to be independent and achieve personal success. Herz and Rosen (1982) write, "Through the child's success, parents are validated; through their defects and wrong-doings parents are disgraced and ashamed" (p. 380). Farber, Mindel, and Lazerwitz (1976) note that Jewish children have an obligation to bring *nakhus,* or pride, to their parents.

The high value that Jewish parents place on achievement creates difficulties when a child has a disability. Children with mental retardation, in particular, pose a threat to the value placed on intellectual accomplishment. Saenger (reported in Zuk, 1962) found that, indeed, Jews are more likely to institutionalize their retarded children than members of other ethnic groups. Jewish values as they reflect on other disabilities may also differ from the American cultural norm. One study (Goodman, Dornbusch, Richardson, & Hastorf, 1963) found, for example, that general

American samples tend to regard deformity and disfigurement more negatively than functional (orthopedic) impairment, whereas Jewish samples regard functional impairment more negatively than facial or bodily aberrations.

In relationships with professionals, Jews tend to be favorably inclined toward reliance on experts, including psychotherapists and counselors of various kinds. However, Jews are also more likely than members of some other groups to question the credentials of professionals (Herz & Rosen, 1982).

RELIGIOUS VARIATION

A number of earlier studies looked at the effect of religion on parental acceptance of children with disabilities. Zuk (1959) found, for example, that Catholic mothers in one sample were more accepting of their children with retardation than Protestants and Jews. On the other hand, Leichman (reported in Zuk, 1962) found no difference in verbalized acceptance between Catholic and Protestant mothers. Zuk (1959) argues that Catholics are absolved from guilt by their religious beliefs and that Catholic doctrine insists that every child is a special gift from God. Yet in another study (Boles, 1959), Catholic mothers of children with cerebral palsy were found to have *more* feelings of guilt than Protestants and Jews.

The relationship between any particular religion and acceptance is thus not clear. Parents who regard themselves as more intense in their religious practices—regardless of their religion—may be more accepting, however. Zuk, Miller, Bartram, and Kling (1961) found that mothers rating themselves as intensely religious were slightly more likely to verbalize attitudes judged to be more accepting of their children with retardation. This correlation may be a spurious one, though. Parents who are more religious are probably more deeply immersed in a religion-based support network, and social support, rather than religion by itself, may be the important variable in determining parental acceptance or coping ability. Although religion has not been the focus of most recent research, additional studies are needed to clarify the relationship between religion and attitudes toward childhood disability.

REGIONAL VARIATION

Virtually no research has been done on variations in family reactions to children with disabilities according to residential background, whether urban or rural, northern, southern, eastern, or western. As mass culture becomes more widespread, these differences probably become quite minimal; however, no documentation of this trend exists with respect to such families.

One study (Dunst et al., 1988) compared Appalachian and non-Appalachian families with children with disabilities and found that, contrary to expectation, non-Appalachian families find their social support systems to be more helpful in caring for their child than Appalachian families. The authors found that SES "rather than 'Appalachianness' accounts for differences in informal social support networks." Although they had less social support, the Appalachian families were able to use the support they had quite effectively. In conclusion, the authors note that social support rather then region is the most important variable in reducing the stress associated with rearing a child with a disability. Heller et al. (1981) also note differences in family support between urban and rural families.

IMPLICATIONS FOR PROFESSIONALS

Professionals who work with families of children with disabilities should be aware of subcultural differences. However, the professional must be careful not to stereotype families on the basis of social class or ethnic, religious, or regional identification. Within most subcultures, a considerable amount of intragroup variation exists. Professionals should not assume that individual members of a group will share all of the values and beliefs commonly held by the group as a whole. In a study of lower-class African American mothers' aspirations for their children, for example, Bell (1965) found aspirations varied *within* a group that was homogeneous in both social class and race.

Intragroup variation was also found in a study of lower-class Anglo, African American, and Chicano couples (Cromwell & Cromwell, 1978). No ethnic differences were found among the groups in styles of conflict resolution. Stereotypical characterizations of African American matriarchy and Chicano patriarchy were thus not supported. The authors conclude that "categorical labeling of family structure based on ethnic group membership is unwarranted and inappropriate" (p. 757). The value of subcultural studies, then, is in making professionals more aware of *possible* characteristics they may encounter.

The need for a better understanding of subcultural differences is demonstrated by a number of studies that reveal misunderstandings between professionals and clients of a different cultural background. One study of therapists and their Spanish-speaking patients (Kline, Acosta, Austin, & Johnson, 1980) found that the therapists did not accurately perceive the patients' wants and feelings and instead projected their own wishes onto the patients. Such misperceptions may persist even when interpreters are used. Marcos (1979) found, for example, that clinicians evaluating non-English-speaking patients through an interpreter were faced with "consistent, clinically relevant, interpreter-related distortions, which may give rise to important misconceptions about the patient's mental status" (p. 173).

Studies with Mexican American groups (Delgado-Gaitan; Ada, reported in Harry, 1992a) have shown that passivity can be overcome by professional techniques that are inclusive rather than exclusive. The parents in these studies were empowered by the realization that their social (nonacademic) skills were valuable. Thus, the process of encouraging families to share their concerns may require special techniques. A number of recommendations emerge to guide professionals who work with culturally diverse families:

1. *If at all possible, the professional should speak the family's native language.* As Laosa (1974) has suggested, abandonment of one's native language may imply abandonment of one's entire culture. Also, as indicated earlier, much misunderstanding occurs when professionals and families do not speak the same language, even when an interpreter is used. Hanson (1981) has also noted the importance of providing written materials in the family's native language. Fracasso (1994) suggests the technique of "back translation," whereby materials that have been translated be translated back to English by an independent translator, to assure that meanings have not been changed. Harry (1992a) suggests that when interpreters must be used, they should always be bicultural as well as bilingual to avoid misunderstandings caused by nuances of meaning. Lynch (1992) provides some excellent guidelines for working with interpreters, and we suggest that the reader consult her work prior to using an interpreter.

2. *Indigenous professionals, paraprofessionals, and consultants should be used as much as possible.* Although professionals can learn about the language and culture of the families they serve, they can never acquire the cultural worldview to the same extent as one raised in the culture. Families also feel more comfortable interacting with their peers. Quesada (1976) thus recommends the use of community representatives as teachers and consultants or the employment of local community representatives at the paraprofessional level.

3. As Marion (1980) and others have suggested, *professionals must meet the needs of culturally diverse parents for information, belonging, and self-esteem.* These parents are often excluded from advocacy organizations and support groups and feel isolated as a result. They may come from powerless segments of society and have little knowledge of their rights to educational and other services for their children. Professionals must be

supportive of these families' cultural values and work toward integrating them into support and service networks located in the cultural mainstream. Harry (1992a) has suggested that information could be disseminated through traditional community supports such as churches or through community leaders.

4. *Scheduling should be flexible.* Families in the early intervention program formerly directed by one of us (R. B. D.) must often travel to the closest large medical center for consultation and treatment. Some of the clinics there schedule only early morning appointments. Because they have no other means of transportation, lower-SES families often must rely on a bus to travel to these clinics, and the earliest bus of the day does not arrive until afternoon. As a result, at least one family has had to spend the night at the bus station. Others simply avoid making the trip. Quesada (1976) notes, too, that people working on an hourly basis may not be able to afford to spend entire days at a clinic. He recommends a system of routine call-backs in order to reschedule missed appointments. In addition, as Harry (1992a) suggests, providing access to supports such as transportation or child care may be necessary in assuring the participation of some families in treatment programs.

5. *Attempts must be made to elicit the family's definition of the situation.* Although important for all professional–family interactions, this guideline is especially important in the case of culturally diverse families. Montalvo (1974) has presented a number of cases of Puerto Rican children who had difficulties in school because well-intentioned school personnel failed to take into account the meanings attached by the family to a child's language or style of dress. Similarly, Anderson (1988) notes that an early intervention program could not be established in a Native American community until the support of the elders was obtained. Similarly, Harry, Allen, and McLaughlin (1995) report that African American parents withdrew their support when their children's preschool program labeled their children in ways they perceived as inappropriately negative.

In general, the professional must take what Mercer (1965) calls a *social system* (rather than a clinical) *perspective* when working with culturally diverse populations. To the greatest extent possible, the professional must assume the family's point of view. Helping cannot occur without understanding. Before the professional can begin to meet the needs of families of children with disabilities, he or she must determine how those needs are defined by the family itself within the context of the subcultural world that shapes its daily round of life.

Professionals can take certain steps to better educate themselves about the subcultures of the families they serve (Harry, 1992b). Harry, Otrguson, Katkavich, and Guerrero (1993) describe, for example, a teacher training program that requires students to spend time with a culturally different family, including interviewing the parents and participating in a community-based activity.

Lynch (1992) suggests five areas that should be addressed in training early interventionists to work with culturally diverse families. These areas are relevant to other helping professionals as well:

a. Self-awareness: The professional should first be able to articulate the relevant norms, values, and beliefs of his or her *own* culture.
b. Awareness of other cultures in general.
c. Awareness of other cultures' views of children and childrearing, disability, family roles and structures, healing practices, and intervention by professionals.
d. Cross-cultural communication, including verbal and nonverbal messages such as eye contact, proximity and touching, gestures, and listening skills.
e. Acknowledgment of cultural differences.

Wayman, Lynch, and Hanson (1991) suggest a series of questions for home visitors in early intervention to ask themselves as an aid in understanding a family's values and lifestyle. The questions address areas such as sleeping patterns, mealtime rituals, and other aspects of life that might be relevant to a family's participation in a program. Eliades and Suitor (1994) also suggest some differences in relation to eating that might have relevance for professional–family interaction.

6. As stated earlier and as Harry (1992a) notes, *professionals must recognize that issues of survival may have to be given precedence over intervention concerns* and be willing to assist families in obtaining material resources. Families with major needs for food, clothing, shelter, or health care will not have the time or energy for, or interest in, discussing their concerns in relation to their child's disability.

7. When possible, *professionals must adapt their communication style to the expectations of the family.* Kavanagh and Kennedy (1992) suggest numerous strategies for communicating with culturally diverse families. Some examples follow:

• Do not discredit folk theories or remedies unless you *know* they are harmful.
• Establish a personalized relationship by means of disclosing selected, culturally appropriate personal information.
• If appropriate, acknowledge unfamiliarity with the family's culture.
• Ask direct questions only if appropriate to the family's cultural and

linguistic expectations. (Direct questioning should be avoided with some Asian, Latino, or Native American families.)

- Adjust the tone of your voice and your body position to synchronize with those of family members.
- Include extended family members or others in an interview if they are normally part of the family's support system.
- Be willing to tolerate periods of silence.

The authors recommend role playing and other exercises to practice these techniques before they are needed in a professional interaction situation.

For professionals who routinely work with culturally diverse families, this overview of principles and techniques should be supplemented with further reading in some of the sources noted above. In addition, the professional may want to consult one or more of the following:

Brislin, R. W., & Yoshida, T. (1993). *Improving intercultural communications: Modules for cross-cultural training programs.* Thousand Oaks, CA: Sage.

Brislin, R. W., & Yoshida, T. (1994). *Intercultural communication training: An introduction.* Thousand Oaks, CA: Sage.

Canino, I. A., & Spurlock, J. (1994). *Culturally diverse children and adolescents: Assessment, diagnosis, and treatment.* New York: Guilford Press.

Chang, H. N. L. (Ed.). (1993). *Affirming children's roots: Cultural and linguistic diversity in early care and education.* San Francisco: California Tomorrow (Fort Mason Center, Building B, San Francisco, CA 94123).

McGoldrick, M. (1993). Ethnicity, cultural diversity, and normality. In F. Walsh (Ed.), *Normal family processes* (2nd ed., pp. 331–360). New York: Guilford Press.

Professional–Family Interaction: Working toward Partnership

Ask any five parents of visually impaired children how they first learned their child had vision problems and you will get five different horror stories. . . . We parents try to be grateful that professionals pay any attention to the imperfect children we have produced, but we cannot avoid feelings of betrayal and anger when we are the recipients of misinformation or of the kind of callous treatment that ignores parental expertise.

—STOTLAND (1984, p. 69)

When I placed Matthew into a strange woman's arms on his first day in the infant program, I didn't know what she hoped to accomplish with my 4-week-old baby. . . . As the weeks and months passed, I sensed my baby's growing attachment to his teacher and his response to her obvious delight whenever he accomplished a new feat. I, too, unconsciously formed my attachment to her. . . . Professionals who work with families in the early months of the child's life can have a profound influence on parents. A mother may hear the first hopeful words about her child from the teacher or therapist. And those words and assurances can become the basis of strong attachments, acknowledged or unrealized, between parents and program staff.

—MOELLER (1986, pp. 151–152)

PROFESSIONALS CAN evoke strong feelings, both positive and negative, in their interactions with parents. During the early months of the child's life especially, both parents and professionals are highly vulnerable: The professional is charged with conveying the "bad news" of a child's disability to parents but is also in a position to offer badly needed information, hope, and support. The parent, on the other hand, is the recipient of the news about the child and looks to the professional as an expert who can provide answers to the many questions raised by the diagnosis. The reactions of professionals during these early months can form the basis for parents' future trust.

In this chapter, we explore the views that professionals and parents have of each other and examine some of the sources of those views. We also look at the parent–professional encounter from a sociological perspective, as an interaction situation. Finally, we discuss the need for a parent–professional partnership and explore some of the new roles available to both parents and professionals in their quest for improved services for children and families. Most of the literature in this area deals with physicians and educators; however, our discussion may apply equally well to counselors, social workers, psychologists, and other professionals.

PROFESSIONALS AND PARENTS: HOW DO THEY VIEW EACH OTHER?

Parents' Predispositions toward Professionals

Long before they become the parents of children with disabilities, individuals have various beliefs about and attitudes toward professionals. They have interacted with physicians, nurses, teachers, and possibly therapists, counselors, or social workers in different contexts; they have also been exposed to media images of these professionals. As a result, when their children are born, they have expectations about professional behavior that may or may not be fulfilled by the actual professionals with whom they come into contact. As one mother wrote, "The last thing I wanted was a home visitor. . . . I thought Public Health Nurses were for people who beat their kids and drink too much" (Judge, 1987, p. 20).

PROFESSIONAL DOMINANCE

The most common image associated with physicians and other professionals in our society has been one of *professional dominance* (Freidson, 1970). By virtue of their education and high status in the community, professionals, especially physicians, have been expected to play a dominant role in their interactions with clients or patients. Dominance generally includes elements of paternalism and control: The professional determines "what is best" for the client and provides only as much information to the client as is necessary for the clinical management of the case. Parents who have been exposed to this image may view physicians and other professionals with respect, even awe, and submit to their recommendations without question. As we will show later, such submission is becoming less common in society today. In addition, as the last chapter has shown, subcultural values and beliefs play an important role in shaping parents' views of and behavior toward professionals.

Studies (Barsch; Shapiro; both reported in Seligman, 1979) indicate that parents may be more positively predisposed toward teachers than toward other professionals. On the other hand, as Seligman has noted, parents' perceptions of teachers may be colored by negative experiences *they* had in school. In addition, teachers spend many hours with their pupils and may be regarded as being in competition with parents for their children's time, attention, respect, or affection. Lortie (reported in Seligman, 1979) has also suggested that parents may resent a teacher's control over their children when the teacher's values are different from those of the parent.

A number of studies have indicated that professional dominance in general may be declining somewhat in today's society as part of a trend toward greater consumer control in the marketplace. Gallup and Harris polls (reported in Betz & O'Connell, 1983) indicate that the public's confidence in and respect for physicians has declined markedly since 1950. In 1966, 72% of the public expressed confidence in doctors, but only 43% expressed such confidence in 1975. Betz and O'Connell suggest that the sense of trust is diminished as the physician–patient relationship becomes more specialized, impersonal, and shortlived as a result of population mobility, professionalization, and bureaucratization. Haug and Lavin (1983) suggest further that "in the dialectic of power relations, the increasing monopolization of medical knowledge and medical practice could only call forth a countervailing force in the form of patient consumerism" (p. 16).

Prior to their child's birth, then, parents are likely to have been exposed to both professional dominance and consumerism. Shortly after the birth and initial diagnosis, they are likely to defer to the expertise of the professional. As indicated in Chapter 2, parents are typically in a state of anomie when they first realize that their child has a problem. Because they are ill prepared for the birth of a child with a disability, they are likely to rely heavily on the advice of the professionals they encounter at that time. Later, especially in cases in which professionals are not able to provide appropriate information and guidance, parents' awareness of consumerism may lead them to challenge professional authority. Such changes in attitude and behavior toward professionals are discussed later in this chapter.

THE PROFESSIONAL ROLE AS AN IDEAL TYPE

Professional dominance is one of several images of professionals common in society today. Parsons (1951) classically described the role of the professional as being characterized by the traits of achievement, universalism, functional specificity, and affective neutrality. Although real professionals only approximate these traits to greater or lesser degrees, the public image of the ideal–typical professional may be a composite of all of them.

The professional role is achieved rather than ascribed, that is, to become a professional, one must successfully complete a program of education and training. Professionals who work with families of children with disabilities have *chosen* that specialty. Unlike the parent who has given birth to a child with a disability, the professional works in this field because of interest, altruism, monetary or other reward, or convenience. Parents may resent the professional, who deals with their problems only during working hours, while they deal with them 24 hours a day.

The professional role is also universalistic, that is, the professional is expected to be fair. Ideally, all children will receive treatment of the same quality. In reality, though, many parents discover that their children with disabilities are *not* treated like their nondisabled children. These parental reports are illustrative:

> [Our pediatrician] seemed to feel that Brian was an unnecessary burden. . . . He didn't take my complaints seriously. . . . I feel that Brian's sore throat is just as important as [my nondisabled daughter's] sore throat.

> She has a problem with her knee, and we took her to_____Children's Hospital. . . . They said, "There's nothing we can do with one of *these* children." (Parent of child with Down syndrome)

> Our pediatrician. . . . says, "She's retarded, and there's nothing you can do about it. You're wasting your time going to specialists." He blames all of her [medical] problems on retardation instead of treating them. (Darling, 1979, pp. 151–152)

Such experiences may eventually result in parental challenges to professional authority. As we will show later in the chapter, newer training programs for physicians and other professionals are resulting in fewer such experiences today than in the past.

The professional role is also functionally specific and continues to become increasingly more specialized. Parents expect teachers to be experts in the field of education but do not expect them to be experts in the field of medicine as well. Teachers, physicians, therapists, and other professionals who work with children and families all have their own areas of expertise. Parents, however, are not always aware of the distinctions among disciplines and may not be sure whether a question about feeding skills, for example, would be more appropriately asked of a pediatrician, speech therapist, occupational therapist, or teacher.

Parents are also interested in the whole child. They see their children playing many roles—child, grandchild, playmate, pupil—as well as "child with a disability." Most parents appreciate physicians who take the time to inquire about how their child is doing in school or teachers who show an interest in their child's medical problems. Likewise, they may come to resent professionals who do not show an interest in the whole child. As one father remarked, "The pediatrician . . . would keep him alive but he wasn't interested in Brian as a *person*" (Darling, 1979, p. 152).

Finally, professionals are expected to be affectively neutral and not become emotionally involved with their clients. Again, the professional role is the antithesis of the parental role in this regard, and regardless of ideal–typical role expectations, many parents appreciate professionals who do become attached to their children. Matthew's mother, quoted at the beginning of the chapter, described a strong bond between her infant program teacher, her child, and herself. Because of the frequency and intensity of contact, parents are more likely to develop such a bond with teachers and therapists in a home-based program than with physicians seen only during brief clinic or office visits.

THE NEED TO BE AWARE OF PARENTAL EXPECTATIONS

Professionals who work with families, then, should be aware that parents have preconceived notions about the nature of the professional role. The degree to which professionals are able to meet parents' expectations may determine the nature of the relationship they will have with a family. Parents' expectations are shaped both by the views of the larger society and, as the last chapter has shown, by their subculture as well. Attitudes toward professionals differ among the various social classes, and parents may react differently to professionals who are of different ethnic groups. An awareness of these differing parental perceptions and expectations can help professionals improve the services they provide to families.

Professionals' Predispositions toward Children with Disabilities and Their Families

STIGMATIZING ATTITUDES

Families with children who have disabilities come into contact with a variety of professionals. Some of these professionals, such as pediatric physical therapists, have chosen their specialty because they want to work with this population. Other professionals, such as pediatricians or teachers in regular classrooms, may not enjoy working with children with disabilities at all. As one pediatrician said:

> I don't enjoy it. . . . I don't really enjoy a really handicapped child who comes in drooling, can't walk, and so forth. . . . Medicine is geared to the perfect human body. Something you can't do anything about challenges the doctor and reminds him of his own inabilities. (Darling, 1979, p. 215)

Like others in society, these professionals have been exposed to stigmatizing attitudes toward individuals with disabilities. Most have not had any direct experience with such individuals either in their training or in their personal lives. As a result, they may not be able to understand the positive aspects of relationships between parents and children with disabilities. They may also feel inadequate in their ability to work with such families. These concerns are evident in this pediatrician's comments:

> There are personal hang-ups. You go home and see three beautiful, perfect children; then you see this "dud." You can relate more easily to those with three beautiful perfect kids. . . . If somebody comes in with a cerebral palsy or a Down's, I'm not comfortable. . . . My inadequacy to the task bothers me. . . .
> I liked problems as a resident but I can't say that I enjoy sick kids anymore. It's hard to find much happiness in this area. The subject of deformed children is depressing. . . . As far as having a Mongoloid child, I can't come up with anything good it does. There's nothing fun or pleasant. It's somebody's tragedy. I can find good things in practically anything—even dying—but birth defects are roaring tragedies. (Darling, 1979, pp. 214–215)

With newer training programs, such attitudes may be less common today than in the past, especially among recently trained physicians.

Professionals may have more negative views of families than families have of themselves. One study (Blackard & Barsh, 1982) found significant differences between parents' and professionals' responses to a questionnaire about the impact of the child on the family. As compared with parents' responses, the professionals tended to overestimate the negative impact of the child on family relationships. The professionals overestimated the extent to which parents reported community rejection and lack of support and underestimated parents' ability to use appropriate teaching and behavior management techniques. A study by Sloper and Turner (1991) also showed how professionals overestimate the negative impact of a child with a disability on the family.

Rousso (1985) has suggested that when professionals without disabilities have difficulty identifying with clients with disabilities, their attitudes
do not help to promote their clients' self-esteem:

> When, as professionals, we find ourselves feeling too tragic, too
> despairing about our disabled patients' lives . . . we need to look at our
> own attitudes and our own history regarding disability. We may be
> imagining how our lives would be if we were suddenly disabled. . . .
> But keep in mind that congenitally disabled people are not newly
> disabled. . . .
>   Being disabled and being intact at the same time is an extremely
> difficult notion for nondisabled people to make sense of. I keep thinking
> of my mother's words: "Why wouldn't you want to walk straight?" Even
> now, it is hard to explain that I may have wanted to walk straight, but I
> did not want to lose my sense of self in the process. . . . Fostering
> self-esteem in our congenitally disabled children and clients means
> helping them reconnect and reclaim these scattered pieces of their
> identities and once again feel whole, as they deserve. (p. 12)

In some cases, professionals have recommended institutionalization
of children with disabilities, more because of *their* negative views of these
children than because of parents' inability to cope (MacKeith, 1973).
These professionals may project their negative views onto parents without
knowing with certainty how the parents perceive their situation.

In the well-publicized "Baby Doe" cases, physicians' negative attitudes
may have contributed to their recommending against treatment in some
cases (United States Commission on Civil Rights, 1986). When such
decisions are made shortly after a child's birth, most parents, like most
physicians, have been exposed only to society's stigmatizing attitudes
toward people with disabilities. They have not had any of the positive
experiences reported by families who have lived with disability for any
length of time. In addition, parents are vulnerable in the immediate
postpartum period and likely to accept the advice of an authority figure
or expert. A physician's recommendation, then, about whether or not an
infant with a disability should receive life-saving treatment may strongly
influence the parents' decision. Consequently, physicians and other professionals who may be involved in these situations have an obligation to
be as fully informed as possible about the consequences—*both positive and
negative*—of such decisions for families.

Apart from a child's disability, professionals may have negative
attitudes toward parents because of their ethnicity, race, gender, or social
class. Like others in society, professionals may have stereotypical views of
various minority groups and have difficulty relating to families from those
groups. Some strategies for assisting professionals in relating to those who
are "different" are suggested in Chapter 7.

The nature of a child's disability may also affect the attitudes of professionals toward the family. Some professionals may have more negative views of mental retardation than of physical disability, for example. Certain disabilities appear to be more stigmatizing than others. Wasow and Wikler (1983) found, for example, that professionals tended to react more positively toward parents of children with mental retardation than toward parents of children with mental illness. Whereas parents of children with retardation were viewed as part of the treatment team, parents of children with mental illness were seen as part of the problem, even though chronic mental illness is recognized to be largely organic in etiology. With respect to mental illness, such views may be changing thanks to newer "CASSP" models (Cohen & Lavach, 1995). The attitudes of professionals noted by Wasow and Wikler are an example of victim blaming, which is discussed further in the next section.

THE CLINICAL PERSPECTIVE: BLAMING THE VICTIM

In addition to their exposure to stigmatizing attitudes in everyday life, professionals, especially those out of school for more than 10 years, may in fact have been *trained* to have negative views of individuals with disabilities and their families as part of their professional education. As Seligman and Seligman (1980) have noted, much of the early professional literature in this field characterized both children with disabilities and their parents as deficient.

Some social workers, psychologists, and other professionals have been trained in a psychoanalytic perspective, which locates the source of human problems within the psyche of the client (or the client's parents) rather than in the structure of the social system. When seen from this perspective, parents' concerns about their children are interpreted as indications of parental pathology. In much of the literature, this pathology is traced to parental guilt over having given birth to an "imperfect" child (see, e.g., Forrer, 1959; J. D. Powell, 1975; Zuk, 1959). When such an interpretive framework is used, expressions of parental love may be defined as "idealization" and treating a child as normal may be seen as "denial." Regardless of whether parents apparently accept or reject their children, their actions are believed in either case to be based on guilt.

Within this perspective, when parents are unable to cope, their failure is blamed on a supposed neurotic inability to accept the child. Real, systems-based needs for financial aid, help with child care, or medical or educational services tend to be discounted and attributed to parental inadequacy rather than to a lack of societal resources. Although some parents certainly do have neurotic tendencies, the victim-blaming model is inadequate to explain the many problems faced by parents of children with disabilities. Because society is structured largely to meet the needs of people without disabilities, goods and services for those with disabilities are often difficult, if not impossible, to find. Many older textbooks stressed guilt-based theories of parental behavior, and as a result, professionals often completed their education with the belief that parents of children with disabilities are responsible for their own problems.

Gliedman and Roth (1980) argue that the nature of the parent–professional encounter encourages the professional to see the parent, in addition to the child, as the patient. They suggest that parents are expected to play the classic "sick role," that is, to be passive, cooperative, and in agreement with the decisions of the "experts." When parents disagree, they are sometimes treated like recalcitrant children, and efforts are made to convert them to the "correct" position. Victim blaming and professional dominance can combine to render the parent powerless. "As for the parent . . . he finds himself in a double bind: either submit to professional dominance (and be operationally defined as a patient) or stand up for one's rights and risk being labeled emotionally maladjusted (and therefore patientlike)" (Gliedman & Roth, 1980, p. 150). Such views are sometimes perpetuated when young professionals learn them from their older colleagues.

As a result of their training and experience, then, professionals may come to adopt a *clinical* perspective. Mercer (1965) suggests that this perspective has the following components:

- The development of a diagnostic nomenclature.
- The creation of diagnostic instruments.
- The professionalization of the diagnostic function.
- [The] assumption that the official definition is somehow the "right" definition. If persons in other social systems, especially the family, do not concur with official findings, . . . the clinical perspective assumes that they are either unenlightened or are evidencing psychological denial.
- Finally, . . . social action tends to center upon changing the individual. . . . Seldom considered [is] the alternative . . . of . . . modifying the norms of the social system or of attempting to locate the individual in the structure of social systems which will not perceive his behavior as pathological. (pp. 18–20)

Mercer suggests an alternative *social system perspective,* which "attempts to see the definition of an individual's behavior as a function of the values of the social system within which he is being evaluated" (p. 20).

The clinical perspective has persisted in services to families of children with disabilities for a number of reasons, including professional socialization, transdisciplinary understanding, rewards for the clinician, ease of intervention, and the maintenance of professional dominance. Each of these will be considered in turn.

Professional Socialization. As indicated earlier, the clinical perspective has been a part of professional training in schools of medicine, education, and social work, as well as in courses in psychology and other related fields. Courses in sociology or a social system perspective have not always been included in curricula used in training professionals in these fields, although such curricula have been changing in recent years to include such courses.

Transdisciplinary Understanding. Most intervention programs in medical and educational settings employ a team of professionals. A variety of individuals, including a pediatrician, speech therapist, physical therapist, occupational therapist, and social worker, for example, may work together to provide services to each child and family. All of these professionals may have tended to share the clinical perspective as a result of their training and have consequently been able to communicate with one another fairly easily. Although the instruments of each specialty have varied, they have all used some sort of assessment tool to measure the child's or family's dysfunction and then developed a course of remediation involving changing the child or family to meet professionally defined goals. Recently, team members have been trained in a systems-oriented perspective in a variety of disciplines (Darling & Baxter, 1996; Darling & Peter, 1994); Intervention strategies are changing as a result.

Rewards for the Clinician. The clinical perspective tends to quantify its concepts. Children can be placed at a specific point along a developmental scale; even family coping skills can be quantified. As a result, progress in a treatment program can be readily measured. When a child or family makes measurable progress, the professional feels rewarded. Social system variables (the availability of financial resources, for example) are not as easy to control, and methods for their measurement are not widely taught in professional schools.

Ease of Intervention. A consideration of all of the systems within which a family interacts complicates the intervention process. Treating the family in isolation is easier for the clinician and allows for more variables to be controlled. The system of categorical labels associated with the clinical perspective also facilitates intervention. Once a family is labeled, a known treatment method can be applied.

Maintenance of Professional Dominance. If they recognized the family's perspective as valid, professionals would have to yield some of their dominance. Many clinicians believe that their dominant status is justified because of their education and clinical experience (Goodman, 1994).

In some cases, professionals may actually fear parents because of the threat they pose to the professionals' dominance. Lortie (reported in Seligman, 1979) notes that teachers, in particular, experience a sense of vulnerability because of parents' rights in the educational realm. Other professionals, such as physicians (the increase of malpractice suits not withstanding), may feel more secure, but those in private practice must always be sensitive to the need to please the client.

LIMITATIONS OF THE CLINICAL PERSPECTIVE

The clinical perspective is limited in its value as a holistic approach to the treatment of children and their families. By extracting the child and family from their situational context and evaluating them using professionally constructed instruments, the clinician may be attaching meanings to their situation that are different from those attached to it by the family members themselves. When clinicians place children and families in diagnostic categories, they lose some of the uniqueness of any particular family. When the child and family are the primary focus of attention, social system-created problems, whose causes are external to the family system, may be overlooked.

The interaction between parents and children, and professionals is only one of many interaction situations encountered by families. While their child is in a treatment program, parents continue to interact with relatives, friends, strangers, and other professionals. In some cases, the demands of a program may even conflict with the family's pursuit of a normalized lifestyle in other areas. The professional in such a program cannot understand a family's failure to cooperate without an understanding of that family's competing needs. The following quote from the mother of four teenagers with disabilities illustrates the gap that sometimes exists between parent and professional:

> I'm seeing [a new psychologist] now. He's kind of giving me the blame for the way I am: "It's your fault you feel the way you do about things." I don't *want* to feel this way. . . . He says, "You create your own problems." My problem is that I have four handicapped children, and that has nothing to do with the fact that I had an unhappy childhood. . . . I'm nervous because I have reason to be nervous. . . . That very night we were supposed to go someplace, and the van at the CP Center broke down, so suddenly we had four kids to worry about. . . . We had to change our plans. . . . That's the problem with these professionals. . . . They have a job. . . . They don't live with the parents 24 hours a day. What sounds nice at the office just doesn't work in real life. (Darling, 1979, pp. 179–180)

Parents' priorities may be different from those of professionals, and, as a result, professionals often have little success when they try to intervene in these cases. As one professional who became a parent remarked, "Before I had Peter I gave out [physical therapy] programs that would have taken all day. I don't know when I expected mothers to change diapers, sort laundry, or buy groceries" (Featherstone, 1980, p. 57).

The following anecdote was related by the parent of a child with a disability:

> One parent . . . told me of her initial clinic visit where the social worker assured her that guilt in a parent was natural and that she shouldn't feel bad about it. . . . Stunned, she allowed the social worker to go on at some length before informing her that the child, in fact, was adopted. (Pieper, in Darling & Darling, 1982, p. viii)

Although this anecdote is extreme, professionals can overlook important individual and contextual differences by making parents and children fit into clinical categories. Each family's situation is unique and derives from that family's particular place in society. A preconceived diagnostic nomen-clature tends to prevent the clinician from seeing the client in a new or creative way.

When families are seen outside of their situational context in a school, clinic, or treatment center, the cause of their problems is more likely to be sought within the family itself. When the family's situation is not completely understood, parents' neurotic symptoms may be attributed to their inability to cope with the child rather than to some external cause. As earlier chapters have shown, however, such symptoms are as likely to result from lack of social support or community resources as from the child's disability. Parents are expected to *accept* and *adjust* to their situation, and the professional role is perceived as one of helping parents cope. This view assumes that the situation of most families cannot or should not be changed.

In fact, sometimes the situation *can* be changed. The child can be placed in a more appropriate program; respite care can be provided; financial aid may be available. (See Chapter 10 for additional systems-based interventions.) Parenting a child with a disability is expensive and exhaust-ing, because society does not have sufficient resources available to help ease the burden for parents. Society's lack of resources is not the parents' fault. Learning to cope may not be a more appropriate response than learning to work to bring about social change. In an early study of 50 Australian families who did not have access to any kind of program for their children with retardation, Schonell and Watts (1956) found that the parents were "almost desperate." After a training center was established in the city, however, the parents' "neurotic symptoms" virtually disappeared (Schonell & Rorke, 1960).

Gliedman and Roth (1980) remind us that professionals exist to serve their clients:

> The parents' rights over the child take precedence over the profes-
> sional's personal moral views. To put it bluntly, the professional exists
> to further the parent's vision of the handicapped child's future. Should
> the professional disagree, he has every right to try to *persuade* the
> parent to adopt a different view. . . . But except in the most extreme
> cases of parental incompetence and brutality, such as child abuse, the
> professional has no right to use his immense moral and practical
> power to intimidate or to manipulate the parent. (p. 145)

As noted earlier, some newer approaches in this field have taken a social system, rather than clinical, perspective. Changing service models are discussed more fully later in the chapter.

THE PARENT-PROFESSIONAL ENCOUNTER: ROLE TAKING AND ROLE PLAYING

Both parents and professionals, then, bring preconceived ideas and views with them when they interact for the first time. Because of their differing life experiences, parents and professionals tend to view children with disabilities differently. The parenting experience is a powerful means of socialization and, as earlier chapters have shown, may shape parents' perceptions and definitions in unique ways. A professional who is not a parent cannot readily "understand" parenthood in the same way as a parent. The divergent views of parents and professionals sometimes result in strained interaction between them. As Freidson (1961) has written, "the separate worlds of experience and reference of the layman and the professional worker are always in potential conflict with each other" (p. 175).

The Setting

Although a number of intervention programs operate in the homes of the families they serve, many parent–professional encounters take place in clinics, hospitals, offices, schools, and treatment centers, which are natural habitats for professionals but not for parents. Many parents are intimidated by such settings. They may recall prior experiences in schools or hospitals that made them feel uncomfortable during their own childhood or at some other time in their lives. They may also feel powerless because the setting is professionally controlled. Large treatment facilities also tend to have a bureaucratic atmosphere, which depersonalizes families and their problems.

Presentation of Self

Goffman (1959) and other sociologists have looked at how people attempt to create images of themselves in the course of interaction with others. Individuals act in a manner they believe will convey a desired impression. Parents and professionals also engage in self-presentation in their interactions with each other.

One of us (R. B. D.) once made an unscheduled home visit to a family in her early intervention program to find the usually neat and clean home in complete disarray. Toys were strewn about the floor, and dirty dishes filled the kitchen. The mother was extremely embarrassed and uneasy throughout the visit. The interventionist realized, as a result of this experience, that all of her previous, scheduled visits had been preceded by much house cleaning and preparation by the family. Activities such as cleaning the house, dressing the child for the visit, and reporting about having worked on therapeutic or educational programs are all forms of self-presentation. Parents' awareness of such presentation is variable, although, as the following parental statement suggests, parents may deliberately and consciously attempt to convey a certain impression to the professional:

> I was conscious of the need to make these doctors identify with us as strongly and as quickly as possible. . . . I made sure that Julian and I dressed in a way that we imagined the doctor's family might dress. We were meticulous about showing up for appointments, at least 15 minutes early, to prove that we were concerned, responsible parents. We paid our bills promptly at the end of each visit. I tried to elicit personal comments from the doctor by referring to topics that might interest him. . . . Finally, I worked with David to make sure he was a cooperative and likable patient. (Stotland, 1984, p. 72)

The need to have the professional see them as "good" parents may be very stressful to some.

Professionals also engage in self-presentation in their interactions with parents. They may want to be perceived as authority figures, or as friends, or as sympathetic listeners. Self-presentation is learned in the course of professional training and experience. Professionals should try to become more aware of the images they are creating and of those they wish to create.

Role Taking

The concept of *role-taking ability* suggests that people are able to see a situation from another person's perspective in the course of interaction. As the above discussion has indicated, our definitions of any situation are products of our unique life experiences. As a result, professionals may have difficulty "taking the role" of the parent, and parents likewise may have difficulty understanding the professional's point of view. This difficulty is summarized by Dembo (1984): "[T]he professionals frequently appear to be insensitive to the parents because the professionals' position and values as outsiders stand in opposition to the position and values of the parents as insiders" (p. 93).

THE DIAGNOSTIC ENCOUNTER

The literature suggests that the situation of first informing parents of a child's disability has often been characterized by the poor role taking of professionals. As Chapter 2 indicated, until fairly recently professionals tended to delay in providing such information to parents because they did not want to be the bearers of "bad news." Many physicians also incorrectly believed that parents did not want to receive this information shortly after a child's birth (see Darling, 1979, for pediatricians' statements expressing this belief). Studies (Berg, Gilderdale, & Way, 1969; Carr, 1970; Drillien & Wilkinson, 1964; Gayton & Walker, 1974; McMichael, 1971; Quine & Pahl, 1986) have indicated, however, that most parents *do* want diagnostic information as soon as possible.

Parents' reactions to lack of information resulting from poor role taking by professionals are illustrated by this mother's story:

> On our third visit, the neurologist said, "I think I know what's wrong with your son but I'm not going to tell you because I don't want to frighten you." Well, I think that's about the worst thing anyone could say. . . . We didn't go back to him. . . . We insisted that [our pediatrician] refer us to_____Children's Hospital. He said, "He's little. Why don't you wait—you don't need to take him there yet." I have a feeling that he knew what the diagnosis was going to be and he didn't really think that we needed to know yet. . . . The chief of pediatrics at_____Children's Hospital told us he was retarded. . . . That was the first person we talked to that we really felt we could trust. . . . Everyone was pablum-feeding us, and we wanted the truth. [Story

related to the author (R. B. D.) in 1978 by the parent of a 6-year-old
child with mental retardation and cerebral palsy]

During the last 10 or 15 years, programs have been developed in
medical schools to aid physicians in role taking during the diagnostic
encounter (see Darling & Peter, 1994, for descriptions of some of these).
McDonald, Carson, Palmer, and Slay (1982) found, perhaps because of
such programs, that 88% of physicians surveyed stated that they presented
diagnostic information to both parents immediately after birth. Gill and
Maynard (1995) suggest that professionals today still do not generally
present diagnostic information outright; rather they present small
amounts of information at a time, waiting for reactions from parents
before proceeding. By taking the role of the parent they are able to adjust
their statements to take parents' expectations into account. Interactions
between physicians and parents in the diagnostic situation will be discussed further in the section on role playing below.

OTHER ENCOUNTERS

Examples of poor role taking can also be found in later encounters
between parents and professionals, after a diagnosis has been established.
Misperceptions of parents' desires for information continue to occur,
primarily in interactions involving physicians. Raimbault, Cachin, Limal,
Eliacheff, and Rappaport (1975) report, for example, that in a study of
interactions between pediatric endocrinologists and parents of children
with Turner syndrome, the physicians tended to avoid concerns raised by
parents. Instead, they offered quasi-scientific explanations that parents
did not understand.

Studies of the doctor–patient relationship in general have indicated
that misconceptions of patients' needs for information are common.
Waitzkin (1985) found, for example, in an analysis of 336 outpatient
encounters, that physicians overestimated the time they spent in information giving and underestimated patients' desires for information. Class-
based patterns tended to predominate, with patients of upper SES getting
more information. Patients' *desires* for information were comparable in all
social classes, however. In a British study (Boulton, Tuckett, Olson, &
Williams, 1986), on the other hand, similar proportions of working- and
middle-class patients received explanations in general practice consultations.

One suggestion for improving the receipt of information during
parent–professional encounters has been tape recording. During an
electronic mail exchange on this subject, some physicians expressed

concern with liability issues and with the self-censoring that sometimes occurs when statements are being recorded. However, the advantages to families of this method might encourage some practitioners at least to offer a recording option to their patients or clients. One physician wrote:

> One I remember best was a young couple with . . . a poor prognosis and some difficult therapeutic choices including amputation. . . .They asked for my permission [to tape] and then we talked for more than thirty minutes. At subsequent [and non-taped] visits they noted how helpful the taped session had been as they listened to it many times prior to making a decision regarding further treatment. (Internet, Children with Special Health Needs List, June 27, 1995)

Another area of misperception involves parents' psychosocial concerns and needs for emotional support. One study of mothers seeking care in private pediatric offices (Hickson, Altemeier, & O'Connor, 1983) found that only 30% of the mothers were most worried about their child's physical health; the others were more concerned with parenting, behavioral, developmental, or psychosocial issues. Yet most parent–physician communication involved only health issues. Mothers were not aware that pediatricians could help them with these concerns or they believed that pediatricians were not interested in helping them. Pediatricians, on the other hand, assumed incorrectly that mothers who did not raise such issues were not concerned about them. Lack of physician interest was also a barrier to communication, leading some mothers to "cloak psychosocial worries in physical terms to gain the attention of the physician" (Hickson et al., 1983, p. 623). In another study (Cadman et al., reported in Bailey & Simeonsson, 1984), clinicians rated interactions within the family as the most important outcomes of intervention, whereas families rated these as next to least important.

Role Playing

The behavior, or role playing, of parents and professionals is based on their role-taking ability. They will act in a manner they believe will evoke the desired response on the part of the other. Role playing is based not only on preexisting perceptions but also on what actually happens in the course of a conversation. Both parents and professionals constantly adjust their behavior as they engage in an ongoing process of redefinition of the situation.

With regard to the parent–professional encounter, Gliedman and

Roth (1980) have written, "Most people adjust their behavior unconsciously to reflect the prevailing structural asymmetries in a relationship"
(p. 170). When parents perceive a difference in status between themselves
and professionals, they may defer to the expertise of the professional and
not express some of their questions or concerns. As Strong (1979) notes
in a study of two hospital outpatient departments:

> Many parents disagreed strongly with the doctors' verdict at one time
> or another. Nevertheless all but a handful made no direct challenge
> to their authority. Most maintained an outward pose of agreement with
> what they were told, even though they might say rather different things
> to ancillary staff such as therapists or social workers. (p. 87)

Studies in the medical sociology literature reveal a rather high rate of
noncompliance with doctors' orders among patients who do not openly
express any disagreement while they are in the doctors' offices.

Noncompliance with medical advice appears to be related, at least
in part, to lack of satisfaction during the parent–physician encounter.
Francis, Korsch, and Morris (1968) found in a study of outpatient visits
to a children's hospital that the extent to which parents' expectations were
not met, the lack of warmth in the physician–parent relation, and the
failure to receive a diagnostic explanation were key factors in noncompliance. Compliance was significantly related to parents' satisfaction.

Professional dominance of the parent–professional encounter also
varies in response to parental role playing and the degree of professional uncertainty present in the situation. Fox (1959) found that in a
situation of medical uncertainty, patients had a more collegial relationship with their physicians, and Sorenson (1974) has noted that, in
genetic counseling, patients can play an important role in decision
making.

Many childhood disabilities also fall within the realm of "physician
uncertainty." Diagnosis of mental retardation is very difficult, if not
impossible, in very young children with cerebral palsy and other motor
disabilities or sensory impairments, such as blindness or deafness. More
subtle conditions, such as learning disabilities, are also difficult to diag-
nose at young ages. In one study of children who appeared to have mental
retardation at 8 months of age (Holden, 1972), great variability in the
children's IQ scores at 4 and 7 led the author to conclude that mental
retardation is not predictable in infancy. In such cases, physicians are
likely to communicate their uncertainty to parents and not issue a firm
prognosis.

Davis (1960), however, has noted a distinction between *clinical* and *functional* uncertainty, the former a "real" phenomenon and the latter a patient management technique. Davis found that in the case of paralytic polio convalescence, treatment staff tended to be evasive with parents, avoiding the truth even after clinical uncertainty had disappeared. Such avoidance served to prevent emotional confrontations with parents. Functional uncertainty is also apparent in this statement from the medical report (in 1986) of a child with severe brain damage in one of our (R. B. D.'s) programs:

> I have discussed the above results with John's parents but have not emphasized his very poor developmental outlook. I feel it is more humane and would be easier for them to accept this child if they observe and come to understand his slow progress for themselves. [Identifying information has been changed for the purpose of ensuring anonymity.]

Similarly, in a study of a neonatal intensive care unit, Sosnowitz (1984) notes that "the staff wanted a chance to observe how the parents would react to the crisis. When the staff was unable to predict the parents' reactions, they usually gave just enough information to keep the parents involved" (p. 396).

Functional uncertainty is especially characteristic of the diagnostic encounter. As noted earlier, physicians sometimes delay in providing complete diagnostic information to parents because they believe that parents "are not ready" to hear the truth. Such delays also have the function of avoiding an emotional confrontation. As one of the authors has noted elsewhere (see, e.g., Darling, 1979, 1994), physicians have used four stalling strategies to delay the sharing of diagnostic or prognostic information: avoidance, hinting, mystification, and passing the buck. As earlier chapters have shown, these techniques can increase rather than alleviate parental anxiety. Svarstad and Lipton (1977) found that parents who received specific, clear, and frank communication were better able to accept a diagnosis of mental retardation in their children than those who received vague or evasive information.

The variability in parent roles can also be a potential source of conflict between parents and professionals. In many intervention programs, parents are expected to play the role of teacher with their children and are trained for this role by program professionals. As Farber and Lewis (1975) have argued, however, some parents may not *want* to play a pedagogical role, and "such parental training subordinates the uniquely personalized component of the parent–child relationship" (p. 40). In order to be effective in their interactions with families, professionals must develop realistic role expectations for parents that are compatible with parents' expectations for themselves.

THE EMERGENCE OF A PARENT–PROFESSIONAL PARTNERSHIP: NEWER ROLES FOR PARENTS AND PROFESSIONALS

Although parent and professional roles have historically been in conflict, some newer directions have been emerging that are helping to bring them closer together.

New Roles for Parents: The Emergence of Parent Activism

Ayer (1984) and others have suggested that the failure of professionals to meet family needs has resulted in self-help activities by families. Although most parents begin by acquiescing to professional authority, many come to play an *entrepreneurial* role (Darling, 1979, 1988) in order to secure needed services. This role includes (1) seeking information, (2) seeking control, and (3) challenging authority.

As noted earlier in this chapter, parents of children with disabilities, like others in society, have been socialized to accept professional dominance. Haug and Lavin reported in 1983 that the large majority (72%) of their general population sample had never challenged their physicians in any way. However, the consumerist movement has been growing, and parents have been becoming more aware of the possibility of challenging professional authority.

Parents' disillusionment with professionals may begin to occur shortly after a child's birth, when professionals fail to provide desired diagnostic or treatment information or deny parents' control over their child's management and care. Parents may come to resent their role as helpless bystanders:

> We were always going back and forth to_____Children's Hospital. . . . It was a constantly pulling away. We could never be a family. . . . It was always, "We have to go to the hospital." We had to go to doctors, doctors, doctors. . . . We could never get to know our child. . . . We got to the point where we hated doctors, we hated_____Children's Hospital. (Darling, 1979, p. 154)

On the other hand, some professionals willingly share information with and seek advice from parents:

> The most important aspect of the doctor's presentation was that he involved us as equals in the decision-making process. . . . By involving us in the process and by giving us his professional opinion as an opinion, he returned to us our parental rights of making the important

decision that would affect our child's life. *We were in control,* but we were no longer alone. (Stotland, 1984, p. 72, emphasis added)

The staff at the early intervention center knew we wanted Aric to attend a regular kindergarten class. . . . They gave us ideas to get him into the setting. They never took control out of our hands, and we always did the steps ourselves. They were there as a resource and support. The staff at the early intervention center helped me to gel the vision. But it didn't take the Family and Child Learning Center to show me promise [in Aric]; I could see that when he was born. (Leifield & Murray, 1995, pp. 246–247)

As noted in earlier chapters, the more parents interact with their children, the more committed they become to their children's welfare. The emotional bond that develops between parent and child is a strong catalyst to parental activism. Pizzo (1983) has suggested that the bond "energizes" parent advocacy. She writes:

The most universal shared experience we have as parents is the struggle to protect children and to get them the resources they need to develop well. Listening to parent activists describe their work, one soon learns that their organizational activities are not radically different from the basic task we undertake as parents. In self-help and advocacy, parents take the intimate, nurturing vigilance needed for effective child-rearing into a social and political domain. (p. 19)

When parents encounter difficulties in meeting their children's needs, they are likely to continue to search for appropriate services and helpful professionals. Negative experiences with professionals can be a catalyst for further action. Pizzo (1983) argues that parent advocacy derives from "acute, painful experiences," and Haug and Lavin (1983) report that the most important variable in consumerist challenges to medical authority is the *experience of medical error.* Such an experience erodes trust in professional authority and may provide the needed turning point to launch parents on a career of activism.

Parents of children with disabilities are more likely than other people to encounter medical error or errors in professional judgment because of the frequency and intensity of their contacts with the many professionals involved in their children's care. They have more opportunities to encounter professional failure. Haug and Lavin (1983) have suggested that "chronic patients, who live with their conditions for long stretches of time, often learn by their own experience which therapies are helpful and which are not" (p. 33). The mother of a child with multiple medical problems explains her actions:

There is so much confusion. Each doctor tells me something different.

. . . I wish they would talk to each other. I have requested that all communication between doctors be carbon copied to me, in the hopes of deciphering what is being said. . . . I have purchased some medical dictionaries so I can better understand the terminology and discuss Michael's condition with my doctors on a more realistic level. I'm starting to wonder if perhaps Michael doesn't need to see some other specialists. . . . I keep asking my cardiologist, and he finally responds, "It's your dime. If you want to see one, go ahead." I want to trust him, but at the same time I don't feel that he is taking Michael's condition seriously enough. . . . I refuse to simply wait for him to die. (Spano, 1994, pp. 38–39)

Through their children's medical treatment or educational programs, most parents meet other parents of children with disabilities, with whom they exchange stories and thereby learn that their problems are shared. They also learn about the possibilities for activism and advocacy through the relationships they develop in support groups and other disability organizations. When they interact with others, parents learn about techniques that have worked and come to realize that authority can be successfully challenged. As an article about the Parents' Union of Philadelphia noted (Wice & Fernandez, 1984), "Mrs. Thomas was powerful when she was linked to others through an alert advocacy group. . . . Alone, a parent may be tempted to give up. Together, parents have power" (p. 40).

Pizzo (1983) notes that many parents become involved in self-help groups after seeing something in the media. In addition to general newspapers, magazines, and television programs, specialized publications are targeted specifically at parents of children with disabilities. *The Exceptional Parent* magazine, for example, prints success stories about and by parents who have actively challenged professional authority. When Mary Tatro received *The Exceptional Parent* Award of 1984, her merits were described as follows:

Mrs. Tatro was able to persist more than five years to get the services necessary for her child, although this meant sustaining personal hardship, a prolonged struggle, and an eventual confrontation at the United States Supreme Court. ("Related Services," 1984, p. 36)

Such stories may inspire other parents to pursue more or better services for their own children.

In addition to opportunities to learn from experience and informal socialization in parent groups, more formalized training in assertiveness and advocacy is available to parents. A number of books and manuals have been published that familiarize parents with their legal rights and teach strategies for interacting with professionals and bringing about social change (see, e.g., Biklen, 1974; DesJardins, 1971; Dickman & Gordon, 1985; Lurie, 1970). Courses are also being offered in activist techniques.

Increasing parent awareness of rights and methods for acting on those rights is an important step toward the creation of a true parent–professional partnership. Parents and professionals must work together to meet the needs of children with disabilities. The changing roles of professionals are explored in the next section.

New Roles for Professionals: Advocacy and a Social System Perspective

DEVELOPING ROLE-TAKING ABILITY

In order to be truly effective, the professional must learn to take the role of the parent. The professional exists to help families achieve their goals. To serve that purpose, the professional must understand, as well as possible, the *family's* definition of what its members want and need and must take what Mercer (1965) has called a social system perspective.

Professional awareness of the point of view of families has certainly been increasing in recent years, as evidenced by a growing body of literature in professional journals and books about the family experience. Professional training programs have been using videotapes, trained parents, and other techniques for making professionals more aware of parent perceptions (see, e.g., Bailey et al., 1987; Darling & Peter, 1994; Guralnick, Bennett, Heiser, & Richardson, 1987; H. B. Richardson, Guralnick, & Tupper, 1978; Stillman, Sabers, & Redfield, 1977). New programs for medical students and residents (Cooley, 1994; DiVenere, 1994; Lewis & Greenstein, 1994) have involved them in the lives of families in various ways, and the field of early intervention has moved toward a family-centered approach in both legislation and practice (Darling, 1989; Darling & Darling, 1992).

The helping professions in general have been rapidly shifting during the past decade from a clinical perspective to a "partnership" model, in which the client's perspective is highly valued by the professional. This shift is evident in the fields of early intervention (Darling & Darling, 1992; Chapter 10, this volume), social work (Adams & Nelson, 1995), and medicine (Darling & Peter, 1994), among others. The recent proliferation of home visits and family centers as service models attests to the growing acceptance of a system-based, partnership paradigm. The special expertise of professionals has always been recognized; the special expertise of clients is now being recognized as well. Some professionals have not been comfortable with the shift from professional dominance to partnership (see, e.g., Goodman, 1994); most, however, are discovering that the newer, community-based, family-centered models are working because they enable families to participate in their "treatment" in a meaningful way. In Chapter 10 we illustrate the application of a partnership model in early intervention.

In order to become more effective in taking the role of family members, professionals must explore their own attitudes, accept their own limitations, and try to share the experience of the families they are trying to help. Some practical exercises for increasing role-taking ability are suggested below (adapted from Darling & Darling, 1982, pp. 184–189):

1. *Write a sociological autobiography.* Think about your own background and the experiences that have shaped your attitudes. Try to remember your earliest experiences with children or adults with disabilities. Do you recall any individuals with disabilities in your family, your neighborhood, your school, your church, or your Scout troop? What did you think of them? How did you feel in their presence? What did your parents, friends, and other significant others tell you about them?

How have your other group affiliations shaped your attitudes toward disabilities? Do your religious values affect your attitudes? Did your social-class background stress hard work, achievement, and "getting ahead" and deprecate those who were dependent on others for a livelihood? How has your gender-role socialization affected your attitudes? Did you learn that males are supposed to be physically and emotionally strong or that females are supposed to be physically attractive?

Think about the strangers with disabilities you have seen in public places or on television and those about whom you have read in books or magazines. Have you watched telethons on behalf of various disabilities? As a child, did you read *A Christmas Carol, The Prince and the Pauper,* or *Heidi*? Have you seen televised faith healings or read any of the publications of the Christian Science church?

Have you ever deliberately avoided interacting with a person with a disability? Have you walked away from an opportunity to help a person with blindness? Have you avoided a friendship with a neighbor who has a child with retardation? Why do you think you acted the way you did in these situations?

Make a list of all of your group affiliations and experiences with disability and examine how each has affected your attitudes toward people with disabilities. Use your list to write an autobiography that traces your experiences and shows how they shaped your present attitudes.

2. *Design and conduct in-depth interviews with (a) one or more adolescents or adults with disabilities and (b) one or more parents of children with disabilities.*

Get to know someone with a disability. Make a list of questions that will serve as the basis for an in-depth conversation so that your respondents tell you how they feel about their disability. Do they welcome questions about their disability? What kinds of questions are upsetting or offensive? What kinds of questions are helpful?

In interviewing parents, questions should include the following topics: (1) their expectations prior to their child's birth (e.g., Did they want their unborn son to be a football player or a doctor?); (2) their experiences during labor and delivery (Did they suspect that something was wrong with the baby?); (3) their reactions to the first information that their child had a disability (How were they told? How did they feel?); (4) their attitudes toward professionals (Which professionals have been helpful to them? Why?); (5) their feelings about their children (What negative and positive effects have they had on their lives?); (6) their experiences with friends, relatives, and strangers (Have grandparents been supportive? How do people react to their children in restaurants, shopping malls?); (7) their perceptions of their child's effect on family relationships (Has their marriage been strengthened or weakened? How have siblings reacted?); and (8) their expectations and hopes for the future (What do they think/hope will happen to their children when they grow up?)

Students and others not currently involved professionally with people with disabilities can usually find respondents in parent groups affiliated with hospitals, clinics, preschool programs, or organizations such as the ARC (formerly known as the Association for Retarded Citizens), or the United Cerebral Palsy Association. Adults with disabilities may be located through associations such as the Easter Seal Society, the Spina Bifida Association of America, or United Cerebral Palsy Association; at workshops, such as those operated by Goodwill Industries; or through group homes and other community-based housing facilities for people with disabilities. Organized groups for students with disabilities can be found on some college campuses.

These interviews are not intended to provide a complete picture of individuals with disabilities, and you must be careful not to generalize from your respondents to others with similar disabilities. Individuals with disabilities are just as different from one another as individuals without disabilities. This exercise is only intended to make you more aware of how *one person* or *a few people* feel about their situation.

3. *Observe a special situation.* You may want to spend some time observing any or all of the following: meetings of an association of parents of children with disabilities, a preschool center for children with disabilities, a special-education class in the public schools (or an inclusive classroom that includes students with disabilities), a vocational training program for adults with mental retardation, a support group for adoles-

cents or adults with disabilities, a group home for adults with physical disabilities or mental retardation, a day program for adults with mental retardation.

4. *Read some personal accounts written by parents of children with disabilities.* The following is a small sample of such books. Many others are available as well:

Killilea, M. (1952). *Karen.* Englewood Cliffs, NJ: Prentice-Hall. [Written by the mother of a child with cerebral palsy.]
Meyer, D. J. (1995). *Uncommon fathers.* Bethesda, MD: Woodbine House.
Pieper, E. (1977). *Sticks and stones.* Syracuse, NY: Human Policy Press. [Written by the mother of a young adult with spina bifida.]
Roberts, N. (1968). *David.* Richmond, VA: John Knox Press. [Written by the mother of a child with Down syndrome.]
Ulrich, S. (1972). *Elizabeth.* Ann Arbor: University of Michigan Press. [Written by the mother of a preschool child with blindness.]

5. *Read some literature written from the parents' perspective.* Magazines and newsletters written for parents provide insight into the parents' point of view. See, for example, *The Exceptional Parent,* a magazine written especially for the parents of children with special needs. Newsletters such as those of the National Down Syndrome Society, the Spina Bifida Association of America, and United Cerebral Palsy Associations are also valuable.

6. *Participate in simulation experiences or other awareness-promoting programs.* Spend a day in a wheelchair or wearing a blindfold—or spend some time pushing a wheelchair or escorting someone with blindness. Accompany a child with an obvious disability to a shopping mall, restaurant, or other public place. Watch the reactions of waitresses, store clerks, and other customers. (Some individuals with disabilities disagree about the value of simulation experiences.) Packaged programs that promote disability awareness are also available.

7. *Evaluate your goals.* Why have you decided to enter the helping professions? Why have you chosen a field that brings you into contact with families with children with disabilities? Make a list of your personal professional goals. Evaluate each of your goals in terms of its potential beneficial or negative effect on the families you serve.

PROFESSIONALS AS ADVOCATES

Traditionally, helping professionals worked to change their *clients,* to cure them, to improve their functional abilities, to make them more comfortable, to aid them in adjusting to their situation. In recent years, we have learned that changing the "client" is not always enough. Sometimes, the family's *social situation* needs to be changed. Because society is designed primarily to meet the needs of those without disabilities, structural barriers exist that prevent those with disabilities from achieving full integration. These barriers include the following:

- Physical barriers, such as curbs, stairs, and narrow doorways
- Cultural barriers, such as stigma and "handicapism"
- Social barriers, such as lack of needed services

These barriers cannot be eliminated without social change to produce access, public awareness, and resources to meet the needs of families whose children have disabilities.

Advocacy involves working to bring about social change. Is advocacy an appropriate part of the professional role? Wolfensburger (reported in Kurtz, 1977) argues that "the advocacy concept demands that advocacy for an impaired person is to be exercised *not* by agencies,and *not* by professionals acting in professional roles, but by *competent and suitable citizens*" (p. 146, emphasis in original). Adams (1973) argues that professional advocacy poses ethical dilemmas. The professional must decide whether to support the rights of the individual or the rights of society when the two are in conflict. Kurtz (1977) has noted that advocacy may produce role conflict, involving the professional's agency of employment, as well as parents, children, and others who may be deprived of services, and Frith (1981) states that "it is becoming increasingly difficult for professionals in the field [of special education] to assume the role of child advocate, while simultaneously attempting to support their employing agency" (p. 487).

Two professional organizations, the Council for Exceptional Children and the Ad Hoc Committee on Advocacy of the National Association of Social Workers, have taken the position that, in the case of advocacy dilemmas, the professional *should act as an advocate for the client.* The Council for Exceptional Children (1981) has issued the following statement:

> The Council for Exceptional Children firmly believes that the role of the professional as an employee should not conflict with the professional's advocate role. Rather, these roles should complement each other. . . . Failing to assume responsibility [as an advocate], the professional can only play the role of participant in whatever injustice may befall the child. (pp. 492–493)

When they become advocates for vulnerable families, professionals become partners with their clients in working toward social change.

Professionals should certainly not usurp advocacy roles that families can play themselves; however, even the most "empowered" families sometimes need help in negotiating a system that was not created with their needs in mind. Unlike the professional dominance that characterized parent–professional interaction in the past, today's parent–professional partnerships are marked by equality and mutual respect. Although we must continue to help families adjust to situations that cannot be changed, we cannot continue to blame families for their problems when society *can* be changed. Social action rather than passive adjustment may be the hallmark of parent–professional interaction in the future. Together, professionals and families can work to eliminate the physical, cultural, and social barriers that prevent families from attaining the best possible quality of life.

The next two chapters suggest some concrete ways that professionals can help families. Chapter 9 reviews counseling techniques that respect the family's perspective and empower families to optimize their life situation. Chapter 10 illustrates the application of family-centered principles in the field of early intervention through methods for the development of Individualized Family Service Plans. Both chapters reflect the systems approach that has been advocated throughout this book.

Therapeutic Approaches

THIS CHAPTER explores various approaches to working with families who have children with disabilities. The interventions that are examined are primarily designed to promote healthy family relationships; however, some of the approaches used to achieve this goal are not necessarily family interventions per se. That is, individual, marital, or group counseling approaches can be employed while keeping the family system in mind. The systems approach advocated in this book is considered central to both theoretical and treatment aspects of families in that when disability occurs, it affects all family members. Therefore, when working with family members, it is essential, we believe, to maintain a family systems mindset irrespective of the therapeutic modality employed.

Therapeutic approaches include interventions that are designed to change families. However, we preface the remainder of this chapter with the important reminder that *not all families need to be changed.* For too long, professionals in the helping professions have embraced a pathology orientation and assumed that the birth of a child with special needs would necessarily result in pathology in a family's functioning. When families neither need nor desire therapeutic intervention, some therapeutic approaches may be more intrusive than helpful. On the other hand, some families *do* need psychotherapeutic help, and professionals must be able to meet that need when it arises. The reader should keep in mind, then, that the following discussion applies in varying degrees to the families the professional will encounter.

This chapter presents an overview of existing interventions along with references for further reading. Some of the strategies discussed require extensive knowledge and training and it is our assumption that readers already have or are in the process of acquiring requisite training. Some therapeutic approaches are beyond the scope of the reader. In such instances, referrals to other professionals are indicated. We begin our discussion by examining the characteristics of effective helpers.

EFFECTIVE HELPERS AND THE HELPER–FAMILY RELATIONSHIP

The literature informs us that effective helpers have certain qualities, skills, and values. Indeed, as Ross (1964) points out, persons who lack certain characteristics should not work with families of children with disabilities:

> A student may be able to develop these [characteristics] in the course of closely supervised experience but some people lack these qualities in sufficient measure and these should probably not enter a profession whose central task is helping other people. No amount of exhortation can make a rejecting person accepting, a frigid person warm, or a narrow-minded person understanding. Those charged with the selection, education and training of new members of the helping professions will need to keep in mind that the presence or absence of certain personality characteristics make the difference between a truly helpful professional and one who leaves a trace of misery and confusion in the wake of his activities. (pp. 75–76)

Based on their research at the University of Florida, Combs and Avila (1985) found that effective helpers share certain attributes:

1. *Knowledge*: To be effective, practitioners must be personally committed to acquiring specialized knowledge in their field. Professionals who work with families should have at least rudimentary knowledge of family dynamics, issues pertaining to disability, and how childhood disability affects family functioning (McDaniel et al., 1992; Seligman, 1979).
2. *People*: Effective helpers view people as being able rather than unable, worthy rather than unworthy, internally rather than externally motivated, dependable rather than undependable, helpful rather than hindering.
3. *Self-concept*: Effective helpers feel personally adequate, identify readily with others, feel trustworthy, wanted, and worthy.
4. *Helping purposes*: Successful helpers are freeing rather than controlling, deal with larger rather than smaller issues, are more self-revealing, are involved with clients, and are process oriented in helping relationships.

5. *Approaches to helping*: Effective helpers are more oriented to people than things, and are more likely to approach clients subjectively or phenomenologically than objectively or factually.

Others (Carkhuff & Berenson, 1967; Egan, 1986; Ivey & Simek-Downing, 1980; Rogers, 1958) consider the following to be important helper characteristics:

1. *Positive regard*: Helpers should communicate acceptance of clients as worthwhile persons, regardless of who they are or what they say or do.
2. *Empathy*: Professionals must be able to communicate that they feel and understand the client's concerns from the client's point of view.
3. *Concreteness*: Professionals should respond accurately, clearly, specifically, and immediately to clients.
4. *Warmth*: Professionals should show their concern through verbal and nonverbal expression. This concept appears often in the counseling literature but has not been well defined, yet one "knows" when someone is warm and accepting—or cold and distant.

Self-awareness is an essential characteristic for the professional helper (Sommers-Flanagan & Sommers-Flanagan, 1993). An awareness of one's attitudes toward persons with a disability, as well as toward families with children who have disabilities, is essential (Marshak & Seligman, 1993). We have discussed and in this chapter will discuss further the negative attitudes that the general public *and* professionals hold toward persons with disabilities (see also Chapter 4). These negative attitudes from professionals become manifest in behaviors that communicate coldness, distance, abruptness, and rejection. Such behaviors, in turn, can generate, reinforce, or deepen feelings of guilt, depression, and shame in family members. Therefore, professionals need to examine their attitudes carefully so that they do not interfere with efforts to be helpful to families.

The evidence to date regarding the quality of relationships families experience with professionals is indeed discouraging (Darling, 1991; Darling & Peter, 1994). Telford and Sawrey (1977) report that parents of children with disabilities are almost universally dissatisfied with their experiences with professionals. The authors quote a mother who characterized her contacts with professionals as "a masterful combination of dishonesty, condescension, misinformation and bad manners" (p. 143). Sometimes parents are perceived as problems with which professionals need to contend, or are blamed for causing or at least not preventing their child's disability (Seligman, 1979). Parents are sometimes considered a nuisance rather than a resource and are frequently criticized, analyzed, or made to feel responsible for their child's problems (Seligman & Seligman, 1980). Furthermore, it is not unusual to hear of parents being called lazy, stupid, demanding, greedy, conniving, or angry and defensive (Rubin & Quinn-Curran, 1983). Holden and Lewine (reported in Bernheim & Lehman, 1985) found in their research that there are high levels of dissatisfaction with mental health services. In their survey of families in five different locales, families reported that professionals increased their feelings of guilt, confusion, and frustration. The net result was that 74% were dissatisfied with the services received, for reasons including lack of information about diagnosis and treatment, vague and evasive responses, professional avoidance of labeling the illness (which increased families' confusion), lack of support during critical periods, lack of help in locating community resources, and little or no advice about how to cope with their child's symptoms or problem behaviors. Although some believe that parent–professional relationships have improved in recent years (Darling & Peter, 1994; Marsh, 1992), the professional community is currently experiencing massive changes in systems of service delivery that are affecting the quality of existing services. These changes, rooted in mandates to reduce medical and other service charges, are resulting in confusion, added burden, and frustration for professionals. One might expect that as stress increases, relationships between professionals and their patients will again become less satisfactory until efforts are made to combine cost containment with efficient, effective, high-quality services.

Such negative indicators of professional–family relationships should constitute a strong stimulus for professionals to reexamine how they view and treat families of children who have disabilities (Bernheim & Lehman, 1985). Although professionals must be held responsible for much of the tension between families and themselves, Gargiulo (1985) holds that some of the blame falls on family members. Sometimes family members condemn professionals for not recognizing the disability sooner and occasionally accuse the professional of causing the disability. Some parents, Gargiulo argues, inhibit the growth of the relationship with professionals by withdrawing, while other families prematurely judge professionals to be insensitive, offensive, and incapable of understanding their situation. Many professionals who are attempting to help may not realize that the very proliferation of specialists sometimes complicates rather than clarifies issues. Furthermore, help should be free from petty professional jealousies that may cause one group to attempt to keep another from giving help.

Another source of difficulty is to be found in the anxieties the child's disability may arouse in the professional (Darling, 1979; Ross, 1964;

Seligman & Seligman, 1980). Due to their discomfort, professionals may withdraw from certain families and rationalize that "someone else" will talk with them about their problems. The difficulty is that other professionals may have similar anxieties so that in the end the family is not helped by anyone. Such difficulties are being addressed by current curricula in medical schools and other professional education programs (see Chapter 8).

There is also the tendency to concentrate on specifics and disregard the whole picture: "All too often the physician will concentrate on the medical aspects, the therapist on rehabilitation, and the teacher on education—each carefully avoiding the problem of the family by focusing on the problem of the child" (Ross, 1964, p. 74). Such a view disdains the family systems view that we advocate in this book.

Moreover, parents may have visited numerous professionals but remain poorly informed about the nature and implications of their child's disability. For many families this problem is not due to their resistance to facts but rather the failure of the professional to inform the family adequately. A parent's lack of knowledge about a child's disability may be attributed to the professional's anxiety and withdrawal from the family.

Another reason for the family's confusion or lack of information may be the professional's use of jargon, which can render communication relatively worthless. Professionals need to be concrete (yet not condescending) with their clients or patients, and be sensitive to nonverbal cues that suggest that they are not being understood. When a professional believes a message is misunderstood he or she can say, "I'm not sure if I made myself understood. If it didn't make sense to you, I'd be happy to try again." The use of professional jargon does not generate respect; it causes distance and implies aloofness and insensitivity.

The timing of professional interventions is a key barometer of the success of relationships between professionals and families. Professionals need to be sensitive to a family's receptiveness to a particular intervention. For example, parents may not be ready to explore their feelings about their child and what the disability means to them when they are confronted with the practical implications of the child's disability and need to know what services are available to help with immediate problems. Conversely, when parents need to sort out their feelings, professionals, threatened by affective disclosures, should not hide behind a laundry list of agencies and services and avoid discussing emotional responses. The timing of an intervention determines whether family members truly hear what is being said; it also affects their level of trust in the professional and their perception of his or her expertise.

Although we acknowledge that family members can contribute to tension between themselves and professionals (Gargiulo, 1985), we would argue that professionals must shoulder most of the responsibility. To avoid problems, we believe that professionals should (1) gain a thorough understanding of family systems and especially the dynamics of families of children with disabilities, (2) be expert in effective interpersonal relationship skills, and (3) acquire extensive experience working with families of children who are disabled.

BARRIERS TO EFFECTIVE HELPING

In any type of helping endeavor it is imperative that professionals interpret parents' circumstances from *the family members'* point of view. This means that the professional must listen to them carefully and try to experience or at least deeply understand what they may be feeling. Empathic listeners have an ability to put their own biases and opinions aside as they try to understand what is being said and felt. Family members intuitively know when they are in the presence of an empathic helper because they feel understood and valued. Many preparation programs help train professionals to develop empathy skills, and the best way to learn them is to be in the presence of a good professional model. A primary obstacle to good communication skills is graduate school education, where students may be exposed to poor role models. As Yalom (1975) observes, "Pipe-smoking therapists often beget pipe-smoking patients. Patients during psychotherapy may sit, walk, talk and even think like their therapists" (p. 17). Likewise, professional educators often discount the social-modeling effects they have on the people they train.

Professionals in medical, educational, and social service occupations are often burdened because of the nature of their work and the demands placed on them. Professionals in stressful occupations are often so fatigued psychologically and physically that they are hard pressed to interact comfortably and productively with family members. If we wish to help promote healthier parent–professional relationships, we must create less stressful job environments for professionals who typically begin their careers with energy, high goals, and positive expectations and attitudes.

Preoccupation with personal concerns is another barrier to effective helping. When a family member is speaking, novice professionals often "think ahead," thereby making it difficult to empathize with the client. Preoccupation with personal problems also tends to distract from careful listening. Because the lives of professionals may sometimes be difficult, like those of the people they serve, it is not surprising that occasional personal concerns can interfere with one's effectiveness. Occasional preoccupation is not a serious problem but chronic distractions can result in communication impasses. When the latter occur, it helps to talk with a trustworthy colleague, supervisor, or psychotherapist.

Strong feelings about the family member(s) one is working with can be a major barrier to effective listening and rapport building. Angry or anxious feelings toward someone we are trying to communicate with generally limit our ability to be helpful. In regard to physicians, Darling (1979) provides compelling evidence that some medical practitioners view families with at least some degree of personal discomfort.

Professionals sometimes allow themselves to be distracted by phone calls or interruptions from secretaries and other colleagues. Such behavior conveys a lack of concern and respect as well as inattentiveness to family members. Families should be given a predetermined period of time all to themselves. Phone calls or a colleague "just wanting a word" with you tend to interrupt and are often considered discourteous. We might reflect on how we feel when our conversation with someone is marked by a series of disruptive breaks.

THE FAMILY'S NEED FOR COUNSELING

Lesley Max (1985), a mother of a child with mental retardation and a New Zealand freelance writer, says, "No need is more clearly or more frequently expressed when the parents of the retarded gather than the need to talk to, and be counseled by, an informed, accessible, mature and sympathetic person" (p. 252). She goes on to describe some of the factors that make counseling necessary and valuable:

1. Figures relating to the incidence of maternal postnatal depression in the population at large support the contention that birth is frequently a time of emotional turmoil, even when no handicap is present.
2. Family disintegration can be initiated or worsened by the birth of an intellectually handicapped baby. Informal observations of families with a handicapped child suggest a rate of friction and desertion that deserves close study, with a view to effective intervention.
3. Grandparents can be the staunchest support of parents of the handicapped yet the birth of an intellectually handicapped child can be the cause of a complete breakdown in the relationship between the generations. Since neighbours and other relatives are not seen as a source of either emotional or practical support, it makes sense to facilitate adjustment to the new child together with the grandparents, who are themselves often burdened with outdated fear and shame-laden prejudice.
4. Current concepts of care of the intellectually handicapped are predicated firmly on the basis of a normally functioning family,

yet professional neglect of family members is nowhere more grossly in evidence than in the case of siblings. (pp. 252–253)

Throughout the book we have indicated the challenges families must contend with in the face of disability, although we acknowledge that many families adapt remarkably well. We have discussed how a major event to one family member reverberates throughout the family unit, leading us to emphasize the wisdom of a systems perspective. The family must come to terms with its destiny—that of frustrated expectations and thwarted life goals. Depending on the nature and severity of the child's disability, his or her capacity to achieve independence may be limited and therefore not allow family members to live out a "normal" family life cycle.

Family members experience many and mixed feelings, such as love and hate, joy and sorrow, elation and depression. In addition, there are guilt and anger and frustration in dealing with a remarkably complex and difficult service delivery system (Upshur, 1991). There are concerns about the future—about a child's educational and vocational endeavors as well as prospects for independence. In addition, families will need to confront the stigmatizing attitudes of others in professional, educational, social, and public contexts.

For some parents, financial burdens may be the major problem. Medication, special equipment, physical therapy, speech therapy, physician visits, and, perhaps, counseling sessions all reflect potential sources of financial drain. Severe financial problems can, in themselves, create great strain within the family system (see Chapter 3).

S. L. Harris (1983) discusses *accepting the diagnosis* as a problem some families face. Seeking second, third, and fourth opinions regarding a child's diagnosis is to be expected and sometimes encouraged. However, when guilt and denial are present, there may be an endless round of visits to professionals for a "cure."

Burnout is another problem experienced by some families over time when a child's gains may slow down or plateau. The family's hope for a cure or significant improvement may decline as they begin to accept the chronicity of their child's disability. Not only do family members need to work, study, and find time for leisure and pleasure but they must also attend to the increasing needs of their disabled family member. When these tasks strain the family's resources, behaviors symptomatic of burnout begin to emerge and threaten the family's ability to cope.

Fatigue, according to S. L. Harris, is related to burnout and derives from the many tasks parents must assume such as feeding, toileting, and managing disruptive behavior. Fatigued and burned-out family members need help from professionals to help explore the demand characteristics of the child and family dynamics that may have contributed to this state of affairs. Professionals can also help families obtain needed services such as respite care to help relieve stress.

S. L. Harris (1983) believes that families need to know how to find professional services:

> One source of frequent frustration for parents is the problem of finding professional services for their child. Locating a pediatrician, neurologist, dentist, ophthalmologist, audiologist, and other specialists who are good at what they do, who understand the special needs of the developmentally disabled child, and who take time to communicate with parents, is exceedingly difficult. (p. 83)

To help parents locate the services and professionals familiar with childhood disability, professionals ought to have the names of competent service providers at hand to pass on to family members.

Some family members may become clinically depressed, while others may be occasionally dispirited. The professional can help parents accept the fact that one's distress is a reasonable response to a difficult situation. For family members who are seriously depressed, however, psychotherapy (and perhaps even medication) may be indicated. As noted earlier, professionals need to be able to distinguish serious clinical depression from temporary and mild "blues," and make appropriate referrals when indicated.

Other feelings, such as guilt and anger, and other problems, such as marital dysfunction, need to be dealt with by the professional (S.L. Harris, 1983). In addition, professionals should be alert to problems that may develop in more peripherally involved family members, such as siblings or grandparents.

Rolland (1993) argues that all families facing disability or chronic illness should routinely have a family consultation as a preventive measure. Such a consultation demonstrates that a psychosocial consultant is a member of the health care team, it normalizes the expectation of psychosocial stress in a nonpejorative manner, it reduces feelings of helplessness, and it promotes open communication among professionals and family members alike. However, some families may feel no need for help of this kind, and their wishes should be respected.

INDIVIDUAL INTERVENTIONS

Opirhory and Peters Model

Employing a stage model, Opirhory and Peters (1982) provide a useful guide to interventions with parents of newborns with disabilities. As noted earlier, stage theory holds that parents generally follow a fairly predictable series of feelings and actions after a child's diagnosis has been communicated. These authors believe that the sequence of phases are useful general benchmarks for considering appropriate interventions.

During the *denial* stage, professionals should gently provide an honest evaluation of the situation the parents are confronting. They should simply describe the child objectively and indicate the care that is needed. They should not remove the parents' hope or interfere with their coping style unless it is inappropriate or dysfunctional for the family.

When parents reach the *anger* stage, professionals must create an open and permissive atmosphere so that parents can vent their anger and pain. They must be accepting of the parents' criticism, even if it is directed toward them, without personalizing the parents' remarks or defending other professionals or themselves. It is important to keep in mind that projected anger reflects the parents' anxiety in the face of a situation that will significantly change their lives. They should be mindful, too, that some parents have been treated so badly by professionals that their anger and frustration derive from thoroughly objective circumstances.

Opirhory and Peters recommend that professionals discourage parents from dwelling on a review of the pregnancy during the *bargaining* phase. During this phase, parents feel that they can reverse their child's condition by engaging in certain redemptive activities. The authors advise the professional to point out the child's positive characteristics, encourage involvement, and remain optimistic without giving any guarantees about the child's potential progress. It is also essential that while parents continue to establish a warm and loving relationship with their child they nonetheless balance their lives with personally fulfilling goals and activities. Professionals need to be wary of parents who either fill their lives with a variety of outside activities at the expense of their child or are so involved with the child that their lives become severely restricted and they begin to withdraw from others.

The *depression* stage can be characterized by mild or severe mood swings. Again, the professional needs to be able to distinguish between clinical depression and milder forms of dysphoria. Mild, situational, and time-limited depression is common and liable to emerge at various points in the child's development. Parents need to be reassured that what they are experiencing is normal. They should not be criticized or made to feel that they have a major psychological problem when they experience occasional mood changes. Opirhory and Peters believe that one needs to be especially alert to signs of regression to earlier stages, although we do not necessarily view this with alarm. Anger and mild denial, for example, can resurface and should be considered normal unless these feelings become chronic, excessive, and rigidly held.

During the *acceptance* stage, the professional should continue to reinforce the positive aspects of the parent–child relationship. Because a realistic adjustment to the family member who is disabled is achieved during this stage, it is typically characterized by fulfilling family relationships. Therefore, the need for professional help and support is unlikely to be crucial, although problems can emerge when the child reaches certain developmental milestones.

Laborde and Seligman Model

Laborde and Seligman (1991) propose a model comprised of three somewhat distinct counseling interventions: educative, personal advocacy, and facilitative counseling. *Educative counseling* is appropriate when families need information about their child's disability. This approach is based on the premise that families know little about disability until they are confronted by it in their own child. As Chapter 2 shows, parents' need for information tends to be stronger than their need for support early in the infancy period. Especially early on, and particularly relevant to health care professionals, educative counseling can be used to inform parents, to lessen their sense of confusion and ambiguity, and to decrease the stress that is partially a result of not knowing essential information and where to turn.

As noted elsewhere in this volume, in addition to being informed about their child's disability, its etiology and prognosis, family members may need to know about available services, reading materials germane to their situation, and specialized equipment for their child. Family members should know about their legal rights for service or education as well as about parent organizations, self-help groups, and local professionals who can help with problems of a more psychological nature.

Educative counseling is not just for family members of newborns. Concrete information and guidance is needed at all stages of the child's development as the disabling condition stabilizes, worsens, or improves. After the initial hospital stay, professionals such as social workers, rehabilitation counselors, and psychologists are often in a position to help family members gain access to community resources.

Darling and Darling (1982) argue that psychotherapy is not a substitute for practical help when such help is called for. They cite Australian research reporting that the parents studied were "almost desperate" in their plea for help until a training center for children with retardation was established in their community. As a consequence of this resource, parents reported being much happier and more relaxed, and their "neurotic symptoms" virtually disappeared.

Ferhold and Solnit (1978) sound a note of caution regarding a guidance-oriented educative approach:

The counselor is more a facilitator of learning and problem solving than a teacher of facts or an instructor in child-rearing effectiveness. The counselor [should] avoid too many specific directions, even when they appear to be helpful in the short run, because they dilute the process of enabling parents and child to be active on their own behalf—the counselor needs to have faith that parents will make sound choices allowing for some mistakes along the way; when the counselor can no longer accept the parents' decisions, he should withdraw. (pp. 160–162)

This brings us to the next element in Laborde and Seligman's (1991) model, *personal advocacy counseling*. We have already established that families need guidance in finding relevant information and in locating appropriate services. Furthermore, we concur with Ferhold and Solnit (1978) that parents should normally be their own case managers. Parents are, after all, the logical choice to serve as chief coordinators and evaluators of service with the *assistance* of a competent professional. To fill this guidance role adequately, the professional must become familiar with general referral procedures and must be knowledgeable about how the various local service agencies operate.

The professional acts as a broker of services by assisting the family in formulating a clear idea of which needs they wish to have met and in deciding where to receive services. With information on hand, the professional can help the family members develop a plan of action for obtaining needed assistance.

The primary goal of personal advocacy counseling is to help parents to experience a sense of control over events in their own lives and their children's lives. Family members, by experiencing more control, can act with greater confidence and purpose when confronted with various choices or situations. Personal advocacy counseling can help parents work for their family's welfare in a positive and assertive manner. Family members are encouraged to ask questions of their service providers, to question a provider's responses to inquiries, to seek out second opinions, and to request services they believe they need and are entitled to. In short, parents are given the support and "permission" to obtain the professional help they need without feeling guilt or feeling that they do not have the right to ask questions. Family members are encouraged to seek out professionals who are knowledgeable and candid yet compassionate, and to feel confident enough to dismiss professionals who do not meet these requirements.

Facilitative counseling, the third and final component of Laborde and Seligman's model, resembles relationship counseling, wherein a professional helps a family member accept or change distressing feelings or behaviors in the context of a trusting relationship.

As noted previously, parents experience a plethora of contradictory emotions when they first learn their child has a disability. The professional should acknowledge to the parents that their dreams and plans for their child may be severely shaken. It is essential that the professional accept these distressing feelings and not encourage family members to deny or repress them. The family requires time to overcome their grief, and the most helpful professional behavior is to be accepting and available, yet not intrusive.

When the parents are ready to move on they can be helped to see that they can still, to a large degree, live normal, productive, and comfortable lives. It is important to encourage the necessary parent–child bonding while also encouraging family members to pursue their own interests and aspirations. If some differentiation between parent and child does not occur, then parents may become angry, resentful, and withdrawn or enmeshed.

Although it is important to be accepting of feelings, the professional must also encourage parents to seek help for their child as soon as they feel able. In this regard, Pines (1982) reports that, when some children with Down syndrome receive adequate infant stimulation, receive appropriate medical intervention, and are monitored for imbalances (such as thyroid deficiency), the degree of mental retardation can be minimized. Early intervention programs are important for infants with disabilities so that the disabilities recognized at birth are held to a minimum (Meyer & Bailey, 1993).

Parents sometimes blame themselves for their child's disability, but they are rarely at fault (fetal alcoholism syndrome and disabilities resulting from physical abuse of the mother during pregnancy are two exceptions). It is important that the professional help parents understand that their child's condition is not their doing.

Unable to shed their guilt feelings, some parents begin an endless and unproductive search for the cause of their child's disorder or for a "cure." Parents may base their feelings on perceived "misdeeds" or they may focus on behaviors or even "bad" thoughts that occurred during pregnancy. Professionals need to listen and not pass off such ruminations as unimportant.

Parents may also wish to "make up" for supposed past indiscretions by overprotecting their child, or holding the child back from activities that can facilitate his or her growth and independence. Professionals need to help parents explore their guilt, understand its negative effect on the family, and, ideally, curb their overprotective behavior. At the very least, the professional needs to understand that as an overprotective bond develops between a parent and child, the other parent and other children are generally adversely affected. The boundaries of the parent–child relationship may become so impermeable that other family members feel abandoned and look to other sources for affiliation and gratification.

In terms of rejection, a professional can help parents separate their confused feelings of anger about becoming the parent of a child with a disability from their generally positive feelings toward their child. It is helpful that parents find appropriate outlets for expressing anger and feelings of rejection so that these feelings are not inappropriately directed toward their child with a disability, the other children, or each other.

Family members may deeply love their child but find aspects of the child's condition difficult to accept. Also, feelings of rejection, like other emotions, are cyclical—they come and go over time. It is important for professionals to help family members realize that feelings of anger and occasional or limited rejection are normal and that their expression is acceptable.

Laborde and Seligman's (1991) facilitative counseling model encourages professionals to help parents cope with their feelings of shame, which involve the expectation of ridicule or criticism from others. As noted in earlier chapters, some families must deal with community and public attitudes and behaviors that are negative. A useful strategy is to help family members locate self-help groups, which can reduce feelings of isolation and where they can discover how others cope with negative public attitudes. It is particularly important that families of children with disabilities reduce their contact with professionals who hold negative attitudes. Furthermore, it is helpful if professionals can help family members consider strategies that facilitate involvement in activities that they may have withdrawn from, such as family outings, sporting events, movies, and associating with friends (Marshak & Seligman, 1993). Family members can be helped by understanding that there are few actual risks involved in certain activities. They can also learn cognitive techniques that help to correct inaccurate perceptions and reduce stress, learn social skills, and develop strategies to help reduce stress. Where social embarrassment and uncomfortable social situations lead to withdrawal, family members can learn "stigma management" or "impression management" skills (Marshak & Seligman, 1993).

Parental denial of a child's disability is a defense mechanism that operates on an unconscious level to ward off excessive anxiety (Ross, 1964). For some, the mere idea of being the parent of a child with a disability is so fearful that they deny the reality of their child's disability. These parents fight unconsciously to keep their pain hidden from their own awareness. Parental denial is one of the more difficult coping mechanisms for the professional to contend with. A reasonable approach would be to accept the parents' view of their child while gently, when appropriate, pointing out where the child may need special help. A general rule is to never force parents to cast aside a defense mechanism that is rigidly held. The abrupt unveiling of what is being kept from conscious awareness can have a negative effect, for example, to deepen denial. Also, it is not unusual for parents to seek out appropriate interventions for their child while simultaneously denying the disability. Some parents seem to be able to provide for and deeply love their child while holding on to the unrealistic hope that the child will make dramatic improvements. For most parents, the reality of their child's situation becomes clearer over time.

Shopping behavior, usually attributed to feelings of guilt and rejection and manifested through the coping mechanism of denial, must be carefully evaluated. Such behavior may indeed be caused by the threat the disability presents to the family, but alternatively it may reflect a realistic appraisal of the situation due to the nature of the disability and/or the quality of professional care available.

Family problems can emerge when one parent begins to realize the implications of their child's disability while the other continues firmly to deny it. Such tensions may specifically reflect the parents' differing views of their child, or they may represent a chronically dysfunctional family dynamic. To intervene successfully, the professional needs to know about family interactional patterns and issues of power and control. A child's disability can serve as a handy vehicle for acting out dysfunctional family patterns, and the child can be wrongly identified as the cause of family problems.

Facilitative counseling must also attend to concerns that surface—or resurface—as the child approaches various milestones, such as beginning or completing school. The professional should not be alarmed if parents need to cover "old territory" at different times of their child's development. As noted in earlier chapters, key periods that may trigger the family's anxiety include the following:

1. When parents first learn about or suspect that their child has a disability
2. At about age 5 or 6, when a decision must be reached regarding the child's education
3. When the time has arrived for the child to leave school
4. When the parents become older and possibly unable to care for the child

As the child grows into adolescence and young adulthood, parents may have a difficult time giving up their child, either to a residential treatment setting or to independent living. For a number of reasons parents may be so invested in their child that they find it exceedingly difficult to let go. Letting go is especially difficult for overprotective or enmeshed parents who view their son's or daughter's growing independence with apprehension. As the children differentiate from their parents and begin to live more independent lives, professionals can remind parents that independence is in the best interest of the child and that contact between them and their child will not cease. Furthermore, for parents who are uneasy about this stage of the family's life cycle, some attempt should be made to help them understand why their child's emerging independence is so anxiety provoking.

Professionals must help family members cope with disturbing thoughts and puzzling, unacceptable feelings. Depressive ruminations, such as wishing the child were dead, may occur and need to be expressed and explored. Professionals can only be effective during such emotionally charged moments when they themselves have come to terms with feelings often condemned by society.

Although children with disabilities differ from their nondisabled counterparts in some ways, they are alike in other ways—a point for the professional to keep in mind when working with family members. By focusing on similarities rather than on differences, parents can view their child in a more normal fashion. For example, parents of an adolescent who is physically disabled can note how typical it is for their child to enjoy rock music, show an interest in the opposite sex, display occasional moodiness, and be more secretive.

By concentrating on normal aspects of childhood disability, the professional must be careful not to inadvertently reinforce denial, which means that a decision to follow such a course of action must be based on a careful assessment of the family. A denying family will not be aided by a professional who *unrealistically* concentrates on a child's normative qualities. Dispirited families, who tend to evaluate their circumstances negatively and need to restructure their thinking along more optimistic and hopeful lines, can find such a focus helpful. These families also need to explore how their negative outlook serves unspoken family values or rules.

Ross (1964) argues that professionals who work with families of children with disabilities need to have an appreciation for the existence of ambivalence. We may find it difficult to understand that positive and negative emotions exist at the same time. Instances of ambivalence occur often in working with families. For example, families may want help, but are unable to ask for it; they may request advice but not follow through on it when it is given; they may agree to certain plans but fail to carry them out; and then there are those who tell us one thing, but manifest the opposite by their behavior.

A family's ambivalent behavior can indeed be puzzling and even annoying. However, a deeper appreciation of this behavior along with a greater tolerance of it can be developed by understanding the unconscious motivation that lies behind behavior. What family members verbalize may be what they believe on a conscious level, but what they do is often motivated by unconscious needs that become manifest in the ambivalent behavior they display. It is the professional's task, then, to help family members understand their contradictory behavior, which, incidentally, may be as enigmatic to them as it is to the professional.

BEHAVIORAL PARENT TRAINING

Behavioral parent training (BPT) has been used rather extensively (S. L. Harris, 1983; Kaiser & Fox, 1986) and has been the subject of numerous studies (Marsh, 1992). BPT has specific applications and tends to be used and recommended by professionals with a strong behavioral bent.

For some families, the presenting behavioral problems of their children are so severe and disruptive that parent training is a particularly useful intervention. Focusing on the disruptive behavior of children with mental retardation, Kaiser and Fox (1986) report that parents have been trained successfully to modify diverse behavioral problems and to teach such adaptive abilities as chewing and feeding skills, motor imitation, self-help skills, appropriate play behaviors and social interaction with parents, articulation and vocabulary skills, and compliance behavior. Rose (1974) has described a program designed to train parents in groups as behavior modifiers of their children. This program involved becoming familiar with behavioral principles, learning about behavioral assessment, monitoring behaviors weekly, and developing treatment plans. An evaluation of this program showed that parents who varied in educational level and social class were able to acquire the skills needed to modify their children's behavior.

Baker's (1989) model, Parents as Teachers, included such goals as reducing problem behaviors, increasing the child's involvement in activities, and building basic self-help skills as well as teaching play, speech, and language skills. The program constituted 10 training sessions where the above-mentioned skills were taught and applied. The sessions employed minilectures, small group problem-solving sessions, focused discussion, and role-playing demonstrations, as well as other activities. Baker (1989) evaluated the program and found that the parents and children benefited from it.

Effective BPT can decrease some of the stress that parents of children with disabilities experience (Kaiser & Fox, 1986). With this in mind, we believe that it is important for professionals either to be trained in BPT or to be able to make an appropriate referral to someone who specializes in working with disruptive behavior in children. It is beyond the scope of this chapter to elaborate further on the BPT model; however, an excellent resource for professionals who wish to learn more about individual and group models of BPT is S. L. Harris's (1983) book, *Families of the Developmentally Disabled: A Guide to Behavioral Intervention,* and Baker and Brightman's (1989) *Steps to Independence: A Skills Training Guide for Parents and Teachers of Children with Special Needs.*

A major problem with the BPT model is that some families fail to acquire or maintain newly learned skills. Rose (1974) indicates that some parents "never completed contracts but were either changing the responses to be observed or ineffectively implementing unauthorized procedures" (pp. 138–139). Reasons for parental noncompliance include parents' lack of time to do the training, lack of spouse support, limited materials for teaching, and lack of confidence. Another possible reason for parental noncompliance may be the presence of severely disruptive life events, such as death, divorce, illness, or substance abuse in the family. Some parents may not believe that the program is necessary or that they can actually influence their child's behavior after years of trying and failing. Other limitations include the assumption that all parents want or need BPT, that BPT may limit other forms of parental involvement, and that such training may fail to address other parent needs (Lyon & Lyon, 1991). Others caution that parent training can be a narrow approach to facilitating family adaptation in that it fails to embrace the whole family and the intricate dynamics that characterize family functioning (Marsh, 1992). Further, as Chapter 7 indicates, in some cultures, the "parent as teacher" role is not an appropriate model. Many parents of lower SES are so preoccupied by survival activities that they do not have time to be their children's teachers or therapists.

Caution must be exercised in asking parents to engage in "homework" or to act as their child's therapist. Consider the situation of parents who must follow the prescriptions of the special education teacher, the speech therapist, the hearing specialist, the vision specialist, the physical therapist, and the doctor. Max (1985) notes that the pendulum of fashion might be swinging too far, so that parents' onerous burden of impotence has been replaced by an equally heavy one of great expectations. "You feel that you have to do it all and it is so exhausting. But if you don't do everything they tell you to do, you feel that you're letting down all these highly qualified people who are giving up their good time to help your child" (p. 255)

GROUP FORMATS

Until World War II, when the necessity to treat war casualties overwhelmed available resources, group interventions were considered a lesser form of therapeutic help. Group formats were considered more efficient, in that they could serve more people, but less effective in outcome than existing individual therapies. This early view of groups has changed dramatically (Yalom, 1995). Therapeutic groups are still considered efficient but the central rationale for their use is that, for some persons and certain problems, they are more effective.

The decision to recommend group or individual counseling needs to be carefully considered by the practitioner. The suggestion that parents consider some type of group should be based on the following:

1. The parents feel relatively comfortable in a group context.
2. They are basically mature and emotionally stable but their functioning is temporarily impaired (Ross, 1964).
3. They are not overly self-absorbed and monopolistic (Yalom, 1995).
4. They have pronounced yet well-controlled feelings of hostility (Ross, 1964).
5. They are not overly controlling, masochistic, or passive–aggressive, and do not have psychotic tendencies (Ross, 1964).
6. They have a modicum of empathy for others and they are open to others' opinions and guidance.

Group formats vary greatly in that they may be open or closed in membership, gender or disability; homogeneous or heterogeneous; small or large; professional- or member-led; and so forth. Likewise, the groups purposes differ in that they may be educational or therapeutic (although some would argue that educational groups are also therapeutic), designed to help parents cope immediately after diagnosis or to consider living and working arrangements and problems of their postschool children, or designed to help siblings and extended family members cope.

In terms of purpose, the major distinction is between providing education and information or therapy (Marshak & Seligman, 1993; Seligman, 1993). Groups that are primarily *educative* focus on providing families with information about their child's disability as well as training in effective coping and parenting skills. Educationally oriented groups also serve to inform families about their legal rights and benefits, where to obtain needed services, where to purchase and how to operate special equipment, and the like. In these groups, parents learn from each other, from the leader, and from guest speakers. This model assumes that family problems arise from deficiencies in skills or information and that families function adaptively to meet their own needs when provided with accurate and relevant information. This view further assumes that parents' emotional reactions and coping skills are not problematic when they have the resources to perform adequately as parents.

Although professionally led groups meet informational and skill needs and help parents discuss their emotional burdens, such groups are less likely to foster family leadership and advocacy (Marsh, 1992). Group facilitation by parents, in contrast, is likely to reinforce family leadership and advocacy; professionals can serve as consultants who offer technical assistance or present educationally focused workshops. Marsh (1992) advocates for professional–parent cofacilitation, which can increase the likelihood that all of the families' needs can be addressed.

With regard to homogeneity, some groups are composed of parents with children who have a particular disorder. As long as the child's condition falls within a recognized diagnostic category—for example, mental retardation—parents may be invited to join. However, some groups may be composed of parents with children from a subcategory of a major disorder, for example, Down syndrome. Some time ago Baus, Letson, and Russell (1958) proposed a group model for parents of children with epilepsy, but excluded parents whose children also had other problems such as cerebral palsy, blindness, marked mental retardation, severe hearing loss, or diabetes. The group leaders felt that the group discussions would become too complex if such additional conditions were brought up by the parents. Because many disabling conditions are accompanied by other problems, we would discourage group leaders from using such an exclusionary model.

An early group program with parents of children with physical disabilities used a heterogeneous model by including parents of children with a variety of disabilities (Milman, 1952). The reports by Baus and colleagues (1958) and Milman (1952) reflect the diversity of approaches available, but we suspect that the most prevalent model falls somewhere in between, with parents of children with a particular primary disorder invited to join, irrespective of the child's other problems.

In terms of a structured group experience, Baus and colleagues' (1958) description of a time-limited, information-oriented group for parents of children with epilepsy is a useful model and one that continues to be used. Hornby (1994) believes that an ideal number of sessions is between six and eight weekly 2-hour evening sessions. Less than six sessions is too few to cover the relevant material and to benefit from the therapeutic process. More than eight sessions is considered to be too great a commitment of time and too tiring for parents and professional leaders. Furthermore, parent dropout tends to occur more often when meetings are spaced more than a week apart. Evening meetings are preferred so that both parents can attend. According to Hornby, the 2-hour time period is ideal for a presentation followed by discussion and parent interaction.

Returning to Baus and colleagues' model, a physician attends the first two sessions and discusses the medical aspects of epilepsy. The next two sessions are led by a psychologist who discusses management and behavioral concerns of children with epilepsy, and the final session is devoted to the family's emotional response to the child. Questions are encouraged throughout.

This basic model can be expanded and made more flexible by inviting other specialists, such as the following:

1. A physician to explain more fully the medical implications of a child's condition
2. A physical therapist to discuss exercise and strengthening regimens that may be helpful
3. A psychologist or other mental health worker to help with problems of management and also assist parents to understand their emotional reactions
4. An attorney to elaborate on legal aspects, guardianship, and parent rights, as well as to help interpret relevant legislation
5. A local or state politician to discuss community/state policies regarding disability issues

Hornby (1994), a pioneer in developing and conducting parent groups and workshops in Great Britain and New Zealand, describes a typical 2-hour meeting:

7:30–7:45 P.M. *Socializing.* Tea and coffee are served while parents talk informally with professionals and each other.
7:45–8:05 P.M. *Lecture presentation.* A 20-minute lecture on a topic of concern to the parents is presented by a professional.
8:05–9:15 P.M. *Small group discussion.* Parents are divided into small groups in order to participate in discussion. Opportunity is provided for discussion of the applications of the lecture content to specific problems brought forward by parents. Parents are encouraged to express and explore any problems, concerns, or feelings regarding their children with disabilities.
9:15–9:30 P.M. *Summary, handouts, and homework.* The large group is re-formed so that issues raised in small group discussions can be summarized and shared, homework tasks explained, and handouts summarizing the content of lectures distributed. (p. 156)

The model can be even further expanded to incorporate a series of more therapeutically oriented sessions regarding parental stress, coping behavior, and emotional responses. It may be advantageous to have several open-ended sessions after the more structured program to allow parents to express feelings, to achieve closure, and to terminate the friendships they have developed in the group. There are always some group members that continue relationships begun in the group, thereby adding to their support network (Hornby & Murray, 1983).

Support groups can either be led by professionals or by members, the latter either with or without professional consultation available (Darling & Darling, 1982; Friedlander & Watkins, 1985). The enormous growth of support groups for almost any type of disability has been well documented (Lieberman, 1990; Seligman & Meyerson, 1982). Support groups can benefit their members in several ways:

1. The quick identification with others who are experiencing similar problems
2. The 24-hour availability of group members to assist during critical periods
3. The development of a network of friends to help reduce isolation
4. The lack of costly fees

Also, such groups offer long-term support, an opportunity to develop skills and coping mechanisms, a forum to share concerns and problems, and a sense of belonging.

One of the more prominent types of support groups that are currently flourishing are those for siblings of children with disabilities. Although evaluations of the effectiveness of these groups has not been a major priority, clinical reports and personal accounts of the effects of such groups have been promising (see Chapter 5 for more on siblings). At the University of Washington, a support group model, which has an educational component, has been reported for siblings, fathers, and grandparents (see Chapters 5 and 6 for discussion of these groups).

Agee, Innocenti, and Boyce (1995) report on a recent study designed to assess whether a group for parents who were involved in an early intervention program helped reduce stress. Half of the parents in the early intervention program were asked to participate in a parent group that was chiefly educationally oriented. The parents participated in groups of 8 to 12 members and met for 90- to 120-minute sessions one time a week for 15 or 16 weeks. The results showed that both "highly stressed" and "typically stressed" parents experienced significantly lower levels of stress than parents who were not in the groups.

In addition to educationally oriented groups and peer support groups, Seligman and Meyerson (1982) note that another approach is the *therapy model,* which stresses self-exploration and the disclosure of emotional issues. Such groups can help parents and other family members gain an awareness of attitudes and behaviors that might bear on the family member who has the disability. In addition to exploring feelings, family members can examine how the family is coping with the member who has the disability. Furthermore, group members can explore how they are personally being affected now and how their hopes for future may be affected.

Most parent groups that are reported in the literature combine elements of both education and therapy (Hornby, 1994; Seligman & Meyerson, 1982). At face value this model speaks to the reported needs of families, yet very little research is available to support this or any other approach. Support of the integrated model is based on the premise that group formats should be based on the needs of families and that the family's response to the child is multidetermined. Group goals and content should be based on a careful assessment of parent needs. It is probably true that families need knowledge *and* emotional support in order to cope with the stresses that occur in raising a child with a disability. Families need to know the dimensions of their child's disabling condition and the parameters of his or her growth potential. They need to know what medical, educational, and other services are available within their community. Above all, they need understanding and support for both their wish to raise their child and their need to believe that this task is a hopeful, necessary, and worthwhile commitment.

A crucial attribute of support groups is the experience that negative emotions are more universal and normal than parents may think. This is reflected in the following comment made to group leader Marsh (1992):

> Meeting other mothers with similar experiences was wonderful. As much as we love our handicapped children, it was such an eye-opener to learn that other mothers had intense feelings at times of guilt, anger toward the child, resentment toward an abnormal lifestyle, and other negative feelings. I thought I was the only one that still felt this way after so many years. I left the meetings uplifted that my feelings were quite typical and really normal considering what our family has gone through. (p. 195)

Parent-to-parent models have become popular in the United States (Mott, Jenkins, Justice, & Moon, n.d.) and elsewhere (Hornby, 1994; Hornby & Murray, 1983). Although they were first established in the United States, they have subsequently spread to Canada, Australia, New Zealand, Great Britain, and Ireland (Hornby, 1994). In this model, a parent assists another parent on an individual basis. The success of this approach is predicated on careful screening and group-based training.

A program that illustrates this model is reported by Mott and colleagues (n.d.). Project Hope, which is located in North Carolina, postulates that specific environmental factors are critical in the overall development of the child with a disability. Project Hope is based on a premise characteristic of more educationally oriented models, that is, that social support plays a significant role in decreasing the amount of stress experienced by families. Other rationales for Project Hope include the notion that parents may learn more from each other than from professionals; the belief that in-depth understanding of raising a child with a disability is best understood by other families; the need to help to alleviate feelings of isolation and promote realization that others experience similar problems, frustrations, and successes; and the desire to help parents express anger, grief, exhaustion, expectations, and hope. A final goal of Project Hope is to be available to families at the point of initial diagnosis *and* throughout the child's life. The project's goals are far-reaching and actually incorporate both educational and therapeutic elements.

Volunteer parents are carefully screened and are selected to participate if they have the following attributes:

1. Positive valuing and acceptance of their own child
2. An interest and the time to devote to parent-to-parent contacts
3. A willingness to participate in all parent training sessions
4. An open mind to values and feelings of other parents that differ from their own
5. An awareness of family reactions to having a child with a disability
6. A willingness to help parents whose child has a different disability from their own

The group leaders who train Project Hope parents must (1) be familiar with the nature of specific disabilities and their potential impact on the family, (2) have a good working knowledge about services and resources, and (3) be able to model empathy skills (this was regarded as most important).

The two days of training for the parents consists of (1) sensitizing them to the needs of parents whose children have different disabling conditions than their own children, (2) providing them with a basic framework from which to communicate with others in an empathic manner, and (3) providing them with specific information regarding a variety of conditions and available resources.

Hornby (1994), who pioneered parent-to-parent programs in New Zealand and Great Britain, stated that parents who are accepted in the programs are closely monitored to be sure that they are performing without major problems. This scrutiny is based on the belief that parents are often under enough stress without the additional burden of coping with another parent also under stress. He notes that on occasion a parent who was initially accepted into the program is terminated due to inadequate interpersonal skills or unresolved emotional problems. Hornby adds that the trained parents come together periodically for additional training and to discuss dilemmas they encounter in their contact with other parents. A full discussion of recruitment, retention, and training is included in Hornby's (1994) book, *Counselling in Child Disability: Skills for Working with Parents.*

As noted in Chapter 1, family and ecological models have properly taken their place as useful conceptual frameworks. In addition, there has emerged a rather singular concern about the welfare of siblings (see Chapter 5). In families in which a child with a disability resides, nondisabled siblings sometimes do not receive the parenting accorded to their seemingly more needy brother or sister who is disabled. As indicated in Chapter 5, some siblings fare well, while others do not. Some group models for siblings have emerged out of the recognition that some cope poorly, while other groups for young siblings have evolved to help prevent future problems.

Groups for siblings have similar goals to groups that presently exist for parents. In these groups, siblings gain an understanding of their brother's or sister's condition, its etiology and prognosis, and the knowledge that there are others who have siblings with disabilities and that they struggle with similar issues. In the groups, siblings explore feelings of love, hate, and ambivalence; talk about their fear of developing the same condition; and discuss their concerns about how to handle awkward social situations and how to cope with major anxieties about what the future holds for them. Siblings need a safe place to discuss their feelings of guilt and anger, how they feel their unique situation has affected family life, and how being a sibling of a disabled brother or sister may influence their choice of a career (D. J. Meyer & Vadasy, 1994).

In developing support groups for siblings one should carefully consider the following:

1. Whether the group will be heterogeneous or homogeneous regarding age: This issue requires careful thought in that children and adolescents vary considerably over 2–3 year spans.
2. Whether they will be heterogeneous or homogeneous in regard to the type or severity of the disability: There probably is little lost and perhaps a great deal to gain from more heterogeneous groups.
3. What activities will reflect the group's goals and purposes: Some view sibling groups as primarily informational and recreational, while others stress feelings and adjustment. There probably is considerable value in *all* of these goals.
4. Practical issues, such as the length of each session (keeping in mind the children's ages and the activities planned) and the long-term duration of the group: Some groups span a relatively

brief period of time, with each session being well planned, while others meet for longer periods with more open-ended sessions.

5. Whether a follow-up meeting is deemed necessary: Sibling groups may stir up feelings beyond the group's life, and it may be beneficial to have one or two follow-up meetings to help siblings achieve closure.

6. Information content: What information would siblings find useful?

7. Leadership: Leaders should be chosen who have had some experience with disabilities and group process.

8. Discussion materials: One may wish to have participants read certain materials for discussion purposes. Caution needs to exercised so that books and articles are age appropriate.

A sibling group model developed by Reynolds and Zellmer (1985) is an example of a structured, time-limited group experience. The group was co-led by a social worker and preschool teacher. Six siblings, ages 7–14, participated in the 1-hour per week, 6-session experience.

Session I: Participants brought family pictures to the first session to facilitate a discussion about themselves and their families.

Session II: "What is a disability?" was the theme of the second meeting. Siblings explored how every person has some kind of disability. Medical problems of their brothers and sisters with disabilities were also discussed.

Session III: Group members participated in simulating disabilities so that they could empathize with their siblings.

Session IV: This session focused on what it is like to have a brother or sister with a disability. Books and articles, or diaries authored by siblings can be used to stimulate discussion.

Session V: Siblings discussed ways to deal with their feelings. The notion that all feelings have value and are not bad was stressed. Role playing of key problematic situations was employed.

Session VI: This wrap-up session was used to discuss unfinished business. The meeting was held in a relaxed social setting with food available.

DYSFUNCTIONAL FAMILY DYNAMICS

The treatment of families rests on family systems theory elaborated in Chapter 1. It is not our intent to repeat family systems concepts here nor is it our goal to speak with authority about specific family interventions. It is assumed that professionals who plan to conduct family therapy are well grounded in the theory and practice of this intervention. Without question, specialized training is required for successful family therapy. Furthermore, as noted earlier, it is incumbent upon those who work with families with a disabled family member to acquire the requisite knowledge about disability and the families' response to it.

We basically agree with Meyerson (1983), who says that

> problems in families of handicapped children are essentially no different from those in any family. The primary difference between normal and exceptional families is that, in the latter, the additional stresses and strains may highlight existing problems or force them to a higher level of awareness. (p. 293)

Dysfunctional, tension-filled families are in a poor position to cope with a family member who is disabled. Although there have been reports that some families have become more cohesive as a result of a childhood disability, these families probably had a minimum of existing pathology. Troubled families tend to become more dysfunctional in the face of crises and chronic stressors, while strong ones adapt, cope, and grow in the wake of crises.

Johnson (in Turk & Kerns, 1985) writes about a family dynamic that may be especially salient in families with a child who is chronically ill:

> Because chronically ill children are physically vulnerable, the child's illness may encourage over involvement by one parent. This parent, usually the mother, then neglects other family members. Her neglect places strain on the marital relationship and also results in feelings of hostility toward the patient by siblings. However, these feelings of resentment are not expressed openly because the patient is not to be "upset." The parents' focus on the child's symptoms permit them to avoid their own marital conflicts and consequently the patient's symptoms are reinforced. (p. 239)

Responding to the scenario described above requires a sensitivity to both subtle and obvious family dynamics—hence, the need to be well schooled in family systems theory, family dynamics, and family interventions. Below are other potential problematic family patterns:

1. A child with a disability can be the recipient of excessive attention because he or she is seen as the most needy family member. Other family members, such as nondisabled siblings, may experience parental withdrawal and as a result feel angry toward the parents and the privileged (disabled) sib. Siblings may also feel resentful and unloved, and they may

act out their anger in an effort to capture some of the attention they long for. Unfortunately, the methods some nondisabled children use to capture parental attention may further alienate the parents, thus increasing the likelihood of additional disruptive behavior. The professional can assist a family so embroiled by helping them understand that although a child with a disability may appear to be the most needy, in fact, the other children may be the most emotionally deprived. Furthermore, nondisabled siblings can be helped to understand their well-intentioned parents who focused on the child they erroneously thought needed the most attention.

2. Grandparents who cannot accept their grandchild's disability add considerably to the parents' burdens. The parents are torn by their natural inclination to accept and love their child and the pressure they feel to shun (and perhaps institutionalize) him or her. This scenario creates tension within both parents (intrapsychic), between them, and between the parents and the grandparents. It is easy to see how parents can be torn by their pain, because they need to make difficult choices regarding whom they wish to align themselves with. Ideally, an astute therapist can help the family resolve this crisis without excessive damage.

3. Family members who experience themselves as significantly stigmatized by their community are in danger of becoming isolated, bitter, and withdrawn. Although the danger comes from outside of the family, the perception of a hostile community can create major tensions within the family. A major risk factor exists if the family members begin to internalize the perceived negative community evaluations and conclude that they are unworthy. Professionals can help such family members to consider alternative explanations for the behaviors they experience and to become more proficient at detecting their misperceptions of others who are actually supportive of them. They may also be referred to a support group where they can share their perceptions and discover from others that some people are actually supportive, helpful, and kind.

4. Poor relationships with professionals and the absence of important social services can have devastating effects on the family. Families feel unsupported and overburdened, which in turn creates tension and stress in the family. Here families need to seek out professionals who can explore alternative service delivery systems and service providers who devote a portion of their practice to the area of childhood disability (Laborde & Seligman, 1991).

5. As noted earlier, the birth of a child with a disability to a troubled family can exacerbate existing family tension. Fragile families cannot tolerate additional pressures and the presence of a child with a disability is not only an additional burden of some magnitude, but also a chronic one. Some family members find it difficult to be cooperative with and supportive of each other due to conditions of unemployment and poverty.

Families that are significantly troubled can be helped by agencies that provide a full range of services including in-home help.

6. Perhaps the most frequently described situation is the one in which parents, expecting a healthy baby, discover that their newborn is disabled. The potential immediate effects are considerable: shock; the realization that one must make major changes in one's life, in one's expectations, and the like. Most families eventually learn to cope by altering their values, expectations, and goals, without abandoning important life objectives. For those family members who find it difficult to come to grips with their circumstances, professional psychological help combined with support group membership can prove beneficial.

Drotar, Crawford, and Bush (1984) acknowledge that the presence of a chronic illness has a profound effect on family life. Until recently, professionals have attended to the ill child rather than to the family unit. The focus on children has advanced our knowledge of how children with a chronic disability or illness cope, but the neglect of the family in its interaction with the child has produced some undesirable consequences. For example, a narrow child-centered focus fails to recognize the family as a powerful context for socialization and support for the child with a disability. The nature and quality of intrafamilial coping is important to assess because children learn their methods of adaptation from their parents. What these children learn from their parents affects their ability to negotiate the stressful demands of their disability. Being knowledgeable about the family's dynamics helps professionals understand how the family's culture promotes both healthy and unhealthy responses to stress and crisis. Furthermore, an analysis of the family can help determine how the family facilitates illness and disability behaviors (e.g., dependency) or how it encourages adaptation and healthy independence (Rolland, 1994).

In physical disabilities, day-to-day treatment regimens require parents to consider their respective contributions to the care of their child (Drotar et al., 1984). Parental roles and responsibilities must be negotiated and there is a compelling need to reconcile career versus family demands. Furthermore, parental involvement in the physical treatment of their children can violate customary psychological boundaries between parent and child.

Chronic childhood illnesses can intersect with family and individual developmental issues (Rolland, 1994). A child with disabilities can be a considerable burden on a newly married couple that is trying to establish a family identity. Developmental transitions of the child and of family members can create tension as the family is confronted by changes. For example, the decision on the part of an adolescent with a disability to live in a college dormitory can be disturbing to a close-knit, overprotective family. Other developmental milestones, such as when a child first begins school or reaches adolescence, may create family tension.

Parents may have difficulty maintaining appropriate boundaries concerning their child's privacy and they can find it difficult to support each other, especially in the area of how best to manage a child with a chronic illness (Drotar et al., 1984). In general, according to Drotar and his colleagues, although a child's chronic illness can cause family strain, it is not necessarily the cause of marital dysfunction. In this regard, Venter (in Drotar et al., 1984) suggests that the parents' ability to construct meaning from the child's chronic illness experience may help the family's ability to cope. In writing about coping with his son Andrew, who has Down syndrome, Nicholas Kappes (1995) embraces the concept of relativity to help place his son's disability within a broad philosophical context:

> I find peace in relativity. It governs our universe—it also governs our lives. No matter who or where we are we can always look up to greater and down to lower. Presidents and kings have their heroes and their inadequacies. No one is completely happy or has it all figured out to their satisfaction, and even those in tragic, painful circumstances cling to each precious moment of life—so it must be worth it for all. (p. 27)

Despite existing publications about children with disabilities and their families, there have been few attempts to describe intervention models. Bailey and colleagues (1986) have, however, proposed a model referred to as *family-focused intervention*. This model involves assessing family needs, planning goals, providing services for families, and evaluating outcomes. The intervention rests on the assumption that services for families must be individualized. Another key assumption of the family-focused intervention is that, although the child is an essential concern, the family is also viewed as a target client. The interested reader can consult Bailey and colleagues (1986) for a detailed discussion of this comprehensive model of family intervention.

Drotar and colleagues (1984) also focus on the family as the client. These authors assert that, in working with children who are chronically ill, families should be involved immediately after the child's diagnosis is known. They embrace a structural family systems model, which focuses on observable patterns through which family members relate to one another to carry out important roles and functions.

Another essential concept is the family's subsystems, such the parent and sibling subsystem (see Chapter 1 for a fuller discussion). Attention to subsystems allows the professional to evaluate and intervene in the smaller unit within the family that is most dysfunctional, although one cannot lose sight of how the subsystem (e.g., a parent and the child with a disability) can influence the whole family. As already noted, the concept of *boundary* is especially relevant for those who work with chronically ill children and their families. The concepts of boundaries and subsystems go hand-in-hand, because families need to negotiate appropriate space between subsystems.

One of the chief contributors to dysfunctional families is the consistent violation of boundaries by the intrusion of family members into functions that are the domains of other family members (Elman, 1991). An example of this phenomenon is an overprotective, controlling mother's thwarting of the father's involvement with his son who has a disability, which violates the father's parent role. Another illustration is the parents' violation of the sibling subsystems when they interfere with the siblings' methods of solving conflicts among themselves.

If possible, the professional's contact with a family should begin at the point of the child's diagnosis (Bailey et al., 1986; Drotar et al., 1984). However, these initial contacts may give unintended, powerful messages to families. For example, if professionals maintain contact with the mother only, the family may interpret this as an indicator that she should be involved in subsequent contacts. It may further be interpreted that it is the mother who should be the primary caregiver, rather than having shared caregiving. These early interactions between professional staff members and the mother can isolate the father and other children from the mother–child dyad. A more adaptive model is to involve as many family members as possible, especially at the point of initial diagnosis.

Siblings can be the source of considerable support to a brother or sister with a disability. However, it is difficult for siblings to be supportive and to feel a part of the family if they are not included in what the parents are experiencing, informed about the disability, or involved, to some extent, in the disabled child's care. Sibling involvement can be beneficial to the family and can help siblings feel useful, helpful, and a part of the family that is presently coping with a crisis. However, as noted earlier, sibling involvement can be a double-edged sword.

An important element of family-centered care is the family's involvement in decision making. Especially where a child with a disability is involved and where there may be numerous decisions to be made, all salient family members (and this may include grandparents) should be allowed to voice an opinion so that certain members do not take over while others feel left out.

Before intervening in a family, an assessment should be made (Elman, 1991; Rolland, 1993). Rolland, for example, believes that a multigenerational assessment helps clarify the family's strengths and vulnerabilities. It also helps to identify families that exhibit dysfunctional patterns due to unresolved past issues. Such families may find it difficult to absorb the challenges presented by a chronic illness or disability.

Rolland (1993) encourages the family practitioner to explore how the family has dealt with previous stressors. It is helpful to track family illnesses and determine how family members have coped with them in the past. Ascertaining how family members handle affective issues and practical tasks in the face of disability contributes to an understanding of helpful and dysfunctional responses. The practitioner should attempt to understand the roles family members play in handling emotional and practical tasks and explore whether they emerged from coping with disability or illness with a sense of competence or failure.

Another area to assess is whether the family tends to catastrophize events (Elman, 1991). Elman would also inquire about the specific aspects of the disability—for example, is the disability chiefly physical, cognitive, or emotional, or a combination? Relatedly, one might inquire about whether the child is capable of some emotional reciprocity with family members and to what extent the disability impairs the child's functioning. The severity or ambiguity of the diagnosis and the expected level of the child's ongoing dependency should be explored as well as his or her "launchibility." Age and gender of the child should also be determined. These factors may interact with other variables, such as a father's emotional difficulty with a son who has a disability; an adolescent's search for a sense of identity, competence, and self-esteem; or a young adult's continued dependency on the family when independent living is possible. The professional should also inquire about who participates with whom, when, where, and in what ways.

According to Elman (1991), normalizing and reframing are important intervention strategies when there is a disability. Normalizing communicates that the emotions and struggle experienced by the family is both normal and expectable. Normalization can help reduce feelings of isolation and stigma. Support groups are an ideal source for normalizing, in that family members experience others who are struggling similarly. The danger with normalizing is that it can be viewed as trivializing the family's problems. When done by a sensitive professional, normalizing can help reduce anxiety and the sense of catastrophe that some family members experience.

Reframing is a powerful and effective strategy to help family members change the meaning of disability in their lives. Reframing means reinterpreting behavior or putting it into a new "frame." In the area of family therapy, the most useful reframing is to redefine a behavior as benignly motivated and capable of being changed (Hoffman, 1981). Below is an illustration of a helpful reframe:

> For example, if a mother is defined as overinvolved and intrusive, the
> family therapist can respond empathically to how much she cares for

her disabled child and how hard she has tried to find ways to help the child to grow as successfully as possible. The therapist can further comment on the difficulty of knowing how to change in the face of the child's and family's changing needs. This basically simple reframe of the mother's behavior, from intrusive to caring, concerned and confused about change, alters the perception of and meaning attributed to the experience. The mother probably feels more understood than she has in the past and feels that continuing effort is worthwhile, even if it has not always worked. The rest of the family also views the mother in a different perspective. An underinvolved parent or relative may feel more able to choose alternative responses when the behavior is framed as one that encourages self-care or independence. (Elman, 1991, p. 394)

Reframing also allows the family to change its perception of the disabling condition, such as changing the perception of a child from a severely disabled one to a youngster who has abilities and strengths. For example, Elman (1991) relates the story of a young woman, ashamed of her crutches, who was helped to select brightly colored or decorated ones to help her emphasize her strengths rather than discount herself as a crippled person.

Resnick, Reiss, Eyler, and Schauble (1988) describe a family-oriented multidisciplinary program in the School of Medicine at the University of Florida. This family-focused approach was designed to prevent developmental delay in premature and low-birth-weight infants. Professionals from several disciplines are involved with the at-risk infant and the family immediately after diagnosis. Supportive counseling is offered during the initial crisis. Also, while the baby is in intensive care, staff teach such skills to family members as coping with stressful emotions, communication skills, crisis management techniques, and so forth. Instruction in developmental activities is provided to the family as well, so that they can be involved in the care and development of the child.

Staff members are involved with the family during the infant's hospital stay and help prepare the family for the transition to the home environment. A pediatric nurse visits the family to facilitate the infant's homecoming. Also, twice a month, staff members from the early childhood education program at the hospital visit the child's home to help family members learn appropriate interaction activities and to teach other activities and exercises from a detailed curriculum. This service continues until the child is 3 years old or is eligible for nursery school.

A particularly innovative aspect of the program reported by Resnick and colleagues (1988) is the attention paid to the professional staff. Professionals often experience their own grief, guilt, and vulnerability (similar to parents) when an infant fails to thrive, but they tend to suppress their feelings so that they can continue to provide competent care to the infant and the family. Over time, however, such suppressed feelings can lead to personal distress, withdrawal, and depression. In response, group meetings are scheduled to help the professional staff air their feelings and concerns. The meetings provide an important safety valve for dealing with personal stress and other volatile issues.

Professional burnout may need to be addressed more seriously in settings where providing services to children with disabilities and their families is stressful. In Chapter 8, we discuss the adversarial relationship that sometimes exists between families and professionals. Chronic stress and burnout certainly contribute to strained relationships. It is conceivable that, in some encounters, family members are experiencing stress as they attempt to cope with their situation, while at the same time professionals may be anxious and stressed because of their demanding work with families and their stressful work environments. This potentially explosive situation needs to be acknowledged and addressed.

A family-oriented approach can rectify the counterproductive view that the child with a disability should be the sole focus of concern. When the family is considered the client, one must necessarily keep in mind that families differ in terms of culture, ethnicity, and lifestyle. In addition, as structural changes in family life occur over the years, professionals must be cognizant of the special needs of divorced and reconstituted families. And, finally, one must keep in mind that some children with disabilities live in fragmented and highly chaotic situations that do not provide a nurturing environment. In working with families, all of these considerations must be kept in mind.

Finally, one cannot assume that professionals have a right to intervene in families simply because those families happen to have a child with a disability. One parent has written that

> no one ever seemed to examine professionals' reactions . . . *parents* are turned into patients and are endlessly analyzed, scrutinized, and finally packaged into neat stages as if they were one-celled animals going through mitosis. . . . Although parents and people with disabilities do have obligations and responsibilities, they must not be victimized by their status. (Pieper, in Darling & Darling, 1982, p. viii)

Parents must be active participants in determining what kinds of help they need and how much help is needed. When families agree that therapeutic intervention would be beneficial, professionals trained in a family systems perspective can be tremendously helpful to them.

Applying a Systems Approach to the Identification of Family Resources and Concerns: The Individualized Family Service Plan and Beyond

As NOTED repeatedly in this volume, the recognition of the importance of the family as a whole in services to children with disabilities is a relatively recent development in the history of the field. In the past, medical, educational, and therapeutic services were designed to meet only the needs of the child. The needs of parents and other family members were neglected or left to mental health professionals who had little direct influence on the child's educational or therapeutic program. In recent years, professionals have come to recognize that child needs and family concerns are not separate and distinct. This recognition achieved legal acknowledgment with the passage of landmark legislation in 1986, the Education of the Handicapped Act amendments—Public Law 99-457 (since amended and renamed the Individuals with Disabilities Education Act).

Part H of that law, which applies to infants and toddlers with disabilities, established a policy to assist states "to develop and implement a statewide, comprehensive, coordinated, multidisciplinary interagency program of early intervention services for handicapped infants and toddlers *and their families*" (pp. 1–2, emphasis added). Services to families of infants and toddlers are to be provided through an Individualized Family Service Plan (IFSP). Because this requirement highlights the importance of the family as a whole, a discussion of the process of developing an IFSP provides an excellent illustration of the application of system-based principles and methods to an intervention situation.

THE INDIVIDUALIZED FAMILY SERVICE PLAN (IFSP)

For infants and toddlers, the IFSP replaces the Individualized Education Plan (IEP), created under Public Law 94-142. The IEP is a document that lists the strengths and needs of special-education students and develops the long-range goals and short-term objectives that will meet those needs. Although the parent may participate in the development of the IEP, the parent's needs, as distinct from the child's needs, are not addressed. With the passage of Public Law 99-457, very young children do not have IEPs at all. Rather, service providers must take family concerns into account in the preparation of IFSPs.

Among other items, the IFSP must include the following:

- A statement of the family's resources, concerns, and priorities relating to enhancing the development of the child
- A statement of the major outcomes expected to be achieved for the child and the family
- A statement of specific early intervention services necessary to meet the unique needs of the child and the family and timeframes for these services

Because our main concern in this book is with families, we will not address processes for determining *child* outcomes for the IFSP. (We should note, however, that much of the current literature in the early intervention field stresses family involvement in determining these outcomes.) Rather, we will look at methods for identifying the resources, concerns, and priorities of parents and other family members and for developing *family* outcomes based on these concerns and priorities.

The methods that will be illustrated here use a questionnaire and an interview format. Both have been used extensively in early intervention programs and are based on the social system perspective (Mercer, 1965) that has been presented throughout this book. To understand families, professionals must accept the statements of parents and other family members as meaningful, regardless of whether they agree with them or think they are true. Intervention must be based on what is real *for the family*. Parents must not themselves become objects of clinical analysis simply because they happen to be the parents of children with disabilities. Parents of children without disabilities are not required to demonstrate a standardized set of "parenting skills"; parents of children with disabilities should not be subjected to a double standard. Certainly the literature reveals the existence of disordered family relationships in families with children with disabilities, as well as in families whose children are "normal." Such families may need the assistance of trained counselors. Unless we have strong evidence to the contrary, however, we should not assume that family relationships are pathological. Early intervention professionals should limit their intervention to meeting those needs that *families* define as important. The early intervention specialist should help the family help the child and should respect the family's privacy in other areas of family life—unless help is requested in those areas.

THE PARENT NEEDS SURVEY (PNS)

This questionnaire-type instrument is an example of a tool based on a social system perspective, in that needs are defined by the family rather than by the professional. The PNS has been used for 7 years in a program previously directed by one of the authors (R. B. D.) and was also field tested in other early intervention programs around the country (see Darling & Baxter, 1996 for a discussion of the testing process). Figure 10.1 is a sample survey form.

The PNS was developed from an overview of the literature (presented in earlier chapters) on families of young children with disabilities. The literature indicates six major areas of need or concern in this population:

1. *Information* about diagnosis, prognosis, and treatment
2. *Intervention* for the child—medical, therapeutic, and educational
3. *Formal support* from public and private agencies
4. *Informal support* from relatives, friends, neighbors, coworkers, and other parents
5. *Material support,* including financial support and access to resources
6. Elimination of *competing family needs,* that is, needs of other family members (parents, siblings, etc.) that may affect the family's ability to attend to the needs of the child with a disability

Date: _____

Name of person completing form: _____

Relationship to child: _____

Parents of young children have many different needs. Not all parents need the same kinds of help. For each of the needs listed below, please check (x) the space that best describes your need or desire for help in that area. Although we may not be able to help you with all your needs, your answers will help us improve our program.

	I really need some help in this area.	I would like some help, but my need is not that great.	I don't need any help in this area.
1. More information about my child's disability.	I		
2. Someone who can help me feel better about myself.	FS, IS		
3. Help with child care.	FS, IS		
4. More money/financial help.	MS, CN		
5. Someone who can babysit for a day or evening so I can get away.	CN		
6. Better medical care for my child.	T		
7. More information about child development.	I		
8. More information about behavior problems.	I, T		
9. More information about programs that can help my child.	I, T		
10. Counseling to help me cope with my situation.	FS		
11. Better/more frequent teaching or therapy services for my child.	T		
12. Day care so I can get a job.	FS, CN		
13. A bigger or better house or apartment.	CN		
14. More information about how I can help my child.	I, T		
15. More information about nutrition or feeding.	I, T		

(continued)

FIGURE 10.1. Parent Needs Survey

		I really need some help in this area.	I would like some help, but my need is not that great.	I don't need any help in this area.
16. Learning how to handle my other children's jealousy of their brother or sister.	CN			
17. Problems with in-laws or other relatives.	IS, CN			
18. Problems with friends or neighbors.	IS, CN			
19. Special equipment to meet my child's needs.	T, MS			
20. More friends who have a child like mine.	IS			
21. Someone to talk to about my problems.	FS, IS			
22. Problems with my husband (wife).	IS, CN			
23. A car or other form of transportation.	MS, CN			
24. Medical care for myself.	CN			
25. More time for myself.	CN			
26. More time to be with my child.	CN			

Please list any needs we have forgotten:

27.			
28.			
29.			
30.			
31.			
32.			
33.			
34.			

FIGURE 10.1. *cont.*

The PNS contains items that relate to each of these categories of need as follows:

1. Information (I)—items 1, 7, 8, 9, 14, 15
2. Intervention (T)—items 6, 8, 9, 11, 14, 15, 19
3. Formal support (FS)—items 2, 3, 10, 12, 21
4. Informal support (IS)—items 2, 3, 17, 18, 20, 21, 22
5. Material support (MS)—items 4, 19, 23
6. Competing needs (CN)—items 4, 5, 12, 13, 16, 17, 18, 22, 23, 24, 25, 26

Field-test studies of the PNS (reported in Darling & Baxter, 1996) have indicated that information is by far the greatest area of need expressed by parents of very young children with disabilities, followed by concerns relating to intervention for the child. Needs for material support also tend to be relatively high among families of lower SES. In general, needs relating to both formal and informal support are expressed by only a small minority of families, probably because most families already receive some support from family, friends, and community agencies. Needs in all areas tend to decrease over time among families involved in early intervention programs. No doubt these programs provide much of the information, intervention, and support that families need. Information gathered from an instrument like the PNS, along with information from a family interview and from observation, can be used in the development of an IFSP.

THE FAMILY INTERVIEW

No checklist-type instrument provides qualitative, in-depth information about families. True understanding of a family's situation can only be obtained by talking with family members about their resources and concerns or through long-term observation. Observation will be discussed more fully in the next section. Here, we will suggest that a well-constructed depth interview can provide valuable information.

The following interview schedule is a suggested model excerpted from a model used in the program mentioned in the previous section (see Darling & Baxter, 1996, for an extended discussion of interviewing in this context). The interview should be conducted in a relaxed, conversational style, and follow-up questions should be asked to clarify statements made by parents and other family members. The interviewer must be careful to listen empathically and without personal judgment. The interview may be used separately with mothers and fathers, or with other family members, or with both parents or the whole family present together.

I'd like to ask you some questions about your family to help us understand how we can best meet your needs and help you help your child. If I ask you anything you'd rather not answer, just tell me, and we'll skip that question. Please tell me, too, if there's anything you'd like to talk about that I may forget to ask.

First, it would help me to know a little about your (and your husband's or wife's) background.

Where are you from originally?

Was your family large?

Where did you go to school? What was the last grade in school you completed?

While you were growing up, did you know any children or adults with any kind of disability?

Had you ever heard of (child's disability) before _____ was born?

Do you remember the kinds of things you were thinking before _____ was born? Did you ever think he or she might have a problem of any kind?

Is _____ your first child?

When did you first learn that _____ had a problem? How did you feel when you first heard (or suspected) this?

What kinds of things have you worried about since you first learned about _____'s disability?

Have you told other people—siblings, grandparents, friends, minister/priest/rabbi, neighbors, coworkers? How have they reacted to the news? How have they reacted to the baby?

Do you know any other parents of children with special needs? Would you like to talk to other parents?

How did you learn about this program?

Has it been hard to get information about available services?

Have you been satisfied with your child's medical treatment so far?

How about your health; has it been good?

Has anyone else in the family had any medical problems?

Do you work? (if not) Have you worked in the past? What kind of work do you do?

(if not working) Would you work if you had someone to take care of _____?

Does your husband (or wife) help with child care?

Does your family live nearby? Do they help you with anything?

Do any of your other children have any special needs?

Have you had any problems with the baby—with sleeping, feeding, handling, or other areas of care?

Is there anything you need for the baby—furniture, clothing, equipment, toys?

Do you have a car or other means of transportation?

Would you say that you are coping pretty well with your problems right now, or would you like some help with things that are bothering you?

As part of this program, you will be asked to work on some activities with your baby at home. Do you think you will have any difficulty finding enough time to work on these activities? Do you like the idea of being your baby's teacher? Do you think you might have any special experience, skills, or feelings that will make you a good teacher for your baby?

Can you think of anything else right now that our program might be able to help you with?

The reader will note that the areas covered in the family interview are the same as those covered in the PNS—information, intervention, formal support, informal support, material support, competing needs. The interview provides another way of getting at and elaborating on this kind of information and, as such, provides a valuable supplement to the checklist.

Interviewing skills should be part of the training that professionals in the early intervention field receive. Without such training, they may feel uncomfortable asking personal questions and may not be able to elicit valid responses; they may also make families feel uncomfortable. We would recommend that a course in social research methods, counseling techniques, or a similar subject be included as part of the preprofessional curriculum offered to those planning to enter the early intervention field. An alternative for those already working in the field would be appropriate inservice training. The family interview format included here is intended to serve as a guide and should not generally be used by untrained staff.

Regardless of the level of staff training, data from an initial family interview should be regarded with some caution. The interviewer is a stranger to the family and may not be trusted at the beginning of an intervention program. As a relationship develops between an interventionist and a family, the family is likely to reveal additional information about its concerns. Concerns also change over time. Consequently, the identification process should be ongoing, and the interventionist should be sensitive to any changes in family status that occur. Finally, interviews, like other methods of assisting families, should be conducted in a spirit of partnership with family members. In this case, the *family* is the expert, and the professional is the student who needs to learn about the family's resources, concerns, and priorities.

OBSERVATION

Professionals acquire information about families simply by being with them. In the course of interaction, they will observe how the family dresses, how family members interact with one another, what conversational mannerisms are employed, and how feelings are revealed. Professionals who work with families in their homes will also have the privilege of observing furnishings, toys, and other material resources; daily routines; family photos and memorabilia; and more "natural" interactions among family members. Such information may be valuable in developing the IFSP, but the professional should be careful to ask families if they want it to be included; *they* may see it as intrusive and inappropriate.

Observation may be the most appropriate method to use in the case of some culturally different families who are suspicious of questionnaires or who are uncomfortable revealing personal information in the verbal format of an interview. In general though, observation should only be used to *supplement* information obtained in other ways. The observer who is not familiar with a family's lifestyle and interaction patterns may draw incorrect inferences about the family's concerns and priorities. Thus, he or she should always *ask* family members about observed behaviors (e.g., "I see that your children are playing very well together; do they always cooperate so nicely?").

In early intervention, home visits are almost essential for professionals who want to get to know families well. Recommended courses of action that seem to make sense in an office or at a center may not work at all in the home environment. Some homes are very small and cramped, with many people (both related and unrelated) living together. In other cases, the impact of many siblings all needing attention at the same time cannot be fully understood outside the home setting. Only through observation in the home can the professional be reasonably confident that a plan will work for a given child and family.

DEVELOPING THE IFSP

In deciding which methods to use in identifying family concerns and priorities for the IFSP, the interventionist should try to limit the identification process as much as possible. Most families resent having to fill out numerous forms or submit to more than one interview; unfortunately, when a professional first meets a family, the family has probably already been asked many questions by intake workers or professionals in other agencies. Intrusion into a family's private life should be kept to a minimum, and only methods that are truly necessary for an understanding of the family's situation should be used.

After the needs identification process has been completed, the interventionist and the family collaborate to write the IFSP. Many or most of the written outcomes in the plan will relate to the child; many guidelines exist in the educational literature for developing such outcomes based on an assessment of the child. We will not concern ourselves here with outcomes that relate specifically to the child (e.g., "Johnny will learn to walk"). Rather, we will look at the process of developing outcomes that relate to the *family.*

In order to be sure that all possible areas of family concern have been addressed, the interventionist should check to see that all of the areas noted above are included: information; intervention; formal, informal, and material support; and competing needs. Not all families will have concerns in all areas; however, simply listing a family's *resources* can also be helpful in family empowerment. A statement such as the following might be included: "The Smiths are satisfied with Johnny's medical care and are pleased with the progress he has made in the early intervention program; they do not have any concerns in this area at the present time."

Examples of outcomes based on expressed concerns in each area follow:

Area of concern	*Suggested outcome*
I. Information (e.g., parent wants more information about child's disability)	I. Provide information or make referral to appropriate resource or professional.
II. Intervention (e.g., parent wants a program to help the child learn to talk)	II. Provide speech therapy or make appropriate referral.
III. Formal support (e.g., parent is experiencing incapacitating depression because of child's disability	III. Provide counseling or make appropriate referral.
IV. Informal support (e.g., parents report that grandparents do not accept the child)	IV. Provide information to grandparents and provide or make referral to grandparent support group.
V. Material support (e.g., parents do not have enough money to meet child's needs)	V. Refer to appropriate community resources (e.g., Supplemental Security Income).
VI. Competing needs (e.g., mother wants to resume career but feels she must stay home to care for child)	VI. Help the family locate appropriate child care.

In some cases, resources may not be readily available in the community to meet identified needs. For example, babysitters trained to care for children who have seizure disorders or who are dependent on highly technical medical equipment may be difficult to locate. In such instances, professionals may wish to explore the possibility of starting new programs or to help parents advocate for the creation of such programs. (The role of the professional as an advocate is discussed in Chapter 8.) The actual IFSP will also contain timeframes within which outcomes are to be achieved.

The degree to which early intervention programs will be able to meet all of the needs expressed by families will vary considerably. Programs that employ appropriately trained psychologists may be able to provide family counseling in accordance with the model suggested in Chapter 9. Programs without such resources will need to make referrals to other agencies or professionals. Some needs may not be able to be met at all (e.g., the need for a cure in the case of chronic or terminal illness); in such cases, the interventionist may only be able to help the family cope. Other needs are the result of major social problems that cannot be corrected through intervention by helping professionals. For example, many material needs reflect a family's underlying poverty; intervention at the family level cannot change the stratified structure of society or an economy that does not provide enough jobs that pay a living wage for all people (see Bowman, 1992, for a further discussion of the limits of early intervention).

Programs that do have competent psychologists or counselors on staff should not necessarily include clinical treatment outcomes for families on IFSPs. Just as all children do not need physical therapy, all parents do not need counseling. The methods described in this chapter allow the family to define its own needs. In some cases, the professional might not agree with the family's definitions; however, professionals do not have the right to impose their judgments on families. Except in extreme cases such as child abuse, the family's wishes should prevail. As noted earlier, this model of family-centered and family-directed services is supported by recent legislation in the fields of both early intervention and maternal and child health.

The application of the methods of observation, questionnaire administration, and interviewing to IFSP development is best illustrated through a case example. The case described below is a fictitious composite of several real families in an early intervention program. (The complete case description also appears in Darling & Baxter, 1996.)

Case Example: The Torres Family

This family consists of 3-month old Amanda, who was just discharged from a neonatal intensive care unit; her 2-year old brother, Raymond; her

4-year-old sister, Jennifer; and her 21-year-old mother, Elena. Amanda was born prematurely at 32-weeks gestation. She had an intraventricular hemorrhage shortly after birth, developed hydrocephalus, and underwent surgery to have a shunt inserted to drain the fluid from her head. She had seizures right after the surgery, but these seem now to be under control. Amanda has been referred to a local early intervention program.

OBSERVATION

Elena brings the baby to the early intervention center for a team assessment. Kate (child development specialist), Susan (speech therapist), Paul (physical therapist), and Nancy (occupational therapist) are involved. They notice that Elena seems tired and has a bruise under one eye. Raymond and Jennifer seem quiet. Amanda is wearing a pink dress that looks new and a matching bonnet and booties.

Barbara (social worker) makes a home visit. She sees that the family lives in a cramped, sparsely furnished, two-bedroom apartment in a run-down building. She does not see any toys. The paint on the baby's crib is peeling. The older children are sitting at a kitchen table eating their breakfast—cereal and milk. It is 1 o'clock in the afternoon, and they have just awakened. Elena looks as though she has been crying.

INTERVIEW

Because the family has just entered the early intervention program, they are assigned a temporary Service Coordinator, Judy, by the Department of Human Services, which funds the program. Judy meets with the family when they arrive at the center for Amanda's team assessment and asks for some background information, including Amanda's birth history, her hospital course, and how she has been doing since she has been home.

Elena tells her that she seems to be doing all right, although she seems sleepy all the time. Elena is worried about the possibility of another seizure. Judy also asks Elena for some additional information about the family, including household composition and who cares for the baby. She learns that Elena lives alone with the children; Elena is the only caregiver.

Barbara conducts a more in-depth interview during her home visit but does not repeat questions Judy has already asked. The format Barbara follows is the one suggested earlier in this chapter. As a result of this interview, Barbara learns that Elena comes from a large family. One of her sisters lives a few blocks away from her, but the rest of the family lives in another state.

Elena dropped out of high school in her senior year while she was pregnant with Jennifer. She lived with Jennifer's father, Joe, for a while and planned to marry him, but while she was pregnant with Raymond, Joe started seeing other women. They had arguments, which were sometimes violent. Elena says that her mother was not supportive, because "they didn't want me to live with Joe in the first place." As a result, Elena reports that she moved to the state where she currently resides to be near her sister, who paid her moving expenses.

Elena met Amanda's father, Mike, shortly after moving here. He was very nice to her at first and brought presents for her and the children. However, while she was pregnant with Amanda, her history started to repeat itself. Elena and Mike argued often. He would drink and become abusive. Elena says that she does not see Mike very often anymore and that he has no interest in Amanda; however he made one of his infrequent visits the previous night.

When Barbara asks Elena how she feels about Amanda's medical problems, Elena says, "scared." She says she is afraid that the baby will have a seizure or that the shunt will malfunction, and she will not know what to do. She explains that she has no experience with problems of this kind—her other children were "normal."

Barbara asks Elena about her resources. She learns that the family is on welfare, and Elena's sister, who has a clerical job, helps them some, but "we still don't have enough to pay the bills." Elena's sister, Maria, also helps a little with babysitting, but she works full-time and has two school-aged children of her own, including one who is "hyperactive." Elena says she has no close friends. Her neighbors are "nice, but they have enough of their own problems."

Elena reports that her other two children are healthy. Jennifer goes to Head Start and really likes it. She says that although he has never hurt them, the children are afraid of Mike and get upset when he is loud and violent.

As for her own health, Elena notes that she has had intermittent bleeding since Amanda was born and that she always feels tired. When asked, she says she has no regular doctor for herself, but has recently found a pediatrician she likes for the children, and he accepts the medical card. Barbara asks if she has any difficulty getting to medical or early intervention appointments. Elena says she usually takes the bus, but that taking three young children on the bus is not easy.

Barbara asks if Elena needs anything for herself or the children. Elena says she could use a new crib; the one she got from a neighbor is not in good condition. She says she gets food stamps and help from the Women, Infants, and Children Program (WIC) and usually has enough food in the house, "but we can't afford anything extra that the kids want." She says she does not need clothes for the baby—she has "hand-me-downs" from Jennifer and her sister's children. She says she does not have enough money to buy the children the nice toys they should have. Elena says often throughout the interview that she wants the best for her children.

QUESTIONNAIRES

Barbara asks Elena if she would like to fill out the PNS "in case there's something I forgot to ask you about," but Elena declines. Judy has told Barbara that Elena seemed to have difficulty with the intake forms at the early intervention center.

Because she does not see any toys in the home, Barbara asks Elena to complete the toy checklist from the HOME Screening Questionnaire (JFK Child Development Center, 1981). She offers to read it to her, and Elena accepts her offer. The results indicate that the family does not have most of the items on the list. The only age-appropriate toys that Elena has for Amanda are a few rattles.

DEVELOPING FAMILY OUTCOMES

In reviewing all the information that has been gathered, Elena and the team list the family's resources and concerns, as illustrated in Table 10.1.

Priorities
1. Help with medical concerns about the baby.
2. Not having to take the children on the bus for Amanda's physical therapy appointment, scheduled for later this week.

Based on this list, the following IFSP outcomes are written:

1. Barbara will immediately make a referral to the public health nurse, who will make home visits to provide information and support to Elena regarding hydrocephalus and seizure management.
Rationale: Because of Elena's apparent difficulty with printed material, modeling and discussion appear to be better in this case than booklets, handouts, and library references.
2. All early intervention services will be provided through home visits rather than at the center. These services will begin immediately.
3. Barbara will make a referral to the free babysitting program offered by the Association for Children with Special Needs.
4. Barbara will give Elena information about the support group for abused women and other services at the Women's Help Center.
Rationale: During their discussion, Elena indicated to Barbara that she was "not ready" for Barbara to make a referral; she wanted the information so she

TABLE 10.1. The Torres Family's Resources and Concerns

Area	Resources	Concerns
Information	Elena knows about child development in general, because she has two older children.	Elena would like more information about hydrocephalus and seizure management.
Intervention	Elena is satisfied with Amanda's medical care. Elena wants to do the best for Amanda.	Elena is concerned about getting to the early intervention center by bus.
Informal support	Elena's sister helps with babysitting when she can.	Elena could use more help with babysitting and child care. Elena is concerned about the effect of Mike's violence on the children.
Formal support	Elena is interested in learning more about agencies that can help her family.	No concerns.
Material support	Elena receives support from welfare and WIC and some help from her sister and neighbors. Amanda has enough clothes; she has some toys.	Elena would like a new crib and more toys for Amanda. Elena could use more help in meeting household expenses.
Other family members	Jennifer and Raymond are healthy. Jennifer is enrolled in Head Start.	Elena would like medical care for herself.

could call and get help "when she needed it." She said she would call if Mike hit her again, or if Jennifer and Raymond seemed "really upset."

If the children were being abused, Barbara would have an ethical (and probably legal) obligation to report the situation to children's protective services. In the current circumstances, however, she should respect Elena's decision. She will continue to work very closely with her and encourage her to seek help for the children if necessary. Such situations always involve a delicate balance between respecting a family's privacy and doing what the professional considers to be best for the children.

5. Barbara will give Elena information about the "Moms of Tots" support group that meets monthly at a church near her home.

Rationale: Elena expressed considerable interest in this group when Barbara explained that this church-sponsored group included other young mothers like *herself and that babysitting was provided. Elena was not interested in the early intervention program's support group, which included only parents of children with disabilities.*

6. Barbara will assist Elena in locating a crib at the Salvation Army store or another thrift shop.

7. Barbara will assist Elena in applying for SSI for Amanda.

8. Kate [the child development specialist] will review the agency's toy-lending library list with Elena and will bring to the home the toys that Elena selects (both for Amanda and the other children).

9. Barbara will give Elena a list of family doctors and ob–gyn specialists who accept the medical card and are easily accessible with public transportation.

In the case of a two-parent family, the interventionist would identify the concerns and priorities of both parents. Each would be asked about completing a PNS, and both would participate in the interview. Further illustrations of the process of developing family outcomes in early intervention, with families of varying compositions, can be found in Darling and Baxter (1996).

CHILDREN AND FAMILIES: A SUMMARY

Although the IFSP is only required for early intervention programs serving children from birth to age 3, *all* professionals who work with children with disabilities of any age must recognize the resources and concerns of the family as a whole. Professionals working in medical and educational settings have historically developed a kind of tunnel vision— that is, they have focused exclusively on the child as patient, student, or client and ignored the world within which the child lives. The field of early intervention has pioneered a broadening of that focus because of the inescapable recognition that infants and their families are clinically inseparable.

The process described above for the development of IFSPs can be used to some extent in any kind of helping relationship between professionals and families. Regardless of professional discipline, all those who work with families need to address the family's location in society. Not all families have equal access to resources and opportunities; families also differ in their priorities for their children. In the case illustration above, the mother was most concerned about her baby's medical needs. However, a professional evaluating the case might have listed the father's abuse of the mother as the primary concern. Professionals need to take their lead from families. They need to listen to what family members are saying.

In this book, we have tried to show how a child's disability has an impact on mothers, fathers, siblings, grandparents, and all other family members whose lives intersect with the child's life. These family members, in turn, play the most important role in shaping the child's future. Families are circles of interaction, and all of their members affect one another. Professionals who treat children must acknowledge families, the cultural worlds within which those families live, and the right of families to determine their own destiny.

In review, then, we have looked at childhood disability from the broad perspective of both *family systems* and *social systems*. We have looked at the effect of a child's disability on the family as a whole, as well as the family's interaction within a social world of friends, relatives, professionals, and strangers. The family's definition of its situation is the product of all of these interactional experiences. If professionals want to understand families, they must come to understand their interactional worlds.

Specifically, as Chapter 2 suggests, families are located in social worlds long before their children are born. These worlds provide families with definitions of children and of disabilities, and these definitions shape family reactions to a child's birth and diagnosis. Preexisting definitions, however, generally prepare families poorly for the birth of a child with a disability. As a result, families strive to overcome their initial reaction of anomie and to reestablish meaning in and control over their lives. Children themselves play an important role in this definitional process as they grow and develop and respond to their families' attempts at interacting with them.

As Chapter 3 indicates, the period of acute anomie usually ends with infancy. After their initial need for information and intervention for their child has been satisfied, most families are able to maintain a normalized lifestyle. As long as the surrounding social system is supportive, families who have children with disabilities can return to the routines of career, household, and recreational pursuits during the years of childhood and adolescence. New concerns may emerge during adolescence and early adulthood.

For some families, however, normalization remains elusive. When formal and informal sources of support are not available or other family members have overwhelming problems, a child's disability can have a devastating impact on a family's lifestyle. As Chapters 4, 5, and 6 reveal, childhood disability can have both positive and negative effects on mothers, fathers, siblings, grandparents, and other family members. Each of these family members experiences the child's disability in a different way. Yet, these family experiences are always shaped by the availability of resources in the family's social world.

In Chapter 7, the reader is once again reminded of the importance of the larger social system in understanding family beliefs, attitudes, and behavior. Reactions to childhood disability vary across ethnic, socioeconomic, and religious groups. Attitudes toward disability can also vary within the same cultural group over time. Professionals who interact with culturally diverse families must take their clients' cultural backgrounds into account in any interventions they attempt.

The first seven chapters, then, further our understanding of the social world of the family. Chapter 8 shows what happens when this world intersects with that of the professional. Many professionals have been trained to have a clinical worldview, which is different from the perspective of the family. The clinical view tends to define children and families narrowly in terms of a disability category or value-based label. The family, on the other hand, tends to define its situation within the broader parameters of its various interactional contexts. The difference in perspectives can result in conflict when families and professionals interact. Recently, a number of professional fields have been moving away from a clinical worldview toward a more system-based perspective.

Finally, Chapters 9 and 10 attempt to apply the systems perspective developed in earlier chapters to actual interventions with families. Sometimes family relationships become inordinately disturbed, and families express a need for professional intervention. Chapter 9 describes a family systems approach to providing counseling in such situations. In this approach, the interactions among family members become the locus of concern. The present chapter suggests a model for applying the social system perspective in early intervention programs for infants and toddlers and their families. By rejecting a traditional clinical assessment in favor of a process of identification of family-defined concerns and priorities, professionals and families can work together to develop system-based outcomes. Tools such as the PNS described here do not impose an external interpretation on a family's definition of the situation. We hope that an increasing recognition of and respect for the family's point of view will result in the development of similarly based instruments in all professional disciplines in the field.

Since the first edition of this book was published in 1989, a number of professional disciplines seem to have moved closer to a systems model. Examples abound in the fields of education, social work, medicine, and child development, among others, of approaches that take the whole family into account. A growing interest in cultural diversity also reflects increasing awareness of the family's location in a social world. We have tried to record some of these changes throughout the book. We hope that this edition has not only recorded, but will also contribute to, this trend.

Families are our greatest resource. They provide individuals with their earliest emotional and educational experiences. Children from strong families have the opportunity to become strong adults. Profession-als cannot help children without the help of families. Only through a professional–family partnership can effective intervention occur. Profes-sionals, then, must work to understand the world in which a child lives—the world of the family.

Families, in turn, reside within larger social structures. They are parts of systems of beliefs, values, and behaviors that shape their thinking and actions. Reactions to childhood disability are social products resulting from a lifetime of interactional experiences. If we truly want to help families, we must do it on their terms, within the context of *their* system of meaning. Only through such a systems perspective can we hope to improve the quality of life for ordinary families who happen to have children with out-of-the-ordinary needs.

References

Ablon, J. (1982). The parents' auxiliary of Little People of America: A self-help model for social support for families of short-statured children. In L. D. Borman (Ed.), *Helping people to help themselves* (pp. 31–46). New York: Haworth.

Abraham, W. (1958). *Barbara: A prologue.* New York: Rinehart.

Adams, M. (1973). Science, technology, and some dilemmas of advocacy. *Science, 180,* 840–842.

Adams, P., & Nelson, K. (Eds.). (1995). *Reinventing human services: Community- and family-centered practice.* New York: Aldine deGruyter.

Agee, L. C., Innocenti, M., & Boyce, G. C. (1995). I'm all stressed out: The impact of parenting stress on the effectiveness of a parent involvement program. *Center for Persons with Disabilities News, 8,* 4–7.

Alper, S. K., Schloss, P. J., & Schloss, C. N. (1994). *Families of students with disabilities: Consultation and advising.* Boston: Allyn & Bacon.

Alvirez, D., & Bean, F. D. (1976). The Mexican-American family. In C. H. Mindel & R. W. Habenstein (Eds.), *Ethnic families in America: Patterns and variations* (pp. 271–292). New York: Elsevier.

Anderson, P. (1988, June). *Serving culturally diverse populations of infants and toddlers with disabilities.* Paper presented at the meeting of the Society for Disability Studies, Washington, DC.

Anderton, J. M., Elfert, H., & Lai, M. (1989). Ideology in the clinical context: Chronic illness, ethnicity and the discourse of normalisation. *Sociology of Health and Illness, 11,* 253–258.

Andrew, G. (1968). Determinants of Negro family decisions in management of retardation. *Journal of Marriage and the Family, 30,* 612–617.

Appoloni, T. (1987, November/December). Guardianship: New options for parents. *Exceptional Parent,* pp. 24–28.

Attneave, C. (1982). American Indians and Alaska native families: Emigrants in their own homeland. In M. McGoldrick, J. K. Pearce, & J. Giordano (Eds.), *Ethnicity and family therapy* (pp. 55–83). New York: Guilford Press.

Ayer, S. (1984). Community care: The failure of professionals to meet family needs. *Child: Health and Development, 10,* 127–140.

Azar, B. (1994). Research plumbs why the "talking cure" works. *APA Monitor, 25,* 24.

Azziz, R. (1981, July). The Hispanic parent. *Pennsylvania Medicine,* pp. 22–25.

Bailey, D. B., & Wolery, M. R. (1984). *Teaching infants and preschoolers with handicaps.* Columbus, OH: Merrill.

Bailey, D. B., Jr., & Simeonsson, R. J. (1984). Critical issues underlying research and intervention with families of young handicapped children. *Journal of the Division for Early Childhood, 9,* 38–48.

Bailey, D. B., Jr., Simeonsson, R. J., Winton, P. J., Huntington, G. S., Comfort, M., Isbell, P., O'Donnell, K. J., & Helm, J. M. (1986). Family-focused intervention: A functional model for planning, implementing, and evaluating individual family services in early intervention. *Journal of the Division for Early Childhood, 10,* 156–171.

Baker, B. L. (1989). *Parent training and developmental disabilities.* Washington, DC: American Association on Mental Retardation.

Baker, B. L., & Brightman, A. J. (1989). *Steps to independence.* Baltimore: Brookes.

Bank, S. P., & Kahn, M. D. (1982). *The sibling bond.* New York: Basic Books.

Baranowski, M. D. (1982). Grandparent–adolescent relations: Beyond the nuclear family. *Adolescence, 17,* 575–584.

Barnett, W. D. (1995). Effects of children with Down syndrome on parents' activities. *American Journal on Mental Retardation, 100,* 115–127.

Bartz, K. W., & Levine, E. S. (1978). Childbearing by black parents: A description and comparison to Anglo and Chicano parents. *Journal of Marriage and the Family, 40,* 709–719.

Baus, G. J., Letson, L., & Russell, E. (1958). Group sessions for parents of children with epilepsy. *Journal of Pediatrics, 52,* 270–273.

Baxter, C. (1986). *Intellectual disability: Parental perceptions and stigma as stress.* Unpublished doctoral dissertation, Monash University, Victoria Australia.

Beckman, P. J. (1983). Influence of selected child characteristics on stress in families of handicapped infants. *American Journal of Mental Deficiency, 88,* 150–156.

Beckman, P. J., & Pokorni, J. L. (1988). A longitudinal study of families of preterm infants: Change in stress and support over the first two years. *The Journal of Special Education, 22,* 66–65.

Beit-Jones, M. S., & Kapust, L. R. (1986). Temporal lobe epilepsy: Social and psychological considerations. *Social Work in Health Care, 11,* 17–33.

Bell, R. R. (1965). Lower class Negro mothers' aspirations for their children. *Social Forces, 43,* 493–500.

Berg, J. M., Gilderdale, S., & Way, J. (1969). On telling parents of the diagnosis of Mongolism. *British Journal of Psychiatry, 115,* 1195–1196.

Berger, M., & Foster, M. (1986). Applications of family therapy theory to research and interventions with families with mentally retarded children. In J. J.

Gallagher & P. M. Vietze (Eds.), *Families of handicapped persons* (pp. 251–260). Baltimore: Brookes.

Bernard, A. W. (1974). A comparative study of marital integration and sibling role tension differences between families who have a severely mentally retarded child and families of non-handicapped (Doctoral dissertation, University of Cincinnati). *Dissertation Abstracts International, 35A*(5), 2800–2801.

Bernheim, K. F., & Lehman, A. (1985). *Working with families of the mentally ill.* New York: Norton.

Bernstein, N. R. (1978). Mental retardation. In A. M. Nicholi (Ed.), *The Harvard guide to modern psychiatry.* Cambridge, MA: Harvard University Press.

Betz, M., & O'Connell, L. (1983). Changing doctor–patient relationships and the rise in concern for accountability. *Social Problems, 31,* 84–95.

Beyer, H. A. (1986, December). Estate planning: Providing for your child's future. *Exceptional Parent,* pp. 12–18.

Biklen, D. (1974). *Let our children go: An organizing manual for advocates and parents.* Syracuse, NY: Human Policy Press.

Billingsley, A. (1968). *Black families in white America.* Englewood Cliffs, NJ: Prentice Hall.

Birenbaum, A. (1970). On managing a courtesy stigma. *Journal of Health and Social Behavior, 11,* 196–206.

Birenbaum, A. (1971). The mentally retarded child in the home and the family cycle. *Journal of Health and Social Behavior, 12,* 55–65.

Blacher, J. (1984a). A dynamic perspective on the impact of a severely handicapped child on the family. In J. Blacher (Ed.), *Severely handicapped young children and their families: Research in review* (pp. 3–50). Orlando, FL: Academic Press.

Blacher, J. (1984b). Sequential stages of parental adjustment to the birth of a child with handicaps: Fact or artifact? *Mental Retardation, 22,* 55–68.

Blacher, J. (Ed.). (1984c). *Severely handicapped young children and their families: Research in review.* Orlando, FL: Academic Press.

Blacher, J., & Bromley, B. E. (1990). Correlates of out of home placement of handicapped children. *Journal of Children in Contemporary Society, 21,* 3–40.

Blacher, J., Nihira, K., & Meyers, C. E. (1987). Characteristics of home environments of families with mentally retarded children: Comparison across levels of retardation. *American Journal of Mental Deficiency, 91,* 313–320.

Blackard, M. K., & Barsch, E. T. (1982). Parents' and professionals' perceptions of the handicapped child's impact on the family. *TASH Journal, 7,* 62–70.

Blum, R. W. (1992). Chronic illness and disability in adolescence. *Journal of Adolescent Health, 13,* 364–368.

Blumberg, B. D., Lewis, M. J., & Susman, E. J. (1984). Adolescence: A time of transition. In M. G. Eisenberg, L. C. Sutkin, & M. A. Jansen (Eds.), *Chronic illness and disability through the life span: Effects on self and family* (pp. 133–149). New York: Springer.

Boles, G. (1959). Personality factors in mothers of cerebral palsied children. *Genetic Psychology Monographs, 59,* 160–218.

Boulton, M., Tuckett, D., Olson, C., & Williams, A. (1986). Social class and the general practice consultation. *Sociology of Health and Illness, 8,* 325–350.

Bowen, M. (1978). *Family therapy in clinical practice.* New York: Jason Aronson.

Bowlby, J. (1951). *Maternal care and mental health.* Geneva: World Health Organization.

Bowman, B. T. (1992). Who is at risk for what and why? *Journal of Early Intervention, 16*(2), 101–108.

Boyce, G. C., & Barnett, S. W. (1991). *Siblings of persons with mental retardation: A historical perspective and recent findings.* Unpublished manuscript, Utah State University.

Boyce, G. C., Behl, D., Mortensen, L., & Akers, J. (1991). Child characteristics, family demographics and family processes: Their effects on the stress experienced by families of children with disabilities. *Counselling Psychology Quarterly, 4,* 273–288.

Boykin, A. W. (1983). The academic performance of Afro-American children. In J. Spence (Ed.), *Achievement and achievement motives.* San Francisco: Freeman.

Breslau, N. (1982). Siblings of disabled children. *Journal of Abnormal Child Psychology, 10,* 85–96.

Breslau, N., Weitzman, M., & Messenger, K. (1981). Psychologic functioning of siblings of disabled children. *Pediatrics, 67,* 344–353.

Brinthaupt, G. (1991). The family of a child with cystic fibrosis. In M. Seligman (Ed.), *The family with a handicapped child* (2nd ed., pp. 295–336). Needham Heights, MA: Allyn & Bacon.

Bristol, M. M. (1984). Family resources and successful adaptation to autistic children. In E. Schopler & G. B. Mesibov (Eds.), *The effects of autism on the family* (pp. 289–310). New York: Plenum.

Bristol, M. M. (1987). Methodological caveats in the assessment of single-parent families of handicapped children. *Journal of the Division for Early Childhood, 11,* 135–143.

Bristol, M. M., & Schopler, E. (1984). A developmental perspective on stress and coping in families of autistic children. In J. Blacher (Ed.), *Severely handicapped young children and their families: Research in review* (pp. 91–141). Orlando, FL: Academic Press.

Bronfenbrenner, U. (1979). *The ecology of human development.* Cambridge, MA: Harvard University Press.

Brotherson, M. J., Backus, L. H., Summers, J. A., & Turnbull, A. P. (1986). Transition to adulthood. In J.A. Summers (Ed.), *The right to grow up: An introduction to adults with developmental disabilities* (pp. 17–44). Baltimore: Brookes.

Bubolz, M. M., & Whiren, A. P. (1984). The family of the handicapped. An ecological model for policy and practice. *Family Relations, 33,* 5–12.

Butler, J. A., Rosenbaum, S., & Palfrey, J. S. (1987). Ensuring access to health care for children with disabilities. *New England Journal of Medicine, 317*(3), 162–165.

Caldwell, B., & Guze, S. (1960). A study of the adjustment of parents and siblings of institutionalized and non-institutionalized retarded children. *American Journal of Mental Deficiency, 64,* 839–844.

Camp cares for handicapped kids. (1986, April 18). *Johnstown (PA) Tribune Democrat,* p. 5C.

Cantwell, D. P., & Baker, L. (1984). Research concerning families of children with autism. In E. Schopler & G. B. Mesibov (Eds.), *The effects of autism on the family* (pp. 41–63). New York: Plenum.

Capper, C. (1990). Students with low incidence disabilities in disadvantaged, rural settings. *Exceptional Children, 56*(4), 338–344

Carkhuff, R. R., & Berenson, B. G. (1967). *Beyond counseling and therapy.* New York: Holt, Rinehart & Winston.

Carr, J. (1970). Mongolism: Telling the parents. *Developmental Medicine and Child Neurology, 12,* 213.

Carter, B., & McGoldrick, M. (1989). *The changing family life cycle* (2nd ed.). Boston: Allyn & Bacon.

Carter, E., & McGoldrick, M. (Eds.). (1980). *The family life cycle: A framework for family therapy.* New York: Gardner.

Castaneda, A. (1976). Cultural democracy and the educational needs of Mexican-American children. In R. L. Jones (Ed.), *Mainstreaming and the minority child* (pp. 181–194). Reston, VA: Council for Exceptional Children.

Chan, S. (1990). Early intervention with culturally diverse families of infants and toddlers with disabilities. *Infants and Young Children, 3,* 78–87.

Chesler, M. (1965). Ethnocentrism and attitudes toward the physically disabled. *Journal of Personality and Social Psychology, 2,* 877–892.

Chesney, A. P., Thompson, B. L., Guevara, A., Vela, A., & Schottstaedt, M. F. (1980). Mexican-American folk medicine: Implications for the family physician. *Journal of Family Practice, 11,* 567–574.

Chigier, E. (1972). *Down's syndrome.* Lexington, MA: Heath.

Chigier, E., & Chigier, M. (1968). Attitudes to disability of children in the multicultural society of Israel. *Journal of Health and Social Behavior, 9,* 310–317.

Chinn, H., Jr. (1976). *Each step of the way.* Johnstown, PA: Mafex.

Clemens, A. W., & Axelson, L. J. (1985). The not-so-empty nest: The return of the fledgling adult. *Family Relations, 34,* 259–264.

Clemens, S. L. (1963). What is man? In C. Neider (Ed.), *The complete essays of Mark Twain.* New York: Doubleday.

Cleveland, D. W., & Miller, N. (1977). Attitudes and life commitments of older siblings of mentally retarded adults. *Mental Retardation, 15,* 38–41.

Click, J. (1986). Grandparent concerns: Learning to be special. *Sibling Information Network Newsletter, 5,* 3–4.

Cobb, S. (1976). Social support as a moderator of life stress. *Psychosomatic Medicine, 38,* 300–314.

Cohen, R., & Lavach, C. (1995). Strengthening partnerships between families and service providers. In P. Adams & K. Nelson (Eds.), *Reinventing human services: Community- and family-centered practice* (pp. 261–277). New York: Aldine deGruyter.

Coleman, S. V. (1990). The siblings of the retarded child: Self-concept, deficit compensation, and perceived parental behavior (Doctoral dissertation, California School of Professional Psychology, San Diego). *Dissertation Abstracts International, 51*(10-B), 5023. (University Microfilms No. 01147421-AAD91-07868)

Collins-Moore, M. S. (1984). Birth and diagnosis: A family crisis. In M. G. Eisenberg, L. C. Sutkin, & M. A. Jansen (Eds.), *Chronic illness and disability through the life span: Effects on self and family* (pp. 39–46). New York: Springer.

Colón, F. (1980). The family life cycle of the multiproblem poor family. In E. A. Carter & M. McGoldrick (Eds.), *The family life cycle: A framework for family therapy* (pp. 343–381). New York: Gardner.

Combs, A. W., & Avila, D. L. (1985). *Helping relationships: Basic concepts for the helping professions* (3rd ed.). Boston: Allyn & Bacon.

Cooley, W. C. (1994). Graduate medical education in pediatrics: Preparing reliable allies for parents of children with special health care needs. In R. B. Darling & M. I. Peter (Eds.), *Families, physicians, and children with social health needs: Collaborative medical education models* (pp. 109–120). Westport, CT: Auburn House.

Council for Exceptional Children. (1981). Editor's note. *Exceptional Children, 47,* 492–493.

Crnic, K. A., Friedrich, N. W., & Greenberg, M. T. (1983). Adaptation of families with mentally retarded children: A model of stress, coping, and family ecology. *American Journal of Mental Deficiency, 88,* 125–138.

Crnic, K. A., Greenberg, M. T., Ragozin, A. S., Robinson, N. M., & Basham, R. B. (1983). Effects of stress and social support on mothers and premature and full-term infants. *Child Development, 54,* 209–217.

Cromwell, V. L., & Cromwell, R. E. (1978). Perceived dominance in decision making and conflict resolution among Anglo, black, and Chicano couples. *Journal of Marriage and the Family, 19,* 749–759.

Cummings, S. T. (1976). The impact of the child's deficiency on the father: A study of fathers of mentally retarded and of chronically-ill children. *American Journal of Orthopsychiatry, 46,* 246–255.

Danziger, S. K. (1979). Treatment of women in childbirth: Implications for family beginnings. *American Journal of Public Health, 69,* 895–901.

D'Arcy, E. (1968). Congenital defects: Mothers' reactions to children with birth defects. *British Medical Journal, 3,* 796–798.

Darling, R. B. (1979). *Families against society: A study of reactions to children with birth defects.* Beverly Hills: Sage.

Darling, R. B. (1983). The birth defective child and the crisis of parenthood: Redefining the situation. In E. Callahan & K. McCluskey (Eds.), *Lifespan developmental psychology: Nonnormative life events* (pp. 115–143). New York: Academic Press.

Darling, R. B. (1987). The economic and psycho-social consequences of disability: Family–society relationships. In M. Ferrari & M. B. Sussman (Eds.), *Childhood disability and family systems* (pp. 45–61). New York: Haworth.

Darling, R. B. (1988). Parental entrepreneurship: A consumerist response to professional dominance. *Journal of Social Issues, 44,* 141–158.

Darling, R. B. (1989). Using the social system perspective in early intervention: The value of a sociological approach. *Journal of Early Intervention, 13,* 24–35.

Darling, R. B. (1991). Initial and continuing adaptation to the birth of a disabled child. In M. Seligman (Ed.), *The family with a handicapped child* (2nd ed., pp. 55–89). Boston: Allyn & Bacon.

Darling, R. B. (1994). Overcoming obstacles to early intervention referral: The development of a video-based training model for community physicians. In R. B. Darling & M. I. Peter (Eds.), *Families, physicians, and children with special health needs: Collaborative medical education models* (pp. 135–148). Westport, CT: Greenwood.

Darling, R. B., & Baxter, C. (1996). *Families in focus: Sociological methods in early intervention.* Austin, TX: Pro-Ed.

Darling, R. B., & Darling, J. (1982). *Children who are different: Meeting the challenges of birth defects in society.* St. Louis, MO: Mosby.

Darling, R. B., & Darling, J. (1992). Early intervention: A field moving toward a sociological approach. *Sociological Studies in Child Development, 5,* 9–22.

Darling, R. B., & Peter, M. I. (Eds.). (1994). *Families, physicians, and children with special health needs: Collaborative medical education models.* Westport, CT: Greenwood.

Davis, F. (1960). Uncertainty in medical prognosis: Clinical and functional. *American Journal of Sociology, 66,* 41–47.

Davis, F. (1961). Deviance disavowal: The management of strained interaction by the visibly handicapped. *Social Problems, 9,* 120–132.

Dawes, R. M. (1994). *House of cards.* New York: Free Press.

DeCaro, J. J., Dowaliby, F. J., & Maruggi, E. A. (1983). A cross-cultural examination of parents' and teachers' expectations for deaf youth regarding careers. *British Journal of Educational Psychology, 53,* 358–363.

Deluca, K. D., & Solerno, S. C. (1984). *Helping professionals connect with families with handicapped children.* Springfield, IL: Thomas.

Dembo, T. (1984). Sensitivity of one person to another. *Rehabilitation Literature, 45,* 90–95.

Dembo, T., Leviton, G. L., & Wright, B. A. (1956). Adjustment to misfortune: A problem of social–psychological rehabilitation. *Artificial Limbs, 3,* 4–62.

DeMyer, M., & Goldberg, P. (1983). Family needs of the autistic adolescent. In E. Schopler & G. Mesibov (Eds.), *Autism in adolescents and adults* (pp. 228–237). New York: Plenum.

DesJardins, C. (1971). *How to organize an effective parent group and move bureaucracies: For parents of handicapped children and their helpers.* Chicago: Coordinating Council for Handicapped Children.

Dickman, I., & Gordon, S. (1985). *One miracle at a time: How to get help for your disabled child–From the experience of other parents.* New York: Simon & Schuster.

DiVenere, N. J. (1994). Parents as educators of medical students. In R. B. Darling & M. I. Peter (Eds.), *Families, physicians, and children with special health needs: Collaborative medical education models* (pp. 101–108). Westport, CT: Greenwood.

Dodson, J. (1981). Conceptualizations of black families. In H. P. McAdoo (Ed.), *Black families* (pp. 23–36). Beverly Hills: Sage.

Doering, S. G., Entwisle, D. R., & Quinlan, D. (1980). Modeling the quality of women's birth experience. *Journal of Health and Social Behavior, 21,* 12–21.

Doherty, W. J. (1985). Family intervention in health care. *Family Relations, 34,* 129–137.

Dorner, S. (1975). The relationship of physical handicap to stress in families with an adolescent with spina bifida. *Developmental Medicine and Child Neurology, 17,* 765–776.

Dow, T. E., Jr. (1966). Optimism, physique, and social class in reaction to disability. *Journal of Health and Social Behavior, 7,* 14–19.

Down syndrome, difficult behavior. (1991, January/February). *Exceptional Parent,* pp. 12–13.

Downey, K. J. (1963). Parental interest in the institutionalized severely mentally retarded child. *Social problems, 11,* 186–193.

Drillien, C. M., & Wilkinson, E. M. (1964). Mongolism: When should parents be told? *British Medical Journal, 2,* 1306–1307.

Drotar, D., Crawford, P., & Bush, M. (1984). The family context of childhood chronic illness. In M. G. Eisenberg, L. C. Sutkin, & M. A. Jansen (Eds.), *Chronic illness and disability through the life span* (pp. 103–129). New York: Springer.

Duncan, D. (1977, May). *The impact of a handicapped child upon the family.* Paper presented at the Pennsylvania Training Model Sessions, Harrisburg, PA.

Dunst, C. J., Trivette, C. M., & Cross, A. H. (1986). Mediating influences of social support: Personal, family, and child outcomes. *American Journal of Mental Deficiency, 90,* 403–417.

Dunst, C. J., Trivette, C. M., & Cross, A. H. (1988). Social support networks of Appalachian and non-Appalachian families with handicapped children: Relationship to personal and family well-being. In S. Keefe (Ed.), *Mental health in Appalachia.* Lexington: University of Kentucky Press.

Dushenko, T. (1981). Cystic fibrosis: Medical overview and critique of the psychological literature. *Social Science in Medicine, 15B,* 43–56.

Duvall, E. (1957). *Family development.* Philadelphia: J. B. Lippincott.

Dybwad, G. (1970). Treatment of the mentally retarded: A cross-cultural view. In H. C. Haywood (Ed.), *Social-cultural aspects of mental retardation* (pp. 560–572). New York: Appleton-Century-Crofts.

Dyer, E. D. (1963). Parenthood as crisis: A re-study. *Marriage and Family Living, 25,* 196–201.

Dyson, L., & Fewell, R. R. (1986). Stress and adaptation in parents of young handicapped and nonhandicapped children: A comparative study. *Journal of the Division for Early Childhood, 10,* 25–35.

Dyson, L. L. (1989). Adjustment of siblings of handicapped children: A comparison. *Journal of Pediatric Psychology, 14,* 215–229.

Edelman, M. W. (1985). The sea is so wide and my boat is so small: Problems facing black children today. In H. P. McAdoo & J. L. McAdoo (Eds.), *Black children: Social, educational and parental environments* (pp. 72–82). Beverly Hills: Sage.

Edgerton, R. B. (1970). Mental retardation in non-Western societies: Toward a cross-cultural perspective on incompetence. In H. C. Haywood (Ed.), *Social–*

cultural aspects of mental retardation (pp. 532–559). New York: Appleton-Century-Crofts.

Egan, G. (1986). *The skilled helper* (3rd ed.). Monterey, CA: Brooks/Cole.

Eliades, D. C., & Suitor, C. W. (1994). *Celebrating diversity: Approaching families through their food*. Arlington, VA: National Center for Education in Maternal and Child Health.

Ellis, A. (1987). Rational emotive therapy: Current appraisal and future directions. *Journal of Cognitive Psychotherapy, 1,* 73–86.

Ellis, A. (1962). *Reason and emotion in psychotherapy*. New York: Lyle Stuart.

Ellman, N. S. (1991). Family therapy. In M. Seligman (Ed.), *The family with a handicapped child* (2nd ed., pp. 369–406). Boston: Allyn & Bacon.

English, R. W. (1971). Correlates of stigma towards physically disabled persons. *Rehabilitation Research and Practice Review, 2,* 1–17.

Eyer, D. E. (1992). *Mother–infant bonding: A scientific fiction*. New Haven: Yale University Press.

Fagan, J., & Schor, D. (1993). Mothers of children with spina bifida: Factors related to maternal psychosocial functioning. *American Journal of Orthopsychiatry, 63,* 146–152.

Falicov, C. J. (1982). Mexican families. In M. McGoldrick, J. K. Pearce, & J. Giordano (Eds.), *Ethnicity and family therapy* (pp. 134–163). New York: Guilford Press.

Falicov, C. J., & Karrer, B. M. (1980). Cultural variations in the family life cycle: The Mexican-American family. In E. A. Carter & M. McGoldrick (Eds.), *The family life cycle: A framework for family therapy* (pp. 383–426). New York: Gardener.

Farber, B. (1959). Effects of a severely mentally retarded child on family integration. *Monographs of the Society for Research in Child Development, 24*(2, Serial No. 71).

Farber, B. (1960a). Family organization and crisis: Maintenance of integration in families with a severely mentally retarded child. *Monographs of the Society for Research in Child Development, 25*(Whole No. 75).

Farber, B. (1960b). Perceptions of crisis and related variables in the impact of a retarded child on the mother. *Journal of Health and Social Behavior, 1,* 108–118.

Farber, B. (1975). Family adaptations to severely mentally retarded children. In M. J. Begab & S. A. Richardson (Eds.), *The mentally retarded and society: A social science perspective* (pp. 247–266). Baltimore: University Park Press.

Farber, B., & Lewis, M. (1975). The symbolic use of parents: A sociological critique of educational practice. *Journal of Research and Development in Education, 8,* 34–41.

Farber, B., Mindel, C. H., & Lazerwitz, B. (1976). The Jewish American Family. In C. H. Mindel & R. W. Habenstein (Eds.), *Ethnic families in America: Patterns and variations* (pp. 347–378). New York: Elsevier.

Farber, B., & Ryckman, D. B. (1965). Effects of a severely mentally retarded child on family relationships. *Mental Retardation Abstracts, 11,* 1–17.

Featherstone, H. (1980). *A difference in the family: Life with a disabled child*. New York: Basic Books.

Feigon, J. (1981). A sibling group program. *Sibling Information Newsletter, 1,* 2–3.

Femminella, F. X., & Quadangno, J. S. (1976). The Italian-American family. In C. H. Mindel & R. W. Habenstein (Eds.), *Ethnic families in America: Patterns and variations* (pp. 62–88). New York: Elsevier.

Ferhold, J. B., & Solnit, A. (1978). Counseling parents of mentally retarded and learning disordered children. In E. Arnold (Ed.), *Helping parents help their children* (pp. 157–173). New York: Brunner/Mazel.

Fewell, R. (1986). A handicapped child in the family. In R. R. Fewell & P. F. Vadasy (Eds.), *Families of handicapped children* (pp. 3–34). Austin, TX: Pro-Ed.

Fewell, R. R. (1991). Parenting moderately handicapped persons. In M. Seligman (Ed.), *The family with a handicapped child* (2nd ed., pp. 203–232). Boston: Allyn & Bacon.

Fewell, R. R., & Gelb, S. A. (1983). Parenting moderately handicapped persons. In M. Seligman (Ed.), *The family with a handicapped child: Understanding and treatment* (pp. 175–202). Orlando, FL: Grune & Stratton.

Figley, C. R., & McCubbin, H. I. (1983). *Stress and the family: Vol. 2. Coping with catastrophe.* New York: Brunner/Mazel.

Fish, T. (Producer). (1993). *The next step.* [Videotape]. (Available from Publications Office, Nisonger Center, UAP, 434 McCampbell Hall, The Ohio State University, 1581 Dodd Dr., Columbus, OH 43210.)

Fitzpatrick, J. P. (1976). The Puerto Rican family. In C. H. Mindel & R. W. Habenstein (Eds.), *Ethnic families in America: Patterns and variations* (pp. 192–217). New York: Elsevier.

Foley, V. D. (1975). Family therapy with black disadvantaged families: Some observations on roles, communication and technique. *Journal of Marriage and Family Counseling, 1,* 29–38.

Folkman, S., Lazarus, R., Dunkel-Schelter, C., DeLongis, A., & Gruen, R. (1986). The dynamics of a stressful encounter: Cognitive appraisal, coping and encounter outcomes. *Journal of Personality and Social Psychology, 50,* 992–1003.

Forrer, G. R. (1959). The mother of a defective child. *Psychoanalysis Quarterly, 28,* 59–63.

Fox, R. (1959). *Experiment perilous.* Glencoe, IL: Free Press.

Fracasso, M. P. (1994). Studying the social and emotional development of Hispanic children in the United States. *Zero to Three, 15,* 24–27.

Francis, V., Korsch, B. M., & Morris, M. J. (1968). Gaps in doctor–patient communication: Patients' response to medical advice. *New England Journal of Medicine, 280,* 535–540.

Franklin, A. J., & Boyd-Franklin, N. (1985). A psychoeducational perspective on black parenting. In H. P. McAdoo & J. L. McAdoo (Eds.), *Black children: Social, educational, and parental environments* (pp. 194–210). Beverly Hills: Sage.

Freedman, D. G. (1981). Ethnic differences in babies. In E. M. Hetherington & R. D. Parke (Eds.), *Contemporary readings in child psychology* (2nd ed., pp. 6–12). New York: McGraw-Hill.

Freidson, E. (1961). *Patient's views of medical practice.* New York: Russell Sage Foundation.

Freidson, E. (1970). *Professional dominance*. Chicago: Aldine.

Freud, S. (1936). *Inhibitions, symptoms and anxiety*. London: Hogarth Press.

Friedlander, S. R., & Watkins, C. E. (1985). Therapeutic aspects of support groups for parents of the mentally retarded. *International Journal of Group Psychotherapy, 35,* 65–78.

Friedrich, W. N., & Friedrich, W. L. (1981). Psychosocial assets of parents of handicapped and nonhandicapped children. *American Journal of Mental Deficiency, 5,* 551–553.

Friedrich, W. N. (1979). Predictors of the coping behaviors of mothers and handicapped children. *Journal of Consulting and Clinical Psychology, 47,* 486–492.

Frith, C. H. (1981). "Advocate" vs. "professional employee": A question of priorities for special educators. *Exceptional Children, 47,* 486–492.

Frodi, A. M. (1981). Contributions of infant characteristics to child abuse. *American Journal of Mental Deficiency, 85,* 341–349.

Gabel, H., & Kotsch, L. S. (1981). Extended families and young handicapped children. *Topics in Early Childhood Special Education, 1,* 29–35.

Gabel, H., McDowell, J., & Cerreto, M. C. (1983). Family adaptation to the handicapped infant. In S. G. Garwood & R. R. Fewell (Eds.), *Educating handicapped infants* (pp. 455–493). Rockville, MD: Aspen.

García-Preto, N. (1982). Puerto Rican families. In M. McGoldrick, J. K. Pearce, & J. Giordano (Eds.), *Ethnicity and family therapy* (pp. 164–186). New York: Guilford Press.

Gargiulo, R. M. (1985). *Working with parents of exceptional children.* Boston: Houghton-Mifflin.

Gath, A. (1974). Sibling reactions to mental handicap: A comparison of the brothers and sisters of mongol children. *Journal of Child Psychology and Psychiatry, 15,* 187–198.

Gayton, W. F., & Walker, L. (1974). Down's syndrome: Informing the parents. *American Journal of Disabled Children, 127,* 510–512.

George, J. D. (1988). Therapeutic intervention for grandparents and extended family of children with developmental delays. *Mental Retardation, 26,* 369–375.

Gerson, K. (1993). *No man's land: Men's changing commitments to family and work.* New York: Basic Books.

Ghali, S. B. (1977). Culture sensitivity and the Puerto Rican client. *Social Casework, 58,* 459–474.

Gill, V. J., & Maynard, D. W. (1995). On "labeling" in actual interaction: Delivering and receiving diagnoses of developmental disabilities. *Social Problems, 42(1),* 11–37.

Glendinning, C. (1983). *Unshared care.* London: Routeledge & Kegan Paul.

Gliedman, J., & Roth, W. (1980). *The unexpected minority: Handicapped children in America.* New York: Harcourt, Brace, Jovanovich.

Goffman, E. (1959). *The presentation of self in everyday life.* Garden City, NY: Doubleday.

Goffman, E. (1963). *Stigma: Notes on the management of spoiled identity.* Englewood Cliffs, NJ: Prentice Hall.

Goldberg, S., Marcovitch, S., MacGregor, D., & Lojkasek, M. (1986). Family responses to developmentally delayed preschoolers: Etiology and the father's role. *American Journal of Mental Deficiency, 90,* 610–617.

Goode, D. A. (1984). Presentation practices of a family with a deaf–blind child. *Family Relations, 33,* 173–185.

Goodman, C. I. (1980). *A study of alternative therapeutic relationships: Parent groups and their members.* Unpublished doctoral dissertation, Case Western University, Cleveland, OH.

Goodman, J. F. (1994). "Empowerment" versus "best interests": Client–professional relationships. *Infants and Young Children, 6,* vi–x.

Goodman, N., Dornbusch, S. M., Richardson, S. A., & Hastorf, A. H. (1963). Variant reactions to physical disabilities. *American Sociological Review, 28,* 429–435.

Gottlieb, J. (1975). Public, peer, and professional attitudes toward mentally retarded persons. In M. J. Begab & S. A. Richardson (Eds.), *The mentally retarded and society: A social science perspective* (pp. 99–125). Baltimore: University Park Press.

Gould-Martin, K., & Ngin, C. (1981). Chinese Americans. In A. Harwood (Ed.), *Ethnicity and medical care* (pp. 130–171). Cambridge, MA: Harvard University Press.

Gowen, J. W., Christy, D. S., & Sparling, J. (1993). Informational needs of parents of young children with special needs. *Journal of Early Intervention, 17,* 194–210.

Grakliker, B. V., Fishler, K., & Koch, R. (1962). Teenage reactions to a mentally retarded sibling. *American Journal of Mental Deficiency, 66,* 838–843.

Greenfield, J. (1978). *A place for Noah.* New York: Pocket Books.

Groce, N. (1987, Summer). Cross-cultural research, current strengths, future needs. *Disability Studies Quarterly,* pp. 1–3.

Grossman, F. K. (1972). *Brothers and sisters of retarded children.* Syracuse, NY: Syracuse University Press.

Guerra, F. A. (1980, September/October). Hispanic child health issues. *Children Today,* pp. 18–22.

Gundry, M. (1989, November/December). Wanted: A diagnosis for my son. *Exceptional Parent,* pp. 22–24.

Guralnick, M. J., Bennett, F. C., Heiser, K. E., & Richardson, H. B., Jr. (1987). Training future primary care pediatricians to serve handicapped children and their families. *Topics in Early Childhood Special Education, 6,* 1–11.

Guttmacher, S., & Elinson, J. (1971). Ethno-religious variation in perceptions of illness. *Social Science and Medicine, 5,* 117–125.

Hanson, M. J. (1981). A model for early intervention with culturally diverse single and multiparent families. *Topics in Early Childhood Special Education, 1,* 37–44.

Hanson, M. J., & Lynch, E. W. (1992). Family diversity: Implications for policy and practice. *Topics in Early Childhood Special Education, 1,* 37–44.

Harbaugh, G. R. (1984). *Costs and "out of pocket" costs of rearing a handicapped child.* Unpublished manuscript.

Harris, L., & Associates. (1975). *The myth and reality of aging in America*. Washington, DC: National Council on Aging.

Harris, S. (1994). *Siblings of children with autism: A guide for families*. Rockville, MD: Woodbine House.

Harris, S. L. (1983). *Families of the developmentally disabled: A guide to behavioral intervention*. New York: Pergamon.

Harrison, A., Serafica, F., & McAdoo, H. (1984). Ethnic families of color. In R. D. Parke (Ed.), *Review of child development research* (Vol. 7, pp. 329–371). Chicago: University of Chicago Press.

Harry, B. (1992a). *Cultural diversity, families, and the special education system: Communication and empowerment*. New York: Teachers College Press.

Harry, B. (1992b). Developing cultural self-awareness: The first step in values clarification for early interventionists. *Topics in Early Childhood Special Education, 12*, 333–350.

Harry, B. (1992c). Making sense of disability: Low-income Puerto Rican parents' theories of the problem. *Exceptional Children, 59*, 27–40.

Harry, B., Allen, N., & McLaughlin, M. (1995). Communication versus compliance: African-American parents' involvement in special education. *Exceptional Children, 61*, 364–376.

Harry, B., & Kalyanpur, M. (1994). Cultural underpinnings of special education: Implications for professional interactions with culturally diverse families. *Disability and Society, 9*, 145–165.

Harry, B., Otgruson, C., Katkavich, J., & Guerrero, M. (1993). Crossing social class and cultural barriers in working with families: Implications for teacher training. *Teaching Exceptional Children, 26*(1), 48–51.

Hartman, A. (1978, October). Diagrammatic assessment of family relationship. *Social Casework*, pp. 465–476.

Hartman, A., & Laird, J. (1983). *Family-centered social work practice*. New York: Free Press.

Harwood, A. (1981). Mainland Puerto Ricans. In A. Harwood (Ed.), *Ethnicity and medical care* (pp. 397–481). Cambridge, MA: Harvard University Press.

Hauenstein, E. J. (1990). The experience of distress in parents of chronically ill children: Potential or likely outcome? *Journal of Clinical Child Psychology, 19*, 356–364.

Haug, M., & Lavin, B. (1983). *Consumerism in medicine: Challenging physician authority*. Beverly Hills: Sage.

Hayden, V. (1974). The other children. *Exceptional Parent, 4*, 26–29.

Hazi, H. (1992). *Caregiving: Looking to the future with an eye on the past*. Unpublished manuscript.

Heiss, J. (1981). Women's values regarding marriage and the family. In H. P. McAdoo (Ed.), *Black families* (pp. 186–198). Beverly Hills: Sage.

Helge, D. (1984). The state of the art of rural special education. *Exceptional Children, 50*(4), 294–305.

Heller, P. G., Quesada, G. M., Harvey, D. L., & Warner, L. G. (1981). Familism in rural and urban America: Critique and reformulation of a construct. *Rural Sociology, 46*, 446–464.

Helsel, E. (1978). The Helsels' story of Robin. In A. P. Turnbull & H. R. Turnbull (Eds.), *Parents speak out* (pp. 81–98). Columbus, OH: Merrill.

Herz, F. M., & Rosen, E. J. (1982). Jewish families. In M. McGoldrick, J. K. Pearce, & J. Giordano (Eds.), *Ethnicity and family therapy* (pp. 84–107). New York: Guilford Press.

Hess, R. D. (1970). Social class and ethnic influences upon socialization. In P. H. Mussen (Ed.), *Carmichael's manual of child psychology* (pp. 457–557). New York: Wiley.

Hickson, G. B., Altemeier, W. A., & O'Connor, S. (1983). Concerns of mothers seeking care in private pediatrics offices: Opportunities for expanding services. *Pediatrics, 72,* 619–624.

Hill, C. (1982). Our patients have culture. *Clinical Management of Physical Therapy, 2,* 5–10.

Hines, P. M. (1989). The family life cycle of poor black families. In B. Carter & M. McGoldrick (Eds.), *The changing family life cycle* (2nd ed., pp. 513–544). Boston: Allyn & Bacon.

Hines, P. M., & Boyd-Franklin, N. (1982). Black families. In M. McGoldrick, J. K. Pearce, & J. Giordano (Eds.), *Ethnicity and family therapy* (pp. 84–107). New York: Guilford Press.

Hobbs, D. F., Jr., & Wimbish, J. M. (1977). Transition to parenthood by black couples. *Journal of Marriage and the Family, 18,* 677–690.

Hobbs, N., Perrin, A., & Ireys, S. (1986). *Chronically ill children and their families.* San Francisco: Jossey-Bass.

Hoffman, L. (1981). *Foundations of family therapy.* New York: Basic Books.

Holden, R. H. (1972). Prediction of mental retardation in infancy. *Mental Retardation, 10,* 28–30.

Hollingshead, A. B., & Redlich, F. C. (1958). *Social class and mental illness: A community study.* New York: Wiley.

Holroyd, J. (1974). The questionnaire on resources and stress: An instrument to measure family response to a handicapped member. *Journal of Community Psychology, 2,* 92–94.

Holt, K. S. (1958a). Home care of severely retarded children. *Pediatrics, 22,* 744–755.

Holt, K. S. (1958b). *The impact of mentally retarded children upon their families.* Unpublished doctoral dissertation, University of Sheffield, England.

Hormuth, R. P. (1953). Home problems and family care of the mongoloid child. *Quarterly Review of Pediatrics, 8,* 274–280.

Hornby, G. (1988). *Fathers of handicapped children.* Unpublished manuscript, University of Hull, England.

Hornby, G. (1994). *Counselling in child disability: Skills for working with parents.* London: Chapman & Hall.

Hornby, G., & Ashworth, T. (1994). Grandparent support for families who have children with disabilities: A survey of parents. *Journal of Child and Family Studies, 3,* 403–412.

Hornby, G., & Murray, R. (1983). Group programmes for parents of children with various handicaps. *Child Care Health and Development, 9,* 185–198.

Houser, R., & Seligman, M. (1991). A comparison of stress and coping by fathers of adolescents with mental retardation and fathers of adolescents without mental retardation. *Research in Developmental Disabilities, 12,* 251–260.

Huang, L. J. (1976). The Chinese-American family. In C. H. Mindel & R. W. Habenstein (Eds.), *Ethnic families in America: Patterns and variations* (pp. 124–147). New York: Elsevier.

Illes, J. (1979). Children with cancer: Healthy siblings' experience during the illness experience. *Cancer Nursing, 2,* 371–377.

Israelite, N. (1985). Sibling reaction to a hearing-impaired child in the family. *Journal of Rehabilitation of the Deaf, 18,* 1–5.

Ivey, A. E., & Simek-Downing, B. (1980). *Counseling and psychotherapy: Theories and practice.* Englewood Cliffs, NJ: Prentice-Hall.

Jackson, J. J. (1981). Urban black Americans. In A. Harwood (Ed.), *Ethnicity and medical care* (pp. 37–129). Cambridge, MA: Harvard University Press.

Jacobson, R. B., & Humphrey, R. A. (1979). Families in crisis: Research and theory in child mental retardation. *Social Casework, 60,* 597–601.

JFK Child Development Center. (1981). *HOME Screening Questionnaire.* Denver, CO: LADOCA.

Joe, J. R., & Malach, R. S. (1992). Families with Native American roots. In E. W. Lynch & M. J. Hanson (Eds.), *Developing cross-cultural competence: A guide for working with young children and their families* (pp. 89–119). Baltimore: Brookes.

Jones, R. L., & Wilderson, F. B., Jr. (1976). Mainstreaming and the minority child: An overview of issues and a perspective. In R. L. Jones (Ed.), *Mainstreaming and the minority child* (pp. 1–13). Reston, VA: Council for Exceptional Children.

Judge, G. (1987). Knock, knock. . . . It's no joke. *Zero to Three, 8,* 20–21.

Kahana, G., & Kahana, E. (1970). Grandparenthood from the perspective of the developing grandchild. *Developmental Psychology, 3,* 98–105.

Kahn, M. D., & Lewis, K. G. (1988). *Siblings in therapy: Life span and clinical issues.* New York: Norton.

Kaiser, A. P., & Fox, J. J. (1986). Behavioral parent training research. In J. J. Gallagher & P. M. Vietze (Eds.), *Families of handicapped persons* (pp. 219–235). Baltimore: Brookes.

Kappes, N. (1995). Matrix. In D. L. Meyer (Ed.), *Uncommon fathers: Reflections on raising a child with a disability* (pp. 13–18). Bethesda, MD: Woodbine.

Kavanagh, K. H., & Kennedy, P. H. (1992). *Promoting cultural diversity: Strategies for health care professionals.* Newbury Park, CA: Sage.

Kazak, A. E. (1987). Professional helper and families with disabled children: A social network perspective. *Marriage and Family Review, 11,* 177–191.

Kazak, A. E., & Marvin, R. S. (1984). Differences, difficulties, and adaptation: Stress and social networks in families with a handicapped child. *Family Relations, 33,* 67–77.

Kazak, A., & Wilcox, B. (1984). The structure and function of social support networks in families with handicapped children. *American Journal of Community Psychology, 12,* 645–661.

Keefe, S. E., Padilla, A. M., & Carlos, M. L. (1979). The Mexican American extended family as an emotional support system. *Human Organization, 38,* 144–152.

Kelker, K., Garthwait, C., & Seligman, M. (1992). Rural special education options. *Human Services in the Rural Environment, 15,* 14–17.

Kennedy, J. F. (1970). Maternal reactions to the birth of a defective baby. *Social Casework, 51,* 410–416.

Kibert, R. P. (1986). *A descriptive study of the perceptions of normal college age siblings in families with a mentally retarded child.* Unpublished doctoral dissertation, University of Pittsburgh.

Kirkman, M. (1985). The perceived impact of a sibling with a disability on family relationships: A survey of adult siblings in Victoria, Australia. *Sibling Information Network Newsletter, 4,* 2–5.

Kiser, B. (1974). *New light of hope.* New Canaan, CT: Keats.

Kitano, H. H. L., & Kikumura, A. (1976). The Japanese-American family. In C. H. Mindel & R. W. Habenstein (Eds.), *Ethnic families in America: Patterns and variations* (pp. 41–60). New York: Elsevier.

Klein, C. (1977). Coping patterns of parents of deaf–blind children. *American Annals of the Deaf, 122,* 310–312.

Klein, S. D. (1972). Brother to sister: Sister to brother. *Exceptional Parent, 2,* 10–15.

Klein, S. D. (1994). The challenge of communication with parents. In R. B. Darling & M. I. Peter (Eds.), *Families, physicians, and children with special health needs: Collaborative medical education models* (pp. 51–74). Westport, CT: Greenwood.

Kleinman, A., Eisenberg, L., & Good, B. (1978). Culture, illness and care: Clinical lessons from anthropologic and cross-cultural research. *Annals of Internal Medicine, 88,* 251–258.

Kline, F., Acosta, F. X., Austin, W., & Johnson, R. G., Jr. (1980). The misunderstood Spanish-speaking patient. *American Journal of Psychiatry, 137*(12), 1530–1533.

Kohn, M. L. (1969). *Class and conformity: A study in values.* Homewood, IL: Dorsey.

Konstam, V., Drainoni, M., Mitchell, G., Houser, R., Reddington, D., & Eaton, D. (1993). Career choices and values of siblings with individuals with developmental disabilities. *School Counselor, 40,* 287–292.

Korn, S. J., Chess, S., & Fernandez, P. (1978). The impact of children's physical handicaps on marital quality and family interaction. In R. M. Lerner & G. B. Spanier (Eds.), *Child influences on marital and family interaction: A life-span perspective* (pp. 299–326). New York: Academic Press.

Krahn, G. L. (1993). Conceptualizing social support in families of children with special health needs. *Family Process, 32,* 235–248.

Krauss, M. W., & Giele, J. Z. (1987). Services to families during three stages of a handicapped person's life. In M. Ferrari & M. B. Sussman (Eds.), *Childhood disability and family systems* (pp. 213–229). New York: Haworth.

Krauss, M. W., & Seltzer, M. M. (1993). Coping strategies among older mothers of adults with retardation: A life-span developmental perspective. In A. P. Turnbull, J. M. Patterson, S. K. Behr, D. L. Murphy, J. G. Marquis, & M. J.

Blue-Banning (Eds.), *Cognitive coping, families, and disability* (pp. 173–182). Baltimore: Brookes.

Kübler-Ross, E. (1969). *On death and dying.* New York: Macmillan.

Kunitz, S. J., & Levy, J. E. (1981). Navajos. In A. Harwood (Ed.), *Ethnicity and medical care* (pp. 337–396). Cambridge, MA: Harvard University Press.

Kurtz, R. A. (1977). Advocacy for the mentally retarded: The development of a new social role. In M. J. Begab & S. A. Richardson (Eds.), *The mentally retarded and society: A social science perspective* (pp. 377–394). Baltimore: University Park Press.

Kurtz, R. A. (1975). *Social aspects of mental retardation.* Lexington, MA: Heath.

Laborde, P. R., & Seligman, M. (1991). Counseling parents with children with disabilities. In M. Seligman (Ed.), *The family with a handicapped child* (2nd ed., pp. 337–369). Boston: Allyn & Bacon.

Lamb, M. E. (1983). Fathers of exceptional children. In M. Seligman (Ed.), *The family with a handicapped child: Understanding and treatment* (pp. 125–146). Orlando, FL: Grune & Stratton.

Lamb, M. E., & Meyer, D. J. (1991). Fathers of children with special needs. In M. Seligman (Ed.), *The family with a handicapped child* (2nd ed., pp. 151–179). Boston: Allyn & Bacon.

Landers, A. (1986, October). *Ann Landers advice column.*

Laosa, L. M. (1974). Child care and the culturally different child. *Child Care Quarterly, 3,* 214–224.

Laosa, L. M. (1978). Maternal teaching strategies in Chicano families of varied socioeconomic levels. *Child Development, 49,* 1129–1135.

LaRossa, R. (1977). *Conflict and power in marriage: Expecting the first child.* Beverly Hills: Sage.

Laureys, K. (1984). Growing up with Brian. *Sibling Information Network Newsletter, 3,* 5–6.

Lazerson, M. (1975). Educational institutions and mental subnormality: Notes on writing a history. In M. J. Begab & S. A. Richardson (Eds.), *The mentally retarded and society: A social science perspective* (pp. 33–52). Baltimore: University Park Press.

Lechtenberg, R. (1984). *Epilepsy and the family.* Cambridge, MA: Harvard University Press.

Lee, E. (1982). A social systems approach to assessment and treatment for Chinese American families. In M. McGoldrick, J. K. Pearce, & J. Giordano (Eds.), *Ethnicity and family therapy* (pp. 527–551). New York: Guilford Press.

Leifield, L., & Murray, T. (1995). Advocating for Aric: Strategies for full inclusion. In B. B. Swadener & S. Lubeck (Eds.), *Children and families "at promise": Deconstructing the discourse of risk* (pp. 238–261). Albany: State University of New York Press.

LeMasters, E. E. (1957). Parenthood as crisis. *Marriage and Family Living, 19,* 352–355.

LePontois, J., Moel, D. I., & Cohn, R. A. (1987). Family adjustment to pediatric ambulatory dialysis. *American Journal of Orthopsychiatry, 57,* 78–83.

Levine, E. S. (1960). *Psychology of deafness.* New York: Columbia University Press.

Lewis, J., & Greenstein, R. M. (1994). A first-year medical student curriculum about family views of chronic and disabling conditions. In R. B. Darling & M. I. Peter (Eds.), *Families, physicians, and children with special health needs: Collaborative medical education models* (pp. 77–100). Westport, CT: Greenwood.

Lewis, O. (1959). *Five families: An intimate and objective revelation of family life in Mexico today–A dramatic study of the culture of poverty.* New York: Basic Books.

Lieberman, A. F. (1990). Infant–parent intervention with recent immigrants: Reflections on a study with Latino families. *Zero to Three, 10,* 8–11.

Lipscomb, J., Kolimaga, J. T., Sperduto, P. W., Minnich, J. K., & Fontenot, K. J. (1983). *Cost–benefit and cost-effectiveness analyses of screening for neural tube defects in North Carolina.* Unpublished manuscript, Duke University, Institute for Policy Sciences, Durham, NC.

Lobato, D. (1983). Siblings of handicapped children: A review. *Journal of Autism and Developmental Disorders, 13,* 347–364.

Lobato, D. J. (1990) *Brothers and sisters with special needs.* Baltimore: Brookes.

Locust, C. (1988, June). *Integration of American Indian and scientific concepts of disability: Cross-cultural perspectives.* Paper presented at the meeting of the Society for Disability Studies, Washington, DC.

Lorber, J. (1971). Results of treatment of myelomeningocele. *Developmental Medicine and Child Neurology, 13,* 279–303.

Lurie, E. (1970). *How to change the schools: A parent's action handbook on how to fight the system.* New York: Vintage.

Luterman, D. (1984). *Counseling the communicatively disordered and their families.* Boston: Little, Brown.

Luterman, D. J. (1979). *Counseling parents of hearing-impaired children.* Boston: Little, Brown.

Lynch, E. W. (1992). Developing cross-cultural competence. In E. W. Lynch & M. J. Hanson (Eds.), *Developing cross-cultural competence: A guide for working with young children and their families* (pp. 33–59). Baltimore: Brookes.

Lynch, E. W., & Hanson, M. J. (1992). *Developing cross-cultural competence: A guide for working with young children and their families.* Baltimore: Brookes.

Lyon, S., & Lyon, G. (1991). Collaboration with families of persons with severe disabilities. In M. Seligman (Ed.), *The family with a handicapped child* (2nd ed., pp. 237–264). Boston: Allyn & Bacon.

Lyon, S., & Preis, A. (1983). Working with families of severely handicapped persons. In M. Seligman, (Ed.) *The family with a handicapped child: Understanding and treatment* (pp. 203–232). Orlando, FL: Grune & Stratton.

MacGregor, P. (1994). Grief: The unrecognized parental response to mental illness in a child. *Social Work, 39,* 160–166.

MacKeith, R. (1973). The feelings and behavior of parents of handicapped children. *Developmental Medicine and Child Neurology, 15,* 524–527.

Manns, W. (1981). Support systems of significant others in black families. In H. P. McAdoo (Ed.), *Black families* (pp. 238–251). Beverly Hills: Sage.

Marcos, L. R. (1979). Effects of interpreters on the evaluation of psychopathology in non-English-speaking patients. *American Journal of Psychiatry, 136*(2), 171–174.

Marion, R. L. (1980). Communicating with parents of culturally diverse exceptional children. *Exceptional Children, 46,* 616–623.

Marion, R. L. (1981). *Educators, parents, and exceptional children.* Rockville, MD: Aspen.

Marsh, D. T. (1992). *Families and mental retardation.* New York: Praeger.

Marshak, L. (1982). Group therapy with adolescents. In M. Seligman (Ed.), *Group psychotherapy and counseling with special populations* (pp. 185–213). Baltimore: University Park Press.

Marshak, L. E., & Seligman, M. (1993). *Counseling persons with disabilities: Theoretical and clinical perspectives.* Austin, TX: Pro-Ed.

Martin, P. (1975). Marital breakdown in families of patients with spina bifida cystica. *Developmental Medicine and Child Neurology, 17,* 757–764.

Martinez, C., & Martin, H. W. (1966). Folk diseases among urban Mexican-Americans: Etiology, symptoms, and treatment. *Journal of the American Medical Association, 196,* 161–164.

Mary, N. L. (1990). Reactions of black, Hispanic, and white mothers to having a child with handicaps. *Mental Retardation, 28,* 1–5.

Matheny, K. B., Aycock, D. W., Pugh, J. L., Curlette, W. L., & Canella, K. S. (1986). Stress coping: A qualitative and quantitative synthesis with implications for treatment. *Counseling Psychologist, 14,* 499–549.

Max, L. (1985). Parents' views of provisions, services, and research. In N. N. Singh & K. M. Wilton (Eds.), *Mental retardation in New Zealand* (pp. 250–262). Christchurch, New Zealand: Whitcoulls.

May, J. (1991). *Fathers of children with special needs: New horizons.* Bethesda, MD: ACCH.

McAdoo, J. L. (1981). Involvement of fathers in the socialization of black children. In H. P. McAdoo (Ed.), *Black families.* Beverly Hills: Sage.

McAnaney, K. (1990, July/August). How did I get this tough? Fighting for your child's rights. *Exceptional Parent,* pp. 20–22.

McCracken, M. J. (1984). Cystic fibrosis in adolescence. In R. W. Blum (Ed.), *Chronic illness and disabilities in childhood and adolescence* (pp. 397–411). Orlando, FL: Grune & Stratton.

McCubbin, H. I., & Patterson, J. M. (1981). *Systematic assessment of family stress, resources, and coping: Tools for research, education and clinical intervention.* St. Paul: University of Minnesota, Department of Family Social Science, Family Stress and Coping Project.

McCubbin, H. I., & Patterson, J. M. (1983). The family stress process: The double ABCX model of adjustment and adaptation. *Marriage and Family Review, 6,* 7–37.

McDaniel, S. H., Hepworth, J., & Doherty, W. J. (1992). *Medical family therapy.* New York: Basic Books.

McDonald, A. C., Carson, K. L., Palmer, D. J., & Slay, T. (1982). Physicians' diagnostic information to parents of handicapped neonates. *Mental Retardation, 20,* 12–14.

McGoldrick, M. (1982). Ethnicity and family therapy: An overview. In M. McGoldrick, J. K. Pearce, & J. Giordano (Eds.), *Ethnicity and family therapy* (pp. 3–30). New York: Guilford Press.

298   References

McGoldrick, M., & Gerson, R. (1985). *Genograms in family assessment.* New York: Norton.

McGoldrick, M., Pearce, J. K., & Giordano, J. (1982). *Ethnicity and family therapy.* New York: Guilford Press.

McHale, S. M., & Gamble, W. C. (1987). Sibling relationships and adjustment of children with disabled brothers and sisters. *Journal of Children in Contemporary Society, 19,* 131–158.

McHale, S. M., Sloan, J., & Simeonsson, R. J. (1986). Sibling relationships with autistic, mentally retarded, and non-handicapped brothers and sisters. *Journal of Autism and Developmental Disorders, 16,* 399–414.

McHugh, P. (1968). *Defining the situation.* Indianapolis: Bobbs-Merrill.

McMichael, J. K. (1971). *Handicap: A study of physically handicapped children and their families.* Pittsburgh: University of Pittsburgh Press.

McPhee, N. (1982, June). A very special magic: A grandparent's delight. *Exceptional Parent,* pp. 13–16.

Mercer, J. R. (1965). Social system perspective and clinical perspective: Frames of reference for understanding career patterns of persons labeled as mentally retarded. *Social Problems, 13,* 18–34.

Meyer, D., Vadasy, P., & Fewell, R. R. (1985). *Living with a brother or sister with special needs: A book for sibs.* Seattle, WA: University of Washington Press.

Meyer, D. J. (1995). *Uncommon fathers: Reflections on raising a child with a disability.* Bethesda, MD: Woodbine.

Meyer, D. J., & Vadasy, P. F. (1986). *Grandparent workshops: How to organize workshops for grandparents of children with handicaps.* Seattle: University of Washington Press.

Meyer, D. J., & Vadasy, P. F. (1994). *Sibshops: Workshops for siblings of children with special needs.* Baltimore: Brookes.

Meyer, D. J., Vadasy, P. F., Fewell, R. R., & Schell, G. (1985). *A handbook for the fathers program.* Seattle: University of Washington Press.

Meyer, E. C., & Bailey, D. B. (1993). Family-centered care in early intervention: Community and hospital settings. In J. L. Paul & R. J. Simeonsson (Eds.), *Children with special needs: Family, culture, and society* (pp. 181–209). New York: Harcourt, Brace, Jovanovich.

Meyer, J. Y. (1978). One of the family. In S. L. Brown & M. S. Moersch (Eds.), *Parents on the team* (pp. 103–111). Ann Arbor: University of Michigan Press.

Meyerson, R. C. (1983). Family and parent group therapy. In M. Seligman (Ed.), *The family with a handicapped child: Understanding and treatment* (pp. 285–305). Orlando, FL: Grune & Stratton.

Michaelis, C. T. (1980). *Home and school partnerships in exceptional children.* Rockville, MD: Aspen.

Miller, S. (1974). *An exploratory study of sibling relationships in families with retarded children.* Unpublished doctoral dissertation, Columbia University, New York.

Milman, D. H. (1952). Group therapy with parents: An approach to the rehabilitation of physically disabled children. *Journal of Pediatrics, 41,* 113–116.

Minkler, M., & Roe, K. M. (1993). *Grandmothers as caregivers: Raising the children of the crack cocaine epidemic.* Thousand Oaks, CA: Sage.

Minuchin, S. (1974). *Families and family therapy*. Cambridge, MA: Harvard University Press.

Minuchin, S. (1978). *Psychosomatic families*. Cambridge, MA: Harvard University Press.

Mitchell, D. (1983). Guidance needs and counseling of parents of mentally retarded persons. In N. N. Singh & K. M. Wilton (Eds.), *Mental retardation: Research and services in New Zealand* (pp. 136–156). Christchurch, New Zealand: Whitcoulls.

Mitchell, D. (1985). Guidance needs and counselling of parents of persons with intellectual handicaps. In N. N. Singh & K. M. Wilton (Eds.), *Mental retardation in New Zealand* (pp. 136–156). Christchurch, New Zealand: Whitcoulls.

Mizio, E. (1974). Impact of external systems on the Puerto Rican family. *Social Casework, 55,* 76–83.

Moeller, C. J. (1986). The effect of professionals on the family of a handicapped child. In R. R. Fewell & P. F. Vadasy (Eds.), *Families of handicapped children* (pp. 149–166). Austin, TX: Pro-Ed.

Montalvo, B. (1974). Home–school conflict and the Puerto Rican child. *Social Casework, 55,* 76–83.

Moore, E. K. (1981). Policies affecting the status of black children and families. In H. P. McAdoo (Ed.), *Black families* (pp. 278–290). Beverly Hills: Sage.

Moorman, M. (1992, January/February). My sister's keeper. *Family Therapy Networker,* 41–47.

Morgan, S. (1987). *Abuse and neglect of handicapped children*. Boston: College-Hill.

Mori, A. A. (1983). *Families of children with special needs: Early intervention*. Rockville, MD: Aspen.

Morris, M. M. (1987, July). Health care: Who pays the bills? *Exceptional Parent,* pp. 38–42.

Mott, D. W., Jenkins, V. L., Justice, E. F., & Moon, R. M. (n.d.) *Project Hope*. Family, Infant and Preschool Program, Western Carolina Center, Morganton, NC.

Mullins, J. (1979). *A teacher's guide to management of physically handicapped students*. Springfield, IL: Thomas.

Murphy, A., Paeschel, S., Duffy, T., & Brady, E. (1976). Meeting with brothers and sisters of Down's syndrome children. *Children Today, 5,* 20–23.

Myers, R. (1978). *Like normal people*. New York: McGraw-Hill.

NCHS studies health insurance and chronically ill children. (1992, October). *Nation's Health,* p. 13.

Neugarten, B. L. (1976). Adaptation and the life cycle. *Counseling Psychologist, 6,* 16–20.

Newman, J. (1983). Handicapped persons and their families: Philosophical, historical, and legislative perspectives. In M. Seligman (Ed.), *The family with a handicapped child* (pp. 3–25). Orlando, FL: Grune & Stratton.

Newman, J. (1991). Handicapped persons and their families: Philosophical, historical, and legislative perspectives. In M. Seligman (Ed.), *The family with a handicapped child* (2nd ed., pp. 1–26). Boston: Allyn & Bacon.

Newman, M. A. (1983). A continuing evolution: A history of nursing science. In N. L. Chaska (Ed.), *Time to speak* (pp. 385–393). New York: McGraw-Hill.

Norr, K. L., Block, C. R., Charles, A., Meyering, S., & Meyers, E. (1977). Explaining pain and enjoyment in childbirth. *Journal of Health and Social Behavior, 18,* 260–275.

Offer, D., Ostrov, E., & Howard, K. I. (1984). Body image, self-perception, and chronic illness in adolescence. In R. W. Blum (Ed.), *Chronic illness and disabilities in childhood and adolescence* (pp. 59–73). Orlando, FL: Grune & Stratton.

Olshansky, S. (1962). Chronic sorrow: A response to having a mentally defective child. *Social Casework, 43,* 190–193.

Olson, D. H., McCubbin, H. I., Barnes, H., Larsen, A., Muxen, M., & Wilson, M. (1984). *One thousand families: A national survey.* Beverly Hills: Sage.

Olson, D. H., Russell, C. S., & Sprenkle, D. H. (1980). Circumplex model of marital and family systems II: Empirical studies and clinical intervention. In J. P. Vincent (Ed.), *Advances in family intervention assessment and theory* (Vol. 1, pp. 129–179). Greenwich, CT: JAI Press.

Opirhory, G., & Peters, G. A. (1982). Counseling intervention strategies for families with the less than perfect newborn. *Personnel and Guidance Journal, 60,* 451–455.

Orenstein, A. (1979). *Organizational issues in implementing special educational legislation.* Paper presented at the annual meeting of the Society for the Study of Social Problems, Boston, MA.

Parke, R. D. (1981). *Fathers.* Cambridge, MA: Harvard University Press.

Parsons, T. (1951). *The social system.* NY: Free Press.

Patterson, J. M. (1985). Critical factors affecting family compliance with home treatment for children with cystic fibrosis. *Family Relations, 34,* 79–89.

Patterson, J. M. (1988). Chronic illness in children and the impact on families. In C. Chilman, E. Nunnally, & E. Cox (Eds.), *Chronic illness and disability* (pp. 69–107). Beverly Hills: Sage.

Patterson, J. M. (1991). A family systems perspective for working with youth with disability. *Pediatrician, 18,* 129–141.

Pearlman, L., & Scott, K. A. (1981). *Raising the handicapped child.* Englewood Cliffs, NJ: Prentice-Hall.

Peck, J. R., & Stephens, W. B. (1960). A study of the relationship between the attitudes and behavior of parents and that of their mentally defective child. *American Journal of Mental Deficiency, 64,* 839–844.

Pepper, F. C. (1976). Teaching the American Indian child in mainstream settings. In R. L. Jones (Ed.), *Mainstreaming and the minority child* (pp. 108–122). Reston, VA: Council for Exceptional Children.

Pieper, E. (1976, April). Grandparents can help. *Exceptional Parent,* pp. 7–9.

Pinderhughes, E. (1982). Afro-American families and the victim system. In M. McGoldrick, J. K. Pearce, & J. Giordano (Eds.), *Ethnicity and family therapy* (pp. 133–158). New York: Guilford Press.

Pines, M. (1982). Infant-stim: It's changing the lives of handicapped kids. *Psychology Today, 16,* 48–53.

Pizzo, P. (1983). *Parent to parent: Working together for ourselves and our children.* Boston: Beacon.

Powell, J. D. (1975). *Theory of coping systems: Changes in supportive health organizations.* Cambridge, MA: Schenkman.

Powell, T. H., & Gallagher, P. E. (1993). *Brothers and sisters: A special part of exceptional families* (2nd ed.). Baltimore: Brookes.

Poznanski, E. (1969). Psychiatric difficulties in siblings of handicapped children. *Pediatrics, 8,* 232–234.

Prattes, O. (1973). Section A: Beliefs of the Mexican-American family. In D. Hymovich & M. Barnard (Eds.), *Family health care* (pp. 128–137). New York: McGraw-Hill.

Price, J. A. (1976). North American Indian families. In C. H. Mindel & R. W. Habenstein (Eds.), *Ethnic families in America: Patterns and variations* (pp. 248–270). New York: Elsevier.

Pruett, K. D. (1987). *The nurturing father.* New York: Warner.

Quesada, G. M. (1976). Language and communication barriers for health delivery to a minority group. *Social Science and Medicine, 10,* 323–327.

Quine, L., & Pahl, J. (1986). First diagnosis of severe mental handicap: Characteristics of unsatisfactory encounters between doctors and parents. *Social Science and Medicine, 22,* 53–62.

Radley, A., & Green, R. (1987). Illness as adjustment: A methodology and conceptual framework. *Sociology of Health and Illness, 9,* 179–207.

Ragucci, A. T. (1981). Italian Americans. In A. Harwood (Ed.), *Ethnicity and medical care* (pp. 211–263). Cambridge, MA: Harvard University Press.

Raimbault, G., Cachin, O., Limal, J. M., Eliacheff, C., & Rappaport, R. (1975). Aspects of communication between patients and doctors: An analysis of the discourse in medical interviews. *Pediatrics, 55,* 401–405.

Ramsey, C. N., (Ed.). (1989). *Family systems in medicine.* New York: Guilford Press.

Reader's forum. (October, 1985). *Exceptional Parent,* p. 7.

Related Services and the Supreme Court: A family's story. (1984, October). *Exceptional Parent,* pp. 36–41.

Resnick, M. D. (1984). The social construction of disability. In R. W. Blum (Ed.), *Chronic illness and disabilities in childhood and adolescence* (pp. 29–46). Orlando, FL: Grune & Stratton.

Resnick, M. D., Reiss, K., Eyler, F. D., & Schauble, P. (1988). Children's developmental services: A multidisciplinary program of psychological and educational services for neonatal intensive care. *Journal of Counseling and Development, 66,* 279–282.

Reynolds, T., & Zellmer, D. D. (1985). Group for siblings of preschool age children with handicaps. *Sibling Information Network Newsletter, 4,* 2.

Rhoades, E. A. (1975). A grandparents' workshop. *Volta Review, 77,* 557–560.

Richardson, H. B. (1945). *Patients have families.* New York: Commonwealth Fund.

Richardson, H. B., Guralnick, M. J., & Tupper, D. B. (1978). Training pediatricians for effective involvement with preschool handicapped children and their families. *Mental Retardation, 16,* 3–7.

Richardson, S. A. (1970). Age and sex differences in values toward physical handicaps. *Journal of Health and Social Behavior, 11,* 207–214.

Richardson, S. A. (1972). People with cerebral palsy talk for themselves. *Developmental Medicine and Child Neurology, 14,* 521–535.

Richardson, S. A., Goodman, N., Hastorf, A. H., & Dornbusch, S. M. (1961).

Cultural uniformity in reaction to physical disabilities. *American Sociological Review, 26,* 241–247.

Richardson, S. A., Goodman, N., Hastorf, A. H., & Dornbusch, S. M. (1963). Variant reactions to physical disabilities. *American Sociological Review, 28,* 429–435.

Robson, K. S., & Moss, H. A. (1970). Patterns and determinants of maternal attachment. *Journal of Pediatrics, 77,* 976–985.

Rogers, C. R. (1958). The characteristics of a helping relationship. *Personnel and Guidance Journal, 37,* 6–16.

Rolland, J. S. (1993). Mastering family challenges in series illness & disability. In F. Walsh (Ed.), *Normal family processes* (2nd ed., pp. 444–473). New York: Guilford Press.

Rolland, J. S. (1994). *Families, illness, and disability: An integrative treatment model.* New York: Basic Books.

Romaine, M. E. (1982). Clinical management of the Spanish-speaking patient: Pleasures and pitfalls. *Clinical Management in Physical Therapy, 2,* 9–10.

Rose, S. (1974). Training parents in groups as behavior modifiers of their mentally retarded children. *Journal of Behavior Therapy and Experimental Psychiatry, 5,* 135–140.

Rose, S. D. (1974). Training parents in groups as behavior modifiers of their mentally retarded children. In L. Wikler & M. P. Keenan (Eds.), *Developmental disabilities: No longer a private tragedy* (pp. 159–165). Silver Spring, MD: NASW.

Rosengren, W. R. (1962). The sick role during pregnancy: A note on research in progress. *Journal of Health and Human Behavior, 3,* 213–218.

Roskies, E. (1972). *Abnormality and normality: The mothering of thalidomide children.* Ithaca, NY: Cornell University Press.

Ross, A. O. (1964). *The exceptional child in the family.* New York: Grune & Stratton.

Rothman, B. K. (1978). Childbirth as negotiated reality. *Symbolic Interaction, 1,* 124–137.

Rotunno, M., & McGoldrick, M. (1982). Italian families. In M. McGoldrick, J. K. Pearce, & J. Giordano (Eds.), *Ethnicity and family therapy* (pp. 340–363). New York: Guilford Press.

Rousso, H. (February, 1984). Fostering healthy self-esteem. *Exceptional Parent,* pp. 9–14.

Rubel, A. J. (1960). Concepts of disease in Mexican-American culture. *American Anthropologist, 62,* 795–816.

Rubin, S., & Quinn-Curran, N. (1983). Lost, then found: Parent's journey through the community service maze. In M. Seligman (Ed.), *The family with a handicapped child: Understanding and treatment* (pp. 63–94). Orlando, FL: Grune & Stratton.

Safilios-Rothschild, C. (1970). *The sociology and social psychology of disability and rehabilitation.* New York: Random House.

San Martino, M., & Newman, M. B. (1974). Siblings of retarded children: A population at risk. *Child Psychiatry and Human Development, 4,* 168–177.

Scanlon, C. A., Arick, J., & Phelps, N. (1981). Participation in the development of the IEP: Parents' perspective. *Exceptional Children, 47,* 373–374.

Scanzoni, J. (1975). *Sex roles, lifestyles, and childbearing: Changing patterns in marriage and family.* New York: Free Press.

Scanzoni, J. (1985). Black parental values and expectations of children's occupational and educational success: Theoretical implications. In H. P. McAdoo & J. L. McAdoo (Eds.), *Black children: Social, educational and parental environments* (pp. 113–122). Beverly Hills: Sage.

Schilling, R. F., Gilchrist, L. D., & Schinke, S. P. (1984). Coping and social support in families of developmentally disabled children. *Family Relations, 33,* 47–54.

Schipper, M. T. (1959). The child with mongolism in the home. *Pediatrics, 24,* 132–144.

Schonell, F. J., & Rorke, M. (1960). A second survey of the effects of a subnormal child on the family unit. *American Journal of Mental Deficiency, 64,* 862–868.

Schonell, F. J., & Watts, B. H. (1956). A first survey of the effects of a subnormal child on the family unit. *American Journal of Mental Deficiency, 61,* 210–219.

Schopler, E., & Mesibov, G. B. (1984). *The effects of autism on the family.* New York: Plenum.

Schorr-Ribera, H. K. (1987). *Ethnicity and culture as relevant rehabilitation factors in families with children with disabilities.* Unpublished manuscript, University of Pittsburgh.

Schreiber, J. M., & Homiak, J. P. (1981). Mexican Americans. In A. Harwood (Ed.), *Ethnicity and medical care* (pp. 264–336). Cambridge, MA: Harvard University Press.

Schreiber, M., & Feeley, M. (1965). A guided group experience. *Children, 12,* 221–225.

Schulz, D. A. (1969). *Coming up black: Patterns of ghetto socialization.* Englewood Cliffs, NJ: Prentice-Hall.

Schulz, J. B. (1987). *Parents and professionals in special education.* Boston: Allyn & Bacon.

Schulz, J. B. (1993). Heroes in disguise. In A. P. Turnbull, J. M. Patterson, S. K. Behr, D. L. Murphy, J. G. Marquis, & M. J. Blue-Banning (Eds.), *Cognitive coping, families, and disability.* Baltimore: Brookes.

Schwab, L. O. (1989). Strengths of families having a member with a disability. *Journal of the Multihandicapped Person, 2,* 105–117.

Searle, S. J. (1978). Stages of parents reaction. *Exceptional Parent, 8,* 27–29.

Seligman, M. (1979). *Strategies for helping parents of exceptional children: A guide for teachers.* New York: Free Press.

Seligman, M. (1991a). Grandparents of disabled grandchildren: Hopes, fears, and adaptation. *Families in Society, 72,* 147–152.

Seligman, M. (Ed.). (1991b). *The family with a handicapped child* (2nd ed.). Boston: Allyn & Bacon.

Seligman, M. (1993). Group work with parents of children with disabilities. *Journal for Specialists in Group Work, 18,* 115–126.

Seligman, M. (1995). Confessions of a professional/father. In D. Meyer (Ed.), *Uncommon fathers: Reflections on raising a child with a disability* (pp. 169–183). Bethesda, MD: Woodbine.

Seligman, M., & Meyerson, R. (1982). Group approaches for parents of handicapped children. In M. Seligman (Ed.), *Group psychotherapy and counseling with special populations* (pp. 99–116). Baltimore: University Park Press.

Seligman, M., & Seligman, P. A. (1980, October). The professional's dilemma: Learning to work with parents. *Exceptional Parent, 10,* 511–513.

Seltzer, M. M., & Krauss, M. W. (1984). Placement alternatives for mentally retarded children and their families. In J. Blacher (Ed.), *Severely handicapped young children and their families: Research in review* (pp. 143–175). Orlando, FL: Academic Press.

Shapiro, J., & Tittle, K. (1986). Psychosocial adjustment of poor Mexican mothers of disabled and nondisabled children. *American Journal of Orthopsychiatry, 56,* 289–302.

Shereshefsky, P. M., Liebenberg, B., & Lockman, R. F. (1973). Maternal adaptation. In P. M. Shereshefsky & L. J. Yarrow (Eds.), *Psychological aspects of a first pregnancy and early postnatal adaptation.* New York: Raven.

Shon, S. P., & Ja, D. Y. (1982). Asian families. In M. McGoldrick, J. K. Pearce, & J. Giordano (Eds.), *Ethnicity and family therapy* (pp. 208–228). New York: Guilford Press.

Shurka, E., & Florian, V. (1983). A study of Israeli Jewish and Arab parental perceptions of their disabled children. *Journal of Comparative Family Studies, 14,* 367–375.

Siegel, B., & Silverstein, S. (1994). *What about me?: Growing up with a developmentally disabled sibling.* New York: Plenum.

Siller, J. (1984). Personality and attitudes toward physical disabilities. In C. J. Golden (Ed.), *Current topics in rehabilitation psychology* (pp. 201–227). New York: Grune & Stratton.

Simeonsson, R. J., & Bailey, D. B. (1986). Siblings of handicapped children. In J. J. Gallagher & W. Vietze (Eds.), *Families of handicapped persons* (pp. 67–77). Baltimore: Brookes.

Simpson, R. L. (1990). *Conferencing parents of exceptional children.* Austin, TX: Pro-Ed.

Simpson, R. L. (1996). *Working with parents and families of exceptional children and youth.* Austin, TX: Pro-Ed.

Singer, G. H. S., & Powers, L. E. (1993). *Families, disability, and empowerment.* Baltimore: Brookes.

Skrtic, T., Summers, J., Brotherson, M. J., & Turnbull, A. (1984). Severely handicapped children and their brothers and sisters. In J. Blacher (Ed.), *Severely handicapped young children and their families: Research in review* (pp. 215–246). Orlando, FL: Academic Press.

Sloman, M. D., Springer, S., & Vachon, M. (1993). Disordered communication and grieving in deaf member families. *Family Process, 32,* 171–181.

Sloper, P., & Turner, S. (1991). Parental and professional views of the needs of families with a child with severe physical disability. *Counseling Psychology Quarterly, 4,* 323–330.

Smith, K. (1981). The influence of the male sex role on discussion groups for fathers of exceptional children. *Michigan Personnel and Guidance Journal, 12,* 11–17.

Sollenberger, E. R. (1974). *Care and education of crippled children in the United States.* New York: Arno.

Solnit, A. J., & Stark, M. H. (1961). Mourning and the birth of a defective child. *Psychoanalytic Study of the Child, 16,* 523–537.

Sommers-Flanagan, J., & Sommers-Flanagan, R. (1993). *Foundations of therapeutic interviewing.* Boston: Allyn & Bacon.

Sonnek, I. M. (1986). Grandparents and the extended family of handicapped children. In R. R. Fewell & P. F. Vadasy (Eds.), *Families of handicapped children* (pp. 99–120). Austin, TX: Pro-Ed.

Sontag, J. C., & Schacht, R. (1994). An ethnic comparison of parent participation and information needs in early intervention. *Exceptional Children, 60,* 422–433.

Sorenson, J. (1974). Biomedical innovation, uncertainty, and doctor–patient interaction. *Journal of Health and Social Behavior, 15,* 366–374.

Sosnowitz, B. G. (1984). Managing parents on neonatal intensive care units. *Social Problems, 31,* 390–402.

Sourkes, B. M. (1987). Siblings of a child with a life-threatening illness. *Journal of Children in Contemporary Society, 19,* 159–184.

Spano, S. L. (1994). The miracle of Michael. In R. B. Darling & M. I. Peter (Eds.), *Families, physicians, and children with special health needs: Collaborative medical education models* (pp. 29–50). Westport, CT: Auburn House.

Spector, R. E. (1979). *Cultural diversity in health and illness.* New York: Appleton-Century-Crofts.

Spock, B. M. (1946). *The common sense book of baby and child care.* New York: Duell, Sloan, Pearce.

Spock, B. M. (1957). *Baby and child care.* New York: Pocket Books.

Spock, B. M., & Rothenberg, M. B. (1985). *Baby and child care.* New York: Dutton.

Staples, R. (1976). The black American family. In C. H. Mindel & R. W. Habenstein (Eds.), *Ethnic families in America: Patterns and variations* (pp. 221–247). New York: Elsevier.

Stax, T. E., & Wolfson, S. D. (1984). Life-cycle crises of the disabled adolescent and young adult. In R. W. Blum (Ed.), *Chronic illness and disabilities in childhood and adolescence* (pp. 47–57). New York: Grune & Stratton.

Stehower, J. (1968). The household and family relations of old people. In E. Shames, D. Townsend, D. Wedderbrunn, H. Friis, P. Michoj, & J. Stehower (Eds.), *Old people in three industrial societies* (pp. 177–226). New York: Atherton.

Stein, R. C. (1983). Hispanic parents' perspectives and participation in their children's special education program: Comparisons by program and race. *Learning Disability Quarterly, 6,* 432–439.

Stillman, P. L., Sabers, D. L., & Redfield, D. L. (1977). Use of trained mothers to teach interviewing skills to first-year medical students: A follow-up study. *Pediatrics, 60,* 165–169.

Stone, N. W., & Chesney, B. H. (1978). Attachment behaviors in handicapped infants, *Mental Retardation, 16,* 8–12.

Stoneman, Z., & Berman, P. W. (1993). *The effects of mental retardation, disability, and illness on sibling relationships.* Baltimore: Brookes.

Stoneman, Z., Brody, G. H., Davis, C. H., Crapps, J. M., & Malone, D. M. (1991). Ascribed role relations between children with mental retardation and their younger siblings. *American Journal on Mental Retardation, 95,* 537–550.

Stonequist, E. V. (1937). *The marginal man: A study in personality and culture conflict.* New York: Scribners.

Stotland, J. (1984, February). Relationship of parents to professionals: A challenge to professionals. *Journal of Visual Impairment and Blindness,* 69–74.

Streib, G., & Beck, R. (1981). Older families: A decade review. *Journal of Marriage and the Family, 42,* 937–956.

Strong, P. M. (1979). *The ceremonial order of the clinic: Parents, doctors, and medical bureaucracies.* London: Routledge & Kegan Paul.

Sudarkasa, N. (1981). Interpreting the African heritage in Afro-American family organization. In H. P. McAdoo (Ed.), *Black families* (pp. 37–53). Beverly Hills: Sage.

Suelzle, M., & Keenan, V. (1981). Changes in family support networks over the life cycle of mentally retarded persons. *American Journal of Mental Deficiency, 86,* 267–274.

Svarstad, B. L., & Lipton, H. L. (1977). Informing parents about mental retardation: A study of professional communication and parent acceptance. *Social Science and Medicine, 11,* 645–651.

Tallman, I. (1965). Spousal role differentiation and the socialization of severely retarded children. *Journal of Marriage and the Family, 27,* 37–42.

Tartar, S. B. (1987). *Traumatic head injury: Parental stress, coping style and emotional adjustment.* Unpublished doctoral dissertation, University of Pittsburgh.

Telford, C. W., & Sawrey, J. M. (1977). *The exceptional individual* (3rd ed.). Englewood Cliffs, NJ: Prentice-Hall.

Tew, B., & Lawrence, K. (1975). Mothers, brothers and sisters of patients with spina bifida. *Developmental Medicine and Child Neurology, 15*(Suppl. 29), 69–76.

Tew, B. J., Lawrence, K. M., Payne, H., & Rawnsley, K. (1977). Marital stability following the birth of a child with spina bifida. *British Journal of Psychiatry, 131,* 79–82.

Thibodeau, S. M. (1988). Sibling response to chronic illness: The role of the clinical nurse specialist. *Issues in Comprehensive Pediatric Nursing, 11,* 17–28.

Tolson, T. F. J., & Wilson, M. N. (1990). The impact of two- and three-generational black family structure on perceived family climate. *Child Development, 61,* 416–428.

Travis, C. (1976). *Chronic illness in children: Its impact on child and family.* Stanford, CA: Stanford University Press.

Trevino, F. (1979). Siblings of handicapped children. *Social Casework, 60,* 488–493.

Tritt, S. G., & Esses, L. M. (1988). Psychological adaptation of siblings of children with chronic medical illness. *American Journal of Orthopsychiatry, 58,* 211–220.

Trivette, C. M., & Dunst, C. J. (1982). *Proactive influences of social support in families of handicapped children.* Unpublished manuscript.

Turk, D. C., & Kerns, R. D. (1985). *Health, illness and families: A life-span perspective.* New York: Wiley.

Turnbull, A. P., Brotherson, M. J., & Summers, J. A. (1985). The impact of deinstitutionalization on families: A family systems approach. In R. H. Bruininks (Ed.), *Living and learning in the least restrictive environment* (pp. 115–152). Baltimore: Brookes.

Turnbull, A. P., Patterson, J. M., Behr, S. K., Murphy, D. L., Marquis, J. G., & Blue-Banning, M. J. (1993). *Cognitive coping, families, and disability.* Baltimore: Brookes.

Turnbull, A. P., Summers, J. A., & Brotherson, M. J. (1986). Family life cycle: Theoretical and empirical implications and future directions for families with mentally retarded members. In J. J. Gallagher & P. M. Vietze (Eds.), *Families of handicapped persons* (pp. 45–65). Baltimore: Brookes.

Turnbull, A. P., & Turnbull, H. R. (1986). *Families, professionals, and exceptionality.* Columbus, OH: Merrill.

Turnbull, A. P., & Turnbull, H. R. (1990). *Families, professionals, and exceptionality* (2nd ed.). Columbus, OH: Merrill.

Turnbull, A. P., & Turnbull, H. R., III (in press). An analysis of self-determination within a culturally responsive family systems perspective: Balancing the family mobile. In J. Sowers (Ed.), *Making our way: Promoting self-competence among children and youth with disabilities.* Baltimore: Brookes.

Turnbull, H. R., & Turnbull, A. P. (Eds.). (1985). *Parents speak out: Then and now.* Columbus, OH: Merrill.

United States Commission on Civil Rights. (1986). *Protection of handicapped newborns: Hearing held in Washington, DC, June 26–27, 1986* (Vol II). Washington, DC: U.S. Government Printing Office.

University of Pittsburgh Office of Child Development. (1991). Black families: An inquiry into the issues. *Developments, 5*(1), 5–8.

Upshur, C. C. (1982). Respite care for mentally retarded and other disabled populations: Program models and family needs. *Mental Retardation, 20,* 2–6.

Upshur, C. C. (1991). Families and the community service maze. In M. Seligman (Ed.), *The family with a handicapped child* (2nd ed., pp. 91–118). Boston: Allyn & Bacon.

Vadasy, P. F. (1986). Single mothers: A social phenomenon and population in need. In R. R. Fewell & P. F. Vadasy (Eds.), *Families of handicapped children* (pp. 221–249). Austin, Texas: Pro-Ed.

Vadasy, P. F., & Fewell, R. R. (1986). Mothers of deaf–blind children. In R. R. Fewell & P. F. Vadasy (Eds.), *Families of handicapped children* (pp. 121–148). Austin, TX: Pro-Ed.

Vadasy, P. F., Fewell, R. R., & Meyer, D. J. (1986). Grandparents of children with special needs: Insights into their experiences and concerns. *Journal of the Division for Early Childhood, 10,* 36–44.

Vadasy, P. F., Fewell, R. R., Greenberg, M. T., Desmond, N. L., & Meyer, D. J. (1986). Follow-up evaluation of the effects of involvement in the fathers program. *Topics in Early Childhood Education, 6,* 16–31.

Vadasy, P. F., Fewell, R. R., Meyer, D. J., & Greenberg, M. T. (1985). Supporting fathers of handicapped young children: Preliminary findings of program effects. *Analysis and Intervention in Developmental Disabilities, 5,* 125–137.

Varekamp, M. A., Suurmeijer, P., Rosendaal, F. R., DiJck, H., Uriends, A., & Briet, E. (1990). Family burden in families with a hemophilic child. *Family Systems Medicine, 8,* 291–301.

Vasta, R. (1982). *Strategies and techniques of child study.* New York: Academic Press.

Vincent, L. J., & Salisbury, C. L. (1988). Changing economic and social influences on family involvement. *Topics in Early Childhood Special Education, 12*, 48–59.

Visher, E., & Visher, J. (1988). *Old loyalties new ties: Therapeutic strategies with step families.* New York: Brunner/Mazel.

Von Bertalanffy, L. (1968). *General systems theory.* New York: Braziller.

Voysey, M. (1972). Impression management by parents with disabled children. *Journal of Health and Social Behavior, 13*, 80–89.

Voysey, M. (1975). *A constant burden: The reconstitution of family life.* London: Routledge & Kegan Paul.

Waechter, E. H. (1977). Bonding problems of infants with congenital anomalies. *Nursing Forum, 16*, 229–318.

Waisbren, E. (1980). Parents' reactions after the birth of a developmentally disabled child. *American Journal of Mental Deficiency, 84*, 345–351.

Waitzkin, H. (1985). Information giving in medical care. *Journal of Health and Social Behavior, 26*, 81–101.

Waitzman, N. J., Romano, P. S., Scheffler, R. M., & Harris, J. A. (1995, September 22). *Morbidity and mortality weekly report.* Atlanta: Centers for Disease Control.

Walker, J. H. (1971). Spina bifida—and the parents. *Developmental Medicine and Child Neurology, 13*, 462–476.

Wallinga, C., Paquio, L., & Skeen, P. (1987). When a brother or sister is ill. *Psychology Today, 42*, 43.

Walsh, F. (1989). The family in later life. In B. Carter & M. McGoldrick (Eds.), *The changing family life cycle* (2nd ed., pp. 311–332). Needham Heights, MA: Allyn & Bacon.

Wasow, M., & Wikler, L. (1983). Reflections on professionals' attitudes toward the severely mentally retarded and the chronically mentally ill: Implications for parents. *Family Therapy, 10*, 299–308.

Wasserman, R. (1983). Identifying the counseling needs of the siblings of mentally retarded children. *Personnel and Guidance Journal, 61*, 622–627.

Watson, R. L., & Midlarsky, E. (1979). Reaction of mothers with mentally retarded children: A social perspective. *Psychological Reports, 45*, 309–310.

Wayman, K. I., Lynch, E. W., & Hanson, M. J. (1991). Home-based early intervention services: Cultural sensitivity in a family systems approach. *Topics in Early Childhood Special Education, 10*, 56–75.

Weisbren, S. E. (1980). Parents' reactions after the birth of a developmentally disabled child. *American Journal of Mental Deficiency, 84*, 345–351.

Wendeborn, J. D. (1982). Administrative considerations in treating the Hispanic patient. *Clinical Management in Physical Therapy 2*, 6–7.

Western Psychiatric Institute and Clinic. (1980). *An intruder in the family: Families with cancer* [Videotape]. Pittsburgh: University of Pittsburgh.

White, R., Benedict, M. I., Wulff, L., & Kelley, M. (1987). Physical disabilities as risk factors for child maltreatment: A selected review. *American Journal of Orthopsychiatry, 57*, 93–101.

Wice, B., & Fernandez, H. (1984, October). Meeting the bureaucracy face to face: Parent power in the Philadelphia schools. *Exceptional Parent*, pp. 36–41.

Wikler, L. (1981). Chronic stresses of families of mentally retarded children. *Family Relations, 30*, 281–288.

Wilcoxon, A. S. (1987). Grandparents and grandchildren: An often neglected relationship between significant others. *Journal of Counseling and Development, 65*, 289–290.

Williams, H. B., & Williams, E. (1979). Some aspects of childrearing practices in three minority subcultures in the United States. *Journal of Negro Education, 48*, 408–418.

Wilton, K., & Barbour, A. (1978). Mother–child interaction in high-risk and contrast preschoolers of low socioeconomic status. *Child Development, 49*, 1136–1145.

Wortis, H. Z., & Margolies, J. A. (1955). Parents of children of cerebral palsy. *Medical Social Work, 4*, 110–120.

Wright, B. A. (1983). *Physical disability: A psychosocial approach* (2nd ed.). New York: Harper and Row.

Yalom, I. (1975). *The theory and practice of group psychotherapy* (2nd ed.). New York: Basic Books.

Yalom, I. (1995). *The theory and practice of group psychotherapy* (4th ed.). New York: Basic Books.

Yee, L. Y. (1988). Asian children. *Teaching Exceptional Children, 20*(4), 49–50.

Young, V. H. (1970). Family and childhood in a southern Negro community. *American Anthropologist, 40*, 269–288.

Zborowski, M. (1952). Cultural components of response to pain. *Journal of Social Issues, 8*, 16–30.

Zinn, M. B., & Eitzen, D. S. (1993). *Diversity in families.* New York: HarperCollins.

Zucman, E. (1982). *Childhood disability in the family.* World Rehabilitation Fund. Monograph No. 14, New York.

Zuk, G. H. (1959). The religious factor and the role of guilt in parental acceptance of the retarded child. *American Journal of Mental Deficiency, 64*, 139–147.

Zuk, G. H., Miller, R. L., Batrum, J. B., & Kling, F. (1961). Maternal acceptance of retarded children: A questionnaire study of attitudes and religious background. *Child Development, 32*, 525–540.

Index